TOEFL® MAP

ACTUAL TEST

New TOEFL® Edition

Writing 2

DARAKWON

TOEFL® MAP
ACTUAL TEST New TOEFL Edition
Writing 2

Publisher Chung Kyudo
Editors Zong Ziin, Cho Sangik
Authors Susan Kim, Michael A. Putlack
Designers Kim Nakyung, Park Narae, Lee Seunghyun

First Published in April 2022
By Darakwon, Inc.
Darakwon Bldg., 211, Munbal-ro, Paju-si, Gyeonggi-do 10881
Republic of Korea
Tel: 82-2-736-2031 (Ext. 250)
Fax: 82-2-732-2037

Price ₩18,000
ISBN 978-89-277-8015-1
        978-89-277-8007-6 (set)

www.darakwon.co.kr

Photo Credits
Shutterstock.com

Components Main Book / Script and Translation Book
7 6 5 4 3 2 1   22 23 24 25 26

TOEFL® MAP
ACTUAL TEST

New TOEFL® Edition

Writing **2**

머리말

미국에 처음 왔을 때, 저녁 모임에서 교수님 한 분께서 제가 한국 학생들에게 토플을 가르쳐 왔다는 말을 듣고, 질문을 하셨습니다. 한국 유학생들은 토플이나 GRE 점수가 만점에 가까운데 왜 토론 수업에 참여를 거의 안 하느냐는 질문이었습니다. 당장 점수를 올려서 좋은 학교를 보내야겠다는 목표만 가지고 학생들을 가르쳤던 저로서는 어떤 대답을 해야 할지 당황스러웠지요.

그 이후, 토플 점수를 내는 것만이 성공적인 유학의 삶을 보장하는 것이 아니라는 사실을 깨닫고, 학생들이 다른 나라로 유학을 가서도 언어로 인해 너무 힘들지 않고 본인들의 전공에 집중할 수 있도록 도와야겠다는 결심을 했습니다. 그리고, 단지 점수를 높이기 위해 토플에서 원하는 형식의 답만 쓰는 것이 아닌 기본적인 문장 구조를 알아가고, 분석을 하고, 그 내용을 다시 스스로 쓸 수 있는 방법을 찾으려 노력해 왔습니다.

이 책에서 저는 기출 지문의 토픽은 물론이고, 현재 일어나고 있는 환경, 기술, 교육 등의 다양한 주제를 다루는데 심혈을 기울였습니다. 그래서 영어권 사람들과 대화를 할 때, 언어뿐 아니라 중요한 이슈에 관련된 단어들과 표현에 익숙해지는 것에도 목적을 두었습니다. 따라서, 제 아이들과 아이들의 친구들에게도 라이팅 실력 향상을 돕기 위해 자신있게 선물할 수 있는 교재를 만들었습니다.

실제로 토플 시험을 볼 때, 화면에 주어진 시간이 1초씩 없어지는 걸 보고 있으면 잘 알고 있는 것들도 머릿속에서 뒤죽박죽 섞이거나 아예 생각이 안 날 수도 있습니다. 제가 가르쳐 온 학생들의 고민과 의견을 토대로 실제 시험을 볼 때 도움이 되는 포인트들을 TIPS for SUCCESS에 담았습니다. 그리고 어떤 주제가 나와도 상대방을 설득시킬 수 있는 능력을 발달시킬 목적으로 독립형 문제에서는 찬반 혹은 선택의 모든 옵션을 샘플 에세이에 실어서 동일한 주제 및 동일한 서론 하에 자신의 주장을 개진해 볼 수 있도록 하였습니다.

본 교재를 통해 토플 시험을 준비하는 여러분들이 반드시 좋은 결과를 얻어 여러분들의 꿈을 향해 조금 더 다가설 수 있게 되기를 진심으로 기원합니다. 학생들에게 조금이나마 도움을 주고자 하는 제 바람을 펼칠 수 있도록 책이 출판되기까지 도움을 주신 다락원 편집부에 감사의 말씀을 전합니다. 마지막으로, 언제나 사랑과 응원으로 제 하루하루를 행복하고 가치 있게 만들어 주는 가족들께 깊이 감사드립니다.

저자 김수진

목차

이 책의 특징

최신 경향의 최다 문제 수록

- 각권 18회분 총 36회분의 문제 수록
- 최신 기출 문제를 분석하여 빈출 주제 및 단어로 문를 재구성

모든 문제에 대한 샘플 에세이 제공

- 수험생에게 실질적인 도움이 될 수 있는 모범 답안 제공
- 독립형 문제의 경우 찬/반에 대한 각각의 샘플 에세이 수록

고득점으로 이어지는 필수 팁 제공

- 고득점을 얻기 위해 에세이 작성시 반드시 알아야 할 팁 제시
- 각 독립형 문제에 관련된 연관 토픽 제시

모든 지문과 스크립트, 그리고 샘플 에세이에 대한 해석 수록

- 리딩 지문과 리스닝 스크립트, 그리고 각 샘플 에세이에 대한 해석 포함

리스닝 MP3 파일

이 책의 구성

TASK

주제들이 한 쪽으로 치우치지 않도록 빈출 주제들을 균형감 있게 재배치하였다.

NOTE-TAKING

통합형의 경우 리딩 및 리스닝에 대한 노트테이킹 요령을 제시하고 있으며, 독립형의 경우에는 노트테이킹 요령뿐만 아니라 브레인스토밍을 원활히 할 수 있는 가이드라인 또한 제시하였다.

WORD REMINDER

해당 주제와 관련되고 실제 토플 시험에서 자주 사용되는 단어들을 일목요연하게 정리해 두어, 수험생들이 빠른 시간 내에 단어 학습에 대한 효과를 볼 수 있게 했다.

SAMPLE ESSAY & TIPS for SUCCESS

수험생들이 실제 쓸 수 있는 레벨을 감안하여 눈높이에 맞춘 샘플 에세이들을 제공하였다. 특히 독립형의 경우, 찬/반에 대한 각각의 샘플 에세이를 제공해 줌으로써, 자신의 의견에 맞는 모범 답안을 분석해 볼 수 있다. 또한 작문에 유용한 문법 사항 등을 TIPS for SUCCESS에 정리하였다.

RELATED TOPICS

독립형의 경우 해당 주제와 관련되어 출제될 수 있는 다양한 문제들을 추가적으로 제시하고, 아울러 간단한 노트테이킹 작성 요령들도 함께 수록하였다.

TOEFL® iBT에 대한 소개

1. 구성

시험 영역	지분 형식과 문제 수	시간	점수
Reading	• **시험당 3~4개의 지문** 　– 지문 하나는 약 700개의 단어로 구성됨 　– 각 지문마다 10개의 문제가 출제됨	54–72분	30점
Listening	• **시험당 2~3개의 대화** 　– 약 3분 동안 12~25차례의 대화가 오고 감 　– 각 대화마다 5개의 문제가 출제됨 • **시험당 3~4개의 강의** 　– 강의는 3~5분 동안 500~800개의 단어로 구성됨 　– 각 강의마다 6개의 문제가 출제됨	41–57분	30점
Break　10 minutes			
Speaking	• **독립형 문제 1개** 　– 15초의 준비 시간과 45초의 응답 시간 　– 선호 및 의견에 근거한 말하기 문제 1개가 출제됨 • **읽고 듣고 말하기의 통합형 문제 2개** 　– 30초의 준비 시간과 60초의 응답 시간 　– 대학 생활과 관련된 문제 1개와 특정 학문과 관련된 문제 1개가 출제됨 • **듣고 말하기의 통합형 문제 1개** 　– 20초의 준비 시간과 60초의 응답 시간 　– 특정 학문과 관련된 문제 1개가 출제됨	17분	30점
Writing	• **읽고 듣고 쓰기의 통합형 문제 1개** 　– 20분간 읽기 및 듣기 내용을 150~225개의 단어로 요약하는 문제가 출제됨 • **독립형 문제 1개** 　– 30분간 제시된 주제에 따라 최소 300개의 단어로 에세이를 작성하는 문제가 출제됨	50분	30점

2. 특징

전 세계의 지정된 시험장에서 인터넷을 통해 실시

TOEFL® iBT에서 iBT란 인터넷 기반 시험을 뜻하는 Internet-based Test의 약자이다. 시험은 인터넷 시설이 갖추어진 지정된 시험장에서만 실시되며, 시차에 따른 문제 유출의 소지를 없애기 위해 전 세계에서 동시에 하루 만에 시행된다. 총 시험 시간은 3시간에서 3시간 30분 사이이고, 읽기와 듣기 영역 시험이 끝난 후 10분간의 휴식 시간이 주어진다.

읽기, 듣기, 말하기, 쓰기 영역을 통합적으로 평가

TOEFL® iBT는 네 가지 언어 영역을 평가하는 시험으로, 일부 영역의 시험만 선택할 수는 없다. 특히 말하기와 쓰기 영역에서는 읽고 듣고 말하기, 듣고 말하기, 읽고 듣고 쓰기 등과 같은 통합적인 언어 구사 능력을 평가한다. 문법은 별도의 평가 항목 없이 위의 네 영역에 나오는 문제와 과제를 통해 간접적으로 평가된다.

노트 필기 허용

TOEFL® iBT는 핵심 사항을 필기할 수 있도록 시험장에 입장할 때 연필과 종이를 나누어 준다. 따라서, 읽기, 듣기, 말하기, 쓰기 영역에서 지문을 읽거나 들으면서 중요한 내용을 메모해 두었다가 문제를 풀 때 참고할 수 있다. 노트 필기한 종이와 연필은 시험장에서 퇴실할 때 반납해야 한다.

미국식 이외의 발음 추가

TOEFL® iBT의 듣기 영역에서는 강의 가운데 한 개가 미국식 발음 이외의 영국, 캐나다 등 다양한 국적의 발음으로 나올 수도 있다. 하지만 실제 시험에서 대체적으로 미국식 발음이 가장 많이 들리기 때문에 수험자가 다국적 발음에 대해 크게 걱정할 필요는 없다.

쓰기 영역과 컴퓨터 자판

TOEFL® iBT의 쓰기 영역은 모든 답안을 컴퓨터 자판을 통해 작성해야 한다. 효율적인 답안 작성을 위해 평소에 영문 자판에 익숙해 있어야 한다.

인터넷을 통한 성적 확인

TOEFL® iBT는 수험자가 시험을 치른 후 15일 정도 지나서 시험 결과를 온라인으로 확인할 수 있다. 시험을 신청할 때 온라인 성적 확인과 함께 우편 확인까지 선택하면 차후에 우편으로도 성적표를 받아볼 수 있다.

TOEFL® iBT의 Writing Section 채점 기준

1. 통합형 문제 (Integrated Writing Task)

Score 5

강의의 내용을 명확하게 요약하고 강의 내용이 주어진 읽기 지문에서 나타난 주장과 어떻게 연관되는지를 명료하게 설명한다. 글의 구성이 우수하고 문법적인 실수가 거의 없기 때문에 그 의미가 모호하지 않다.

Score 4

강의 내용의 주제와 그 주제가 읽기 지문에서 나타나고 있는 주제와 어떻게 연관되는지를 잘 설명한다. 하지만 의미가 모호하거나 부정확한 경우가 간혹 있을 수 있다. 또한 이따금 눈에 띄는 문법적인 실수가 나타나서 의미가 모호해 지는 경우도 이 점수에 해당된다.

Score 3

전체적으로 강의의 주제와 그 주제가 읽기 지문에서 나타난 주제와 어떻게 연관되는지를 설명하나 그 의미가 모호하거나, 불명확하거나, 혹은 때때로 잘못되어 있다. 강의의 요점 중 한 가지를 빠뜨리는 경우도 이 점수에 해당된다. 문법적인 실수가 보다 많이 나타나서 강의 및 읽기 지문에서 나타난 주제들 간의 연관성을 알아보기가 힘들다.

Score 2

강의의 주제 중 일부만을 다루고 있으며 그 주제가 읽기 지문에서 나타난 정보와 어떻게 연관되는지를 설명하지 못한다. 또한 심각한 문법적 실수를 포함하고 있기 때문에 해당 주제를 접해본 적이 없는 독자라면 강의 및 읽기 지문의 주제를 이해할 수가 없게 된다.

Score 1

강의의 내용이 거의 다루어지지 않거나 전혀 다루어지지 않는다. 또한 언어 표현 능력이 매우 낮아서 그 의미를 전혀 이해할 수가 없다.

Score 0

단순히 읽기 지문의 내용을 복사해 쓰거나, 전혀 주제를 나타내지 못하거나, 영어 이외의 언어로 쓰여졌거나, 혹은 내용이 아예 없는 경우가 이 점수에 해당된다.

2. 독립형 문제 (Independent Writing Task)

Score 5

명확하게 주제를 전달한다. 글이 논리적으로 구성되어 있고, 아이디어와 단락이 적절하게 연관되어 있으며, 예들이 각 주제를 뒷받침해 준다. 자연스럽게 읽히고 문장 형식이 다양하며, 적합한 단어들이 사용되고, 관용적인 표현들도 올바르게 사용되었다. 사소한 문법적 실수가 있을 수 있으나, 읽는 사람의 이해를 방해하지는 않는다.

Score 4

주제를 잘 전달한다. 하지만 주장을 뒷받침하는 세부적인 내용이 불충분할 수 있다. 전반적으로 글의 구성은 좋으나 연결이 명확하지 않고, 장황하며, 그리고 혹은 관련이 없는 정보가 들어있을 수 있다. 또한 눈에 띄는 문법적인 실수 및 적절치 못한 단어들이 상대적으로 많을 수 있으나, 의미는 명확하게 전달된다.

Score 3

쉽게 이해할 수 없거나 불완전한 설명 및 예들을 사용하여 주제를 나타낸다. 글에 일관성은 있으나, 아이디어간의 연관성은 명확하지 않을 수 있다. 또한 정확하지만 문장 구조 및 어휘의 사용이 제한적일 수 있으며 문법적인 실수가 보다 자주 나타나기 때문에 때때로 그 의미가 모호해진다.

Score 2

주제를 명확하게 표현하지 못하고 글의 구성이 적절치 못하여 아이디어를 제대로 개진하지 못한다. 예들이 주제를 뒷받침하지 못하는 경우도 있고 보다 많은 문법적 실수로 인해 의미가 모호해지는 경우도 많다.

Score 1

주제를 표현하지 못하고 심각한 문법적 실수가 잦아 대체적으로 의미가 불명확하다.

Score 0

단순히 주제를 복사해 쓰거나, 전혀 주제를 나타내지 못하거나, 영어 이외의 언어로 쓰여졌거나, 혹은 내용이 아예 없는 경우 이 점수에 해당된다.

TOEFL® MAP

ACTUAL TEST Writing 2

01

From roughly 3000 B.C. to 1500 B.C., one of the world's greatest early civilizations existed. Located in the Indus River Valley found in modern-day Pakistan and India, it was known as the Harappan civilization. Harappan society was primarily urban, and its cities were even laid out on grids. The people there also used agricultural techniques advanced for the time, had a form of writing called Indus script, and engaged in widespread regional trade. Yet sometime around 1500 B.C., the Harappan civilization came to a sudden end.

One of the most widely accepted theories for its downfall is that the Harappans were overcome by outside invaders. Many scholars believe that the Aryans, an Indo-European tribe from Central Asia, were responsible for conquering the Harappans. Some evidence exists showing that battles were fought in the region around 1500 B.C., and it is also known that the Aryans began moving into the Harappans' territory during that time period, so this theory is a distinct possibility.

Other scholars claim that the Harappan civilization fell due to natural means. According to them, the Indus River Valley underwent a severe change in climate around 1500 B.C. What was once lush land that supported an extensive farming community was transformed into dry desert from a lack of rainfall. Accordingly, famine struck the region, and those individuals who did not die of starvation migrated to other lands that were able to support them.

A third theory is that various diseases rampaged through Harappan society and caused its collapse. Some posit that cholera, an infectious viral disease, was the culprit. Cholera often spreads through water. Since the Harappan people used the same water sources, it is possible that a cholera epidemic could have devastated the population. With so many dead and dying, the civilization simply vanished from history.

🎧 01-01

Directions You have 20 minutes to plan and write your response. Your response will be judged on the basis of the quality of your writing and on how well your response presents the points in the lecture and their relationship to the passage. Typically, an effective response will be 150-225 words.

Question Summarize the points made in the lecture, being sure to explain how they challenge specific arguments made in the reading passage.

| CUT | PASTE | UNDO | REDO | Hide Word Count : 0 |

From roughly 3000 B.C. to 1500 B.C., one of the world's greatest early civilizations existed. Located in the Indus River Valley found in modern-day Pakistan and India, it was known as the Harappan civilization. Harappan society was primarily urban, and its cities were even laid out on grids. The people there also used agricultural techniques advanced for the time, had a form of writing called Indus script, and engaged in widespread regional trade. Yet sometime around 1500 B.C., the Harappan civilization came to a sudden end.

One of the most widely accepted theories for its downfall is that the Harappans were overcome by outside invaders. Many scholars believe that the Aryans, an Indo-European tribe from Central Asia, were responsible for conquering the Harappans. Some evidence exists showing that battles were fought in the region around 1500 B.C., and it is also known that the Aryans began moving into the Harappans' territory during that time period, so this theory is a distinct possibility.

Other scholars claim that the Harappan civilization fell due to natural means. According to them, the Indus River Valley underwent a severe change in climate around 1500 B.C. What was once lush land that supported an extensive farming community was transformed into dry desert from a lack of rainfall. Accordingly, famine struck the region, and those individuals who did not die of starvation migrated to other lands that were able to support them.

A third theory is that various diseases rampaged through Harappan society and caused its collapse. Some posit that cholera, an infectious viral disease, was the culprit. Cholera often spreads through water. Since the Harappan people used the same water sources, it is possible that a cholera epidemic could have devastated the population. With so many dead and dying, the civilization simply vanished from history.

NOTE-TAKING

the sudden disappearance of the Harrapan Civilization 하라파 문명의 갑작스러운 소멸

❶ *outside invaders* 외부 침략자

- Aryans: battles (around 1500 B.C.) 아라아인들: 전쟁 (기원전 약 1500년)

> **Paraphrasing Example** An invasion by outsiders could have caused the collapse of the Harappan civilization.

❷ *natural means* 자연적인 이유

- the Indus River Valley: severe climate change 인더스 강 계곡: 극심한 기후 변화

> **Paraphrasing Example** Extreme climate change in the Indus River Valley resulted in the demise of the Harappans.

❸ *various diseases* 여러 질병

- shared water sources: cholera epidemic 수자원 공유: 콜레라 전염병

> **Paraphrasing Example** The downfall of the Harappans could be attributed to numerous diseases, including cholera, caused by shared water sources.

WORD REMINDER

primarily 주로 lay out 펼치다 grid 격자 눈금 script 필기 문자 widespread 널리 보급된 downfall 몰락 overcome 압도하다
invader 침략자 conquer 정복하다 territory 영토 distinct 명확한 undergo 겪다 lush 우거진 extensive 광대한 transform 변형시키다
famine 기근 starvation 기아 migrate 이주하다 rampage 사납게 돌진하다 collapse 붕괴 posit 단정하다 infectious 전염성의
culprit 원인 epidemic 유행성의 devastate 황폐시키다 vanish 사라지다

the assumptions on the demise: groundless 멸망에 관한 가설: 근거가 없음

❶ *no evidence found in the major regions* 주요 지역들에 관한 증거 ×

Ex Harappa, Mohenjo-Daro (more than 100 cities) 하라파, 모헨조다로 (100개 이상의 도시)
→ wouldn't have easily collapsed 쉽게 붕괴되지 않았을 것임

> **Paraphrasing Example** There is no evidence showing any proof of an invasion.

❷ *Egypt + Mesopotamia → climate changes* 이집트 + 메소포타미아 → 기후 변화

- Egypt: desert-like → thrived 이집트: 사막같이 변했음 → 번영
- Mesopotamia: tremendous flood → helped Mesopotamian agriculture
  메소포타미아: 거대한 홍수 → 메소포타미아 농업에 도움이 되었음
  ∴ Harappans: would've been able to survive 하라파인들: 생존할 수 있었을 것임

> **Paraphrasing Example** Other contemporary civilizations went through climate changes without being destroyed.

❸ *cholera: spreads through dirty water* 콜레라: 더러운 물로 퍼짐

- H: water system 하라파인: 급수 시설
  sewer system 하수구 시설
  → access to clean water 깨끗한 물 이용 가능

> **Paraphrasing Example** Cholera could not have been the cause of the destruction.

WORD REMINDER

virtually 사실상 precisely 정확히 brilliant 훌륭한 primary 주요한 overwhelm 압도하다 minor 작은 settlement 정착
contemporary 같은 시대의 endure 견디다 tremendous 대단한 thrive 번영하다 speculate 추측하다 wipe out 전멸하다 sewer 하수구
entire 전체의

The lecturer argues that the assumptions on the demise of the Harappans are groundless. This contradicts the reading passage's claim that there are possible theories which could explain the sudden disappearance of the civilization.

First, there is no evidence showing any proof of an invasion. In major cities, including Harappa and Mohenjo-Daro, no proof of Aryan encroachment has been found. This casts serious doubts on the reading passage's claim that an invasion by outsiders could have caused the collapse of the Harappan civilization.

Next, the lecturer contends that other contemporary civilizations went through climate changes without being destroyed. While Egypt thrived despite its aridity, Mesopotamia was actually aided by flooding. Resultantly, the Harappans would have been able to sustain themselves even if there had been a dramatic change in climate. This fact contradicts the reading passage's claim that extreme climate change in the Indus River Valley resulted in the demise of the Harappans.

Finally, the lecturer asserts that cholera could not have been the cause. The Harappans had a sewer system as well as a water system that could provide their people with clean water. This goes against the idea presented in the reading passage that the downfall of the Harappans could be attributed to numerous diseases, including cholera, caused by shared water sources.

WORD REMINDER

assumption 가정   demise 소멸   groundless 근거가 없는   proof 증거   encroachment 침략   go through ~을 겪다
despite ~에도 불구하고   aridity 건조   sustain 유지하다   dramatic 극적인   attribute to ~의 탓으로 돌리다

TIPS for SUCCESS

\<there is> vs. \<there are>

〈There + be동사〉는 '~이 존재한다'는 뜻을 가진 표현이다. be동사는 뒤에 나오는 주어가 단수냐 복수냐에 따라 달라진다.

첫 번째 단락의 문장들을 살펴보자.

This contradicts the reading passage's claim that **there are** theories which could explain the sudden disappearance of the civilization.

that절 뒤에 나오는 theories가 복수이므로 there 다음에 is가 아닌 are가 쓰였다.

반면, 두 번째 단락의 문장을 살펴보자.

First, **there is** no evidence showing any proof of an invasion.

no evidence는 증거가 아예 없다는 뜻이므로 단수 동사인 is가 붙었다. 덧붙여, evidence는 불가산명사이므로 만약 '두 가지 증거가 있다' 라는 문장을 쓰고 싶다면 there are two pieces of evidence ~ 즉, piece(s)를 붙여서 셀 수 있도록 만들 수 있다.

TOEFL® MAP **ACTUAL TEST**

VOLUME
HELP
NEXT

WRITING | Question 2 of 2

00:30:00 ● HIDE TIME

ACTUAL TEST 01

Directions Read the question below. You have 30 minutes to plan, write, and revise your essay. Typically, an effective response will contain a minimum of 300 words.

Question

Do you agree or disagree with the following statement?

People who leave their hometowns have a higher chance of becoming happier and more successful than people who stay in their hometowns.

Use specific reasons and examples to support your answer.

CUT   PASTE   UNDO   REDO   Hide Word Count : 0

AGREE

- ***various experiences + interpersonal relationships*** 다양한 경험 + 대인 관계
  - broader perspectives + more opportunities 더 넓은 견해 + 더 많은 기회
    Ex moving to a new place: diff. lifestyles + thoughts 새로운 지역으로의 이주: 다른 생활 방식 + 생각
    → shared diverse point of views → helpful at work 다양한 관점을 공유 → 일에 도움이 되었음

- ***adaptation skills*** 적응 능력
  - new customs + unacquainted people 새로운 관습 + 만나보지 못한 사람들
    Ex cousin: introvert → moved to a diff. state → learned new skills
    사촌: 내성적 → 새로운 주로 이사 → 새로운 능력을 배웠음
    → enjoys getting along w/unacquainted people 처음 보는 사람들과 어울리는 것을 좋아함

INTRODUCTION

generalization: whether to stay or leave their hometowns
일반화: 고향에 머무를 것인지 떠날 것인지

⬇

school / work, financial status, desire to live in a diff. environment
학교 / 직장, 재정 상태, 다른 환경에서 살고자 하는 바람

⬇

thesis: agree (broader perspectives, ability to adapt to a new life)
논제: 찬성 (더 넓은 견해, 새로운 삶에 적응하는 능력)

DISAGREE

- ***comfort + stability*** 편안함 + 안정
  - new place: more effort + time → anxiousness + intimidation 새로운 장소: 더 많은 노력 + 시간 → 불안 + 두려움
    Ex friend: job in a diff. state 친구: 다른 주에서 직장을 구했음
    → start from scratch → waste of time 새로 시작 → 시간 낭비

- ***stronger bond*** 더 강한 유대
  - extend already formed relationships 이미 형성된 관계를 넓힘
    Ex cousin: new job → busy adjusting to work 사촌: 새 직장 → 일에 적응하느라 바빴음
    → coworkers: residing in the same hometown → familiarity: helpful
    동료들: 같은 고향에 거주 → 친숙함: 도움이 되었음

INTRODUCTION

generalization: whether to stay or leave their hometowns
일반화: 고향에 머무를 것인지 떠날 것인지

⬇

school / work, financial status, desire to live in a diff. environment
학교 / 직장, 재정 상태, 다른 환경에서 살고자 하는 바람

⬇

thesis: disagree (mental security, stronger interpersonal relationship)
논제: 반대 (정신적 안정감, 더욱 확고한 대인 관계)

CUT PASTE UNDO REDO

Most people face a time when they have to decide whether to stay in or leave their hometowns. School, work, financial status, or simply a desire to live in a different environment affects their decisions, and the consequences depend on how they adapt to new surroundings. Some contend that people are happier and more successful when they stay in their hometowns. However, I strongly believe living in an unfamiliar place opens people to more opportunities because it lets them develop extensive perspectives and develop the ability to adjust to a novel life.

First of all, people can get various experiences and form extensive relationships with others when moving to a different place. This will aid them in developing broader perspectives and expose them to more opportunities. For instance, when I moved to an unfamiliar town, I realized that not only did the people there have dissimilar lifestyles, but they also had a way of thinking distinct from that of my hometown. Thus I had a chance to share diverse points of view with other people that were very helpful at work.

On top of that, moving to an unfamiliar place can give people a great chance to get used to their new surroundings. By grasping new customs and by interacting with new people, they can develop competence in dealing with certain types of circumstances and individuals. For instance, my cousin was an introvert and had difficulty getting along with those whom she had not met before. However, she had to move to another state for work. Thanks to the new skills she learned, she now enjoys meeting new people in numerous types of gatherings.

It is true that staying in the town where one grew up provides comfort and stability. Conversely, too much relaxation may result in a lack of motivation, and a person may become apathetic. Having diverse experiences and building broader interpersonal relationships can help people gain a wider perspective. Furthermore, experiencing a new culture can give them a chance to acquire necessary skills in particular situations as well as in interpersonal relationships. For the above reasons, I firmly agree with the statement that people who leave their hometowns have a higher chance of becoming happier and more successful than people who stay in their hometowns.

WORD REMINDER

extensive 광범위한 perspective 견해 novel 새로운 dissimilar 다른 interact 서로 영향을 끼치다 competence 능력 circumstance 상황
introvert 내성적인 thanks to ~의 덕택으로 apathetic 무감각한 interpersonal relationship 대인 관계 acquire 얻다

Most people face a time when they have to decide whether to stay in or leave their hometowns. School, work, financial status, or simply a desire to live in a different environment affects their decision, and the consequences depend on how they adapt to new surroundings. Some contend that moving to a different place helps people succeed and become happier. However, I strongly believe it is better for people to stay in their hometowns because it contributes to mental security and enables them to build stronger interpersonal relationships with others.

First of all, unlike the feeling of comfort and stability that comes from staying in one's hometown, leaving for a new place can cause anxiety and intimidate many people. For example, my friend got a job in a different state and was very stressed out because she had to start from scratch. This included finding a grocery store, getting to know her new neighbors, and searching for a new doctor. As a result, she wasted a lot of time getting used to her local circumstances instead of putting effort into work for success and happiness.

On top of that, people can form stronger bonds with others in the region where they grew up. Rather than starting to build friendships by establishing personal relationships with new people, it would be much easier to keep and extend the relationships one has already formed. To illustrate, my cousin was hired by a company right after graduating from college and was very busy adjusting to her new job. However, most of her coworkers were familiar to her since they resided in the same hometown, and that familiarity helped her easily adapt to the company.

It is true that living in a new environment provides people with a chance to learn a new culture. On the other hand, it can also create stress and a feeling of wasting time. Moreover, people are able to build deeper interpersonal relationships with others they have already known for years, resulting in more opportunities for success. For the above reasons, I firmly disagree with the statement that people who leave their hometowns have a higher chance to become happier and more successful than people who stay in their hometowns.

WORD REMINDER

contribute 기여하다   anxiety 불안   intimidate 두려움   get used to ~하는데 익숙해지다   start from scratch 처음부터 다시 시작하다 bond 유대
adjust 맞추다   reside 거주하다

■ TIPS for SUCCESS

부정접속사

neither A nor B: A도 B도 아닌
not only A but also B: A 뿐만 아니라 B도
no sooner A than B: A를 하자마자 B하다
not A but B: A가 아닌 B

1 Nowadays, it is more important to work fast and to risk making mistakes than to work slowly and to make sure everything is correct.
오늘날, 천천히 일하고 모든 것이 맞는지 확인하는 것보다 일을 빨리 하며 실수의 위험을 무릅쓰는 것이 더 중요하다.

AGREE	DISAGREE
- work: more demanding 업무: 더욱 많은 것을 요함 - effectiveness: able to get a lot of work done in a short period of time → advantageous for company 효율성: 빠른 시간 내에 많은 일을 할 수 있음 → 회사에 이익	- making mistakes could delay the overall process 실수는 전체적인 진행을 늦출 수 있음 - less pressure → supplementation + improvement 압박감이 덜함 → 보완 + 향상

2 Successful people try new things and take risks rather than do what they can already do well.
성공한 사람들은 이미 잘할 수 있는 것보다 새로운 것을 시도한다.

AGREE	DISAGREE
- always look for challenges → become an innovator 항상 도전을 찾음 → 혁신가가 됨 - enjoy a sense of accomplishment 성취감을 즐김	- improve what they are good / gifted at 그들이 잘하는 / 재능이 있는 부분을 발전시킴 - start from scratch → taking too much time 처음부터 새로 시작 → 너무 많은 시간 소요

3 Which do you prefer, a job with a high salary but a higher risk of getting fired or a job with a low salary but with stability? 급여는 높지만 해고될 가능성이 높은 직장과 급여는 낮지만 안정적인 직장 중 어느 것을 더 선호하는가?

HIGH SALARY	STABILITY
- more motivated to work harder 더욱 열심히 일하도록 동기 부여를 받음 - financial advantage + accomplishment 재정적 이득 + 성취감	- less stress 스트레스 ↓ - able to make plans (no unexpected situation of getting fired) 계획을 세울 수 있음 (해고당하는 예상치 못한 상황 ✗)

TOEFL® MAP

ACTUAL TEST Writing 2

02

TOEFL® MAP **ACTUAL TEST**

VOLUME

HELP

NEXT

WRITING | Question 1 of 2   00:03:00 ⊖ HIDE TIME

ACTUAL TEST **02**

The narwhal is one of nature's most unique creatures. A species of toothed whale, it grows to around five meters in length. But the most fascinating feature of the narwhal is the single tusk that protrudes from its head. Narwhal tusk can be almost three meters long. For centuries, people have marveled at them. They were once highly valued and even believed to be magical in nature. Modern-day scientists have determined that the tusks probably serve multiple purposes.

The first use of the tusk is highly utilitarian in nature. Narwhals live in the cold waters of the Arctic Ocean. The waters in which they reside are frequently covered by thick sheets of ice. Narwhals, being mammals, must surface to breathe, or they will drown. So when the water is covered by ice, they use their tusks to break through the ice whenever they need to breathe fresh air.

In general, male narwhals have tusks while females rarely possess them. Many marine biologists therefore believe that male narwhals must use their tusks when fighting one another. Males of many species commonly fight when competing either for territory or females. With their tusks making perfect weapons, narwhal males likely engage in battle with them in their fights for dominance.

Finally, scientists from Harvard and other institutes made a recent discovery about the narwhal's tusks. They learned that there are millions of nerve endings on the outer part of the tusk. This enables the tusk to operate as a sensor of sorts. Narwhals can detect changes in the water temperature and pressure and notice what kinds of particles are in the water, and they probably have other functions as well. By having a highly perceptive sensory organ, narwhals are equipped with a very useful appendage.

🎧 02-01

Directions You have 20 minutes to plan and write your response. Your response will be judged on the basis of the quality of your writing and on how well your response presents the points in the lecture and their relationship to the passage. Typically, an effective response will be 150-225 words.

Question Summarize the points made in the lecture, being sure to explain how they challenge specific claims made in the reading passage.

CUT   PASTE   UNDO   REDO   Hide Word Count : 0

The narwhal is one of nature's most unique creatures. A species of toothed whale, it grows to around five meters in length. But the most fascinating feature of the narwhal is the single tusk that protrudes from its head. Narwhal tusk can be almost three meters long. For centuries, people have marveled at them. They were once highly valued and even believed to be magical in nature. Modern-day scientists have determined that the tusks probably serve multiple purposes.

The first use of the tusk is highly utilitarian in nature. Narwhals live in the cold waters of the Arctic Ocean. The waters in which they reside are frequently covered by thick sheets of ice. Narwhals, being mammals, must surface to breathe, or they will drown. So when the water is covered by ice, they use their tusks to break through the ice whenever they need to breathe fresh air.

In general, male narwhals have tusks while females rarely possess them. Many marine biologists therefore believe that male narwhals must use their tusks when fighting one another. Males of many species commonly fight when competing either for territory or females. With their tusks making perfect weapons, narwhal males likely engage in battle with them in their fights for dominance.

Finally, scientists from Harvard and other institutes made a recent discovery about the narwhal's tusks. They learned that there are millions of nerve endings on the outer part of the tusk. This enables the tusk to operate as a sensor of sorts. Narwhals can detect changes in the water temperature and pressure and notice what kinds of particles are in the water, and they probably have other functions as well. By having a highly perceptive sensory organ, narwhals are equipped with a very useful appendage.

✎ NOTE-TAKING

READING

a narwhal's unique tusk has evolved to serve some purpose
일각돌고래의 특이한 엄니는 몇몇 용도로 사용되기 위해 진화해 왔음

❶ *for breaking through the ice* 얼음을 깨기 위해

- need to breathe air ∵ mammals 공기를 마시기 위해 ∵ 포유 동물

> **Paraphrasing Example** Narwhals need to breathe air, and a tusk can be utilized to shatter the ice.

❷ *for fighting* 싸우기 위해

- competing for territory / females 영역 / 암컷에 대한 경쟁

> **Paraphrasing Example** The tusk is also used in fights to take territory or females from other competitors.

❸ *for sensing* 감지를 위해

- water temperature + pressure 수온 + 수압
- kinds of particles in the water 물 속의 입자의 종류

> **Paraphrasing Example** Its millions of nerve endings make the tusk a sensory organ.

WORD REMINDER

feature 특성 tusk 엄니 protrude 돌출하다 marvel 경탄하다 determine 결정하다 utilitarian 실용의 in nature 사실상 reside 거주하다 mammal 포유 동물 breathe 호흡하다 drown 익사하다 possess 소유하다 territory 영토 engage in ~에 종사하다 dominance 지배 institute 기관 nerve ending 신경 종말 pressure 압력 particle 입자 perceptive 지각이 예민한 equip 채비를 하다 appendage 부속물

LISTENING

the uses of a tusk: doubtful 엄니의 사용: 의심스러움

❶ *fragile* 깨지기 쉬움

- length: up to 3m / weight: only 10kg 길이: 최대 3미터 / 무게: 단 10킬로그램
- often swim in areas w/thick ice 종종 두꺼운 얼음이 있는 지역에서 수영
  → impossible to break through the ice 얼음을 깨는 것은 불가능

> **Paraphrasing Example** The utility of a tusk in breaking through the ice is unconvincing in that the tusk is too fragile.

❷ *peaceful* 온순함

- fights: only on rare occasions 싸움: 드문 경우에만 발생
- scars + wounds ✕ 흉터 + 상처 ✕
- used for social ranking 사회 계급에 사용됨

> **Paraphrasing Example** Narwhals do not often engage in fights.

❸ *nerves do not act like sensors* 신경은 감각 기관 역할을 하지 않음

- F: only few possess a tusk 암컷: 몇몇만이 엄니를 소유
- F: outlive M 암컷: 수컷보다 오래 삶

> **Paraphrasing Example** Two pieces of evidence show that the nerve endings attached to the tusk are not used as sensors.

WORD REMINDER

obviously 분명히 entire 전체의 sort 종류 dwell 거주하다 logical 논리적인 assume 추측하다 despite ~에도 불구하고 fragile 부서지기 쉬운 extremely 매우 absolutely 완전히 occasion 경우 lack 결핍 scar 흉터 wound 상처 common practice 흔한 일 pod 작은 떼 intrigue 흥미를 돋우다 evolve 진화하다 so-called 소위 alive 살아 있는

The lecturer argues that many findings concerning the use of a narwhal's tusk are doubtful. This directly refutes the reading passage's claim that a narwhal's unique tusk has evolved to serve some purpose.

Firstly, the utility of a tusk in breaking through the ice is unconvincing in that the tusk is too fragile. In addition, narwhals often swim in places where there are thick layers of ice making it unlikely that narwhals use their tusks to shatter the ice. This contradicts the reading passage's claim that narwhals need to breathe air and that a tusk can be utilized to shatter the ice.

Next, narwhals do not often engage in fights. This assertion is supported by the fact that there are usually no scars and wounds to be found on narwhals. This rebuts the point presented in the reading passage that the tusk is also used in fights to take territory or females from other competitors.

Lastly, two pieces of evidence show that the nerve endings attached to the tusk are not used as sensors. First of all, few females possess a tusk. Furthermore, female narwhals outlive males, which makes its uses by males uncertain. These two facts contradict the reading passage's claim that its millions of nerve endings make the tusk a sensory organ.

WORD REMINDER

finding 연구 결과   concerning ~에 관하여   unconvincing 설득력 없는   shatter 산산이 부수다   utilize 이용하다   outlive ~보다 더 오래 살다

TIPS for SUCCESS

주어와 동사의 일치 Subject-Verb Agreement

주어와 동사의 일치에 유의하자. 주어가 단수일 때에는 단수동사를, 복수일 때에는 복수동사를 맞추어 사용해야 한다는 점을 항상 기억해야 한다. 첫 번째 단락의 문장의 일부를 살펴보자.

Many findings concerning the use of a narwhal's tusk **are** doubtful.

위의 문장에서 주어는 many findings이므로 복수동사인 are를 쓴다. 동사 바로 전에 나온 the use of a narwhal's tusk를 주어로 혼동하여 is를 쓰지 않도록 조심하지.

CUT   PASTE   UNDO   REDO   Hide Word Count : 0

Directions Read the question below. You have 30 minutes to plan, write, and revise your essay. Typically, an effective response will contain a minimum of 300 words.

Question

Do you agree or disagree with the following statement?

Students should have a part-time job while they are attending college.

Use specific reasons and examples to support your answer.

AGREE

- *working experience* 일의 경험
  - preparing for the future 미래에 대한 준비
    Ex uncle: majored in chemistry → worked at a pharmaceutical company
    삼촌: 화학 전공 → 제약 회사에서 근무
    → realized he was better at marketing products 제품 홍보에 더 능력이 있다는 것을 깨달았음

- *developing responsibility / commitment* 책임감 / 헌신 발전시킴
  - dealing w/coworkers + accomplishing given tasks 동료들 상대 + 주어진 일 성취
    Ex exam: tired → still had to go to work 시험: 피곤 → 여전히 일을 하러 가야 했음
    → learned to manage time more effectively 시간을 더 효율적으로 관리하는 것을 배움

INTRODUCTION

generalization: many have a part-time job while studying
일반화: 많은 학생들이 공부하며 아르바이트를 함

⬇

various reasons: tuition, experience, entertainment
여러 가지 이유: 학비, 경험, 여가

⬇

thesis: agree (preparation for the future, responsibility)
논제: 찬성 (미래를 위한 준비, 책임감)

DISAGREE

- *studying: basic part of student life* 공부: 학생의 기본
  - try to get deeper knowledge 더 깊은 지식을 쌓기 위한 노력
    Ex friend w/scholarship → part-time job → lost scholarship 장학금 받던 친구 → 아르바이트 → 장학금 중단
    → wasting time / not helpful for future career 시간 낭비 / 미래 경력에 도움 ✗

- *most part-time jobs: not related to major* 대부분의 아르바이트: 전공과 무관
  - not helpful in future job 미래 직업에 도움 ✗
    Ex cousin majoring in archaeology → coffee shop ∵ space availability + time
    고고학 전공 사촌 → 커피숍 ∵ 자리 유효성 + 시간
    → only learned basic responsibilities 기본적 책임감만 배움

INTRODUCTION

generalization: many have a part-time job while studying
일반화: 많은 학생들이 공부하며 아르바이트를 함

⬇

various reasons: tuition, experience, entertainment
여러 가지 이유: 학비, 경험, 여가

⬇

thesis: disagree (fundamental part of student life, no relationship btwn job + major)
논제: 반대 (학생의 기본적인 부분, 직업과 전공의 연관성 ✗)

Nowadays, many students have part-time jobs while studying at school. They may need money to pay for tuition, want to gain some working experience, or simply wish to work to earn money for entertainment. Though some say students should concentrate on studying, I strongly believe they should do part-time work while attending college because of experience and responsibility.

First of all, students can prepare for the future by working and cooperating with others. To illustrate, my uncle was majoring in chemistry, and he had a part-time job at a pharmaceutical company as a researcher. Later, he realized he was better at marketing products by using the knowledge he had gained in college than by sitting in a lab and doing experiments. As a result, he changed his major to marketing and found his ultimate career.

Moreover, students can develop responsibility and commitment by having part-time jobs. For instance, one of my friends had a part-time job during his last semester, and he worked for a company which was an hour away from his dormitory. One day, he was tired from cramming for his midterm exams; nevertheless, he had no choice but to make the hour-long commute even though he was exhausted. He said he learned to be more disciplined and to more effectively manage his time on a daily basis.

It is true that building in-depth knowledge is crucial for students, and, in a sense, university might be the last stage for many of them to develop their skills. On the other hand, a lack of experience or responsibility would make them confused when they enter the real world, and they might have a hard time adapting themselves to work. Therefore, I believe a part-time job would help them make the transition into the society, and I assert that students should get a part-time job while studying at university.

WORD REMINDER

pharmaceutical company 제약 회사   commitment 의무, 책임   cram 벼락치기 공부를 하다   commute 통근[통학] 하다   disciplined 잘 훈련된
in-depth 심층의   crucial 중대한   transition 변화, 변천

TIPS for SUCCESS

and, but, so로 시작되는 문장을 쓰는 습관은 좋지 않다. 바꿔 쓸 수 있는 단어를 살펴보자.

and	but	so
in addition	however	thus
furthermore	nevertheless	consequently
moreover	conversely	therefore
on top of that	on the other hand	as a result
also	though	hence

Nowadays, many students have part-time jobs while studying at school. They may need money to pay for tuition, want to gain some working experience, or simply wish to work to earn money for entertainment. Though some say it is crucial for students to have a job, I strongly believe they should concentrate on studying because studying is a fundamental part of student life; in addition, part-time jobs are not always related to a student's major.

First of all, a part-time job would not only take away one's study time but also keep one from concentrating. For instance, my friend could not keep a scholarship after one year because she could not concentrate on her studies as much as she used to due to her part-time job. It would have been better for both her future career and for keeping her source of funding had she focused only on her studies instead of her part-time job.

Moreover, many part-time jobs that students have are not related to their majors. To illustrate, my cousin had a part-time job in her sophomore year at university. Since she was majoring in archaeology, the jobs she was looking for were either very limited or offered only to those looking for full-time positions. Consequently, she worked at a coffee shop and learned basic responsibilities, which she could have easily learned in her future workplace after graduation.

It is true that developing responsibility and working with others are important to preparing for a future career. However, as mentioned above, students can develop social skills and a sense of responsibility when they enter the actual job field. Obtaining in-depth knowledge is the fundamental reason for being in college. In addition, many part-time jobs have nothing to do with students' majors. Therefore, I assert that students should concentrate on studying while attending college.

WORD REMINDER

fundamental 기본적인   scholarship 장학금   source 근원   sophomore 2학년생   archaeology 고고학   obtain 얻다

TIPS for SUCCESS

두 번째 단락의 문장을 살펴보며 유용하게 쓰일 수 있는 표현들을 알아보자.

not only A but also B: A뿐만 아니라 B도

First of all, a part-time job would **not only** take away one's study time **but also** keep one from concentrating.

take A away from B: B로부터 A를 제거하다

First of all, a part-time job would not only **take away** one's study time but also keep one **from** concentrating.

keep A from B: B로부터 A를 삼가다

First of all, a part-time job would not only take away one's study time but also **keep** one **from** concentrating.

※ 〈keep + 목적어 + -ing〉는 '~를 계속 ~하게 하다'라는 뜻을 가지고 있으므로 위의 keep A from B와 혼동하지 않게 조심하자.

RELATED TOPICS

1 It is more important for students to understand ideas and concepts than to learn facts.
학생들에게 있어, 의견과 개념을 이해하는 것은 사실을 배우는 것보다 중요하다.

AGREE	DISAGREE
- fact: requires memory skills only → able to learn facts on one's own 사실: 암기 능력만 필요함 → 사실에 관한 것은 스스로 배울 수 있음 - able to develop one's own ideas 본인의 아이디어를 발전시킬 수 있음	- most ideas and concepts should be based on facts 대부분의 의견과 개념은 사실에 바탕을 두고 있음 - could result in misunderstanding → facts should be taught first 오해를 초래할 수 있음 → 사실에 관한 것을 먼저 가르쳐야 함

2 High school graduates should take a year off before entering a university.
고등학교 졸업생들은 대학을 가기 전 일 년을 쉬어야 한다.

AGREE	DISAGREE
- need time to think about one's ultimate goal 본인의 궁극적 목표를 생각할 시간 필요 - gain diverse perspectives through experiences 경험을 통해 다양한 견해를 쌓음 ex) working, traveling 아르바이트, 여행	- able to take some time off during summer + winter breaks 여름, 겨울 방학 동안 시간을 낼 수 있음 - importance of continuity → could affect one's pace and habit of studying 지속성 중요 → 공부하는 속도와 습관에 영향을 미칠 수 있음

3 In order to succeed, it is more important to get along with others well at school than to study hard.
성공하기 위해서는 공부하는 것보다 학교에서 다른 이들과 잘 지내는 것이 더 중요하다.

AGREE	DISAGREE
- social skills 사회성 - forming personality + communication skills 성격 + 의사소통 능력 형성	- study: basic part of student life 공부: 학생의 기본적인 부분 - many jobs require in-depth knowledge 다수의 직업은 심도 있는 지식을 필요로 함

4 The most important factor in succeeding in life is to get a higher education.
인생에서 성공하는데 있어 가장 중요한 요소는 고등 교육을 받는 것이다.

AGREE	DISAGREE
- gaining in-depth knowledge w/people who share the same interests → interpersonal relationships 같은 흥미를 가진 사람들과 함께 심도 있는 지식을 공유하는 것 → 대인 관계 - many opportunities 많은 기회 ex) internship 인턴십	- some jobs: learning in the actual working field is essential 일부 직업: 실제 작업 환경에서 배우는 것이 필요 ex) fishing 어업 - developing one's talent is more important in some cases 어떤 경우에는 본인의 재능을 발달시키는 것이 더욱 중요함 ex) Steve Jobs 스티브 잡스

5 It is better to take the most difficult courses at university even if one does not get good grades.
좋은 성적을 받지 못하더라도 대학에서 가장 어려운 수업들을 듣는 것이 좋다.

AGREE	DISAGREE
- learn to deal with difficulties 어려움에 대처하는 것을 배움 - challenge: opportunity to test one's own learning capacity 도전: 본인의 배움에 대한 능력을 시험할 수 있는 기회	- grade: important when getting a job 성적: 취업할 때 중요함 - most difficult course does not necessarily mean the best course if it does not suit one's aptitude 본인의 적성에 맞지 않는다면, 가장 어려운 수업이 가장 좋은 수업이라고 할 수 없음

TOEFL MAP

ACTUAL TEST Writing 2

03

Thanks to improved lifestyles, consumers have a variety of options to choose from when purchasing goods or services. As each person has his own style and taste, companies strive to suit customers' preferences by providing a large selection of goods. Most people have experienced excitement when they visit a store with a wide range of choices, any of which could be theirs.

Consumers with many choices can shop according to their personal preferences. Having multiple options also means individuals have more freedom to express themselves. This results in happiness and creativity. For example, a vast selection of Lego bricks motivates kids to come up with countless ideas, developing their creativity and imagination.

Better-quality goods and services is another advantage of having many choices. In order to suit each customer's taste, companies continuously work to improve quality. Not only do companies try to improve the quality of their products, but they also compete for better prices. Since there are websites which show the prices of similar items, consumers can easily compare and see which companies offer better options. This helps consumers avoid overpriced items.

With a wide range of choices, people also feel that they have more power and control over what they buy or choose, providing satisfaction. This is common in the workplace as well. Many studies have found that employees are more engaged when they have greater control over their work. A greater amount of autonomy and decision-making leads to higher satisfaction and, hence, healthier bodies.

🎧 03-01

Directions You have 20 minutes to plan and write your response. Your response will be judged on the basis of the quality of your writing and on how well your response presents the points in the lecture and their relationship to the passage. Typically, an effective response will be 150-225 words.

Question Summarize the points made in the lecture, being sure to explain how they challenge specific claims made in the reading passage.

CUT PASTE UNDO REDO   Hide Word Count : 0

Thanks to improved lifestyles, consumers have a variety of options to choose from when purchasing goods or services. As each person has his own style and taste, companies strive to suit customers' preferences by providing a large selection of goods. Most people have experienced excitement when they visit a store with a wide range of choices, any of which could be theirs.

Consumers with many choices can shop according to their personal preferences. Having multiple options also means individuals have more freedom to express themselves. This results in happiness and creativity. For example, a vast selection of Lego bricks motivates kids to come up with countless ideas, developing their creativity and imagination.

Better-quality goods and services is another advantage of having many choices. In order to suit each customer's taste, companies continuously work to improve quality. Not only do companies try to improve the quality of their products, but they also compete for better prices. Since there are websites which show the prices of similar items, consumers can easily compare and see which companies offer better options. This helps consumers avoid overpriced items.

With a wide range of choices, people also feel that they have more power and control over what they buy or choose, providing satisfaction. This is common in the workplace as well. Many studies have found that employees are more engaged when they have greater control over their work. A greater amount of autonomy and decision-making leads to higher satisfaction and, hence, healthier bodies.

📝 NOTE-TAKING

READING

individuals: own style + taste → companies: large selection of goods + services
개인: 자신만의 스타일 + 취향 → 기업: 많은 종류의 상품 + 서비스

❶ able to shop according to preferences 개인의 취향에 따라 쇼핑 가능

Ex many kinds of Lego blocks: motivate kids, developing creativity + imagination
다양한 종류의 레고 블록: 아이들에게 동기 부여, 창의력 + 상상력 발달

> **Paraphrasing Example** A variety of choices provide consumers a chance to shop according to their personal preferences.

❷ many choices → better quality + price 다양한 선택 → 더 나은 질 + 가격

– companies → detailed info → consumers: knowledgeable / able to avoid overpriced items
기업 → 자세한 정보 → 소비자: 지식 / 바가지를 막을 수 있음

> **Paraphrasing Example** Consumers are left with better prices and quality when there are more similar items to choose from.

❸ more choices → power + control 다양한 선택 → 힘 + 지배력

– workplace → more engaged → satisfaction ↑ / healthier body 일터 → 의욕 상승 → 만족 ↑ / 더욱 건강한 몸

> **Paraphrasing Example** Having a feeling of control and power makes consumers satisfied.

WORD REMINDER
consumer 소비자 goods 상품 strive 노력하다 suit 맞추다 preference 선호 range 범위 vast 광대한 motivate ~에 동기를 주다
avoid 막다, 피하다 overpriced 값이 너무 비싸게 매겨진 engaged 몰두해 있는 autonomy 자율

LISTENING

experience at shoe store → too many questions → good or bad?
신발 가게에서의 경험 → 너무 많은 질문들 → 좋을까 나쁠까?

❶ study @ supermarket 슈퍼마켓에서의 연구

– consumers: (1) 24 kinds of jams (2) 6 jams 소비자: (1) 24종류의 잼 (2) 6종류의 잼

– result: consumers less likely to purchase (1) even put off purchases indefinitely
결과: 소비자가 (1)을 구입할 가능성은 낮음 / 심지어는 무기한으로 구매 보류

> **Paraphrasing Example** A study found that consumers with more choices postponed their purchases.

❷ many kinds → more expertise in the field → better quality → chance to make bias and error in decision making 많은 종류 → 그 분야에서 더 전문적 → 더 나은 질 → 결정하는데 있어 편견과 오류를 범할 가능성

– consumers: (1) many kinds of chocolate (2) a few kinds ← both from same brand
소비자: (1) 많은 종류의 초콜릿 (2) 몇 종류의 초콜릿 ← 두 그룹 모두 같은 브랜드의 초콜릿

– result: people chose (1) over (2) 결과: 사람들은 (2)가 아닌 (1) 선택

> **Paraphrasing Example** Giving lots of choices to consumers can lead to misconceptions about a particular brand being of good quality.

❸ dissatisfaction + regrets 불만족 + 후회

– overthink → "what if?" → residual stress → disappointment 계속 생각 → "만약 …했다면?" → 미련에서 오는 스트레스 → 실망감

> **Paraphrasing Example** Shoppers tend to be disappointed with products after choosing one from among many. This happens because people experience residual stress.

WORD REMINDER
occasion 때, 경우 feature 기능 insole 구두의 안창 orthotic (정형용) 지지대 waterproof 방수의 overwhelmed (정신적으로) 압도되다
exhausted 기진맥진한 put off ~을 연기하다 indefinitely 무기한으로 in terms of ~인 면에서 expertise 전문적 기술 particular 특정한
field 분야 bias 편견 overthink 과하게 고민하다 residual 잔여의

The professor says that too many choices can make our lives unhappy. This directly refutes the idea in the reading passage that consumers get numerous advantages by having lots of choices.

First, the professor mentions a study done at a supermarket where one group of shoppers had a choice of twenty-four different jams while the other group had only six. It found that consumers with more choices postponed their purchases. This goes against the reading passage's idea that a variety of choices provide consumers a chance to shop according to their personal preferences.

Secondly, giving lots of choices to consumers can lead to misconceptions about a particular brand being of good quality. In a study, shoppers were shown two groups of chocolates from the same brand: one with many choices and the other with only a few choices. Without knowing all the chocolates were from the same brand, consumers chose the former group as having a better taste. This refutes the reading passage's claim that consumers are left with better prices and quality when there are more similar items to choose from.

Lastly, shoppers tend to be disappointed with products after choosing one from among many. This happens because people experience residual stress, leading to discontent and regret. This directly rebuts the reading passage's idea that having a feeling of control and power makes consumers satisfied.

▶ **WORD REMINDER**

numerous 수많은   postpone 미루다   misconception 잘못된 생각   tend to ~하는 경향이 있다

■ **TIPS for SUCCESS**

나열 Listing

독립형 에세이에서 본론을 시작할 수 있는 표현과 결론을 알려 주는 표현들을 살펴보자.

본론 1을 시작할 수 있는 표현	본론 2를 시작할 수 있는 표현	결론을 알리는 표현
First	Apart from that	To summarize / To conclude
To begin with	On top of that	To sum up
First of all	Moreover	In summary / In conclusion
For one	In addition	All in all
Firstly	Furthermore	Given the above points
First off	Next	Lastly
In the first place	For another	Accordingly

CUT   PASTE   UNDO   REDO   Hide Word Count : 0

Directions Read the question below. You have 30 minutes to plan, write, and revise your essay. Typically, an effective response will contain a minimum of 300 words.

Question

Do you agree or disagree with the following statement?

If a person wants to succeed, developing many skills is better than focusing on one skill.

Use specific reasons and examples to support your answer.

ACTUAL TEST **03**

AGREE

- *interrelated* 서로 연관성이 있음
  - communication + persuasiveness → mandatory in workplace 의사소통 + 설득력 → 직장에서 필수
    - **Ex** person w/comprehensive knowledge → no use if he cannot express ideas
      포괄적인 지식을 가진 사람 → 표현을 못한다면 쓸모가 없음
      → certain skills: closely related + a synergistic effect 특정 능력: 밀접한 관련이 있음 + 시너지 효과

- *helpful in discovering interests + abilities / changing main field*
  능력 + 흥미를 발견 / 전문 분야를 바꾸는데 도움이 됨
  - **Ex** cousin: scuba diving instructor → injured → quit job 사촌: 스쿠버다이빙 강사 → 부상 → 일 중단
    → had a certificate that he had earned in the past → able to get another job easily
    과거에 땄던 자격증이 있었음 → 쉽게 다른 직업을 얻을 수 있었음

INTRODUCTION

generalization: whether to develop many skills or focus on a specific skill → always been present
일반화: 많은 능력을 발달시킬지 하나의 능력에 집중할 것인지 → 언제나 있던 문제

⬇

each w/advantages + disadvantages
각각은 장점 + 단점이 있음

⬇

thesis: agree (interrelated, changeable)
논제: 찬성 (서로 연관되어 있음, 바꿀 수 있음)

DISAGREE

- *most jobs → employees w/a specific skill* 대부분의 직업: 하나의 특정한 능력을 가진 직원들
  - ∵ tasks: segmented among diff. divisions 업무: 다른 부서들로 나뉘어 있음
    - **Ex** employee w/many abilities / not as competent as others 많은 능력을 가졌으나 / 다른 이들만큼 능력이 있지 않은 직원
      → corporation: needs someone w/professional capacity in a specific field
      회사: 특정 분야에 전문적인 능력을 가진 사람이 필요함

- *cultivating different skills → may be a waste of time* 다른 능력을 키우는 것 → 시간 낭비일 수 있음
  - time: could be used to improve one's specific skill 시간: 하나의 특정한 능력을 향상시키는데 쓰일 수 있음
    - **Ex** studies: students studying diverse disciplines 연구: 다양한 학문을 공부했던 학생들
      → lower chance of getting a decent job than those focusing on one field
      한 분야에 초점을 맞추었던 학생들에 비해 훌륭한 직업을 가질 확률이 낮음

INTRODUCTION

generalization: whether to develop many skills or focus on a specific skill → always been present
일반화: 많은 능력을 발달시킬지 하나의 능력에 집중할 것인지 → 언제나 있던 문제

⬇

each w/advantages + disadvantages
각각은 장점 + 단점이 있음

⬇

thesis: disagree (become professional, save time)
논제: 반대 (전문화됨, 시간 절약)

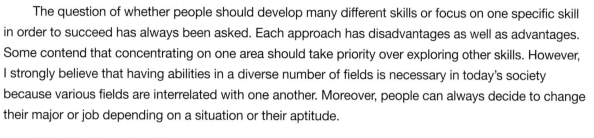

The question of whether people should develop many different skills or focus on one specific skill in order to succeed has always been asked. Each approach has disadvantages as well as advantages. Some contend that concentrating on one area should take priority over exploring other skills. However, I strongly believe that having abilities in a diverse number of fields is necessary in today's society because various fields are interrelated with one another. Moreover, people can always decide to change their major or job depending on a situation or their aptitude.

To begin with, such skills as communication and persuasiveness are mandatory in the workplace as presenting an idea must come before a person can implement it as an actual project. For instance, even if a person is an outstanding employee with comprehensive knowledge, it is impossible for him to give shape to a plan if he cannot express his ideas. Thus certain skills are closely related to each other and create a synergistic effect.

Furthermore, developing many skills is helpful in discovering one's interests and abilities. In addition, sometimes a person may have to change his main field because of dissatisfaction or a change in his situation. To illustrate, my cousin was a scuba diving instructor and was injured as a result of his work. Although he had to quit his job, he was easily able to get a job at an accounting company thanks to a certificate he had earned in the past. Had he not had such a skill, he could have been frustrated and discouraged as a consequence of losing his previous job and moving farther away from succeeding in his career.

It is true that concentrating on a skill helps a person acquire in-depth knowledge in a specific area. However, if that skill becomes useless due to circumstances or if a person loses interest in using the skill, that individual may face hardship and confusion. Furthermore, exploring other skills can create a synergistic effect. For these two reasons, I firmly agree with the statement that if a person wants to succeed, developing many different skills is better than focusing on one skill.

WORD REMINDER

approach 접근법   priority 우위   interrelated 밀접한 관계의   aptitude 적성   persuasiveness 설득력   mandatory 의무의   present 나타내다
implement 이행하다   outstanding 우수한   comprehensive 포괄적인   give shape to a plan 계획을 구체화하다   synergistic 상승적인
accounting 회계(학)   certificate 면허증   frustrated 좌절한   acquire 얻다   in-depth 심층의   confusion 혼돈

■ TIPS for SUCCESS

in + -ing

〈in + -ing〉는 '~를 할 때' 또는 '~함에 있어'라고 해석이 되며 동작 표현을 나타낼 때 쓰인다.

세 번째 단락의 문장을 살펴보자.

Furthermore, developing many skills is helpful **in discovering** one's interests and abilities.

위의 문장에서 helpful in discovering는 '발견함에 있어 도움을 준다'고 해석된다.

cf. 이와 비슷한 표현들로는 〈by + -ing〉 (~을 함으로써: 1권 Test 06 참고)와 〈on/upon + -ing〉 (~ 하자마자: 1권 Test 11 참고) 등이 있다.

The question of whether a person should develop many different skills or focus on one specific skill in order to succeed has always been asked. Each approach has disadvantages as well as advantages. Some contend that having abilities in a diverse number of fields is necessary in today's society. However, I strongly believe that concentrating on one area should take priority over exploring other skills because a person can gain in-depth knowledge by focusing on a particular area. Moreover, concentrating on one skill can save time.

To begin with, most jobs require an employee with a specific skill. Tasks are segmented among different divisions of a company, making it necessary for workers to develop in-depth knowledge in a particular area. For instance, an employee at a company may have a great number of abilities in various areas but not be as competent in a specific area as other workers. Although he possesses diverse skills, what the corporation needs is someone with a professional capacity in a specific field.

Furthermore, cultivating different skills may be a waste of time. Having broad knowledge in various areas may help a person; however, it would take a certain amount of time away which could otherwise be used to improve one specific skill for success in a particular field. To illustrate, many studies have shown that students studying multiple disciplines in university have a lower chance of getting a decent job after graduation than those focusing on one academic field.

It is true that various skills are interrelated with one another. However, corporations and other organizations have different departments in which employees specialize in particular fields, and each worker is expected to possess in-depth knowledge in his area. Furthermore, building many kinds of skills may waste a person's time and effort. For these two reasons, I firmly disagree with the statement that if a person wants to succeed, developing many different skills is better than focusing on one skill.

WORD REMINDER

centralize ~에 집중되다   segment 분할하다   division 부, 과   competent 유능한   possess 소유하다   corporation 기업
capacity 재능, 역량   cultivate 양성하다   otherwise 만약 그렇지 않으면   discipline (학문의) 분야   decent 남부럽지 않은   department 부서, 과
specialize 전문화하다

TIPS for SUCCESS

a number of와 the number of의 차이점에 대해서 알아보자.

a number of는 '얼마간의(some)'의 의미를 지니고 있으며 복수명사와 복수동사를 동반한다. '많다'는 표현으로 a great number of가 쓰이며 동의어로는 many, numerous, a lot of, an enormous number of 등이 있다. 두 번째 단락의 문장을 살펴보자.

For instance, an employee at a company may have **a** great **number of** abilities in various areas but not be as competent in those areas as other workers.

'많은 능력(many abilities)'과 바꾸어 쓸 수 있는 a great number of abilities가 쓰였다. 만약 great을 제외한다면 '몇몇 능력'이라고 해석이 된다.

the number of는 특정 숫자를 나타내며 복수명사와 단수동사를 동반한다. 다음의 예문을 살펴보자.

The number of people developing abilities in various areas has been increasing lately.

(최근 여러 분야에서 능력을 키우는 사람들의 숫자가 많아졌다.)

주어가 사람들을 가리키는 것이 아니라 사람들의 '숫자'를 가리키기 때문에 단수동사가 와야만 한다.

RELATED TOPICS

1 People are busy doing many different things so that they do only a few things well.

사람들은 많은 것을 하느라 바쁘기 때문에 몇 가지만을 잘 한다.

AGREE	DISAGREE
- focus ↓ 집중력 ↓ - haste: chance of making mistakes ↑ 서두름: 실수를 할 가능성 ↑	- many people are skilled at multiple tasks 많은 사람들이 여러 업무에 능력이 있음 ex) working while doing housework 집안일도 하면서 일도 함 - many routine chores → no special skill involved 많은 일상적인 잡일 → 특별한 능력을 필요로 하지 않음 ex) watching TV, having a meal, driving a car TV 시청, 식사, 운전

2 Some people prefer to have broad knowledge in many academic fields while others prefer to specialize in one specific area.

어떤 이들은 하나의 특정한 분야에 전문화하는 것을 선호하는 반면 어떤 이들은 많은 학문에 폭넓은 지식을 가지는 것을 선호한다.

HAVE BROAD KNOWLEDGE	SPECIALIZE
- diverse choices in jobs 직업 선택의 폭이 큼 - many disciplines → interrelated 많은 학문 → 서로 연관되어 있음	- specialize in one field → higher chance of succeeding 한 분야에서의 전문화 → 성공의 가능성 ↑ - able to gain in-depth knowledge 깊이 있는 지식을 얻을 수 있음

3 It is better to complete a task before starting a new one instead of doing various tasks simultaneously. 동시에 여러 가지 일을 하는 것보다 하나의 일을 끝내고 새로운 일을 하는 것이 더 낫다.

AGREE	DISAGREE
- able to concentrate on one task → time saving 하나의 일에 집중할 수 있음 → 시간 절약 - motivation to do the next task after feeling a sense of accomplishment upon finishing one task 하나의 임무를 마치고 성취감을 느낀 후 다음 일을 시작할 동기 부여	- less boring / refreshing 덜 지루함 / 새로운 기분 - many tasks: interrelated → doing similar tasks will save time 많은 업무들: 서로 연관성이 있음 → 비슷한 일을 하면 시간을 절약하게 됨

TOEFL MAP

ACTUAL
TEST Writing 2

04

Thanks to the development of technology, people have been able to share their daily lives with others in different parts of the world. Though social media has made it feasible to communicate with people around the world simultaneously, it has also brought about a number of problems, some of which are serious and require immediate attention.

There have been numerous studies done on how social media affects health. Instead of spending time having face-to-face conversations with one another, people become more isolated and more dependent on social media. A study has found that reducing time on social media has decreased feelings of loneliness and improved people's overall well-being. It has also been discovered that social media interaction over in-person relationships has exacerbated feelings of depression or the fear of missing out, commonly known as FOMO.

There is also a danger of losing creativity due to the prevalence of social media. Rather than coming up with ideas on their own, people simply type in keywords on social media and look for ideas, choose ones that they like, and duplicate them. Many ideas used to be devised when people met in person for discussions. However, social media has hampered this, and it is difficult for people to share their opinions before producing their own ideas.

Misinformation is another serious problem that cannot be easily solved. The reason is that some media organizations or individuals abuse the nature of social media. Once inaccurate information has been released, it continues to spread rampantly even after corrections are made. There are people who distribute misinformation intentionally because it gets clicks. This can even result in innocent victims who need to go through extremely challenging times and situations even though they are not related to the incidents.

🎧 04-01

ACTUAL TEST 04

Directions You have 20 minutes to plan and write your response. Your response will be judged on the basis of the quality of your writing and on how well your response presents the points in the lecture and their relationship to the passage. Typically, an effective response will be 150-225 words.

Question Summarize the points made in the lecture, being sure to explain how they challenge specific claims made in the reading passage.

CUT   PASTE   UNDO   REDO   Hide Word Count : 0

Thanks to the development of technology, people have been able to share their daily lives with others in different parts of the world. Though social media has made it feasible to communicate with people around the world simultaneously, it has also brought about a number of problems, some of which are serious and require immediate attention.

There have been numerous studies done on how social media affects health. Instead of spending time having face-to-face conversations with one another, people become more isolated and more dependent on social media. A study has found that reducing time on social media has decreased feelings of loneliness and improved people's overall well-being. It has also been discovered that social media interaction over in-person relationships has exacerbated feelings of depression or the fear of missing out, commonly known as FOMO.

There is also a danger of losing creativity due to the prevalence of social media. Rather than coming up with ideas on their own, people simply type in keywords on social media and look for ideas, choose ones that they like, and duplicate them. Many ideas used to be devised when people met in person for discussions. However, social media has hampered this, and it is difficult for people to share their opinions before producing their own ideas.

Misinformation is another serious problem that cannot be easily solved. The reason is that some media organizations or individuals abuse the nature of social media. Once inaccurate information has been released, it continues to spread rampantly even after corrections are made. There are people who distribute misinformation intentionally because it gets clicks. This can even result in innocent victims who need to go through extremely challenging times and situations even though they are not related to the incidents.

READING

social media: causes many problems 소셜 미디어: 많은 문제 유발

❶ *affect health-related issues → more isolated + dependent on social media*
건강 관련 문제 → 더욱 고립 + 소셜 미디어에 의존

- study: ↓ time on social media → loneliness ↓ + improved well-being 연구: SNS에 할애하는 시간 ↓ → 외로움 ↓ + 행복감 ↑
- social media interaction → exacerbated depression / FOMO SNS 교류 → 우울증 / 포모증후군을 악화시킴

> **Paraphrasing Example**
> Spending too much time on social media has been said to cause health problems.

❷ *loss of creativity → prevalence of social media* 창의력 상실 ∵ 소셜 미디어의 확산

- type in keywords → look for ideas → choose ones like → duplicate them
  키워드 입력 → 아이디어 탐색 → 좋아하는 것 선택 → 복제
- meeting in person for discussions ✕ → ideas created ✕ 직접 만나 토론하는 미팅 ✕ → 새로운 아이디어 ✕

> **Paraphrasing Example**
> Looking for ideas and duplicating them instead of having discussions while meeting in person can cause a lack of innovation and inventiveness.

❸ *misinformation: media organizations / people → abuse nature of social media*
오보: 언론 조직 / 사람들 → 소셜 미디어의 본질을 악용

- on purpose ∵ # of clicks 일부러 함 ∵ 조회수
- innocent victims → difficult time + situation 무고한 희생자 → 힘든 시간 + 상황

> **Paraphrasing Example**
> Misinformation can cause innocent victims to go through difficult situations.

WORD REMINDER

isolated 고립된   dependent 의존하는   interaction 교류   exacerbate 악화시키다   miss out 놓치다   prevalence 보급, 유행
come up with 떠올리다   duplicate 복제하다   devise 고안하다   hamper 방해하다   abuse 악용하다   release 공개하다   spread 확산되다
rampantly 맹렬히   distribute 공유하다   intentionally 일부러   innocent victim 무고한 희생자

LISTENING

social media: helps people connect with others 소셜 미디어: 다른 이들과 연결되게 도와줌

❶ *Tatuyo: inhabit banks of Amazon River* Tatuyo: 아마존 강둑에 거주

- 6 million followers in 18-month period 18개월 안에 600만 팔로워
- no travelers → upload daily-life pics of indigenous people living in Amazon jungle
  여행객 ✕ → 아마존 정글에서의 원주민의 삶에 대한 일상 생활 사진을 업로드

> **Paraphrasing Example**
> Social media helps people connect with others.

❷ *social media: most effective tool for getting public attention* 소셜 미디어: 대중의 관심을 받는 가장 효율적인 도구

- environmental issues: neglected + ignored 환경 문제: 외면 + 간과 당함
- constant acknowledgement of environmental concerns 환경 문제에 대한 지속적인 인식

> **Paraphrasing Example**
> Continuous engagement on the preservation of nature through social media has brought more attention to the public.

❸ *stay in touch* 연락 가능

- fast-moving society → harder to meet people 빨리 돌아가는 사회 → 사람을 만나기 더 힘듦
- able to see people on pictures → more bond 사진에서 볼 수 있음 → 더욱 단단한 유대감

> **Paraphrasing Example**
> Social media has made it possible for people easily to keep in touch with others whom they do not get to see often.

WORD REMINDER

downside 단점   tolerate 견디다   inhabit 거주하다   pandemic 세계적인 유행병   attract 유치하다   indigenous 토착의   attention 관심
neglect 등한시하다   purposely 고의로   acknowledgement 인식, 확인   concern 우려, 문제, 관심   awareness 경각심
sustainability 지속 가능성   conservation 보존   catch up 따라잡다   close by 인접한

ACTUAL TEST 04

The reading passage claims that social media poses serious problems that require adequate measures. The lecturer, however, contends that since social media has provided people with countless advantages, it is reasonable to tolerate a few drawbacks.

First, the reading passage argues that spending too much time on social media has been said to cause health problems. However, the professor mentions that social media helps people connect with others and gives an example of a woman living on the banks of the Amazon River. She shares the daily lives of indigenous people on social media, and her actions have been successful at getting attention from people.

Moreover, the reading passage makes the point that people are losing creativity. Looking for ideas and duplicating them instead of having discussions while meeting in person can cause a lack of innovation and inventiveness. Nevertheless, the lecturer states that social media can act as a means to attract public awareness. She also says that continuous engagement on the preservation of nature through social media has brought more attention to the public.

Finally, the reading passage elucidates that misinformation can cause innocent victims to go through difficult situations. Yet the professor delineates another advantage on how social media has made it possible for people easily to keep in touch with others whom they do not get to see often.

WORD REMINDER

adequate 적절한   measure 조치   reasonable 합당한   tolerate 견디다   drawback 단점   innovation 혁신   inventiveness 창의력
state 말하다   means 방법   awareness 인식, 경각심   engagement 참여   preservation 보존   elucidate 밝히다   delineate 설명하다

Hide Word Count : 0

Directions Read the question below. You have 30 minutes to plan, write, and revise your essay. Typically, an effective response will contain a minimum of 300 words.

Question

Do you agree or disagree with the following statement?

Overall, the widespread use of the Internet has mostly positive effects on life in today's world.

Use specific reasons and examples to support your answer.

AGREE

- *convenience* 편리함

  Ex past: go to library to find info 과거: 정보를 찾기 위해 도서관으로 감

  now: type in keywords + search for right info 현재: 주요 단어를 입력 + 맞는 정보 검색

  → save time / able to use it anytime 시간 절약 / 아무 때나 사용 가능

- *environmental + social concerns: getting more attention from public*
  환경 + 사회 문제: 대중으로부터 더 많은 관심을 받음

  - prevalence of Internet news + articles → more interests in sustainability + conservation
    인터넷 뉴스와 기사의 보급 → 지속 가능성 + 보존에 대한 더 많은 관심

    Ex renowned companies → detrimental to nature → exposed to social media → spread very fast
    유명한 기업 → 환경에 해를 입힘 → SNS에 노출 → (기사가) 빠르게 퍼짐

    → enactment of law 자연 보호 법의 제정

INTRODUCTION

generalization: hard to imagine life w/out Internet
일반화: 부모: 인터넷 없는 삶을 상상하기 힘듦

⬇

whether widespread use of Internet has +ve effects on life
인터넷의 보급이 삶에 긍정적 영향을 가지는가

⬇

thesis: agree (convenience + aware of environmental matters)
논제: 찬성 (편리함 + 환경 문제 자각)

DISAGREE

- *physical + mental concerns* 신체적 + 정신적 문제

  - more isolated + dependent on electronic communication devices 더욱 고립 + 전자 통신 기계에 의존
    Ex research: time on smartphone / laptop ↓ → feelings of loneliness ↓ + overall well-being ↑
    연구: 스마트폰 / 노트북의 사용 시간 ↓ → 외로움 ↓ + 전체적인 행복감 ↑
  - social media interaction: exacerbated depression / FOMO SNS 교류: 우울증 / FOMO를 악화시킴

- *misinformation* 환경 + 사회 문제: 대중으로부터 더 많은 관심을 받음

  - some media orgs / individuals abuse nature of Internet → once released, continuously spread
    일부 언론 기업 / 개인은 인터넷의 본질을 악용함 → 일단 공개되면, 계속 퍼짐
  - some distribute misinformation intentionally ∵ clicks 일부 사람들은 오보를 일부러 퍼뜨림 ∵ 조회수
  - innocent victims 무고한 희생자

INTRODUCTION

generalization: hard to imagine life w/out Internet
일반화: 부모: 인터넷 없는 삶을 상상하기 힘듦

⬇

whether widespread use of Internet has +ve effects on life
인터넷의 보급이 삶에 긍정적 영향을 가지는가

⬇

thesis: disagree (health problems + misinformation)
논제: 반대 (건강 문제 + 오보)

With the advent of the Internet, our lives have changed, and it is hard to imagine our lives without the Internet. We reply heavily on the Internet from writing an email to making an appointment for a flu shot. Though some people contend that the Internet has caused many negative effects, I strongly agree with the statement that the widespread use of the Internet has mostly positive effects on life in today's world. The reasons have to do with convenience and environmental concerns.

First of all, the Internet has provided us with more convenience than ever before. For instance, in the past, we had to go to a library to find information. However, thanks to the Internet, all we need to do now is type in keywords to search for the right information. This has not only made our lives convenient, but it has also helped us save time. Hence, the Internet has made it feasible for us to look for information without any limitations.

On top of that, environmental and social concerns that would otherwise be neglected get more attention from the public and help people get more interested in the sustainability and conservation of nature. For instance, when renowned companies that operate factories which are detrimental to nature are exposed on social media, the news then spreads very fast. Thanks to the awareness and continuous acknowledgement of environmental concerns, many of those incidents have resulted in people calling for the enactment of justice under environmental law.

It is true that there is a risk of misinformation spreading on the Internet; however, that risk has always been there with newspapers, magazines, and even books. The Internet has provided convenience and has resulted in environmental and social awareness among people. Therefore, I firmly believe the widespread use of the Internet has mostly created advantages in today's world.

WORD REMINDER

advent 출현 type in 타자해서 추가하다 feasible 실현 가능한 limitation 제약 otherwise 그렇지 않으면 neglect 등한시하다
sustainability 지속 가능성 conservation 보존 renowned 유명한 operate 운영하다 detrimental 해로운 expose 폭로하다
spread 확산되다 awareness 경각심 acknowledgement 인식, 확인 incident 사건 call for 요구하다 enactment 법률의 제정

With the advent of the Internet, our lives have changed, and it is hard to imagine our lives without the Internet. We reply heavily on the Internet from writing an email to making an appointment for a flu shot. Though some people contend that the Internet has caused many negative effects, I strongly disagree with the statement that the widespread use of the Internet has mostly positive effects on life in today's world. The reasons have to do with health problems and misinformation that can result in irrevocable consequences.

First of all, the Internet has created physical as well as mental problems. There have been numerous studies conducted on how social media affects health. Instead of spending time having face-to-face conversations with one another, we have become more isolated and more dependent on electronic communication devices. It has been discovered that social media interaction has exacerbated the problems of those who have already been suffering from depression or fear of missing out, commonly known as FOMO. According to research, reducing the amount of time spent using smartphones and laptops has decreased people's feelings of loneliness and improved their overall well-being.

On top of that, misinformation is another serious problem that the Internet has posed. To be specific, some media organizations and individuals abuse the nature of the Internet. Once inaccurate information has been released, it continues to spread rampantly even after corrections are made. This can even result in innocent victims who need to go through extremely challenging situations even though they are not related to the incidents.

It is true that the Internet has made our lives convenient and provided us with a vast amount of knowledge. However, it is not worth it when it comes to people's mental and physical health. In addition, gossip and misinformation can make innocent victims suffer badly. Therefore, I firmly believe that the widespread use of the Internet has numerous negative effects on our lives.

WORD REMINDER

interaction 관계   exacerbate 악화시키다   overall 전반적으로   well-being 행복   pose 야기하다   organization 단체
inaccurate 정확하지 않은   release 공개하다   rampantly 만연하게   vast 방대한   when it comes to ~에 관한 한   gossip 소문
miserable 비참한

RELATED TOPICS

1 Do you agree or disagree with the following statement? It is better to use printed materials such as books and articles to do research than it is to use the Internet. Use specific reasons and examples to support your opinion.

다음 명제에 찬성하는가 반대하는가? 연구를 할 때에는 책이나 기사 같은 인쇄가 된 책을 사용하는 것이 인터넷을 사용하는 것보다 낫다. 구체적인 이유와 예를 들어 자신의 입장을 뒷받침하시오.

PRINTED MATERIALS	INTERNET
- reliable information 믿을 만한 정보 - access to rare documents 희귀한 자료 접근 가능	- save time 시간 절약 - vast amount of information → no need to go to a particular library for specialized documents / books 엄청난 양의 정보 → 전문 문서 / 책을 위해 특정 도서관을 갈 필요가 없음

2 Do you agree or disagree with the following statement? Movies and television programs strongly influence the way people behave. Use specific reasons and examples to support your opinion.

다음 명제에 찬성하는가 반대하는가? 영화와 텔레비전 프로그램은 많은 사람들이 행동하는 방법에 강항 영향을 끼친다. 구체적인 이유와 예를 들어 자신의 입장을 뒷받침하시오.

AGREE	DISAGREE
- visual effects remain in brain 영상 효과가 머릿속에 남음 - sound: changes the way people speak or behave toward others 소리: 다른 사람들을 대하는 사람들의 말이나 행동 방법을 바꿈	- entertainment: leisure for most people 오락: 대부분의 사람들에게는 여가 - so many other factors: books, other people, surroundings 다른 많은 요소들: 책,타인,주위 환경

3 Do you agree or disagree with the following statement? People communicate with one another less than in the past because of the popularity of television. Use specific reasons and examples to support your opinion.

다음 명제에 찬성하는가 반대하는가? 사람들은 TV의 인기 때문에 과거에 비해 서로와 의사소통을 덜 한다. 이유와 예를 들어 자신의 입장을 뒷받침하시오.

AGREE	DISAGREE
- focus on TV: become more individualized TV에 집중: 더 개인주의적으로 변함 - used to watching instead of talking 말하는 것 대신 보는 것에 적응이 됨	- TV has been around for so many years: people communicated well in the past even though TV was popular then TV는 굉장히 오래 되었음: 사람들은 TV가 그 때에도 인기 있었음에도 불구하고 의사소통을 잘 했음 - other culprits: busy life, crimes 다른 요소들: 바쁜 일상,범죄

TOEFL® MAP

ACTUAL TEST Writing 2

05

The Amazon River basin in South America contains the greatest diversity of life on the Earth. Ironically, it has never been an ideal place for large groups of humans to live. In fact, historically, only small groups have managed to survive in the unforgiving rainforest that encompasses the entire area.

The Amazon Rainforest contains abundant plant and animal life yet is incapable of supporting sizable human populations. One reason for this is the poor quality of the soil, which is acidic in nature. Therefore, while farmers can raise crops such as corn and beans for one or two seasons, after that, the soil becomes so depleted that nothing else will grow in it. Even today, when more advanced farming methods are available, not enough food can be grown to support a large number of people in the Amazon.

In the past, there was a lack of sources of protein, which humans need to survive, in the Amazon. Food animals such as cows and sheep only appeared in South America when the Europeans imported them in the 1500s. Even after being introduced to the land, there were never big herds of animals because the poor soil and jungle-covered land could not produce sufficient food to support them.

Three great civilizations once lived in the Americas: the Mayas, the Incas, and the Aztecs. None of them resided in the Amazon. Additionally, the people in all three civilizations constructed stone buildings. Stone was the primary building material for their palaces and temples, which humans in ancient cultures virtually always constructed. Yet there is little stone that can be used for construction anywhere in the Amazon. Likewise, no palaces and temples have been discovered or unearthed by archaeologists, which makes it unlikely that any human settlements of considerable size ever existed there.

ACTUAL TEST 05

🎧 05-01

55

Directions You have 20 minutes to plan and write your response. Your response will be judged on the basis of the quality of your writing and on how well your response presents the points in the lecture and their relationship to the passage. Typically, an effective response will be 150-225 words.

Question Summarize the points made in the lecture, being sure to specifically explain how they answer the problems raised in the reading passage.

CUT PASTE UNDO REDO   Hide Word Count : 0

The Amazon River basin in South America contains the greatest diversity of life on the Earth. Ironically, it has never been an ideal place for large groups of humans to live. In fact, historically, only small groups have managed to survive in the unforgiving rainforest that encompasses the entire area.

The Amazon Rainforest contains abundant plant and animal life yet is incapable of supporting sizable human populations. One reason for this is the poor quality of the soil, which is acidic in nature. Therefore, while farmers can raise crops such as corn and beans for one or two seasons, after that, the soil becomes so depleted that nothing else will grow in it. Even today, when more advanced farming methods are available, not enough food can be grown to support a large number of people in the Amazon.

In the past, there was a lack of sources of protein, which humans need to survive, in the Amazon. Food animals such as cows and sheep only appeared in South America when the Europeans imported them in the 1500s. Even after being introduced to the land, there were never big herds of animals because the poor soil and jungle-covered land could not produce sufficient food to support them.

Three great civilizations once lived in the Americas: the Mayas, the Incas, and the Aztecs. None of them resided in the Amazon. Additionally, the people in all three civilizations constructed stone buildings. Stone was the primary building material for their palaces and temples, which humans in ancient cultures virtually always constructed. Yet there is little stone that can be used for construction anywhere in the Amazon. Likewise, no palaces and temples have been discovered or unearthed by archaeologists, which makes it unlikely that any human settlements of considerable size ever existed there.

no large human population could live in the Amazon 아마존에서는 많은 인구가 거주할 수 없었음

❶ *not enough food* 불충분한 식량

- poor quality of soil 질이 낮은 토양
- advanced farming methods → still not enough food 개선된 농법 → 여전히 불충분한 식량

> **Paraphrasing Example** The poor quality of soil would have made it difficult for enough vegetation to grow.

❷ *lack of sources of protein* 단백질 공급원의 결핍

- poor soil + jungle-covered land = sufficient food for animals ✕
  질이 낮은 토양 + 밀림으로 덮인 땅 = 동물들에게 필요한 충분한 식량 ✕

> **Paraphrasing Example** Poor soil and jungle-covered land makes it difficult for humans to ingest enough protein from animals.

❸ *not enough stones to construct buildings* 건물을 짓기에 불충분한 돌

- no palaces / temples found 궁전 / 사원 발견되지 않음

> **Paraphrasing Example** The lack of palaces or temples proves that no huge civilization dwelled in the Amazon.

WORD REMINDER

basin 유역   unforgiving 험한   encompass 둘러싸다   acidic 산성 물질을 포함한   deplete 고갈시키다   sufficient 충분한   reside 거주하다
temple 사원   virtually 사실상   unearth 발견하다

possibility of the existence of a sizable civilization 큰 문명의 존재 가능성

❶ *plenty of vegetation* 풍부한 식물

Ex nuts, berries, citrus fruits 땅콩, 베리, 감귤류
- parts of Amazon: quite fertile 아마존의 일부: 꽤 비옥함
- volcanic eruption → ash (benefit to soil) 화산 폭발 → 재 (토양에 이득)

> **Paraphrasing Example** Plenty of vegetation would have provided enough food for large human settlements.

❷ *many animals → protein* 많은 동물 → 단백질

- Amazon River: rich in fish → protein 아마존 강: 물고기 풍부 → 단백질
- rainforest: birds, reptiles, mammals 다우림: 새, 파충류, 포유류
  ∴ diverse diet 다양한 식량

> **Paraphrasing Example** The wide variety of animals along with the many fish in the Amazon River were adequate to supply protein for a sizable group of humans.

❸ *very little stone / abundant amount of wood* 약간의 돌 / 많은 양의 나무

- hot + humid weather: destroyed buildings 고온 + 습한 날씨: 건물 파괴
- jungle: overtook the rest 밀림: 나머지를 다 차지
  → impossible to find buildings 건물을 찾는 것은 불가능함

> **Paraphrasing Example** The availability of a lot of wood made it possible for a large human population to dwell in the Amazon.

WORD REMINDER

sparsely 드문드문, 성기게   edible 식용 가능한   citrus fruit 감귤류   fertile 비옥한   copious 풍부한   teem with ~으로 풍부하다
diet 일상의 음식물   humid 습기 있는   overtake 덮치다   practically 사실상

The lecturer discusses the possible existence of a sizable ancient civilization in the Amazon. With three pieces of evidence, she contradicts the reading passage's claim that no large human population could have resided in the area.

First, plenty of vegetation would have provided enough food for large human settlements. Parts of the Amazon are quite fertile, which makes farming feasible. Furthermore, ash from volcanic eruptions added nutrients to the soil. This refutes the reading passage's claim that the poor quality of the soil would have made it difficult for enough vegetation to grow.

In addition, the lecturer says the Amazon River has a lot of fish that can provide protein for humans. Moreover, the wide variety of animals is adequate to supply food for a sizable group of humans. This argument casts doubt on the reading passage's claim that the poor soil and the jungle-covered land made it difficult for humans to get enough protein from animals.

Finally, though there is little stone, the availability of a lot of wood made it possible for a large human population to dwell in the Amazon. According to the professor, no buildings have been found because of the weather conditions and the density of the vegetation. This refutes the reading passage's idea that the lack of palaces or temples proves that no huge civilization dwelled in the Amazon.

WORD REMINDER
sizable 상당한 크기의   settlement 정착   adequate 충분   supply 공급하다   dwell 살다   density 밀도

Hide Word Count : 0

Directions Read the question below. You have 30 minutes to plan, write, and revise your essay. Typically, an effective response will contain a minimum of 300 words.

Question

Do you agree or disagree with the following statement?

The government should invest more money in the educating of children than in the educating of college students.

Use specific reasons and examples to support your answer.

AGREE

- *rudimentary: fundamental basis for further education* 기초: 고등 교육을 위한 근본
  - crucial for building study habits 공부 습관을 기르는데 중요
    Ex Japan: money on children's education → improving the quality of teaching + acquiring learning tools
    일본: 아이들 교육에 투자 → 수업의질 개선 + 학습 도구들의 습득
    → students perform better than average 학생들이 평균보다 잘함

- *college: investments from companies* 대학: 기업들로부터의 투자금
  - research, scholarship, facilities 연구, 장학금, 시설
    Ex cousin: won scholarship 사촌: 장학금을 받음
  - no need to worry about research funds: able to concentrate on studies 연구비 걱정 ✕ : 연구에 전념

INTRODUCTION

generalization: education: one of the most important factors in the development of a country
일반화: 교육: 나라의 발전에 있어서 가장 중요한 요소 중 하나

⬇

government plans the use of funds very carefully
정부는 자금의 사용을 매우 신중히 계획

⬇

thesis: agree (fundamental basis, college: investments from companies)
논제: 찬성 (근본, 대학: 기업으로부터의 투자금)

DISAGREE

- *college: preparation for job field* 대학: 취업 준비
  - developing competency: economic growth 능력 발달: 경제적 성장
    Ex government increased budget on college → quality improved 정부가 대학 예산 ↑ → 질 ↑
    → many graduates work for government 많은 졸업생들이 정부에서 근무

- *investment in children's education: already sufficient* 아이들 교육에 대한 투자: 이미 충분함
  - capacity for in-depth knowledge: limited for children → waste of money
    심층 지식을 얻기 위한 능력: 아이들에겐 한정되어 있음 → 돈 낭비
    Ex government provides funds for kindergarten + elementary schools
    정부에서 유치원과 초등학교에 자금 지원
    → children: no need to research → save money for the future education
    아이들: 연구할 필요 없음 → 미래 교육을 위해 돈 절약

INTRODUCTION

generalization: education: one of the most important factors in the development of a country
일반화: 교육: 나라의 발전에 있어 가장 중요한 요소 중 하나

⬇

government plans the use of funds very carefully
정부는 자금의 사용을 신중히 계획

⬇

thesis: disagree (develop competency, children's education: already sufficient)
논제: 반대 (능숙도 개발, 아이들 교육: 이미 충분함)

Education is one of the most important factors in the development of a country. Therefore, the government plans very carefully where and how it will use its education budget. Some people contend that the government should spend more money on college students. However, I firmly believe the government should spend more money on children's education because children's education provides young students with the foundation for further education. Moreover, college students have many other sources of funding.

First of all, the rudimentary level of schooling is the basis for more profound educational development. Since school is the place where children build their own study habits and routines, it is important that the government focus more on the early years of childhood. For instance, a lot of government funds go toward children's education in Japan. With this money, schools improve the quality of teaching as well as acquire learning tools such as smartboards. Thus children are exposed to various sources of education and learning methods under the guidance of well-qualified instructors. Consequently, their levels of comprehension are higher than those of typical children their age, which opens up opportunities for in-depth training in the future.

Additionally, a number of companies support colleges with funds for students. Since companies need employees with superb educational backgrounds, they invest money in many areas, including research, scholarships, and facilities. For instance, the university my cousin is attending offers various scholarships that students can apply for. Most of those scholarships are from different corporations in Korea. Thus my cousin, who won one of these scholarships, is able to concentrate on his studies without having to worry about funding. In that regard, college students have many opportunities to procure money from sources other than the government.

It is a fact that college education is important in that it is a launching pad for a career. However, preparing children, who develop study habits in their early years, for their further education is more crucial. Moreover, college students already get enough funds from private companies. For these reasons, I agree with the statement that the government should invest money in children's education rather than in college students.

WORD REMINDER

budget 예산   funding 자금 제공   rudimentary 기본의   schooling 학교 교육   profound 깊은   routine 일상의 일   acquire 얻다
in-depth 심층의   in that regard 그 점에 있어서는   procure 조달하다

TIPS for SUCCESS

독립형 에세이: 형식

흔히 설명문 형태의 에세이(expository essay)는 서론, 본론1, 본론2, 본론3, 결론으로 구성되어 있다. 본인도 처음 토플을 가르쳤을 때는, 학교에서 배웠던 위의 방법을 고집했으나, 30분 밖에 주어지지 않는 토플 시험에서는 서론, 본론1, 본론2, 결론의 형식으로도 본인의 생각을 충분히 표현할 수 있다. brainstorming을 할 때, 의견을 논리적으로 펼칠 수 있는 두 가지의 요소를 생각해 내서 두 단락의 본론을 써보도록 하자.

Education is one of the most important factors in the development of a country. Therefore, the government plans very carefully where and how it will use its education budget. Some people contend that the government should spend more money on children's education. However, I firmly believe the government should spend more money on college students because of the in-depth studying and research the college students must do. Moreover, children already receive their primary education through government funding.

First of all, college is an institution where most students prepare to work after graduation. Thus, the more competent they are, the more they can contribute to a company which will eventually promote the economic growth of the country. For example, since the government in Korea started spending a part of its budget on colleges, the quality of education has improved significantly. In return, many of the outstanding graduates of those colleges have gone on to work for the government. Consequently, cultivating a competent workforce can benefit a country.

Additionally, there is no need for the government to invest more money in children's education than it does now. As the capacity for in-depth knowledge is limited for children, investing more in children's education would be excessive spending. For example, the government provides funds for children's fundamental education, such as kindergarten and elementary school. This already includes teacher training and the improvement of facilities. Since children do not need money to condust major research or experiments, investing more money would only result in an overflow of funds.

It is true that children's education is important in that children develop study habits in their early years. However, great study habits come from continuous stimuli from instructors and motivation rather than from constantly changing educational programs. In that sense, the government does not need to increase its spending on children's education. The government should instead put more money into colleges as they help students make the transition to working life. For these reasons, I disagree with the statement that the government should invest money in children rather than in college students.

WORD REMINDER

primary 근본적인   institution 기관, 회관   competent 유능한   contribute 기여하다   promote 촉진하다   outstanding 우수한
cultivate 양성하다   overflow 과다   transition 전환

▌ TIPS for SUCCESS

비교 강조 (the more ~ the more...)

'더 ~할수록 더욱 …하다'라는 뜻을 가지고 있으며 The more, the better.(많을수록 좋다.) 혹은 The smarter, the more advantageous. (급할수록 천천히.)처럼 단순히 형용사만 올 수도 있고 뒤에 절을 동반할 수도 있다. 두 번째 단락의 문장을 살펴보자.

Thus, **the more** competent they are, **the more** they can contribute to a company which will eventually promote the economic growth of the country.

위의 문장에서 볼 수 있듯이, the more competent라는 비교급 형용사와 they are라는 절이 the more라는 비교급 형용사와 they can contribute라는 절을 동반해서, '그들이 더욱 유능할수록, 회사에 더욱 기여할 수 있다'라고 표현되고 있다.

RELATED TOPICS

1 **The government should focus more on the preservation of the natural environment than on economic development.** 정부는 경제 개발보다 환경 보호에 더욱 초점을 맞추어야 한다.

AGREE	DISAGREE
- long-term consequence → more money will be required in the future 장기적 결과 → 미래에 더 많은 돈이 들어갈 것임 ex) custom 관습 - environmental damage: might cause diseases 환경 파괴: 질병을 일으킬 수 있음	- basic rights of people outweigh environmental concerns 인간의 기본적인 권리는 환경 문제보다 우선함 - strong econ. status → invest money for preservation of environment 탄탄한 경제 상태 → 환경 보호를 위해 투자

2 **The government should invest more in supporting artists than in sponsoring athletes, including the Olympic team.** 정부는 올림픽 팀을 포함한 운동선수들을 지원하는 것보다 예술가들을 지원하는 일에 투자를 해야 한다.

AGREE	DISAGREE
- crimes ↓ 범죄 ↓ ex) El Sistema in Venezuela 베네수엘라의 El Sistema - sponsoring athletes: large profit → enough support from corporations 운동선수 후원: 큰 이윤 → 기업들의 충분한 지원 ex) owning a pro baseball team 프로 야구 구단 소유	- promotes sports among citizens → helpful at maintaining health 시민들 사이에 운동 장려 → 건강 유지에 도움 - unifies people 사람들을 단합시킴 ex) cheer for a team during the Olympic Games 올림픽 경기 중의 팀 응원

3 **The government should support scientific research even if it has no practical use to people.**
정부는 사람들에게 실용성이 없더라도 과학 연구를 지원해야 한다.

AGREE	DISAGREE
- may be essential in the future 미래에 필요할 수 있음 ex) treatment for some cancers: requires a lot of time 일부 암 치료법: 많은 시간이 필요 - can apply research to other fields 다른 분야에 응용 ex) substitute for fire to heat food in outer space → invented microwave 우주에서 음식을 가열시킬 대용품 → 전자레인지 발명	- more urgent matters to be solved 더 시급히 해결해야 할 문제들 ex) disaster at the nuclear power plant in Japan vs. exploration of outer space 일본 원자력 발전소의 재앙 vs. 우주 개발 - waste of government funds 정부 예산 낭비

4 **The best way to preserve energy is to increase gas and electricity charges.**
에너지를 보존하는 가장 효율적인 방법은 가스와 전기 요금을 인상하는 것이다.

AGREE	DISAGREE
- the quickest means to get immediate results 단시간 내에 빠른 결과를 얻기 위한 방법 - no significant investment needed for the policy 정책 수립에 많은 비용이 들지 않음	- basic infrastructure: the poor will suffer 기본 인프라: 가난한 사람들이 고통 받을 것임 - alternative energy: under development 대체 에너지: 개발 단계에 있음

5 **The government should not charge people for public transportation.** 정부는 대중교통 요금을 부과하지 말아야 한다.

AGREE	DISAGREE
- for environment → more people will use public transportation 환경 → 더 많은 사람들이 대중교통을 이용할 것임 - fewer cars → an effective way to conserve energy (gasoline) 차량 감소 → 에너지(휘발유)를 보존하는데 효율적인 방법	- tax ↑: unfair for people not using public transportation 세금 ↑: 대중교통을 사용하지 않는 사람들에게 불공평 - overcrowded: people will take public transportation even when they do not need to use it 만원: 사람들이 필요하지 않아도 대중교통을 이용할 것임

TOEFL® MAP

ACTUAL TEST Writing 2

06

Distance learning has become more popular than ever with the advent of the new coronavirus, and many platforms have been developed and improved. A number of schools around the world have chosen to switch from traditional classrooms for elementary and secondary students to virtual classes. Despite many controversies as to whether distance learning will actually work, it has been proven that a majority of parents, students, and teachers are satisfied with the new implementation.

Students can study at their own pace. In the typical traditional classroom environment, students are expected to follow a lesson plan a teacher has set regardless of their learning ability or speed. On the other hand, distance learning provides students with the advantages of choosing their own pace or method, making it feasible for hands-on and experiential learning. In fact, they can study more complicated questions and skip already known topics in some subjects while watching other video lectures several times or leaving messages for teachers. Additional resources or further explanations on other subjects they struggle with can be available to them.

Virtual learning can also help maintain interactions between teachers and students. Since some programs like Zoom allow live online classes, teachers and students can connect with one another simultaneously. Thanks to the chatting function, students can ask questions or get feedback right away, not to mention speak aloud by turning a microphone on. There is even a feature called "breakout rooms" that allow students to meet in smaller groups for discussions.

The most appealing of all factors in distance learning is its convenience. It is possible to study anywhere in the world as long as a person has access to the Internet. Students can choose the most optimal time and place for studying. As a matter of fact, this has let students coordinate and manage their academic and extracurricular activities more effectively. Numerous studies have shown that being able to study any place at any time provides students with great fulfillment, leading to better performance in the end.

🎧 06-01

Directions You have 20 minutes to plan and write your response. Your response will be judged on the basis of the quality of your writing and on how well your response presents the points in the lecture and their relationship to the passage. Typically, an effective response will be 150-225 words.

Question Summarize the points made in the lecture, being sure to explain how they challenge specific arguments made in the reading passage.

CUT PASTE UNDO REDO Hide Word Count : 0

Distance learning has become more popular than ever with the advent of the new coronavirus, and many platforms have been developed and improved. A number of schools around the world have chosen to switch from traditional classrooms for elementary and secondary students to virtual classes. Despite many controversies as to whether distance learning will actually work, it has been proven that a majority of parents, students, and teachers are satisfied with the new implementation.

Students can study at their own pace. In the typical traditional classroom environment, students are expected to follow a lesson plan a teacher has set regardless of their learning ability or speed. On the other hand, distance learning provides students with the advantages of choosing their own pace or method, making it feasible for hands-on and experiential learning. In fact, they can study more complicated questions and skip already known topics in some subjects while watching other video lectures several times or leaving messages for teachers. Additional resources or further explanations on other subjects they struggle with can be available to them.

Virtual learning can also help maintain interactions between teachers and students. Since some programs like Zoom allow live online classes, teachers and students can connect with one another simultaneously. Thanks to the chatting function, students can ask questions or get feedback right away, not to mention speak aloud by turning a microphone on. There is even a feature called "breakout rooms" that allow students to meet in smaller groups for discussions.

The most appealing of all factors in distance learning is its convenience. It is possible to study anywhere in the world as long as a person has access to the Internet. Students can choose the most optimal time and place for studying. As a matter of fact, this has let students coordinate and manage their academic and extracurricular activities more effectively. Numerous studies have shown that being able to study any place at any time provides students with great fulfillment, leading to better performance in the end.

📝 NOTE-TAKING

DL (distance learning): great learning method 원격 학습: 좋은 교육 수단

❶ students can study @ own pace 학생들은 자신의 속도로 공부할 수 있음

- skip already known topics / watch video lectures many times 이미 아는 주제는 생략함 / 비디오 강의를 여러 번 봄

 Virtual learning gives students a chance to study at their own pace.

❷ interactions w/teachers + students 교사와 학생 사이의 상호 작용

- breakout rooms: discussions in small groups 소회의실: 소규모 그룹 토론

 Virtual learning can keep students interacting with one another.

❸ convenience 편의성

- balance academic + EC more effectively 더 효과적으로 학업 + 과외 활동의 균형을 유지함

Paraphrasing Example The convenience of the learning method has helped students balance their academic and extracurricular activities better.

WORD REMINDER

advent 출현 school district 학군 virtual 가상의 implementation 실행 pace 속도 regardless 상관없이 feasible 실현 가능한 experiential 경험적인 struggle 애쓰다 interaction 교류 simultaneously 동시에 appealing 매력적인 optimal 최선의 coordinate 조정하다 extracurricular activity 과외 활동 fulfillment 성취감

DL: many drawbacks 원격 학습: 많은 문제점

❶ lack of motivation 동기 부여의 부족

- only works with students who've already done well in traditional classrooms
  오직 전통적인 교실에서 이미 잘하는 학생들에게만 해당됨
  → easily distracted by others (YouTube, shopping, desserts) 쉽게 다른 것들에 의해 산만해짐 (유튜브, 쇼핑, 간식)
  → can affect academic performance 학업 성취에 영향을 줄 수 있음

 Students can easily get distracted by many things, such as watching YouTube.

❷ development of communications + teamwork skills ✕ 의사소통의 발달 + 팀워크 능력 ✕

- breakout rooms: diff. from interacting in person 소회의실: 직접 교류와는 다름
  → lack of peer interaction → poor academic + social skills 또래와의 교류 결핍 → 더 좋지 않은 성적 + 사회성
- Not suitable for improving interpersonal RS 대인 관계 개선에 적합하지 않음

Paraphrasing Example Insufficient interaction with other peers or teachers will eventually result in a dissatisfying academic performance as well as poor social skills.

❸ health problems 건강 문제들

- commuting / walking around campus → vitamin 통근 / 캠퍼스 주변을 걷기 → 비타민
  → obesity, ingestion, diabetes 비만, 소화 불량, 당뇨
  → kids wearing glasses: ↑ 25% 아동 안경 착용: 25% ↑

Paraphrasing Example Distance learning can even cause serious health problems.

WORD REMINDER

unprecedented 전례 없는 pandemic 세계적인 유행병 tremendous 엄청난 introduction 도입 innovative 혁신적인 pose 야기하다 motivation 동기 부여 flexibility 융통성 challenging 힘든 feature 기능 interact 교류하다 suitable 적합한 commute 통근하다 expose 노출하다 obesity 비만 consequence 결과 indigestion 소화 불량 diabetes 당뇨병

The lecturer argues that distance learning poses many significant drawbacks. This directly contradicts the reading passage's claim that distance learning has been an ideal and successful learning method.

First, in spite of the fact that virtual learning gives students a chance to study at their own pace, it is very hard for students to stay motivated since they can easily get distracted by many things, such as watching YouTube. As a result, a lack of motivation can have a negative effect on a student's overall performance. This refutes the reading passage's claim that all students have an advantage with customized learning styles.

Furthermore, the lecturer says distance learning hinders the development of social skills among students, especially younger kids. Insufficient interaction with other peers or teachers will eventually result in a dissatisfying academic performance as well as poor social skills. This fact contradicts the point made in the reading passage that virtual learning can keep students interacting with one another.

Finally, she points out that distance learning can even cause serious health problems. For example, students can suffer from a lack of vitamin D, obesity, and indigestion. Moreover, statistics show that the number of kids wearing glasses has escalated by 25%. This refutes the reading passage's claim that the convenience of the learning method has helped students balance their academic and extracurricular activities better.

WORD REMINDER

significant 상당한   drawback 단점   ideal 이상적인   customized 맞춘, 특화된   hinder 막다   insufficient 불충분한   escalate 증가시키다

TIPS for SUCCESS

Reading 지문을 반박하는 표현법들을 익혀두자.

This counters the reading passage's claim that ~
This rebuts the reading passage's claim that ~
This refutes the reading passage's claim that ~
This casts doubt on the reading passage's claim that ~
This goes against the reading passage's claim that ~
This disputes the reading passage's claim that ~
This contradicts the reading passage's claim that ~

*강조를 하고 싶으면 clearly, strongly, apparently, explicitly, firmly 등의 강조를 나타내는 단어를 동사 앞에 쓰면 된다.

Hide Word Count : 0

Directions Read the question below. You have 30 minutes to plan, write, and revise your essay. Typically, an effective response will contain a minimum of 300 words.

Question

Do you agree or disagree with the following statement?

It is better to work alone at home than to work with others at a company.

Use specific reasons and examples to support your answer.

ACTUAL TEST **06**

AGREE

- *more freedom* 보다 많은 자유
  - able to establish own rules / system 스스로의 규칙 / 시스템을 구축할 수 있음
    Ex friend: taking a nap → feels more rejuvenated 친구: 낮잠 → 더욱 원기 회복되는 느낌을 받음
    → past: drowsy + lethargic after lunch at a company 과거: 직장에서 점심 식사 후에 졸림 + 나른함

- *save time* 시간 절약
  - takes long to get ready + commute 준비 + 출퇴근 시간이 많이 걸림
    Ex cousin: 1 hour prep. + 40 min driving 사촌: 1시간 준비 + 40분 운전
    → exhausted when gets to workplace 회사에 도착할 때쯤 지쳐 있음

INTRODUCTION

generalization: each possess own lifestyle
일반화: 개인은 다른 삶의 방식을 가지고 있음

⬇

customized way of working: feasible / i.e. able to work at home
맞춤 방식의 근무: 가능 / 즉, 자택 근무 가능

⬇

thesis: agree (flexibility, saving time)
논제: 찬성 (융통성, 시간 절약)

DISAGREE

- *sense of competition* 경쟁을 느낌
  - act as self-motivator 동기 부여 역할
    Ex cousin participated in a presentation contest at a company 사촌이 회사의 발표 대회에 참가했음
    → put in a lot of effort + learned a lot 많은 노력 투자 + 많이 배웠음

- *employees have diff. skills + abilities* 직원들은 다른 기술과 능력을 가지고 있음
  - cooperate w/each other using knowledge + skills 지식과 기술을 사용해서 서로 협력
    Ex friend: skilled w/Excel / not as skilled w/PPT 친구: 엑셀에 뛰어남 / 파워포인트에는 그리 뛰어나지 않음
    → help each other: productivity ↑ + synergistic effect 서로 도움: 생산성 ↑ + 시너지 효과

INTRODUCTION

generalization: each possess own lifestyle
일반화: 개인은 다른 삶의 방식을 가지고 있음

⬇

customized way of working: feasible / i.e. able to work at home
맞춤 방식의 근무: 가능 / 즉, 자택 근무 가능

⬇

thesis: disagree (competition, cooperation)
논제: 반대 (경쟁, 협력)

CUT PASTE UNDO REDO

People have their own lifestyles. Some people prefer starting and finishing their day early while others choose to sleep in. With the development of technology, a customized way of working has now become feasible. In other words, it is no longer uncommon to see employees working in their own homes. Although some people contend that working at home has many drawbacks, I strongly believe that it is better to work alone at home rather than to work with others at a company because this approach offers more freedom for employees. In addition, it saves time for them.

Firstly, workers can have more freedom when working at home. To be specific, employees are able to establish their own rules or systems. For instance, my friend who works at home always takes a nap in the afternoon. He says he feels rejuvenated after getting some rest, which results in better outcomes. According to him, when he worked at a company, he used to feel very drowsy and lethargic after lunch. Thus, working at home allows people to customize their working environments for themselves.

Secondly, employees can save time. It often takes a lot of time to get ready for work and to commute to one's workplace. To illustrate, my cousin says she has to spend more than an hour to get ready, including applying makeup and getting dressed. In addition, it takes her forty minutes to get from her house to her workplace. Consequently, by the time she gets to work, she is already exhausted. Therefore, people can save not only time but also energy by working at home.

Some argue that working with coworkers gives people a chance to work in a competitive environment where they can be motivated. However, competition often creates a stressful atmosphere among workers, which could harm their health. For the reasons of flexibility and saving time, I agree with the statement that working alone at home is better than working with others at a workplace.

WORD REMINDER

sleep in 늦잠 자다   customize 주인이 원하는 대로 만들다[바꾸다]   drawback 결점   approach 접근법   take a nap 낮잠을 자다
rejuvenate 원기를 회복하다   outcome 결과   drowsy 졸리는   lethargic 무기력한   commute 통근하다   exhausted 지칠 대로 지친
motivate 동기를 부여하다   atmosphere 분위기   flexibility 융통성

ACTUAL TEST 06

■ TIPS for SUCCESS

일반적인 사람들에 관한 주어는 people, one, individual(s), you 등을 사용할 수 있다.

많은 학생들이 one, a person 등을 사용하는데, 현재형 동사에 s 또는 es를 붙여야 할 뿐 아니라 he/she/himself/herself/him/her/his 등의 성별을 일치해야 하는 불편함이 있다. 단수형으로 고치는 것이 걱정이 된다면 people을 사용하도록 하자. 현재형 동사는 언제나 원형을 사용하면 되고, they, them, themselves, their만 사용하면 된다. 첫 번째 문단의 첫 문장을 살펴보자.

People have their own lifestyles.

동사는 원형을 사용하면 되고, 복수형 소유대명사로는 their를 적어 주면 된다.

People have their own lifestyles. Some people prefer starting and finishing their day early while others choose to sleep in. With the development of technology, a customized way of working has now become feasible. Although some people contend that working at home offers many advantages, I strongly believe that it is better to work with others at a workplace rather than to work alone at home. This has to do with the working environment and cooperation.

Firstly, one can feel a sense of competition that can act as a self-motivator. To illustrate, the company for which my cousin works once had a contest. Every employee had to present the results of a given task and to compete with the others. The winner's work was to become a future project at the company. Although my cousin's work was not selected for the actual project, he said he put a great deal of effort into the work and learned from it.

Secondly, not every employee has the same abilities. Some are superb at a particular skill while others are talented in different fields. Hence, workers can learn from and cooperate with each other by using their own knowledge and skills. For instance, my friend is proficient in the use of Excel but not as skilled with PowerPoint. Consequently, she helps her coworkers who are experiencing difficulties with Excel. In return, she gets help from others whenever she has trouble with PowerPoint. This results in a synergistic effect as well as better productivity within her department.

It is true that working alone at home provides one with more freedom. However, with too much freedom, it might be difficult for workers to stay focused on the tasks they are working on. This can result in slower productivity. Working with others can help one become disciplined in a more competitive environment. Moreover, one can cooperate and share one's knowledge and skills with one's coworkers. Therefore, I disagree with the statement that working alone at home is better than working with others at a workplace.

WORD REMINDER
present 표현하다   a great deal of 다량의   superb 훌륭한   proficient 능숙한   synergistic 상승적인   productivity 생산성   department 부서
lenient 관대한   in terms of ~에 관하여   disciplined 잘 통솔된, 엄격한

RELATED TOPICS

1 Do you prefer to attend large parties with many people or small parties with a few close friends and relatives? 당신은 많은 사람들과 함께하는 큰 파티를 선호하는가, 몇몇의 친한 친구 및 친지들과 함께하는 작은 파티를 선호하는가?

LARGE PARTY	SMALL PARTY
- broader interpersonal relationships 폭넓은 대인 관계 - less attention + responsibility 더 적은 관심 + 책임	- spending more time together 더 많은 시간을 함께 보냄 - more controlled atmosphere (harder to control many people) 더욱 절제되는 분위기 (많은 사람들을 컨트롤하는 것은 더욱 어려움)

2 It is better to work alone at home by using a computer or telephone rather than to work with others at a company. 컴퓨터나 전화를 사용해서 집에서 혼자 일하는 것이 회사에서 다른 이들과 함께 일하는 것보다 낫다.

AGREE	DISAGREE
- able to concentrate better 더욱 집중할 수 있음 - freedom: schedule, dress code, working hours 자유: 일정, 복장 규정, 근무 시간	- interpersonal relationship 대인 관계 - cooperation → efficiency ↑ 협력 → 효율성 ↑

3 Most people prefer decisions made by others to those made by themselves.
대부분의 사람들은 그들 스스로 내리는 결정보다는 타인이 내려주는 결정을 선호한다.

AGREE	DISAGREE
- various opinions / many indirect experiences 다양한 의견 / 다수의 간접 경험 - objective 객관적	- different solutions may confuse a person 다른 해결책들이 사람을 혼란스럽게 만들 수 있음 - even a good decision may not work for a person 훌륭한 결정이라도 사람에게 맞지 않을 수 있음

4 Making others happy is a way to make oneself happy. 타인을 행복하게 만드는 것은 본인을 행복하게 만드는 것이다.

AGREE	DISAGREE
- payback: others make you happy 보상: 다른 사람들도 당사자를 행복하게 만들어 줌 - emotion: directly delivered back to the person 감정: 본인에게 바로 다시 전달이 됨	- unethical way of making others happy: guilty 비도덕적인 방법으로 다른 이들을 행복하게 만드는 것: 양심의 가책 - competition: making others happy may make people feel overly self-conscious 경쟁: 다른 이들을 행복하게 만드는 것은 사람들이 남의 눈을 지나치게 의식하게 만드는 것일 수 있음

5 Using one's own knowledge and experience is better than listening to advice from others when solving a problem. 문제를 풀 때, 자신의 지식과 경험을 이용하는 것이 다른 이들의 충고를 듣는 것보다 낫다.

AGREE	DISAGREE
- each has own way of handling difficulties 각 개인은 문제를 다루는 본인만의 방법이 있음 - easier to apply → others' advice: may be hard to understand 적용하기 쉬움 → 다른 이들의 충고: 이해하기 힘들 수 있음	- one's own experience: may be too subjective 개인만의 경험: 너무 주관적일 수 있음 - indirect experiences from other people 다른 이들로부터의 간접 경험

TOEFL® MAP
ACTUAL
TEST Writing 2

07

For years, researchers have studied animal behavior. One aspect of it they have observed is that young animals appear to play just like human children do. Through careful examination, scientists have determined that there are three main reasons why young animals play.

First, they believe that animals play to burn off surplus energy. The vast majority of the playing which animals do involves physical activities, such as running and jumping, with their littermates or other animals. Some animals, particularly dogs and cats, also play with toys like balls and sticks, which they may bat around with their paws. As they play either with others or by themselves, young animals expend unneeded energy in a relatively safe way. This, in turn, helps the animals relieve themselves of various types of stress that they may experience.

Playing also helps young animals prepare for adulthood. Virtually all animals in the wild are predators or prey. Lions, which are predators, often stage mock fights with one another when playing in their youth. During these play fights, they learn different fighting methods as well as how to stalk and attack prey. As cubs, they learn critical skills they will require to be able to feed themselves as adults. On the other hand, prey animals such as deer learn to run fast and to jump high, necessary skills for eluding predators hunting them, when they are young.

Furthermore, young animals develop social skills when playing together. Puppies and kittens that play with others of their kind are typically more sociable than those that grow up without interacting and playing with others. And laboratory studies of young rats have shown that their brains secrete certain chemicals when they play. These chemicals help them develop various social skills needed to deal with other rats when they become adults.

🎧 07-01

Directions You have 20 minutes to plan and write your response. Your response will be judged on the basis of the quality of your writing and on how well your response presents the points in the lecture and their relationship to the passage. Typically, an effective response will be 150-225 words.

Question Summarize the points made in the lecture, being sure to explain how they cast doubt on specific points made in the reading passage.

CUT | PASTE | UNDO | REDO | Hide Word Count : 0

For years, researchers have studied animal behavior. One aspect of it they have observed is that young animals appear to play just like human children do. Through careful examination, scientists have determined that there are three main reasons why young animals play.

First, they believe that animals play to burn off surplus energy. The vast majority of the playing which animals do involves physical activities, such as running and jumping, with their littermates or other animals. Some animals, particularly dogs and cats, also play with toys like balls and sticks, which they may bat around with their paws. As they play either with others or by themselves, young animals expend unneeded energy in a relatively safe way. This, in turn, helps the animals relieve themselves of various types of stress that they may experience.

Playing also helps young animals prepare for adulthood. Virtually all animals in the wild are predators or prey. Lions, which are predators, often stage mock fights with one another when playing in their youth. During these play fights, they learn different fighting methods as well as how to stalk and attack prey. As cubs, they learn critical skills they will require to be able to feed themselves as adults. On the other hand, prey animals such as deer learn to run fast and to jump high, necessary skills for eluding predators hunting them, when they are young.

Furthermore, young animals develop social skills when playing together. Puppies and kittens that play with others of their kind are typically more sociable than those that grow up without interacting and playing with others. And laboratory studies of young rats have shown that their brains secrete certain chemicals when they play. These chemicals help them develop various social skills needed to deal with other rats when they become adults.

📝 NOTE-TAKING

three reasons why young animals play 왜 어린 동물들이 노는지에 관한 세 가지 이유

❶ *to burn off surplus E* 남는 에너지를 소모하기 위함
  - relieve themselves of stress 스트레스 해소

   Young animals play in order to consume extra energy.

❷ *to prepare for adulthood* 성인기에 대한 준비
  - learning diff. survival / hunting methods 생존 / 사냥의 다른 방법들을 배움

   Playing teaches young animals a number of survival and hunting techniques, helping them get ready to enter adulthood.

❸ *to develop social skills* 사회적 능력 개발
  - brains secrete certain chemicals 뇌가 특정 화학 물질을 분비

  Paraphrasing Example Certain chemicals released while playing help young animals socialize with others.

WORD REMINDER
burn off 태워서 없애 버리다 surplus 여분의 vast 막대한 majority 대부분 littermate 한배 새끼 particularly 특히
paw (개, 고양이 등의 갈고리 발톱이 있는) 발 expend 소비하다 relieve 완화하다 virtually 사실상 the wild 야생 predator 포식 동물
prey 먹이 stage 상연하다 mock fight 모의 전투 stalk 몰래 접근하다 cub 짐승 새끼 critical 중요한 elude 피하다 sociable 사교적인
interact 상호 작용하다 secrete 분비하다 chemical 화학의

no particular reason for play behavior 노는 행동에 대한 특별한 이유 ×

❶ *do not necessarily play to get rid of extra E* 남는 에너지를 사용하기 위해 노는 것만은 아님
  Ex baby seals: hungry → still play 새끼 물개: 배고픔 → 여전히 놀았음
    ∵ playful nature 명랑한 본성

  Paraphrasing Example There is no correlation between playing and exhausting surplus energy.

❷ *survival skills: instinctive* 생존 능력: 본능
  Ex cats: - playing together 고양이: 같이 노는 그룹
    - no group playing 같이 놀지 않는 그룹
    → hunting skill: no difference 사냥 능력: 다른 점 ×

  Paraphrasing Example Survival skills are inborn traits.

❸ *chemicals from the brain: released when needed* 뇌에서 나오는 화학 물질: 필요할 때 분비됨
  Ex rats: raised alone until reaching adulthood 쥐: 성인기에 다다를 때까지 홀로 자람
    → no problem integrating / socializing w/others 다른 쥐들과 동화되거나 사회화하는데 문제 없음

  Paraphrasing Example Chemicals thought to provide young animals with social skills are released when necessary.

WORD REMINDER
yarn 뜨개실 excess 초과한 disprove 논박하다 seal 바다표범 nature 본성 rid 없애다 discernable 식별할 수 있는 survival 생존을 위한
instinctive 본능적인 raise 기르다 reach ~에 도달하다 community 공동 사회 integrate 통합하다 release 방출하다

The lecturer argues that the theory from the reading passage on the play behavior of young animals is erroneous and that there is no specific reason for this play behavior. This directly refutes the reading passage's claim that there are three reasons why young animals play.

First, there is no correlation between playing and exhausting surplus energy. For example, baby seals play even when they are hungry and keep playing when their mother comes back with food, suggesting they have a playful nature. This contradicts the reading passage's claim that young animals play in order to consume extra energy.

In addition, the lecturer contends that survival skills are inborn traits. She cites a case study explaining that there was no significant difference between a group of cats allowed to play and another kept from playing together. This negates the assertion from the reading passage that playing teaches young animals a number of survival and hunting techniques, helping them get ready to enter adulthood.

Finally, the lecturer asserts that chemicals thought to provide young animals with social skills are released when necessary. In a set of experiments, rats that were raised alone displayed no problem getting along with other rats later. This contradicts the idea presented in the reading passage that certain chemicals released while playing help young animals socialize with others.

WORD REMINDER

exhaust 소진시키다 consume 소모하다 inborn 선천적인 trait 특성 cite 언급하다 significant 현저한 negate 부정하다

TIPS for SUCCESS

'예'를 나타내는 표현법을 살펴보자.

For example, / To illustrate, / For instance,

위의 세 가지 표현법 다음에는 반드시 주어와 동사가 나와야 한다. 가끔 명사나 명사구를 쓰는 학생들이 있는데, 이들은 독립된 절을 이끄는 표현이라는 점을 기억하자.

명사, 동명사, 대명사, 명사구, 명사절을 동반하는 표현법을 살펴보자.

such as / in the case of / including / as shown / revealed by

위의 표현법 다음에는 주어와 동사가 나올 수 없다.

Directions Read the question below. You have 30 minutes to plan, write, and revise your essay. Typically, an effective response will contain a minimum of 300 words.

Question

Do you agree or disagree with the following statement?

Teachers should be paid according to their students' performances.

Use specific reasons and examples to support your answer.

AGREE

- **+ve reinforcement** 긍정적 강화
    - enthusiasm + accomplishment, pride 의욕 + 성취감, 자신감
        Ex studies: outcome-based salary → students' performance ↑ 연구: 결과에 바탕을 둔 보수 → 학생들의 성적 ↑
            → more responsibility + passion 더 많은 책임감 + 열정

- **quality of education improves** 교육의 질 향상
    - encourages teachers to use diff. approaches 교사들이 다양한 접근 방법을 사용하도록 장려
        Ex uncle: always comes up w/new methods 삼촌: 항상 새로운 방법을 연구
            → students learn and understand easily 학생들은 더 쉽게 배우고 이해함

INTRODUCTION

generalization: quality of teaching → issue in education
일반화: 수업의 질 → 교육의 논점

⬇

method + enthusiasm: affect students' performances
방법 + 열의: 학생의 성적에 영향을 끼침

⬇

thesis: agree (recognition, improvement of teaching techniques)
논제: 찬성 (인정, 수업 방법의 향상)

DISAGREE

- **outcome-based salary: class may become too results oriented**
결과에 바탕을 둔 보수: 수업이 결과지향적으로 될 수 있음
    - learning strategies > gaining knowledge 전략을 배우는 것 > 지식을 얻는 것
        Ex studies: teachers focused on materials related to exams 연구: 교사들이 시험에 관련된 자료에 초점을 맞추었음
            → value: outcome > process 가치: 결과 > 과정

- **results: do not always reflect knowledge** 결과: 항상 지식을 반영하는 것은 아님
    - some materials require more time 일부 학습 자료는 더 많은 시간을 필요로 함
        Ex grammatical terms + concepts: took time to apply the skills in actual compositions
        문법 용어 + 개념: 실제 작문에 적용하는데 시간이 걸렸음
            → stress + frustration for instructors and students 교사들 및 학생들에게 스트레스 + 좌절감

INTRODUCTION

generalization: quality of teaching → issue in education
일반화: 수업의 질 → 교육의 논점

⬇

method + enthusiasm: affect students' performances
방법 + 열의: 학생의 성적에 영향을 끼침

⬇

thesis: disagree (diff. objective, anxiety)
논제: 반대 (다른 목적, 불안감)

The quality of teaching has always been an issue in education. How well and enthusiastically an instructor teaches can have a great deal of influence on a student's performance. Some contend that student outcome is not an appropriate method for determining a teacher's salary. However, I strongly believe teachers should get paid according to their students' performances. This is a way to recognize teachers' efforts. In addition, this system would stimulate teachers to constantly improve and develop their teaching methods.

First of all, one's salary can act as positive reinforcement in a capitalist society. Merit pay motivates instructors to teach with more enthusiasm and makes them feel a sense of accomplishment and pride for being acknowledged for their hard work. To illustrate, studies show that students' overall performances improved significantly after their teacher's salaries were based on students' exam results. This situation also leads teachers to feel more responsibility and passion about educating students.

On top of that, the quality of education improves when teachers' salaries are set according to student outcomes. As each instructor specializes in a particular subject, teaching similar materials every year may lead them to teach in a habitual way. On the other hand, an outcome-based salary system would encourage instructors to approach topics differently. For instance, my uncle, a teacher, always comes up with new teaching methods and resources that will help students grasp the class materials more easily. Thus, up-to-date teaching tools and references aid students in learning concepts more effectively and doing better on exams.

It is true that students' performances may not improve soon. Student learning is also affected by many factors outside teachers' control. These include inattentive, absent, or abusive parents and students with learning disabilities. Nonetheless, an outcome-based salary system will stimulate and motivate instructors to work harder. Furthermore, it will push teachers to continuously work and improve their teaching techniques. For the above reasons, I firmly agree with the statement that teachers should get paid according to their students' performances.

WORD REMINDER

enthusiastically 매우 열심히   performance 성적   outcome 결과   appropriate 적당한   method 방법   determine 결정하다
recognize 인정하다   stimulate 자극하다   positive reinforcement 긍정적 강화   capitalist 자본주의자   merit 공로
motivate ～에게 동기를 주다   accomplishment 성취   acknowledged 인정된   overall 총체적인   significantly 상당히   specialize 전문화하다
particular 특정한   habitual 습관적인   encourage 장려하다   approach 접근법   resource 재료   grasp 이해하다   up-to-date 최신의
reference 참고 문헌   concept 개념   inattentive 태만한   abusive 학대하는   disability 무능, 무력

ACTUAL TEST **07**

TIPS for SUCCESS

독립형 에세이: 글자수

독립형 에세이는 약 300단어를 요구한다. 독립형 에세이 역시 단어 개수와 점수가 비례한다고 오해하는 학생들이 많다. 물론 본인은 라이팅 점수가 28~29점 정도 나오는 학생들이 에세이를 조금 더 길게 써서 30점을 만드는 경우는 본 적이 있다. 하지만, 이는 보다 구체적인 아이디어로 의견이 뒷받침되는 경우이다. 즉, 탄탄한 글이 형성되지 않은 상태에서 글자 수만 늘린다고 해서 점수가 올라가지는 않는다.

The quality of teaching has always been an issue in education. How well and enthusiastically an instructor teaches can have a great deal of influence on a student's performance. Some contend that teachers should get paid according to their students' performances. However, I strongly believe student outcome is not an appropriate method for determining a teacher's salary because a class may become too results oriented, and in an outcome-based system, it might create tension among instructors.

First of all, a class may end up focusing only on the results of exams and assignments. This could cause students to concentrate on learning strategies to get better scores on tests rather than on gaining knowledge. To illustrate, many studies show that most teachers concentrate only on material related to exams when they are paid according to student performance, suggesting that students learned only important points rather than getting a comprehensive understanding of a particular topic. Not only that, but both teachers and students also tend to put more value on outcomes than on processes.

On top of that, students' results do not always reflect the knowledge they have gained. Some material requires more time and practice. For instance, I learned a lot of grammatical terms and concepts in English class. Though I knew what they were and how to use them in writing, it took me a long time to apply the skills in actual compositions. Hence, this approach will result in stress and frustration for students as well as instructors who might eventually lose enthusiasm.

It is true that an outcome-based salary system would encourage teachers to improve their teaching skills. However, student learning is affected by many factors outside teachers' control. These include inattentive, absent, or abusive parents and students with learning disabilities. In addition, teachers may put too much emphasis on exam results rather than on knowledge itself, and improvements may become apparent slowly in some subjects, causing pressure and anxiety among teachers. For the above reasons, I firmly disagree with the statement that teachers should get paid according to their students' performances.

WORD REMINDER

tension 긴장, 불안   end up (~으로) 되다   assignment 숙제   strategy 전략   comprehensive 포괄적인   tend to ~하는 경향이 있다
reflect 반영하다   grammatical 문법적인   term 용어   apply 적용하다   composition 한 편의 작문   frustration 좌절   eventually 결국
emphasis 강조   apparent 명백한   pressure 압박감   anxiety 걱정, 불안

TIPS for SUCCESS

most vs. most of the ~

종종 most와 most of the를 혼동하는 학생들이 있다. 두 번째 단락의 문장을 살펴보자.

To illustrate, many studies show that **most** teachers concentrate only on material related to exams when they are paid according to student performance.

위의 most teachers는 '대부분의 교사들', 즉 일반적인 교사들을 가리킨다. 아래의 문장을 살펴보자.

To illustrate, many studies show that **most of the** teachers concentrate only on material related to exams when they are paid according to student performance.

위의 문장에서 most of the teachers는 '특정 교사들 중의 대부분'을 가리키므로 일반적인 교사들을 지칭하는 것이 아니라는 점을 기억하자.

RELATED TOPICS

1 Serious and strict teachers are more effective at educating students than friendly and fun teachers.
진지하고 엄격한 교사들이 친근하고 재미있는 교사들보다 학생들을 가르치는데 있어서 더 효과적이다.

AGREE	DISAGREE
- students tend to concentrate more 학생들이 더욱 집중하는 경향이 있음 - class: more academic → more knowledge delivered 수업: 더욱 학구적 → 더 많은 지식 전달	- able to deliver knowledge in interesting ways 지식을 보다 흥미로운 방법으로 전달할 수 있음 - able to draw questions / ideas from students 학생들로부터 질문이나 의견을 이끌어낼 수 있음

2 It is more important for teachers to get along with their students than to have a lot of knowledge.
교사들은 많은 지식을 가지고 있는 것보다 학생들과 잘 어울릴 수 있는 것이 더 중요하다.

AGREE	DISAGREE
- students: feel more comfortable asking questions / participate in discussions 학생들: 질문 + 토론 참여에 더욱 편안함을 느낌 - students: more interested in studying 학생들: 공부에 더욱 흥미를 가짐	- purpose of learning: to gain a lot of knowledge 배움의 목적: 많은 지식 습득 - students may not take studying seriously if they are too comfortable w/their teachers 교사와 너무 친할 경우 학생들은 공부를 진지하게 받아들이지 않을 수 있음

3 Teachers should assign homework to their students every day. 교사들은 학생들에게 매일 숙제를 내주어야 한다.

AGREE	DISAGREE
- building study habits 공부하는 습관을 기름 - a way to make students review 학생들이 복습하도록 만드는 방법	- students may become passive in studying 학생들은 공부하는데 수동적으로 변할 수 있음 - pressure to do homework every day 매일 숙제를 하는 것에 대한 압박감

4 All teachers should take special courses to improve their knowledge and teaching skills.
모든 교사들은 지식과 교수법을 향상시키기 위해 특별한 수업을 들어야 한다.

AGREE	DISAGREE
- new teaching methods 새로운 교육 방법 - sharing own skills + strategies w/other teachers 다른 교사들과 자신만의 능력 + 전략을 공유	- freedom of taking a course 수업을 수강하는 자유 - all teachers have their own ways of teaching 모든 교사는 자신만의 교육 방식이 있음

5 The quality of education will improve if teachers' salaries become higher.
교사들의 급여가 인상된다면 교육의 질이 높아질 것이다.

AGREE	DISAGREE
- motivation + recognition among teachers 동기 부여 + 교사들 사이에서의 인정 - greater responsibility to teach well 더욱 무거운 책임감	- frustration + competition among teachers 교사들 사이에서의 좌절 + 경쟁 - enthusiasm should come from one's will to teach well 열성은 잘 가르치고자 하는 개인의 의지로부터 비롯되어야 함

TOEFL® MAP
ACTUAL TEST Writing 2

08

The mystery of whether humans are alone in the universe may have been answered by a 1.9-kilogram meteorite discovered in Antarctica in 1984. After careful analysis, scientists from NASA announced that the meteorite, which they say came from Mars, once contained organic matter that was extraterrestrial in origin.

While the meteorite was found in 1984, it was not until 2009 that NASA scientists claimed that it possessed strong evidence that life existed on Mars billions of years in the past. The reason for the delay is that recent advances in electron microscopy made it possible for scientists to see various features on the meteorite that had previously been overlooked. What they found with a high-powered electron microscope was evidence of extremely tiny fossils of bacteria-like organisms on the meteorite. This was a clear indicator that Mars once held life at least on the microscopic level.

Scientists believe the meteorite formed on Mars around 3.6 to four billion years ago. Then, Mars was much warmer and wetter than it is today. Water likely entered fractures in the rock. Then, living organisms soon followed and made their homes inside these fissures. Scientists defend their theory by citing the carbonate minerals found in the rock. These minerals, they speculate, could only have been formed by living organisms.

Further proof of the existence of life is that the meteorite contains magnetite. Studies have determined that roughly one quarter of the magnetite in the meteorite is in the guise of small crystals. These crystals are chemically pure and structurally perfect, and they have unique three-dimensional shapes that could only have been formed by living organisms, not by organic matter. Taken altogether, these scientists are convinced they have proof that life exists—or at least existed—elsewhere in the universe.

🎧 08-01

Directions You have 20 minutes to plan and write your response. Your response will be judged on the basis of the quality of your writing and on how well your response presents the points in the lecture and their relationship to the passage. Typically, an effective response will be 150-225 words.

Question Summarize the points made in the lecture, being sure to explain how they cast doubt on specific points made in the reading passage.

CUT PASTE UNDO REDO   Hide Word Count : 0

The mystery of whether humans are alone in the universe may have been answered by a 1.9-kilogram meteorite discovered in Antarctica in 1984. After careful analysis, scientists from NASA announced that the meteorite, which they say came from Mars, once contained organic matter that was extraterrestrial in origin.

While the meteorite was found in 1984, it was not until 2009 that NASA scientists claimed that it possessed strong evidence that life existed on Mars billions of years in the past. The reason for the delay is that recent advances in electron microscopy made it possible for scientists to see various features on the meteorite that had previously been overlooked. What they found with a high-powered electron microscope was evidence of extremely tiny fossils of bacteria-like organisms on the meteorite. This was a clear indicator that Mars once held life at least on the microscopic level.

Scientists believe the meteorite formed on Mars around 3.6 to four billion years ago. Then, Mars was much warmer and wetter than it is today. Water likely entered fractures in the rock. Then, living organisms soon followed and made their homes inside these fissures. Scientists defend their theory by citing the carbonate minerals found in the rock. These minerals, they speculate, could only have been formed by living organisms.

Further proof of the existence of life is that the meteorite contains magnetite. Studies have determined that roughly one quarter of the magnetite in the meteorite is in the guise of small crystals. These crystals are chemically pure and structurally perfect, and they have unique three-dimensional shapes that could only have been formed by living organisms, not by organic matter. Taken altogether, these scientists are convinced they have proof that life exists—or at least existed—elsewhere in the universe.

📝 NOTE-TAKING

a meteorite discovered on Earth: life once existed on Mars
지구에서 발견된 운석: 화성에 한때 생명체가 존재했음

❶ *use of electron microscope* 전자 현미경의 사용

- evidence of extremely tiny fossils of bacteria-like organisms on the meteorite
  운석에 있었던 박테리아처럼 보이는 매우 작은 화석 증거

 By looking at the meteorite through an electron microscope, scientists found fossils of bacteria-like organisms.

❷ *minerals from living organisms found in the rock* 암석에서 발견된 생명체로부터의 광물

- water entered fractures → living organisms made homes in the fissures
  틈으로 스며든 물 → 틈 안에 생명체가 보금자리를 만들었음

 Carbonate minerals, which could only be formed by living organisms, were spotted in the rock.

❸ *magnetite in the meteorite* 운석의 자철광

- magnetite: crystals → distinctions: only formed by living organisms 자철광: 결정체 → 특성: 오직 생명체로부터 형성될 수 있음

 The features found in the magnetite crystals could have been formed only by living organisms.

WORD REMINDER

meteorite 운석   analysis 분석   announce 발표하다   organic 생물의   extraterrestrial 지구 밖의   billion 10억
microscopy 현미경 사용(법)   feature 특성   overlook 못 보고 지나치다, 간과하다   extremely 극단적으로   fossil 화석   indicator 지표
fracture 갈라진 틈   fissure 갈라진 틈   defend 지지하다   cite 언급하다   speculate 추측하다   roughly 대충   guise 외관   crystal 결정(체)
structuraly 구조적으로

existence of living organisms on Mars: doubtful 화성의 생명체 존재: 의심스러움

❶ *problems with electron microscope* 전자 현미경의 문제

- tech: not perfect → EM: easily contaminated during prep process
  과학 기술: 완벽 ✗ → 전자 현미경: 준비 과정에서 쉽게 오염될 수 있음
  → bacteria: could've been from microscope 박테리아: 현미경에서 생겼을 수 있음
- photographic process: imperfect → confusion in distinguishing bacteria
  사진 촬영의 과정: 완벽 ✗ → 박테리아를 구분하는데 혼동

There were errors in using an electron microscope.

❷ *bacteria from Earth could've gotten into the meteorite* 지구의 박테리아가 운석으로 들어갔을 수 있음

- meteorite: from Mars 운석: 화성으로부터 왔음
- bacteria: terrestrial 박테리아: 지구에서 왔음

It is doubtful that the bacteria are from Mars since there is a possibility that they are from Earth.

❸ *magnetite: extremely tiny* 자철광: 상당히 미세함

- ∴cannot trust images 이미지를 신뢰할 수 없음
- scientists: manipulated pictures 과학자들: 사진을 조작

The size of the magnetite found in the rock is too small to verify the images.

WORD REMINDER

countless 무수한   article 기사   offer 제공하다   magnification 확대   contaminate 오염시키다   reach ~에 도착하다   estimate 추정하다
land 도착하다   plenty 풍부   terrestrial 지구의   presence 존재   microscopic 미시적인   manipulate 조작하다   flimsy 박약한

ACTUAL TEST 08

The lecturer argues that it is unlikely that living organisms once existed on Mars and provides three reasons for his assertion. This directly contradicts the reading passage's claim that a meteorite discovered on the Earth proves that life once existed there.

First, the professor contends that there were errors in using an electron microscope since the technology was not perfect and was susceptible to contamination. Furthermore, the pictures taken were unclear, so it is not possible to say that what the scientists saw were bacteria. This refutes the reading passage's claim that by looking at the meteorite through an electron microscope, scientists found fossils of bacteria-like organisms.

Secondly, the lecturer emphasizes that it is doubtful that the bacteria are from Mars since there is a possibility that they are from Earth. Even though the meteorite is from Mars, bacteria could have gotten into it. This argument casts doubt on the reading passage's claim that carbonate minerals, which could only be formed by living organisms, were spotted in the rock.

Finally, the magnetite found in the rock was too small for good images of it to be taken. In addition, scientists modified the pictures taken by microscopes that were still under development, making them less reliable. This firmly rebuts the reading passage's claim that the features found in the magnetite crystals could have been formed only by living organisms.

WORD REMINDER

once 한때   assertion 단언   susceptible 영향을 받기 쉬운   sufficiently 충분히   emphasize 강조하다   spot 발견하다   verify 증명하다
feature 특성

TIPS for SUCCESS

통합형 에세이에서는 어떠한 사실을 근거로 주장을 증명했다는 내용이 자주 쓰인다. 다양한 표현법들을 살펴보자.
⟨It is supported by the fact that 주어 + 동사⟩ / ⟨It is proved that 주어 + 동사⟩ / ⟨It is approved that 주어 + 동사⟩ / ⟨It is verified that 주어 + 동사⟩ / ⟨It is validated that 주어 + 동사⟩ / ⟨It is authenticated 주어 + 동사⟩
동사 다음에 by the fact that이 오면 '～라는 사실에 의해 뒷받침되다'라고 해석이 되고 동사 다음 by가 올 경우 '～에 의해 증명이 되다'라고 해석이 되며 모두 생략 가능하다. 또한 It has been supported/proved/approved/verified/validated/authenticated ～라고 표현해서 현재완료형으로 쓸 수도 있으며 '증명되어 왔다'라고 해석할 수 있다. 또한 '무엇이 무엇을 증명했다' 등의 표현을 나타내기 위해 능동태를 쓸 수도 있다. 첫 단락의 문장을 살펴보자.
A meteorite discovered on the Earth proves that life once existed on Mars.
위의 문장을 앞에 나온 표현법들 중 하나를 사용해서 만들어 보면 다음과 같다.
With the discovery of a meteorite on the Earth, **it is verified** that life once existed on Mars.
위의 다양한 표현법들을 응용해서 에세이를 쓸 때 같은 표현을 반복하지 않도록 하자.

CUT   PASTE   UNDO   REDO   Hide Word Count : 0

Directions Read the question below. You have 30 minutes to plan, write, and revise your essay. Typically, an effective response will contain a minimum of 300 words.

Question

When you face a difficult problem, what do you feel the best way to solve it is?

- Finding information about the problem by using the Internet
- Taking a long time to think about the problem
- Asking someone with more experience for advice about the problem

Use specific reasons and examples to support your answer.

✎ NOTE-TAKING

Finding Information about the Problem by Using the Internet

- **save time + effort** 시간 + 노력 절약
  - people go through similar problems → how others think and deal with
    사람들은 비슷한 문제를 겪음 → 다른 이들이 생각하고 처리하는 방법
    Ex conflict w/peer → reading similar cases / getting recommendations on books
    직장 동료와 마찰 → 비슷한 경우에 대해 읽음 / 책에서 충고를 얻음

- **objective perspectives** 객관적인 관점
  - people see problems from own point of view 사람들은 자기만의 관점에서 문제를 봄
    Ex studies → close friends + families 연구들 → 가까운 친구 + 식구들
    → biased advice / story from only 1 person's standpoint 편향된 충고 / 오직 한 사람의 관점으로부터의 이야기

INTRODUCTION

generalization: everyone faces problems
일반화: 기업: 모든 이들은 문제를 겪음

⬇

complicated issues → require more thought
좀더 복잡한 문제 → 더 많은 생각을 필요로 함

⬇

thesis: information using the Internet (save time + more objective point of view)
논제: 인터넷을 이용해서 정보를 얻기 (시간 절약 + 좀 더 객관적)

Taking a Long Time to Think about the Problem

- **worth solving by oneself** 스스로 해결하는 것은 가치가 있음
  - essence of problems (repetition ✖) 문제의 본질 (재발 ✖)
    Ex always spend a lot of time → identify potential elements 언제나 많은 시간을 보냄 → 잠재적 요소를 찾음
    → avoid future potential conflicts 미래의 잠재적 충돌을 피함

- **everyone is different** 모든 사람은 다름
  - the solution might not work for another person 해결책이 다른 사람에게는 적용되지 않을 수 있음
    → possibility of unexpected consequences 예상치 못한 결과가 나올 가능함
    Ex conflict w/coworker → many things to consider 동료와의 충돌 → 고려할 많은 것들

Asking Someone with More Experience for Advice about the Problem

- ● ***save time + effort*** 시간 + 노력 절약
  - – avoid unnecessary steps 불필요한 단계를 피함
    Ex problem at company → ask a boss with more experience 회사에서의 문제 → 더 경험이 많은 상사에게 문의함
    employee: never asks Q's → more time to be promoted 고용인: 절대 질문하지 않음 → 승진하는 데 더 시간이 걸림

- ● ***objective perspective*** 객관적 관점
  - – people see problems from own point of view 사람들은 그들 자신의 관점으로 문제를 봄
    Ex listening to a diff. person: more rational + impartial 다른 사람의 말을 경청함: 더 합리적 + 공정한

INTRODUCTION

generalization: everyone faces problems
일반화: 기업: 모든 이들은 문제를 겪음

⬇

complicated issues ➡ require more thought
좀더 복잡한 문제 → 더 많은 생각을 필요로 함

⬇

thesis: asking someone w/more experience for advice (save time + more objective point of view)
논제: 좀 더 경험이 있는 사람에게 조언 요청 (시간 절약 + 좀 더 객관적 관점)

CUT PASTE UNDO REDO

Everyone faces problems each day. Whether it is a trivial matter like spilling coffee or a more serious problem such as having a conflict with a coworker, it is inevitable that trouble occurs in people's lives. When I have a difficult problem, I prefer to solve it by using the Internet to find information. This approach allows me to save time and to look at the problem from more objective points of view.

First of all, looking for information on the Internet could save people a lot of time and effort. Most people go through similar problems, and it is easy to get advice about the matters they face on the Internet. For instance, I can solve a conflict with a peer by reading about similar cases and solutions on the Internet or even by getting recommendations on certain books. Hence, rather than wasting time struggling to resolve a predicament, finding information by using the Internet is a very effective way to solve a problem.

On top of that, people can look at a problem from a more objective perspective. For example, studies show it is highly likely a person will get biased advice from close friends or families. The reasons could be simply that his friends or family members are closely related or that his friends would hear a story only from that person's standpoint; however, different people can share various ideas about a matter on the Internet, making the suggestions more objective.

People have to deal with problems all the time, and each person has his own opinion and reasons for that opinion about how to solve problems. The Internet helps people save time and effort. In addition, advice and guidance found on the Internet could be more unprejudiced. Therefore, I strongly believe that the most effective way to resolve a problem is to find information on the Internet.

WORD REMINDER
face 직면하다   trivial 사소한   inevitable 불가피한   approach 방법   go through 겪다   struggle 어려움을 겪다   predicament 곤경
biased 편중된   standpoint 입장   guidance 지도   unprejudiced 편견 없는

CUT PASTE UNDO REDO

Everyone faces problems each day. Whether it is a trivial matter like spilling coffee or a more serious problem such as having a conflict with a coworker, it is inevitable that trouble occurs in people's lives. When I have a difficult problem, I prefer to solve it by thinking about the problem for a long time. This approach allows me to look at the essence of the problem and to minimize unexpected results.

First of all, it is always worth solving a problem by myself. Simply finding a solution on the Internet could resolve a particular problem, but it will only result in a short-term solution. For instance, whenever I have trouble with a friend, I spend very much time identifying the fundamental problems between her and myself. Thus, taking some time to think about the predicament will eventually provide me with insight and will help me develop the ability to deal with the same matters in the future.

In addition, everybody is different. Hence, listening to others or looking up information on the Internet may cause unforeseen consequences and make a situation worse. For instance, if I try to solve a conflict between myself and a coworker, I should take many things about the specific situation into account, from finding the right time to talk with the coworker to considering where to have the conversation. In other words, when I want to resolve trouble, it is necessary to take enough time and to examine the problem thoroughly.

Some people might argue that spending a lot of time thinking about trouble could be a waste of time. However, figuring out the real cause of the trouble can keep people from repetitive mistakes in the future. Moreover, this can help people react well to unexpected situations. Therefore, I strongly believe that the best way to solve a problem is to take a long time to think about it.

WORD REMINDER

essence 본질   fundamental 근본적인   insight 통찰력   unforseen 뜻하지 않은   take into account ~를 고려하다   thoroughly 완전히, 면밀히
react 반응하다   unexpected 예상하지 못한

Everyone faces problems each day. Whether it is a trivial matter like spilling coffee or a more serious problem such as having a conflict with a coworker, it is inevitable that trouble occurs in people's lives. When I have a difficult problem, I prefer to solve it by asking someone with more experience for advice about the problem. This approach allows me to save time and effort and to be more objective.

First of all, listening to a person who has had a similar experience can help me save time and effort. In other words, I can avoid unnecessary steps that can lead to failure in dealing with the problem. For instance, if I have a problem with my work at my company, it would be better for me to ask my boss, who has more experience, for advice. Therefore, listening to other people can definitely save time and effort when solving a problem.

Moreover, I can look at a problem from a more objective perspective. According to statistics, it is highly likely that people will tell stories from their own viewpoints, so they are unable to think about their problems objectively. That can make it hard to resolve conflicts. By listening to advice from another person with a different perspective, I can become more rational and impartial. Thus, it is crucial to ask for advice from a person with more experience about a problem.

Though seeking advice from the Internet may seem to be a very good way to deal with a problem, it can be more important for people to hear advice directly. Listening to advice from a person with more experience will not only help people save time and effort but will also guide them to be more reasonable and wiser. Therefore, I strongly believe that the best way to solve a problem is to ask someone with more experience for advice about the problem.

WORD REMINDER
objective 객관적인   perspective 관점   standpoint 입장   rational 이성적인   impartial 공정한   deal with 해결하다

1 Do you agree or disagree with the following statement? Most people can solve important problems by themselves or with their families. Use specific reasons and examples to support your answer.

다음 명제에 찬성하는가 반대하는가? 대부분의 사람들은 그들 자신이나 식구들과 함께 중요한 문제를 풀 수 있다. 구체적인 이유와 예를 들어 자신의 입장을 뒷받침하시오.

AGREE	DISAGREE
- know themselves well: able to pinpoint what is needed 그들 자신을 잘 알고 있음: 무엇이 필요한지 정확히 파악 가능 - families: can look at the problem from an objective point of view 식구들: 객관적인 관점에서 문제를 볼 수 있음	- some problems require professional knowledge / methods 어떤 문제들은 전문적인 지식 / 방법을 요함 ex) health 건강 - families: still subjective → often hard to give rational advice 식구들: 여전히 주관적 → 종종 이성적인 조언을 주기 힘듦

2 Do you agree or disagree with the following statement? The most important things people learn are from their families. Use specific reasons and examples to support your answer.

다음 명제에 찬성하는가 반대하는가? 사람들은 식구들로부터 가장 중요한 것들을 배운다. 구체적인 이유와 예를 들어 자신의 입장을 뒷받침하시오.

AGREE	DISAGREE
- manners / politeness: families spend most time together → able to give constant advice 매너 / 예의: 가족이 가장 많은 시간을 함께 보냄 → 끊임없는 조언을 줄 수 있음 - personality: formed since born 인성: 태어날 때부터 형성됨	- social skills: from friends, classmates, colleagues 사회성: 친구, 학우, 동료로부터 배움 - knowledge: from teachers 지식: 교사로부터 배움

3 Do you agree or disagree with the following statement? Friends should talk with each other even when there is a small problem. Use specific reasons and examples to support your answer.

다음 명제에 찬성하는가 반대하는가? 친구는 작은 문제가 있을지라도 서로 이야기할 수 있어야 한다. 구체적인 이유와 예를 들어 자신의 입장을 뒷받침하시오.

AGREE	DISAGREE
- small problems could get bigger → might affect friendship 작은 문제가 크게 될 수 있음 → 우정에 영향을 끼칠 가능성 - help each other correct / change weaknesses 서로 단점을 고치거나 변화하게 도와줌	- should understand / cover a small problem if she / he is a close friend 친한 친구라면 작은 문제를 이해 / 덮어줘야 함 - bringing up a problem constantly can result in a conflict 끊임없는 문제 제기는 마찰을 초래함

TOEFL® MAP

ACTUAL TEST Writing 2

09

Food irradiation is the process by which certain types of food are subjected to low doses of radiation to render any microorganisms in the food harmless and to improve the food's shelf life. Among the foods that are commonly irradiated are root tubers such as potatoes, tropical fruits like mangoes and papayas, and meat products, including poultry and fish. There is a perception among many in the public that irradiating food products is unsafe and harmful, yet both notions are incorrect.

Firstly, the products are exposed to low amounts of radiation, which is completely harmless to humans. The radiation is, however, strong enough to damage the DNA of any microorganisms in or on the food. This prevents the microorganisms from causing the food to spoil and from harming those who eat it. In addition, virtually 100% of the bacteria on the food are destroyed in the irradiation process, and so are other pathogens such as viruses and fungi.

Another advantage of irradiation is that it slows the process by which food spoils. This allows foods such as tropical fruits to be shipped great distances from where they are grown to markets all over the world. Resultantly, farmers in Southeast Asian countries can sell fresh produce to consumers in the United States and Europe. Irradiation also gives food a greater shelf life once it reaches supermarkets. Thus food neither rots nor spoils if it is not sold promptly.

Finally, food suffers hardly any losses in its nutritional value when it is exposed to radiation. In fact, the change is negligible. So while microorganisms, bacteria, and other pathogens are eliminated, the food retains the same amounts of vitamins and minerals. The end result of irradiation is food products that are safer, longer lasting, and high in nutrition.

🎧 09-01

Directions You have 20 minutes to plan and write your response. Your response will be judged on the basis of the quality of your writing and on how well your response presents the points in the lecture and their relationship to the passage. Typically, an effective response will be 150-225 words.

Question Summarize the points made in the lecture, being sure to explain how they challenge specific claims made in the reading passage.

CUT PASTE UNDO REDO   Hide Word Count : 0

Food irradiation is the process by which certain types of food are subjected to low doses of radiation to render any microorganisms in the food harmless and to improve the food's shelf life. Among the foods that are commonly irradiated are root tubers such as potatoes, tropical fruits like mangoes and papayas, and meat products, including poultry and fish. There is a perception among many in the public that irradiating food products is unsafe and harmful, yet both notions are incorrect.

Firstly, the products are exposed to low amounts of radiation, which is completely harmless to humans. The radiation is, however, strong enough to damage the DNA of any microorganisms in or on the food. This prevents the microorganisms from causing the food to spoil and from harming those who eat it. In addition, virtually 100% of the bacteria on the food are destroyed in the irradiation process, and so are other pathogens such as viruses and fungi.

Another advantage of irradiation is that it slows the process by which food spoils. This allows foods such as tropical fruits to be shipped great distances from where they are grown to markets all over the world. Resultantly, farmers in Southeast Asian countries can sell fresh produce to consumers in the United States and Europe. Irradiation also gives food a greater shelf life once it reaches supermarkets. Thus food neither rots nor spoils if it is not sold promptly.

Finally, food suffers hardly any losses in its nutritional value when it is exposed to radiation. In fact, the change is negligible. So while microorganisms, bacteria, and other pathogens are eliminated, the food retains the same amounts of vitamins and minerals. The end result of irradiation is food products that are safer, longer lasting, and high in nutrition.

READING

food irradiation: helpful at storing food for a longer period of time
식품 방사선 처리: 음식을 장기 보관하는데 도움을 줌

❶ *effective at killing bacteria* 박테리아를 죽이는데 효율적

- harmless to humans 인간에게 무해함

- damages DNA of microorganisms → prevents food spoilage 미생물의 DNA 파괴 → 음식의 부패 방지

  Paraphrasing Example Food irradiation is an efficient means of sterilizing pathogens since it kills bacteria, the main culprit behind food spoilage.

❷ *slows the process of food spoilage* 음식의 부패 과정을 늦춤

- tropical fruits: shipped great distances 열대 과일: 장거리까지 운송됨

  Paraphrasing Example Irradiation makes the long-distance delivery of food possible because it delays the process of deterioration.

❸ *almost no loss in nutritional value* 영양소 파괴 거의 ×

- change: negligible 변화: 대수롭지 않음

- bacteria: eliminated / vitamins + minerals: remain the same 박테리아: 제거됨 / 비타민 + 무기질: 그대로 유지됨

  Paraphrasing Example Nutritional losses rarely occur in irradiated food since the vitamins and the minerals remain the same while the bacteria are successfully removed.

WORD REMINDER

irradiation 방사   dose 복용량   radiation 방사선   render ~을 ~하게 하다   microorganism 미생물   shelf life 저장 기간   root tuber 덩이뿌리   poultry 가금   perception 인지   notion 개념   expose 노출시키다   pathogen 병원균   fungus 진균류   spoil 상하다   resultantly 결과적으로   consumer 소비자   negligible 하찮은   eliminate 제거하다   retain 계속 유지하다   mineral 무기질

LISTENING

food irradiation: may cause harmful effects to the human body
식품 방사선 처리: 몸에 해로운 영향을 일으킬 수 있음

❶ *impossible to know if all the bacteria are killed* 모든 박테리아가 죽었는지는 알 수 없음

- 1% survived → super resistant to irradiation 살아남은 1% → 방사선에 극도의 저항력 생김

  → reproduce more pathogens w/similar resistance 비슷한 저항력을 가진 더 많은 병균을 번식시킴

  ∴ harm > good 해로움 > 이로움

  Paraphrasing Example Food irradiation may not get rid of all the bacteria present.

❷ *might cause the ripening process to halt* 익는 과정을 중단시킬 수 있음

  Ex irradiated bananas: stop ripening 방사선 처리된 바나나: 익는 것 중단

  → do not taste good / lack vitamins + minerals 맛이 좋지 않음 / 비타민과 무기질 결핍

  Paraphrasing Example Food irradiation may prevent food from ripening.

❸ *nutritional losses: possible* 영양소 파괴: 가능함

- store food for a longer period of time 식품 장기간 보관

  → reduces nutritional value 영양 가치를 감소시킴

  Ex fresh milk: better than milk on the shelf for longer 신선한 우유: 오래 보관된 우유보다 나음

  Paraphrasing Example It is possible that nutritional value may be lost during the process of irradiation.

WORD REMINDER

widespread 널리 보급된   admit 인정하다   supposed 생각되고 있던   resistant 저항하는   reproduce 번식하다   strain 변종   antibody 항체   definitely 확실히   halt 중지하다   ship 수송하다   reach 도착하다   lack 결핍   mention 언급하다   conduct 이행하다

The lecturer argues that food irradiation may have a harmful impact on the human body. This directly refutes the reading passage's claim that irradiation is an effective means to allow the storage of food for a longer period of time.

First, food irradiation may not get rid of all the bacteria present. The surviving pathogens will become resistant to radiation and will pass along a similar resistance to their offspring. This contradicts the reading passage's claim that food irradiation is an efficient way of sterilizing pathogens since it kills bacteria, the main culprit behind food spoilage.

On top of that, the lecturer contends that food irradiation may prevent food from ripening. According to the professor, the ripening process for bananas stops, resulting in a lack of vitamins and minerals as well as an unsatisfying taste. This rebuts the reading passage's claim that irradiation makes the long-distance delivery of food possible because it delays the process of deterioration.

Finally, it is possible that nutritional value may be lost during the process of irradiation. Though the expiration period for food may be extended, it is likely that the nutrients get destroyed. This challenges the idea presented in the reading passage that nutritional losses rarely occur in irradiated food since the vitamins and the minerals remain the same while the bacteria are successfully removed.

WORD REMINDER

get rid of ~을 제거하다   pass along 전해 주다   offspring 자손   efficient 효과가 있는   sterilize 멸균하다   culprit 원인   spoilage 부패
prevent from ~으로부터 막다   deterioration 악화   expiration 만료, 소멸   extend 늘이다

TIPS for SUCCESS

통합형 에세이: 서론과 결론

통합형에서 서론에 자신의 의견을 쓰는 학생들이 있다. 통합형은 지문과 듣기의 요점을 정리하는 문제이므로, 서론에서는 전체적인 main idea를 언급하여 강의가 지문에 어떠한 연관성을 가지고 있는지를 설명해 주면 된다. 따라서 글자수가 많지 않는 것은 이상한 현상이 아니다. 결론의 경우, 쓰는 것도 무관하지만, 결국 서론과 같은 내용이 들어가게 되므로 결론을 쓸 시간을 차라리 본론의 문단들을 더 자세히 쓰는데 사용하는 것이 효과적일 수 있다.

Hide Word Count : 0

Directions Read the question below. You have 30 minutes to plan, write, and revise your essay. Typically, an effective response will contain a minimum of 300 words.

Question

Do you agree or disagree with the following statement?

People will spend less time cooking twenty years from now.

Use specific reasons and examples to support your answer.

AGREE

- *family: hard to gather at dinner table* 가족들: 저녁 식사에 모이기 힘듦
  - demand for instant food ↑ 인스턴트 식품에 대한 수요 ↑
    Ex often get home late: mom prepares instant noodles 종종 늦게 귀가: 엄마가 라면을 준비해 주심
    → saves time for cooking + preparing + cleaning 조리 + 준비 + 정리 시간 절약

- *development of food tech → reduced time for cooking* 요리 기술의 발달 → 조리 시간 단축
  - tastes: very similar to slow-cooked food 맛: 천천히 조리된 음식과 매우 유사
    Ex coworker: buys frozen food + microwaves it 동료: 냉동 음식 구입 + 전자레인지에 돌림
    → time saving + same taste 시간 절약 + 같은 맛

INTRODUCTION

generalization: people have become busier
일반화: 사람들이 더욱 바빠졌음

cooking method + processes: convenient + time saving
조리 방법 + 과정: 편리 + 시간 절약

thesis: agree (demand for instant food, food tech)
논제: 동의 (인스턴트 식품의 수요, 요리 기술)

DISAGREE

- *nutrition: important issue in modern society* 영양: 현대 사회의 중요한 이슈
  - many people realize dangers of instant food (disease + obesity)
    많은 사람들이 인스턴트 식품의 위험을 깨달음 (질병 + 비만)
    Ex many studies: instant food → lack nutritional value / harmful 많은 연구: 인스턴트 식품 → 영양가 부족 / 해로움
    → slow-cooked food → softer + healthier 천천히 조리하는 음식 → 더 부드러움 + 건강에 더 좋음

- *slow-cooked food → brings out one's culture + childhood memory*
  천천히 조리하는 음식 → 개인의 문화 + 어릴 적 기억을 가져다 줌
  - society: more demanding → many people w/nostalgia 사회: 요구가 더 많음 → 많은 사람들이 향수를 가짐
    Ex family gathering: still prefers slow-braised short ribs 가족 모임: 여전히 갈비찜을 선호
    → smell during cooking: reminds of the past 조리될 때의 향: 과거를 상기시켜 줌

INTRODUCTION

generalization: people have become busier
일반화: 사람들이 더욱 바빠졌음

cooking method + processes: convenient + time saving
조리 방법 + 과정: 편리 + 시간 절약

thesis: disagree (concerning for health, culture)
논제: 반대 (건강에 대한 관심, 문화)

As people adapt to today's fast-paced society, they have become busier than ever before. Accordingly, cooking methods and processes have become more convenient and time saving thanks to the development of culinary arts and food technology. Though some people contend that instant food is losing its place to slow-cooked food, I strongly believe that cooking preparation time will be reduced twenty years from now because the demand for instant food is growing and because food technology is improving rapidly.

First of all, many families find it hard to gather at the dinner table. This occurs because each member is busy with his or her own work, which makes it difficult for a person to prepare a meal for each family member at a different time. Thus, the demand for instant food is growing rapidly. To illustrate, I often finish my work late and am unable to have dinner with my family, so my mother prepares instant noodles, which are convenient and fast in terms of cooking time. More people are satisfied with the convenience and speediness of instant food, which saves time on cooking, preparing, and cleaning. As a result, most people will spend less time cooking in the near future.

Moreover, the continuous development of food technology allows people to cook within a shorter period of time. Since instant foods taste very similar to slow-cooked foods, lots of people prefer the easier way of cooking. For instance, my coworker always buys frozen food for dinner after work and simply microwaves it at home. Not only does it save her time on cooking and cleaning, but it also tastes as if it were food served at a restaurant.

It is true that instant food mostly tastes the same even though some of it comes from other countries. However, people can enjoy different-tasting food at restaurants, so people can eat at them if they want. Most people will be accustomed to cooking instant food at home mainly because of its convenience. Furthermore, developing technology will make instant food suit consumers' tastes. For the above reasons, I firmly agree with the statement that people will spend less time cooking twenty years from now.

WORD REMINDER

adapt 적응하다   pace 속도   instant 즉석의   demand 수요   gather 모이다   in terms of ~에 관하여   be satisfied with ~에 만족하다
continuous 끊임없는   frozen 냉동의, 얼린   be accustomed to ~하는데 익숙해지다   suit ~에 적합하게 하다   taste 맛, 취향

TIPS for SUCCESS

부정 도치

도치의 용법 중 한 가지는 부정어에 관한 것이다. 부정부사인 not, barely, seldom, hardly, scarcely, rarely 등이나 부정접속사(TEST 01 참고)가 문장의 맨 앞에 올 경우 주어와 동사의 위치를 바꾸어 주면 된다. be동사나 조동사 등은 단순히 주어와 동사의 위치를 바꾸어 주면 되고, 일반동사의 경우 의문문의 형태로 바꾸어서 did, do, 또는 does를 주어의 앞으로 보낸 후 주어 뒤에 동사원형을 쓰면 된다. 세 번째 단락의 문장을 살펴보자.

Not only does it save her time on cooking and cleaning, but it also tastes as if it were food served at a restaurant.

it save her time on cooking and cleaning이라는 절에서 not only라는 부정접속사가 나왔기 때문에, 조동사 does가 주어인 it 앞에 나와야 한다.

ACTUAL TEST **09**

As people adapt to today's fast-paced society, they have become busier than ever before. Accordingly, cooking methods and processes have become more convenient and time saving thanks to the development of culinary arts and food technology. Some people contend that cooking preparation time will be reduced twenty years from now. However, I strongly believe that the time it takes to prepare food will either remain the same or increase because people are more concerned with their health and because slow-cooked food represents people's cultures.

First of all, nutrition has become of the most important issues in modern society. Instant food is popular in that it satisfies people's needs in terms of convenience and timing. However, since issues, including new diseases and obesity, have surfaced, many people have come to realize the dangers that instant food can pose. For instance, many studies have proved that lots of instant foods lack nutritional value. In fact, some of them even contain harmful chemicals. Conversely, when food is cooked slowly at a lower temperature, it is much softer and more nutritious. Hence, the awareness of health has led people to prefer slow-cooked food.

Moreover, slow cooking preserves people's cultures and childhood memories. As society is becoming more demanding, people feel nostalgic about their childhood. The preparation of food is as important as the taste since each culture has its own recipes and styles of cooking. To illustrate, many people still have slow-braised short ribs when they have family gatherings since the smell while the food cooks reminds them of their past.

It is true that instant food has prevailed in the decades since its advent. However, many people who used to prefer an apartment for its convenience have gone back to a traditional house with a garden nowadays. Likewise, slow-cooked food will find its place again in the future. People are aware that slow-cooked food is superior to instant food. Furthermore, it brings back childhood memories and reflects one's culture. For the above reasons, I disagree with the statement that people will spend less time cooking twenty years from now.

WORD REMINDER

be concerned with ~에 관심이 있다   represent 나타내다   obesity 비만   surface 표면화하다   realize 깨닫다   pose (위험성을) 내포하다
prove 증명하다   lack 결핍되다   chemical 화학 제품   awareness 자각   bring out 불러일으키다   demanding 요구가 많은   recipe 조리법
braise 천천히 익히다   short ribs 갈비   gathering 모임   remind 상기시키다   prevail 유행하다   advent 출현   superior 우수한

RELATED TOPICS

1 Printed books will disappear in the next twenty years. 인쇄된 책은 앞으로 20년 안에 없어질 것이다.

AGREE	DISAGREE
- electronic books → convenient 전자책 → 편리함 - saves space 공간 절약	- some still prefer traditional ways 일부 사람들은 여전히 전통 방식을 선호함 - old books: represent history 오래된 서적: 역사를 나타냄 ex) paper, lettering 종이, 글씨체

2 Renewable energy sources such as the sun, water, and wind will replace fossil fuels such as gas, oil, and coal. 태양, 물, 바람 같은 재생 가능한 에너지는 가스, 휘발유, 석탄 등의 화석 연료를 대체할 것이다.

AGREE	DISAGREE
- eco-friendly 환경친화적임 - many countries: under development → available in the near future 많은 국가: 개발 중 → 가까운 미래에 이용 가능	- demand exceeds capacity to produce the energy 수요가 에너지를 생산할 수 있는 용량을 초과 - too costly to develop → many countries can't afford to build power stations 개발하는데 너무 비쌈 → 많은 국가들은 발전소를 세울 여유가 없음

3 Colleges and universities should help students prepare for the future.
대학과 대학교는 학생들이 미래를 준비할 수 있도록 도와주어야 한다.

AGREE	DISAGREE
- last stage of education before getting a job 직업을 찾기 전 교육의 마지막 단계 - purpose: learning + working (internship opportunities) 목적: 배움 + 일 (인턴십 기회)	- students are responsible for their future 학생들은 자신의 미래에 대한 책임이 있음 - impossible to help every student 모든 학생들을 도와주는 것은 불가능 ∵each has different goal → diff. ways of preparation 각각의 학생은 다른 목표가 있음 → 다른 방식의 준비 과정

TOEFL MAP
ACTUAL TEST Writing 2

10

TOEFL® MAP **ACTUAL TEST**

VOLUME

HELP

NEXT

WRITING | Question 1 of 2

00:03:00 ⊖ HIDE TIME

ACTUAL TEST 10

Fast fashion is a term used to describe clothing that replicates designs from celebrity culture or runways and turns them into clothing at breakneck speed to meet consumers' needs. Fast fashion has made it easier than ever for shoppers to purchase trendy clothes at very affordable prices. Though it has brought incomparable profits to the clothing industry, it has also caused a number of problems that need close attention.

Since fast fashion typically uses low-quality material to minimize production costs, most clothes are made from non-biodegradable materials. For instance, polyester is made out of petroleum, and it can take up to 200 years to decompose. Moreover, growing cotton, one of the most common fabrics, requires a tremendous amount of water, not to mention the use of harmful pesticides.

Poor work ethics have put many employees in danger. Some companies take advantage of the law in developing countries, and most of the time, they do not follow laws regarding working hours or provide workers with any benefits. Even though people experience countless cases of physical as well as mental abuse, a lot of employees, especially children, are reluctant to report these problems since they can be terminated at any time.

Since the clothes are made of low-quality materials, it is apparent that those clothes will not last very long, resulting in more consumption and generating more textile waste. Consumers are encouraged to visit stores more often and end up making purchases as new products are introduced constantly at low prices. A recent study shows that even though people say they are willing to buy from sustainable brands, they rarely do that. It is not easy for many to give up on their desire to stay top of trends.

🎧 10-01

Directions You have 20 minutes to plan and write your response. Your response will be judged on the basis of the quality of your writing and on how well your response presents the points in the lecture and their relationship to the passage. Typically, an effective response will be 150-225 words.

Question Summarize the points made in the lecture, being sure to explain how they challenge specific claims made in the reading passage.

CUT   PASTE   UNDO   REDO   Hide Word Count : 0

Fast fashion is a term used to describe clothing that replicates designs from celebrity culture or runways and turns them into clothing at breakneck speed to meet consumers' needs. Fast fashion has made it easier than ever for shoppers to purchase trendy clothes at very affordable prices. Though it has brought incomparable profits to the clothing industry, it has also caused a number of problems that need close attention.

Since fast fashion typically uses low-quality material to minimize production costs, most clothes are made from non-biodegradable materials. For instance, polyester is made out of petroleum, and it can take up to 200 years to decompose. Moreover, growing cotton, one of the most common fabrics, requires a tremendous amount of water, not to mention the use of harmful pesticides.

Poor work ethics have put many employees in danger. Some companies take advantage of the law in developing countries, and most of the time, they do not follow laws regarding working hours or provide workers with any benefits. Even though people experience countless cases of physical as well as mental abuse, a lot of employees, especially children, are reluctant to report these problems since they can be terminated at any time.

Since the clothes are made of low-quality materials, it is apparent that those clothes will not last very long, resulting in more consumption and generating more textile waste. Consumers are encouraged to visit stores more often and end up making purchases as new products are introduced constantly at low prices. A recent study shows that even though people say they are willing to buy from sustainable brands, they rarely do that. It is not easy for many to give up on their desire to stay top of trends.

📝 NOTE-TAKING

fast fashion → trendy clothes at low prices (environmental concerns)
패스트 패션 → 낮은 가격의 유행하는 옷 (환경 문제)

❶ *use of low-quality materials → production costs ↓ → non-biodegradable*
질 낮은 원료 사용 → 생산 비용↓ → 비생분해성

Ex polyester: petroleum / cotton: uses a lot of water 폴리에스테르: 원유 / 면: 많은 물 사용

 Fast fashion uses non-biodegradable materials which are harmful to the environment.

❷ *poor work ethics → dangerous for workers* 열악한 기업 윤리 → 근로자들에게 위험

– developing countries: benefits for workers ✗ 개발 도상국: 근로자들에게 혜택 ✗

 The fast-fashion industry, where certain companies take advantage of places with no definite rules set for workers.

❸ *low quality → consumption ↑ + waste ↑* 낮은 질 → 소비 ↑ + 쓰레기 ↑

– study: people say they are willing to buy from sustainable brands → rarely do that ∵ want to stay on top of trends 연구: 사람들은 지속 가능한 브랜드에서 구입할 의사가 있다고 말함 → 실천 거의 안됨 ∵ 유행의 정상에 머물고 싶음

 Lots of shoppers are still reluctant to give up on following trends.

WORD REMINDER

replicate 복제하다   celebrity 유명인   breakneck 아주 빠른   needs 수요   trendy 유행의   affordable 저렴한   incomparable 비할 데 없는
profit 이윤   biodegradable 생물 분해성이 있는   petroleum 석유   decompose ~을 분해하다   fabric 직물, 천   pesticide 살충제   ethics 윤리
take advantage of 이용하다   developing country 개발 도상국   benefit 혜택   abuse 학대하다   reluctant 주저하는   terminate 해고하다
apparent 명백한   generate 생산하다   encourage 조장하다   sustainable 환경을 파괴하지 않고 지속될 수 있는

slow fashion → sustainable materials, fair trade, and minimizing waste
슬로우 패션 → 지속 가능한 원료, 공정 무역, 쓰레기의 최소화

❶ *change in materials → biodegradable / cotton: use of rainwater*
재료 변화 → 생물 분해성이 있는 재료 / 면: 빗물 사용

– higher-quality garments → expensive but last longer 높은 질의 옷 → 더 비싸지만 오래 감

 Sustainable materials such as organic cotton and silk are used in slow-fashion textiles.

❷ *bad work ethics → never seen in SFI* 열악한 근무 윤리 → 슬로우 패션 산업에서는 볼 수 없음

– provide good working conditions: forced labor ✗, child labor ✗, discrimination ✗, violence ✗
좋은 근무 조건: 강요된 노동 ✗, 어린이 노동 ✗, 차별 ✗, 폭력 ✗

 Companies in the slow-fashion industry act on their work ethics.

❸ *awareness of –ve environmental consequences* 부정적 환경 결과에 대한 경각심

– everyone has to try: purchase ↓, better quality, sustainable brands, choose clothing made in countries w/strict labor laws 모두가 노력해야 함: 구입 ↓, 더 나은 질, 지속 가능한 브랜드, 엄격한 노동법을 가진 나라에서 만든 옷을 고르는 것

Unless consumers change their attitudes about the environment, it will be challenging to make them buy fewer clothes, pay more for better quality, or look for textiles that are made in places with stricter environmental rules.

WORD REMINDER

inspire 영감을 주다   principle 원칙, 신념   polluter 오염원   linen 린넨   eco-friendly 친환경적인   garment 의류   harass 괴롭히다
supervisor 관리자   local 현지의   labor law 노동법   forced 강요된   discrimination 차별   awareness 의식, 인식   repair 고치다
stringent 엄격한   regulation 규제

The lecturer explains how the slow-fashion movement is practiced. This provides solutions to the concerns presented in the reading passage that fast fashion threatens the environment.

First of all, according to the professor, sustainable materials such as organic cotton and silk are used in slow-fashion textiles. Despite their high prices, the garments do not wear out easily, meaning that consumers can keep them for a long time. This supports the reading passage's idea that fast fashion uses non-biodegradable materials which are harmful to the environment.

On top of that, the lecturer contends that companies in the slow-fashion industry act on their work ethics. Many corporations in the slow-fashion movement follow principles such as no child labor, no discrimination, and no violence. This is the opposite of what is described in the reading passage about the fast-fashion industry, where certain companies take advantage of places with no definite rules set for workers.

Finally, the professor warns that unless consumers change their attitudes about the environment, it will be challenging to make them buy fewer clothes, pay more for better quality, or look for textiles that are made in places with stricter environmental rules. This clearly elaborates on the point made in the reading passage that lots of shoppers are still reluctant to give up on following trends.

WORD REMINDER
practice 실천하다   despite 불구하고   wear out 닳아 없어지다   act on ~에 따르다   definite 확실한   attitude 자세, 의식
elaborate 자세히 설명하다

Hide Word Count : 0

Directions Read the question below. You have 30 minutes to plan, write, and revise your essay. Typically, an effective response will contain a minimum of 300 words.

Question

Do you agree or disagree with the following statement?

People should buy products made in their home country even if the prices are high.

Use specific reasons and examples to support your answer.

AGREE

- *promote economic growth* 경제 성장 장려

  Ex people refusing to buy mainstream goods from their country 사람들이 자국의 주요 제품 구입을 거부

  → corporations + subcontractors will suffer 기업 + 하청업자들이 고통을 받을 것임

  → whole country: economic difficulties 국가 전체: 경제적 어려움

- *development of the products* 제품의 개발

  - companies: motivated to develop + improve qualities 기업: 제품의 질을 향상시키고 개발하도록 동기가 부여됨

    Ex Japanese: known for buying products of Japan 일본인: 일본의 제품을 사는 것으로 알려져 있음

    → synergistic effect: higher profits + standard of products ↑ 시너지 효과: 높은 이득 + 제품의 기준 ↑

INTRODUCTION

generalization: globalization → competition: inevitable
일반화: 세계화 → 경쟁: 불가피

⬇

importing + exporting products: a common practice
제품의 수입 + 수출: 흔히 있는 일

⬇

thesis: agree (development of products, synergistic effect)
논제: 찬성 (제품의 개발, 시너지 효과)

DISAGREE

- *competition promotes advancement* 경쟁: 진보를 장려함

  - companies try to improve qualities 기업들은 질적 향상을 위해 노력

    Ex electronics companies in Korea: compete w/others / invested a lot in superb researchers
    전자 회사: 다른 기업들과 경쟁 / 훌륭한 연구원들을 위해 많이 투자함

    → some of the leading companies in the world 세계를 이끌어 나가는 기업 중 하나

- *freedom of choice* 선택의 자유

  - consumers: right to choose products 소비자: 제품을 선택할 권리

    Ex whenever buying a product: consider the price first 제품을 살 때: 가격을 제일 고려

    → would be displeased if forced to buy a product of the same quality but with a higher price
    만약 같은 제품을 좀 더 비싸게 사도록 강요당한다면 불쾌할 것임

INTRODUCTION

generalization: globalization → competition: inevitable
일반화: 세계화 → 경쟁: 불가피

⬇

importing + exporting products: a common practice
제품의 수입 + 수출: 흔히 있는 일

⬇

thesis: disagree (advancement, freedom of choice)
논제: 반대 (진보, 선택의 자유)

As the world has become globalized, competition between countries is inevitable, and importing and exporting products from one country to another is a common practice. Thus, companies are striving for attention not only from consumers in their own countries but also from those overseas through marketing, promotions, and services. Some contend that shoppers should take advantage of their freedom to choose what they wish to buy. However, for two reasons, I strongly believe purchasers should buy products from their own country even if the prices are high. For one thing, it will cause a synergistic effect by keeping money in the country's economy. Moreover, it will promote the research and development of new products.

First of all, purchasing products from one's own country would promote the economic growth of the country. To illustrate, if people in a nation refuse to buy mainstream goods from their country and favor imported commodities instead, both the corporations manufacturing completed goods and the subcontractors manufacturing specialized parts and components will suffer. The consequence will be that there is a chance that an entire industry will suffer hardship from economic difficulties.

On top of that, companies are motivated to develop and improve their products when customers purchase them. They have a responsibility to meet shoppers' expectations. For instance, the Japanese are well known for buying commodities from their own country even if the prices are higher than those of goods manufactured overseas. This phenomenon has encouraged Japanese companies to produce better products as a way of attracting business. This practice will result in higher profits and inspire companies to improve the quality of their goods, resulting in a synergistic effect.

It is true that one of the notions of a democratic market is that consumers should have the freedom to decide what they want to pay for. However, if most people prefer imported products that are of better quality and have lower prices, it may result in a nation relying only on imported goods. For the reasons of economic growth and improved product development, I agree with the statement that people should buy products from their own country despite higher prices.

WORD REMINDER

inevitable 피할 수 없는   common practice 흔한 일   strive 노력하다   promotion 판촉   take advantage of ~을 이용하다
synergistic 상승적인   refuse 거절하다   mainstream 주류의   favor 호의를 보이다   commodity 상품   subcontractor 하청업자
component 구성 요소   phenomenon 현상   notion 개념   democratic 민주주의의   rely on ~에 의존하다

TIPS for SUCCESS

형용사절 Adjective Clause

형용사절은 통합형 에세이의 TIPS for SUCCESS에서 나열된 관계대명사들 중 알맞은 것을 골라 명사의 뒤에 쓰면 된다. 두 번째 단락의 문장의 일부를 살펴보자.

Both the corporations that manufacture completed goods and the subcontractors **that** manufacture specialized parts and components will suffer.

위의 문장에서 corporations와 subcontractors 모두 사람이 아니므로 which 또는 that을 쓴다. which 전에는 쉼표를 쓰는 것이 일반적이지만 that 앞에는 절대 쉼표가 올 수 없음을 기억하자. that은 전치사 뒤에도 올 수 없다. 위에서 각각의 that은 앞의 corporations와 subcontractors를 수식해 주며 주격으로 쓰였기 때문에 동사만 동반하면 된다.

As the world has become globalized, competition between countries is inevitable, and importing and exporting products from one country to another is a common practice. Thus, companies are striving for attention not only from consumers in their own countries but also from those overseas through marketing, promotions, and services. Some contend that shoppers should buy products from their own country even if the prices are high. However, for two reasons, I strongly believe consumers should take advantage of their freedom to choose what they wish to pay for. For one thing, competition promotes advancement. Moreover, having freedom is a basic notion in a free market.

First of all, competition results in development. It is most likely that customers prefer a better-quality product for the same price. Hence, companies can expend a great amount of effort in order to deliver satisfaction to consumers. For instance, decades ago, people outside Korea hardly knew about electronics companies from Korea. As there were many electronics companies in Korea and competition was getting stronger, each company invested a lot of capital to cultivate excellent researchers and to gain strategic advantages. As a result, the industry is now recognized as one of the leaders in the world.

On top of that, customers should have the right to choose products according to their will because each individual has different tastes and preferences based on their needs. For example, whenever I need to pay for a commodity, I consider the price first. Because I am a student, I go for the product with the lowest price, not the one with better quality and a higher price. Thus, I would be displeased if I had to purchase a product of the same quality but at a higher price.

It is true that buying products from one's own country can motivate companies to upgrade the quality of their products. However, the conviction that consumers would prefer locally made products to imported goods regardless of circumstances might dissuade some corporations from putting forth the effort to improve more. For the reasons of good-faith competition and freedom of choice, I disagree with the statement that people should buy products from their own country at high prices.

WORD REMINDER

advancement 발달   free market 자유 시장   provoke 불러 일으키다   deliver 전하다   capital 자본   cultivate 양성하다   strategic 전략의
right 권리   preference 더 좋아함   go for ~을 좋아하다   displeased 화난   conviction 확신   locally 지방적으로
regardless of ~에 개의치 않고   circumstance 상황   dissuade 단념시키다   good-faith 선의

RELATED TOPICS

1 Improving schools is the most important factor in the successful development of a country.
학교를 개선하는 것은 나라의 성공적인 발전에 있어서 가장 중요한 요소이다.

AGREE	DISAGREE
- cultivating superb workforce: big asset for the future 우수한 인력 양성: 미래에 대한 큰 자산 - education: crime ↓ 교육: 범죄 ↓	- many other factors 다른 많은 요소 ex) environment, investment in corporations, exploration of outer space 환경, 기업에 대한 투자, 우주 개발 - unfair for those who cannot afford to get a higher education 고등 교육을 받을 여유가 없는 사람들에게 불공평함

2 Countries should invest more money in exploring outer space rather than preserving the natural environment. 국가들은 환경 보호보다 우주 개발에 더 많은 돈을 투자해야 한다.

AGREE	DISAGREE
- possibility of resources which are being depleted on the Earth 지구에서 고갈되고 있는 자원의 가능성 - possible habitat for the future 미래에 가능한 주거지	- other urgent matters to be solved 시급히 해결되어야 하는 다른 문제들 ex) pollution 오염 - outer space has resources: not guaranteed 우주의 자원: 확실치 않음

3 It is important for countries to cooperate and to donate money when there is a disaster in another country that can affect the world.
다른 나라에서 일어난, 세계에 영향을 끼칠 수 있는 재앙에 대해 국가들이 협력하고 돈을 기부하는 것은 중요하다.

AGREE	DISAGREE

- everyone might suffer 모두가 고통을 받을 수 있음
  ex) radiation from the nuclear power plant in Japan 일본의 원자력 발전소에서 나오는 방사능
 	
- for future reference + prediction 미래에 대한 참조 + 예상
  ex) research on plate tectonics: help predict earthquakes 판구조론의 연구: 지진을 예측하는데 도움이 됨
	- each country has own capital + ways to deal with problems 각 국가들은 자본 및 자신들만의 문제 해결 방안을 가지고 있음
	
	- many basic problems that need to be solved in each country 각 나라에는 해결되어야 할 기본적인 문제들이 있음
	  ex) helping the poor 가난한 사람들 돕기

TOEFL® MAP

ACTUAL TEST Writing 2

11

One of the three greatest Pre-Columbian American empires—along with the Incas and the Aztecs—was the Mayan Empire. It was located in Central America in land mostly covered by Mexico, Guatemala, and Belize. The Maya were at their strongest from the years 300 to 800. They had well-developed cities, knew about agriculture, had their own calendar, understood advanced mathematics, and developed a unique writing system. Then, from around 800 to 900, they disappeared.

The collapse of the Maya is one of history's greatest mysteries. There are many theories concerning their downfall. A leading one is that the Maya were overcome in war. The Toltec people of Mexico were contemporaries of the Maya. They were a warlike people. Many archaeologists believe that a Toltec invasion—or a series of invasions lasting nearly a century—severely weakened the Maya and caused them to disappear.

Another prominent theory is that the Maya, because of their successful culture, experienced a sudden increase in their population. However, they could not grow enough crops to support everyone. The Maya often used slash-and-burn techniques to clear forests from land they intended to farm. But this method was bad for the soil, so the land frequently became useless after two or three growing seasons. It is possible that the Maya simply could not feed themselves, so a widespread famine resulted.

While much of the land the Maya once lived on is rainforest today, this was not the case centuries ago. It was much drier then. Some speculate that the Maya experienced a long-lasting drought that prevented them from being able to farm the land. Geological studies of the land indicate that there is some truth to this theory. Without water, the Mayan Empire either would have died or would have moved elsewhere in an effort to survive.

🎧 11-01

Directions You have 20 minutes to plan and write your response. Your response will be judged on the basis of the quality of your writing and on how well your response presents the points in the lecture and their relationship to the passage. Typically, an effective response will be 150-225 words.

Question Summarize the points made in the lecture, being sure to explain how they challenge specific arguments made in the reading passage.

One of the three greatest Pre-Columbian American empires—along with the Incas and the Aztecs—was the Mayan Empire. It was located in Central America in land mostly covered by Mexico, Guatemala, and Belize. The Maya were at their strongest from the years 300 to 800. They had well-developed cities, knew about agriculture, had their own calendar, understood advanced mathematics, and developed a unique writing system. Then, from around 800 to 900, they disappeared.

The collapse of the Maya is one of history's greatest mysteries. There are many theories concerning their downfall. A leading one is that the Maya were overcome in war. The Toltec people of Mexico were contemporaries of the Maya. They were a warlike people. Many archaeologists believe that a Toltec invasion—or a series of invasions lasting nearly a century—severely weakened the Maya and caused them to disappear.

Another prominent theory is that the Maya, because of their successful culture, experienced a sudden increase in their population. However, they could not grow enough crops to support everyone. The Maya often used slash-and-burn techniques to clear forests from land they intended to farm. But this method was bad for the soil, so the land frequently became useless after two or three growing seasons. It is possible that the Maya simply could not feed themselves, so a widespread famine resulted.

While much of the land the Maya once lived on is rainforest today, this was not the case centuries ago. It was much drier then. Some speculate that the Maya experienced a long-lasting drought that prevented them from being able to farm the land. Geological studies of the land indicate that there is some truth to this theory. Without water, the Mayan Empire either would have died or would have moved elsewhere in an effort to survive.

READING

three reasons for the demise of the Mayan Empire 마야 문명의 몰락에 관한 세 가지 이유

❶ *defeat in war* 전쟁에서 패배

- Toltec invasion 톨텍의 침략

Paraphrasing Example | A defeat in the war against the Toltec caused the collapse.

❷ *sudden increase in population* 인구의 급증

- not enough crops to support everyone 모두를 부양하기에 부족했던 농작물
- slash-and-burn techniques → land: useless after 2~3 growing seasons → famine
  화전법 → 땅: 2~3번의 생장기 이후 무용 → 기근

Paraphrasing Example | A lack of food due to a sudden population increase resulted in a severe famine.

❸ *long-lasting drought* 장기 가뭄

→ unable to farm the land 땅을 경작하기가 불가능함

Paraphrasing Example | The continuous aridity made it impossible to farm the land.

> **WORD REMINDER**
>
> empire 제국 collapse 붕괴 mystery 수수께끼 concerning ~에 관하여 downfall 몰락 leading 주된 overcome 이기다 contemporary 동시대의 warlike 호전적인 invasion 침략 severe 호된 prominent 중요한, 유명한 slash-and-burn (일시적인 경작을 위해) 나무를 벌채하여 태우는 intend 의도하다 widespread 널리 보급된 rainforest 다우림 speculate 추측하다 drought 가뭄 indicate 나타내다

LISTENING

the causes of the destruction of the Mayan civilization: uncertain
마야 문명의 파괴에 대한 원인: 확실치 않음

❶ *two problems regarding invasion* 침략에 대한 두 가지 문제점

- warfare: two centuries prior to the collapse 전쟁: 멸망하기 2세기 전
- the Toltec: no military adventurism until after 900 톨텍인들: 900년 이후에 이르기 전까지는 군사적 모험 x

Paraphrasing Example | An invasion that caused the collapse is unlikely for two reasons.

❷ *very knowledgeable in farming* 농업에 관해 매우 유식했음

→ would've overcome difficulties 어려움으로부터 극복했을 것임

∴ entire population wouldn't have died 인구 전체가 사망하지는 않았을 것임

Paraphrasing Example | Since the Mayan people were very knowledgeable about agricultural practices, they should have been able to come up with adequate solutions.

❸ *drought: occurred in the N* 가뭄: 북쪽에서 일어났음

- collapse: started in the S 붕괴: 남쪽에서 시작했음

Paraphrasing Example | While the fatal drought took place in the northern part of the empire, the destruction of the civilization started in the southern part.

> **WORD REMINDER**
>
> cease 그만두다 descendant 자손 essentially 본질적으로 flaw 결점 common 공통의 foreign 외국의 invader 침략자 conquer 정복하다 warfare 전쟁 engage in ~에 참여하다 adventurism 모험주의 when it comes to ~에 대해 말하자면 devise 고안하다 inconceivable 터무니없는 tree ring 나이테 extended 장기간에 걸친 territory 영토

The lecturer argues that nobody is certain about the causes of the destruction of the Mayan Civilization. This directly refutes the reading passage's claim that the Mayan Empire collapsed for three main reasons.

First, the theory stating that an invasion caused the collapse is unlikely for two reasons. First of all, the period when the Maya were involved in wars occurred two centuries before their demise. Second, the Toltec did not take part in wars before 900. This contradicts the reading passage's claim that a defeat in a war against the Toltec caused the collapse.

Next, the lecturer contends that since the Mayan people were very knowledgeable about agricultural practices, they should have been able to come up with adequate solutions. The lecturer suggests that it is highly unlikely that the entire population disappeared due to an insufficient supply of crops. This rebuts the reading passage's claim that a lack of food due to a sudden population increase resulted in a severe famine.

Finally, regarding the drought theory, the two locations do not coincide with each other. While the fatal drought took place in the northern part of the empire, the destruction of the civilization started in the southern part. This goes against the idea in the reading passage that the continuous aridity made it impossible to farm the land, causing famine among the people.

WORD REMINDER

destruction 파괴   demise 소멸   defeat 패배   practice 실행   come up with 고안하다   adequate 적당한   insufficient 불충분한
regarding ~에 관해서   fatal 치명적인   take place (일이) 발생하다   aridity 건조

Directions Read the question below. You have 30 minutes to plan, write, and revise your essay. Typically, an effective response will contain a minimum of 300 words.

Question

Which do you prefer, resolving a problem through email and text messages or resolving it through phone calls and voice mail?

Use specific reasons and examples to support your answer.

📝 NOTE-TAKING

- ***organize thoughts in logical ways*** 논리적인 방식으로 생각을 정리
  - many tend to ramble when upset 많은 이들은 언짢으면 두서없이 말하는 경향이 있음
    - **Ex** tour guide: unenthusiastic 여행 가이드: 열성 ✗
      - → email to a manager → got an apology + compensation 책임자에게 이메일 → 사과와 보상을 받았음

- ***control temper*** 감정을 조절
  - direct verbal expression → may hurt others' feelings / create misunderstandings
    직접적인 구두 표현 → 다른 이의 기분을 상하게 할 수 있음 / 오해를 일으킬 수 있음
    - **Ex** friend: upset with classmate 친구: 급우에게 기분이 상했음
      - → revised text messages before sending 전송 전에 문자 메시지를 수정

INTRODUCTION

generalization: many interacting w/one another → problems: inevitable
일반화: 많은 사람들이 서로 교류 → 문제: 불가피

⬇

many ways to express unpleasant feelings
불쾌한 기분을 표현하는 많은 방법

⬇

thesis: prefer email and text messages (time to organize thoughts, impolite / coarse language ✗)
논제: 이메일과 문자 메시지 선호 (생각을 정리할 시간, 무례하거나 거친 언어 ✗)

- ***direct manner: more effective*** 직접적인 방식: 더욱 효과적임
  - many phonetic expressions 많은 음성 표현
    - **Ex** furious at a clerk: stressed words I wanted to emphasize 점원에게 화남: 강조하고 싶었던 단어에 강세를 줌
      - → message + mood: delivered sufficiently 취지 + 감정: 충분히 전달되었음

- ***a lack of intonation + tone → further misunderstanding*** 억양 + 음조 ✗ → 더 큰 오해 가능
  - → circumstances may get worse 상황이 더 악화될 수 있음
    - **Ex** friend: lab partner didn't show up for meeting 친구: 실험 동료가 회의에 나타나지 않았음
      - → sent message saying he had fun while waiting 기다리는 동안 재미있었다는 메시지를 보냈음
      - → lab partner: didn't feel guilty afterward 실험 동료: 후에 죄책감을 느끼지 않았음

INTRODUCTION

generalization: many interacting w/one another → problems: inevitable
일반화: 많은 사람들이 서로 교류 → 문제: 불가피

⬇

many ways to express unpleasant feelings
불쾌한 기분을 표현하는 많은 방법

⬇

thesis: prefer phone calls and voice mail (direct way, further misunderstanding ✗)
논제: 전화 통화와 음성 메시지 선호 (직접적인 방법, 더 큰 오해 ✗)

As there are many people interacting with one another in modern society, it is inevitable that problems between people occur. There are many ways to express unpleasant feelings: People can show their emotions by writing a letter, by speaking to someone in person, or by talking on the phone. I strongly believe writing an email or text message is the most effective way to keep people's thoughts more organized and to maintain politeness.

First of all, when writing an email or text message, people can organize their thoughts in more logical ways. In many cases, people tend to ramble when they are upset. For instance, I went on a trip to Brazil and was very disappointed by the tour guide's unenthusiastic attitude. Thus, I wrote an email to the manager of the travel agency explaining in a sequential manner what had happened and got an apology and compensation.

Additionally, writing an email or text message lets people control their tempers more effectively because a direct verbal expression of one's anger may hurt someone's feelings or create further misunderstanding. For example, my friend was once upset with a classmate and decided to send a text message. At the moment he was writing the message, his rage directly showed in the sentences. However, before he sent the message, he revised the words that might hurt his classmate's feelings.

It is true that phone calls and voice mail are more efficient at delivering people's emotions. However, direct verbalization could worsen a situation. By writing an email or text message, people can be more logical in presenting their upset feelings. Furthermore, people can control their tempers and have time to revise the content before sending it. Therefore, I think resolving a problem through email or text messages is the best way to deal with an issue.

WORD REMINDER

interact 상호 작용하다   inevitable 피할 수 없는   unpleasant 불쾌한   in person 본인이 직접   effective 효율적인   logical 논리적인
ramble 두서없이 말하다   upset 언짢은   unenthusiastic 열성이 없는   attitude 태도   travel agency 여행사   sequential 순차적인
apology 사과   compensation 보상   temper 화, 기분   misunderstanding 오해   rage 분노   verbalization 언어화   present 나타내다
revise 수정하다   content 내용   resolve 해결하다

TIPS for SUCCESS

과거 완료 Past Perfect

과거 완료는 과거의 특정 시점부터 또 다른 시점까지의 일을 설명할 때도 쓰이지만, 과거의 어떠한 일이 일어나기에 앞서 발생했던 일을 설명할 때에도 쓰인다. 두 번째 단락의 문장을 살펴보자.

Thus, I wrote an email to the manager of the travel agency explaining in a sequential manner what **had happened**.
위의 문장에서, 여행 중의 상황이었던 what had happened는 여행 후에 일어난 I wrote an email을 시간상 앞서기 때문에 과거 완료가 쓰였다.

As there are many people interacting with one another in modern society, it is inevitable that problems between people occur. There are many ways to express unpleasant feelings: People can show their emotions by writing a letter, by speaking to someone in person, or by talking on the phone. I strongly believe making a phone call or leaving voice mail is the most effective method to express emotions directly and to avoid misunderstandings.

First of all, talking to a person on the phone or leaving a voicemail message is an effective means to express anger in a rather direct manner. For instance, when I was furious at a clerk in a shop, I stressed every important word that I wanted to emphasize. Consequently, I found that the message and the emotion I wanted to express were delivered sufficiently.

Additionally, a lack of intonation and tone of voice may cause further misunderstandings between people and exacerbate certain situations. To illustrate, my friend's lab partner did not show up for a meeting. Instead, she sent him a message more than an hour after they were supposed to meet only to say she could not make it. My friend sent a message back with a sarcastic twist. He stated that he had a lot of fun while waiting. Though he wrote it in a sarcastic manner, his lab partner interpreted the message literally and did not feel guilty.

It is true that writing email or text messages allows people to organize their thoughts better. However, it is important that people truly express their feelings rather than hide their emotions. Phone calls and voice mail allow people to express their thoughts more directly. Furthermore, they keep people from causing further misunderstandings. Therefore, I think resolving a problem through phone calls or voice mail is the best way to deal with an issue.

WORD REMINDER

avoid 예방하다   means 수단   furious 격노한   clerk 점원   emphasize 강조하다   sufficiently 충분히   lack 결핍   intonation 억양
show up 나타나다   sarcastic twist 비꼬는 말   literally 글자 뜻대로

TIPS for SUCCESS

당위성 형용사 (가정법)

말하는 사람의 요구나 권고 등의 의견을 나타낼 때 쓰이며, 어떠한 일의 당위성 혹은 중요성을 나타내는 형용사가 that절을 동반할 경우 쓰인다. 〈당위성 형용사 + that절 + (should) + 동사원형〉으로 이루어져 있으며, should는 일반적으로 생략하는 경우가 많다. 네 번째 단락의 문장을 살펴보자.

However, it is **important** that one truly **express** one's feelings rather than hiding one's emotions.

위의 문장 중 it is important that tone truly express one's feelings ~에서는 express라는 동사원형 전에 should가 생략되었다. 즉, 단수나 고유명사가 쓰이더라도 should가 생략되었기 때문에 동사원형이 온다는 것을 잊지 말자. 당위성 형용사에는 natural(당연한), imperative, necessary(필요한), vital, essential, important, crucial(중요한), advisable, fit, proper(타당한), obligatory, compulsory (의무적인), right(옳은), desirable(바람직한), urgent(절박한) 등이 있다.

cf. 당위성 동사: TEST 17 참고

RELATED TOPICS

1 Most people can solve important problems on their own. 대부분의 사람들은 중요한 문제를 스스로 해결할 수 있다.

AGREE	DISAGREE
- most problems: centered around the individual (small scale) 대부분의 문제: 개인을 중심으로 일어남 (작은 규모) - government: processing → takes too long (a lot of documents required) 정부: 처리 과정 → 너무 오래 걸림 (많은 서류 필요)	- some problems require a lot of funding 일부 문제는 많은 자금이 필요함 - problems regarding crime 범죄에 관한 문제들

2 When you need to complain about a product or poor service, which do you prefer, complaining in person or complaining in writing?
제품이나 좋지 않은 서비스에 대해 불만을 제기할 때, 직접 불만을 제기하는 것과 글로써 불만을 제기하는 방법 중 어떤 방식을 선호하는가?

IN PERSON	IN WRITING
- immediate response 즉시 반응이 옴 - able to express one's emotion in a direct way 자신의 감정을 직접적으로 표현할 수 있음 ex) facial expression 얼굴 표정	- more organized 더욱 체계적임 - able to save the mail for reference 참조용으로 메일을 보관해 놓을 수 있음

3 Friends should talk with each other even when there is a small problem.
사소한 문제가 있을 때라도 친구 사이라면 서로 이야기를 나누어야 한다.

AGREE	DISAGREE
- avoid misunderstandings 오해를 예방 - for improvement 발전을 위함	- may hurt feelings 기분을 상하게 할 수 있음 - friends should be able to understand each other 친구는 서로를 이해할 수 있어야 함

TOEFL® MAP
ACTUAL TEST Writing **2**

12

TOEFL® MAP **ACTUAL TEST**

VOLUME

HELP

NEXT

WRITING | Question 1 of 2

00:03:00 ⊖ HIDE TIME

ACTUAL TEST **12**

The bonobo is an endangered species of primates native to the area south of the Congo River in Africa. What many primatologists have learned about bonobos is that they are quite meek in temperament. This is a stark contrast to other primates, such as chimpanzees, which can be rather aggressive and violent in nature.

There is plenty of support for bonobos' gentle demeanors. Experts have studied numerous bonobos in captivity and have witnessed little evidence suggesting that they possess violent tendencies. Bonobos in captivity are typically gentle, kind, and sensitive, and zookeepers report that they experience few problems while handling them. In that regard, bonobos are different from other primates, which sometimes attack their handlers or cause other problems.

Bonobos also tend to prevent their young from engaging in violent behavior. For instance, the young of many animal species frequently fight one another or engage in excessive roughhousing. This teaches them how to hunt as well as other survival techniques. However, older bonobos actively quell this behavior in younger bonobos by intervening in fights between their young. As a result, young bonobos neither learn how to fight nor develop aggressive tendencies during their formative years.

Bonobos are often contrasted with their more violent cousins, the chimpanzees. Chimpanzees have been observed hunting small animals and even use rocks and sticks as weapons to attack other troops of primates. No such behavior has ever been witnessed among bonobos. Some researchers believe that the fact that bonobos are herbivores reduces any violent impulses they may possess. Since bonobos only eat vegetation, they have no need to hunt or kill anything except in self-defense. Thus they have evolved into more peaceful animals, especially when compared with chimpanzees.

🎧 12-01

127

Directions You have 20 minutes to plan and write your response. Your response will be judged on the basis of the quality of your writing and on how well your response presents the points in the lecture and their relationship to the passage. Typically, an effective response will be 150-225 words.

Question Summarize the points made in the lecture, being sure to explain how they cast doubt on specific points made in the reading passage.

CUT | PASTE | UNDO | REDO Hide Word Count : 0

The bonobo is an endangered species of primates native to the area south of the Congo River in Africa. What many primatologists have learned about bonobos is that they are quite meek in temperament. This is a stark contrast to other primates, such as chimpanzees, which can be rather aggressive and violent in nature.

There is plenty of support for bonobos' gentle demeanors. Experts have studied numerous bonobos in captivity and have witnessed little evidence suggesting that they possess violent tendencies. Bonobos in captivity are typically gentle, kind, and sensitive, and zookeepers report that they experience few problems while handling them. In that regard, bonobos are different from other primates, which sometimes attack their handlers or cause other problems.

Bonobos also tend to prevent their young from engaging in violent behavior. For instance, the young of many animal species frequently fight one another or engage in excessive roughhousing. This teaches them how to hunt as well as other survival techniques. However, older bonobos actively quell this behavior in younger bonobos by intervening in fights between their young. As a result, young bonobos neither learn how to fight nor develop aggressive tendencies during their formative years.

Bonobos are often contrasted with their more violent cousins, the chimpanzees. Chimpanzees have been observed hunting small animals and even use rocks and sticks as weapons to attack other troops of primates. No such behavior has ever been witnessed among bonobos. Some researchers believe that the fact that bonobos are herbivores reduces any violent impulses they may possess. Since bonobos only eat vegetation, they have no need to hunt or kill anything except in self-defense. Thus they have evolved into more peaceful animals, especially when compared with chimpanzees.

 READING

bonobos are meek in temperament 보노보들은 온순한 성격을 가지고 있음

❶ *studies on bonobos* 보노보에 대한 연구
- bonobos in captivity: gentle 포획된 보노보: 온순함
  → zookeepers: experience few problems 사육사: 문제를 거의 겪지 않음

> **Paraphrasing Example** Studies on bonobos in captivity support the argument that bonobos have a gentle nature.

❷ *prevent the young from violence* 새끼들이 폭력을 사용하지 못하게 함
- older bonobos: intervene in fights btwn their young 나이 든 보노보: 새끼들의 싸움에 개입

> **Paraphrasing Example** Bonobos maintain a peaceful society by keeping their young from violent behavior.

❸ *differ from chimps* 침팬지와 다름
- chimps: hunt small animals / attack other primates 침팬지: 작은 동물 사냥 / 다른 영장류 공격
- reason: herbivores → violent impulses ↓ 이유: 초식 동물 → 난폭한 충동 ↓

> **Paraphrasing Example** Chimps hunt animals and attack other primates whereas bonobos' herbivorous habits reduce the likelihood of their having vicious temperaments.

WORD REMINDER

primatologist 영장류 동물학자   meek 온순한   temperament 성질, 기질   stark 뚜렷한   demeanor 태도   in this regard 이 점에 있어서는
roughhouse 큰 소동, 큰 싸움   quell 진압하다   intervene 중재하다   formative 발달의, 형성의   impulse 충동

 LISTENING

the theory on bonobos' gentle nature poses problems
보노보의 온순한 성격에 관한 이론은 문제점을 가지고 있음

❶ *few long-term studies done* 장기적 연구 거의 없음
- most research: on captive bonobos (100) 대부분의 연구: 포획된 보노보에 이루어짐 (100 마리)
- animals behave differently in captivity 포획된 상태의 동물들은 다르게 행동함
  → not sure of the nature until research is done in natural habitat
  자연 서식지에서 연구가 이루어지기 전까지는 본성에 대해서 확신할 수 없음

> **Paraphrasing Example** Few long-term studies have been conducted on bonobos in the wild, and most research is focused on captive bonobos.

❷ *not always peaceful* 항상 평화로운 것은 아님
- engage in group aggression 집단 공격에 가담함
- young bonobos form groups → attack an older one 새끼 보노보들이 집단을 형성함 → 나이 든 보노보를 공격

> **Paraphrasing Example** Bonobos are not as friendly as they seem to be.

❸ *chimps: product of environment* 침팬지: 환경의 산물
- natural habitat: invaded by humans 자연 서식지: 인간에 의해 침략됨
  → omnivores → violent tendencies ↑ 잡식성 → 난폭한 성향 ↑
- bonobos' natural habitat: not yet destroyed much 보노보의 자연 서식지: 아직 많이 파괴되지 않았음
  → will become more violent if land is invaded 서식지가 파괴되면 더 폭력적으로 변할 것

> **Paraphrasing Example** The nature of chimps is most likely affected by their circumstances.

WORD REMINDER

conduct 수행하다   rave 격찬하다   vicious 포악한   aggression 공격   stalk 몰래 접근하다   subsequently 그 후에   omnivore 잡식성 동물
encroach 침해하다   herbivorous 초식성의

The lecturer argues that the theory on the gentle nature of bonobos poses some problems. This assertion directly contradicts the reading passage's claim that the theory that bonobos are meek animals is supported with three pieces of evidence.

First, the professor says that few long-term studies have been conducted on bonobos in the wild, and most research is focused on captive bonobos. Since animals in captivity react differently, it is uncertain how bonobos behave in their natural habitat. This fact refutes the reading passage's claim that studies on bonobos in captivity support the argument that bonobos have a gentle nature.

On top of that, the lecturer says that bonobos are not as friendly as they seem to be. In fact, young bonobos sometimes form a group and assault an older bonobo that is alone. This argument casts doubt on the reading passage's claim that bonobos maintain a peaceful society by keeping their young from violent behavior.

Finally, the nature of chimps, which is frequently compared to that of bonobos, is most likely affected by their circumstances. In theory, therefore, if bonobos' habitats are destroyed by humans, they too will develop violent behavior like chimps. This firmly rebuts the reading passage's claim that chimps hunt animals and attack other primates whereas bonobos' herbivorous habits reduce the likelihood of their having vicious temperaments.

WORD REMINDER

pose 내포하다   wild 야생   habitat 서식지   assault 공격하다   keep A from B A를 B로부터 억제하다   circumstance 상황

TIPS for SUCCESS

형용사절 Adjective Clause

형용사절을 흔히 관계대명사절이라고 많이 칭하는데, 이는 앞에 나오는 명사를 수식해 주는 역할을 한다. 관계대명사의 종류로는 세 가지가 있다.

	사람	사물	선행사의 제한 없음
주격	who	which	that
소유격	whose	whose / of which	----
목적격	whom	which	that

CUT PASTE UNDO REDO　　　　Hide Word Count : 0

Directions Read the question below. You have 30 minutes to plan, write, and revise your essay. Typically, an effective response will contain a minimum of 300 words.

Question

Some people prefer that one teacher instruct students in every subject while others think there should be a different teacher for each subject. Which do you prefer and why?

Use specific reasons and examples to support your answer.

ACTUAL TEST **12**

Prefer the Same Teacher for Every Subject

- ***more attention from teacher*** 교사로부터 더 많은 관심을 받음
  - stronger relationship → motivation ↑ → academic performance ↑ 유대감 → 동기 부여 ↑ → 학업 성적 ↑
    - **Ex** one teacher: feel more happiness + secure 단일 교사: 더 행복 + 안전한 기분
      - → more effective 더 효율적

- ***correlation among subjects*** 과목들 사이의 연관성
  - apply knowledge to other subjects → successful academic achievement
    지식을 다른 과목에 적용 → 성공적인 학업 성취
    - **Ex** reading skill in liberal arts → historical figure in students
      국어에서 배운 독해 기술 → 사회에서 배우는 역사적 인물
      - → teacher can identify + understand students' abilities and needs
        교사는 학생들의 능력과 필요성을 구별하고 이해할 수 있음

INTRODUCTION

generalization: educational institute: provide the most desirable learning environment
일반화: 교육 기관:가장 바람직한 배움의 환경을 제공

⬇

various methods + systems
다양한 방법 + 제도

⬇

thesis: prefer one teacher (more attention, better class management)
논제: 단일 교사를 선호 (더 많은 관심,학급의 더 나은 관리)

Prefer Different Teachers

- ***various teaching styles → teachers w/specialized skills*** 다른 수업 방식 →전문화된 방법을 가진 교사
  - exposed to various learning techniques 배움의 다양한 형식에 노출됨
    - **Ex** some teachers: utilize technology / others: follow traditional methods
      일부 교사들: 테크놀로지를 활용 / 다른 교사들: 전통 방식 고수
      - → students can develop multiple perspectives 학생은 다양한 관점을 발달시킬 수 있음
      - → students: more disciplined 학생: 더 훈련이 됨

- ***might end up too comfortable w/one teacher*** 한 명의 교사는 너무 편해질 수 있음
  - **Ex** submit assignments late 늦어진 과제 제출
    - → responsibility ✗ + too dependent 책임감 ✗ + 너무 의존적으로 됨

INTRODUCTION

generalization: educational institute: provides the most desirable learning environment
일반화: 부모: 교육 기관:가장 바람직한 배움의 환경을 제공

⬇

various methods + systems
다양한 방법 + 제도

⬇

thesis: prefer diff. teachers (specialized, responsibility)
논제: 다양한 교사를 선호 (전문화,책임감)

Educational institutions try their best to provide students with the most desirable learning environment to create happiness and well-being. Thus, there are various methods and systems that educational organizations implement to achieve these goals. Though there are some advantages to having different teachers for different subjects, I strongly believe that there should only be one teacher for each class in elementary schools. This has to do with students getting more attention and effective classroom management.

Children, especially at an early age, need more attention from a single teacher and need to build a strong bond with their teacher and classmates. The reason is that a strong relationship with a teacher can enhance students' motivation levels. For instance, studies have shown that students who receive the guidance of one teacher in class feel happier and more secure compared to students who have three or four different teachers in one day. This clearly shows that it is effective to have students be taught by a single teacher.

Moreover, since all subjects are correlated with one another, a teacher can apply the knowledge taught in one subject to another subject, leading to successful academic achievement at the end of a year. For example, a teacher might apply the reading skills taught in language arts class when she is teaching the students about an historical figure in social studies class. Thus, if there is one teacher managing the whole class, the teacher can identify the students' needs and abilities more easily and consider them when teaching different subjects.

It is true that learning each subject from a different teacher will expose students to different teaching styles. However, kids are too young to recognize different approaches and perspectives. Rather, students feel more secure and comfortable learning from one teacher. Furthermore, having one teacher instruct students will allow the teacher to meet better learning goals through an integrated curriculum. Therefore, I firmly believe one teacher should teach every subject during elementary school.

WORD REMINDER

institution 기관   well-being 복지, 행복   organization 기구, 단체   implement 실행하다   bond 유대   enhance 향상하다, 강화하다
motivation 동기 부여   guidance 인도   secure 안전한, 확신하는   correlate 서로 관련시키다   achievement 성취, 성적   figure 인물
recognize 인식하다, 알다   approach 방법   perspective 관점   integrated 통합된   curriculum 교과 과정

Educational institutions try their best to provide students with the most desirable learning environment to create happiness and well-being. Thus, there are various methods and systems that educational organizations implement to achieve these goals. Though there are some advantages to having one teacher for every subject, I strongly believe that elementary schools should assign different teachers for each subject. This has to do with the specialization of each teacher and the fact that students may start depending too much on one teacher.

Students can benefit from various teaching styles by different teachers with specialized skills. In other words, rather than getting used to a specific pedagogical approach, students can have opportunities to be exposed to diverse teaching techniques. For instance, some teachers may be experts at utilizing technology during class whereas others might be superb at traditional teaching methods. This will help students experience various approaches and develop multiple perspectives, leading to an improved quality of education.

Furthermore, having different teachers for each subject helps students become more disciplined. Under the guidance of one teacher, a student might end up feeling too comfortable with the teacher. For instance, a student might think it is okay to submit an assignment a little late because the teacher will be more understanding. This may result in a lack of responsibility and make students more dependent on a teacher. Besides, children will eventually learn from different teachers in the future. Thus, it is better to help them get used to having multiple teachers, especially when the academic requirements are not demanding at an early age.

It is true that having one teacher might create a closer relationship between a teacher and a student; however, it is better for students to be exposed to different educational methods. Moreover, if students are used to one teacher, they may become too comfortable with the teacher and then become too dependent. Therefore, I firmly contend that young students should learn each subject from a different teacher.

WORD REMINDER

specialization 전문화   benefit 이익, 혜택   pedagogical 교육의, 교수법의   expose 경험하다   diverse 다양한   expert 전문가   utilize 활용하다
superb 훌륭한   disciplined 훈련된, 올바른   submit 제출하다   assignment 과제   lack 부족, 부재   dependent 의존하는
requirement 요건, 조건   demanding 요구가 많은

1 Do you agree or disagree with the following statement? Parents are the best teachers. Use specific reasons and examples to support your answer.

다음 명제에 찬성하는가 반대하는가? 부모는 최고의 선생이다. 이유와 예를 들어 자신의 입장을 뒷받침하시오.

AGREE	DISAGREE
- role models for kids 아이들에게 모범이 됨 - spend most time with kids 아이들과 대부분의 시간을 보냄	- purpose of education at school: learn from teachers 학교의 목적: 교사로부터의 배움 - many kids have abusive parents 많은 아이들이 학대하는 부모들을 가지고 있음

2 Do you agree or disagree with the following statement? The knowledge we gain from personal experiences is more valuable than the knowledge we gain from books. Use specific reasons and examples to support your answer.

다음 명제에 찬성하는가 반대하는가? 개인적인 경험으로부터 얻은 지식은 책에서 얻은 지식보다 더욱 가치 있다. 이유와 예를 들어 자신의 입장을 뒷받침하시오.

AGREE	DISAGREE
- direct experiences 직접 경험 - stays in mind for longer time 마음속에 더 오랫동안 남아 있음	- indirect experiences: save time + effort 간접 경험: 시간 + 노력 절약 - many that cannot be done through experience (finding venomous animals) 많은 것들은 경험으로 이루어질 수 없음 (맹독의 동물들 찾기)

3 Do you agree or disagree with the following statement? Students do not respect their teachers as much as they did in the past. Use specific reasons and examples to support your answer.

다음 명제에 찬성하는가 반대하는가? 학생들은 과거만큼 선생들을 존경하지 않는다. 이유와 예를 들어 자신의 입장을 뒷받침하시오.

AGREE	DISAGREE
- many other influencers: YouTubers, celebrities, athletes 영향력 있는 다른 사람이 많음: 유튜버, 연예인, 스포츠 선수들 - lose politeness (due to individualism) 예의의 부재 (개인주의 때문)	- role models for many students 많은 학생들에게 모범적인 역할 - many celebrate special days for teachers 많은 이들이 교사들을 위한 특별한 날을 기념함

TOEFL® MAP

ACTUAL TEST Writing 2

13

Coral reefs are underwater structures that protect coastlines from erosion and storms. Coral reefs are home to about 25% of all ocean fish and other marine organisms, and they serve very important roles in marine ecosystems. However, due to numerous factors, coral reefs are now endangered. The destruction of coral reefs is called coral degradation which is an issue that needs to be addressed immediately.

The biggest problem corals encounter is coral bleaching, and the primary culprit for coral bleaching is climate change. The increase in ocean temperature causes corals to expel algae, which live inside corals and provide them with colors, food, and nutrients. Without algae, corals will fade and look white as if they are bleached. Eventually, this will cause them to die unless the temperature decreases and algae go back to corals.

Among the many problems is pollution, including fertilizer, oil, and human and animal waste. Plastic debris can also cause physical damage to coral tissue and destroy corals. Floating garbage also keeps life-giving sunlight from getting to coral reefs. Land-based activities, including mining, road construction, and farming, put corals in danger as well, and the excessive nutrients in fertilizers used in farming are particularly harmful to coral reefs.

Human activities such as overfishing, scuba diving, and coral harvesting also contribute to the loss of coral reefs. Overfishing threatens more than 55% of the world's reefs, and coral reefs in Southeast Asia are especially vulnerable to this activity. Moreover, not only are many corals collected and displayed in aquariums to attract tourists, but they are also broken off and sold as jewelry or souvenirs. The environmental issue has been worsened by tourists as many of them put on sunscreen with a chemical called oxybenzone, which is devastating to corals.

🎧 13-01

ACTUAL TEST **13**

Directions You have 20 minutes to plan and write your response. Your response will be judged on the basis of the quality of your writing and on how well your response presents the points in the lecture and their relationship to the passage. Typically, an effective response will be 150-225 words.

Question Summarize the points made in the lecture, being sure to specifically explain how they support the explanations in the reading passage.

CUT PASTE UNDO REDO   Hide Word Count : 0

Coral reefs are underwater structures that protect coastlines from erosion and storms. Coral reefs are home to about 25% of all ocean fish and other marine organisms, and they serve very important roles in marine ecosystems. However, due to numerous factors, coral reefs are now endangered. The destruction of coral reefs is called coral degradation which is an issue that needs to be addressed immediately.

The biggest problem corals encounter is coral bleaching, and the primary culprit for coral bleaching is climate change. The increase in ocean temperature causes corals to expel algae, which live inside corals and provide them with colors, food, and nutrients. Without algae, corals will fade and look white as if they are bleached. Eventually, this will cause them to die unless the temperature decreases and algae go back to corals.

Among the many problems is pollution, including fertilizer, oil, and human and animal waste. Plastic debris can also cause physical damage to coral tissue and destroy corals. Floating garbage also keeps life-giving sunlight from getting to coral reefs. Land-based activities, including mining, road construction, and farming, put corals in danger as well, and the excessive nutrients in fertilizers used in farming are particularly harmful to coral reefs.

Human activities such as overfishing, scuba diving, and coral harvesting also contribute to the loss of coral reefs. Overfishing threatens more than 55% of the world's reefs, and coral reefs in Southeast Asia are especially vulnerable to this activity. Moreover, not only are many corals collected and displayed in aquariums to attract tourists, but they are also broken off and sold as jewelry or souvenirs. The environmental issue has been worsened by tourists as many of them put on sunscreen with a chemical called oxybenzone, which is devastating to corals.

✎ NOTE-TAKING

coral degradation → endangers coral and needs to be addressed immediately (cause) 산호 붕괴 →멸종 위기에 놓여 있으며 즉시 해결되어야 함 (원인)

❶ *climate change: main cause of coral bleaching (losing color)* 기후 변화: 산호 표백 (색을 잃는 것)의 주된 원인
 – temp. ↑: expel algae (responsible for colors, food, all nutrients) 온도↑: (색깔, 식량, 영양소 담당하는) 조류를 밀어냄

 The increase in the ocean temperature due to climate change will make corals expel algae, resulting in coral bleaching and the death of corals.

❷ *pollution (fertilizer, oil, human / animal waste)* 공해 (비료, 석유, 인간 / 동물의 분뇨)
 Ex excessive nutrients in fertilizers → harmful to corals 비료 안의 과다 영양분 → 산호에 해로움

 Pollution and land-based activities can harm coral reefs.

❸ *human activities (overfishing, scuba diving, and coral harvesting)* 인간 행위 (남획, 스쿠버 다이빙, 산호 수확)
 – overfishing in SA, jewelry, souvenirs, sunscreens w/oxybenzone
 동남아에서의 남획, 보석, 기념품, 옥시벤존이 들어간 자외선 차단제

 Human activities, including water excursions, overfishing, and coral collecting, contribute to the destruction of coral reefs.

WORD REMINDER

erosion 침식 endangered 멸종 위기의 destruction 파괴 degradation 붕괴 address 해결하다 primary 주된 culprit 원인
bleaching 표백 expel 쫓아내다 algae 조류 fade 흐려지다 fertilizer 비료 human waste 분뇨 debris 쓰레기 tissue 조직
life-giving 생명을 주는 mining 채광 excessive 과한 overfishing 남획 harvesting 수확 contribute to ~의 원인이 되다
threaten 위협하다 vulnerable 취약한 aquarium 수족관 souvenir 기념품 devastating 파괴적인

CD → can affect the entire ecosystem (consequences)
산호 붕괴 →생태계 전체에 영향을 끼칠 수 있음 (결과)

❶ *problem for the entire reef ecosystem* 산호 생태계 전체에 문제
 – can affect marine animals (fish, turtles, and sea birds) → depend on corals for food, protection, and shelter
 해양 동물들(물고기, 거북이, 바다 새)에게 영향을 끼칠 수 있음 → 먹이, 보호, 거처를 위해 산호에게 의존

 Coral bleaching can put the entire reef ecosystem in jeopardy.

❷ *human activities: underwater seawall → protect shorelines from storms, floods, and waves*
 인간 행위: 바닷속 → 태풍, 홍수, 파도로부터 해안가를 보호함
 – excess nutrients → algae ↑ → smother corals 과잉 영양분 → 조류↑ → 산호를 질식시킴

 Without corals, shorelines will be vulnerable to storms, floods, and waves.

❸ *impact on economy* 경제에 영향
 Ex fishing industry: not just corals but animals that feed on corals → affect the entire ecosystem
 어업: 산호뿐 아니라, 산호를 먹는 동물들 → 생태계 전체에 영향을 끼침

 Some countries whose economies rely heavily on ocean activities will experience economic crises.

WORD REMINDER

astonishing 놀라운 consequence 결과 possess 소유하다 merely 단순히 aesthetic 미의 pose 야기하다 catastrophic 비극적인
shelter 주거, 거처 bring about 일으키다 seawall 제방 overabundance 과잉 excess 과잉 smother ~을 질식시키다
inevitable 불가피한 crisis 위기, 문제 deprive 결핍 deprive of ~에게서 …을 빼앗다 income 수입 for a living 생계수단으로

The lecturer explains the devastating consequences that coral degradation will bring about in the near future unless proper measures are taken. This supports the ideas presented in the reading passage that coral reefs have become endangered.

First of all, coral bleaching can put an entire reef ecosystem in jeopardy. If corals lose color and die, other ocean creatures will be in danger, too. This advocates the point in the reading passage that the increase in the ocean temperature due to climate change will make corals expel algae, resulting in coral bleaching and the death of corals.

On top of that, the lecturer forewarns that coastal communities will face natural disasters without any natural barriers. Without corals, shorelines will be vulnerable to storms, floods, and waves. Moreover, a nutrient surplus will cause algae proliferation that will smother and kill corals. This explains the reading passage's position that pollution and land-based activities can harm coral reefs.

Finally, some countries whose economies rely heavily on ocean activities will experience economic crises. If corals die, other animals that prey on corals will also suffer or die due to being deprived of their food source. This elucidates the point made in the reading passage that human activities, including water excursions, overfishing, and coral collecting, contribute to the destruction of coral reefs.

◤ WORD REMINDER

proper 적절한 measure 대책 jeopardy 위험 advocate 옹호하다 forewarn 주의를 주다 barrier 장벽 surplus 과잉 proliferation 급증
prey 잡아먹다 deprive 빼앗다 elucidate 설명하다 excursion 여행, 행동

CUT PASTE UNDO REDO   Hide Word Count : 0

Directions Read the question below. You have 30 minutes to plan, write, and revise your essay. Typically, an effective response will contain a minimum of 300 words.

Question

Do you agree or disagree with the following statement?

Young people nowadays have no influence on important decisions that determine the future of society.

Use specific reasons and examples to support your answer.

ACTUAL TEST **13**

AGREE

- *society: more demanding + competitive* 사회: 더 요구가 많음 + 경쟁적

  - young people: more individualistic 젊은이들: 더욱 개인주의적

    Ex not many young people consider environmental consequences
    많지 않은 젊은이들만이 환경적 결과에 대해 생각함

    → reluctant to participate in preservation of nature 자연 보호에 참여하는 것을 주저함

- *some: conscious about social issues + active in expressing thoughts*
  일부: 사회적 쟁점들에 대한 자각 + 생각을 표현하는데 적극적

  - bureaucracy intervenes 관료제가 개입함

    Ex speak out for changes 변화를 외침

    → neglected by those w/social power + a desire to keep old-standing customs
    사회 권력 + 오랜 관습을 유지하고픈 바람을 가진 이들에 의해 무시당함

INTRODUCTION

generalization: young people → lead society in the future
일반화: 젊은이들 → 미래 사회를 이끎

⬇

involvement → great impact
참여 → 상당한 영향

⬇

thesis: agree (lost interest, poor bureaucracy)
논제: 동의 (사라진 관심, 바람직하지 못한 관료제)

DISAGREE

- *prevalence of the Internet: fortifies influence* 인터넷의 유행: 영향을 강화시킴

  - SNS: opinions spread rapidly 소셜 네트워킹 서비스: 의견이 빠르게 퍼짐

    Ex environmental problems: serious issue among young people 환경 문제: 젊은이들 사이에서 심각한 주제

    → discussion + access to many sources: activated a worldwide movement to preserve nature
    토론 + 많은 자료의 이용: 자연을 보호하기 위한 세계적 운동이 활성화됨

- *various ways to express opinions* 의견을 표현하는 여러 가지 방법

  - results in amendment to law 법안 수정의 결과를 낳음

    Ex temporary position at work: disadvantages + unfairness 회사에서의 비정규직: 불이익 + 불공정

    → protest + demonstrate → government: aware of situation + on its way to passing a law to
    protect workers 항의 + 시위 운동 → 정부: 상황 인식 + 근로자를 보호하기 위한 법안을 통과시키는 중

INTRODUCTION

generalization: young people → lead society in the future
일반화: 젊은이들 → 미래 사회를 이끎

⬇

involvement → great impact
참여 → 상당한 영향

⬇

thesis: disagree (power of the Internet, freedom to demonstrate)
논제: 반대 (인터넷의 힘, 시위의 자유)

Young people are the ones who will lead future society. Thus, their involvement in social issues will have a great impact in the future. Some contend that young people nowadays have taken more significant roles in making crucial decisions. However, I strongly believe they rarely have any influence on important decisions that may affect the future of society. For one, many young people have lost interest in social issues. In addition, bureaucracy often keeps young people from voicing their thoughts.

First of all, as society becomes more demanding and competitive, young people have become more individualistic and do not care about social issues which will not have a direct influence on them. For instance, not many young people consider the consequences of environmental damage in the future. Hence, a majority of young people are reluctant to spend time taking part in campaigns to preserve their natural surroundings.

On top of that, even though there still are young people conscious about social issues who step forward to express their opinions, the bureaucracy frequently intervenes for the purpose of sustaining its power and preserving conventional ways. To illustrate, numerous young people wish to experiment with new and innovative social mechanisms. They often speak out for changes. Nevertheless, their ideas are neglected by older people with social power and a desire to keep long-standing customs.

It is true that some young people are aware of important matters facing society and try to participate in events that may influence decisions for the future. However, most of their lives are self-oriented, and they are busy just managing their own work. Furthermore, bureaucracy prevents young people from voicing their thoughts to the public. For the above reasons, I agree with the statement that young people nowadays have no influence on important decisions that determine the future of society.

WORD REMINDER

bureaucracy 관료주의   voice (강력히) 말로 나타내다   demanding 요구가 많은   individualistic 개인주의적인   reluctant 마음 내키지 않는 take part in ~에 참가하다   preserve 보존하다   conscious 자각하고 있는   step forward 앞으로 나가다   intervene 개입하다   sustain 유지하다 conventional 틀에 박힌   innovative 혁신적인   mechanism 절차, 방법   speak out 거리낌없이 말하다   neglect 무시하다 long-standing 오래 계속되는   custom 관습   be aware of ~을 알다   participate in ~에 참여하다

TIPS for SUCCESS

a majority of 다음에는 단수명사가 오느냐 복수명사가 오느냐에 따라 동사의 단수 혹은 복수의 여부가 결정된다.
단수명사가 올 경우 단수동사를, 복수명사가 올 경우 복수명사를 쓴다. 두 번째 단락의 문장을 살펴보자.

Hence, **a majority of young people are** reluctant to spend time taking part in campaigns to preserve their natural surroundings.

위의 문장에서 young people이라는 복수명사가 쓰였기 때문에 are를 썼지만, 만약 a majority of the population이라고 쓸 경우 population은 family와 더불어 집단을 뜻하는 명사이므로, 단수 취급을 한다. 따라서 문장은 다음과 같이 변하게 된다.

Hence, **a majority of the population is** reluctant to spend time taking part in campaigns to preserve their natural surroundings.

뒤에 오는 명사의 단·복수 여부에 따라 동사의 형태가 변하는 다른 표현들도 살펴보자.

the rest of / half of / the part of / a majority of / lots of / plenty of / all of the / any of the / a lot of the / most of the / some of the / none of the

143

Young people are the ones who will lead future society. Thus, their involvement in social issues will have a great impact in the future. Some contend that young people nowadays rarely have any influence on important decisions. However, I strongly believe they have taken on more significant roles in making decisions that will affect the future of society. For one, they use the power of the Internet to connect with one another. In addition, the freedom to demonstrate lets young people express their opinions.

First of all, the prevalence of the Internet fortifies the influence of individuals on crucial issues in society. As a majority of young people are involved in social network services, their thoughts on particular concerns spread very rapidly. For instance, environmental problems have become a serious issue for young people. Hence, they talk with each other on the Internet and have access to many sources of information, including news from around the world. They have activated a worldwide movement to preserve the natural world for the future.

On top of that, young people have a number of ways to express their opinions. Such methods as signature campaigns and demonstrations sometimes result in amendments to laws. To illustrate, many young people have difficulty finding permanent jobs. Instead, their contracts are renewed on a yearly basis. This situation often forces them to tolerate disadvantages and unfair actions by their companies. Today, many young people take action against injustice through protests and demonstrations. Consequently, the government is aware of their situations and is on its way to passing a law that can protect workers from unreasonable treatment.

It is true that pressure to maintain conventional ways for the sake of convenience sometimes keeps young people from voicing their thoughts. Conversely, the rapid propagation of young people's ideas through the Internet has overcome such drawbacks. Furthermore, young people have actively involved themselves in numerous events that may have effects on crucial decisions. For the above reasons, I disagree with the statement that young people nowadays have no influence on important decisions that determine the future of society.

WORD REMINDER

demonstrate 시위하다   prevalence 유행   fortify 강화하다   spread 퍼지다   access 이용할 권리   source 출처   activate 활성화하다
worldwide 세계적인   amendment 개정   permanent 영구적인   renew 갱신하다   tolerate 너그럽게 봐 주다   take action 조치를 취하다
injustice 부당한 조치   protest 항의   pass 통과시키다   unreasonable 불합리한   treatment 취급, 대우   pressure 압박
for the sake of ~을 위해서   propagation 보급   overcome 극복하다   drawback 결점   actively 활발히

TIPS for SUCCESS

to부정사 vs. 전치사 to

to는 수많은 용법을 가지고 있는데도 불구하고, 일단 to가 보이면 동사원형을 먼저 쓰는 학생들이 있다. 전치사로서의 to는 장소를 나타낼 때 쓰인다. 세 번째 단락의 문장을 살펴보자.

Consequently, the government is aware of their situations and is on its way **to** passing a law that can protect workers from unreasonable treatment.

on the way to는 '진행 중의'라는 뜻을 가지고 있으므로 법안을 통과시키기 위해 진행 중이라고 목적을 나타내기 보다는, 법안의 통과를 진행 중이라고 표현해야 한다.

1 Because modern life has become complicated, it is essential for young people to have the ability to plan and organize. 현대의 삶이 복잡해 졌기 때문에, 젊은이들에게 계획을 세우고 정리를 하는 능력은 필수이다.

AGREE	DISAGREE
- organization: saving time → more work can be done 정리: 시간 절약 → 더 많은 일을 할 수 있음 - many things to take care of → a higher chance of making mistakes 해야 할 일이 많음 → 실수를 할 가능성이 높아짐	- life: more complicated → automated machines: no need to plan / organize 삶: 더욱 복잡 → 자동화 기계: 계획을 세우거나 정리할 필요가 없어짐 - getting complicated doesn't mean more tasks for individuals 더욱 복잡해졌다는 것이 개인에게 더 많은 할 일이 생겼다는 뜻은 아님

2 Young people should try several jobs before they decide what job or career to choose in the long term. 젊은이들은 장기적인 직업이나 경력을 결정하기 전에 다양한 직업을 시도해 보아야 한다.

AGREE	DISAGREE
- able to know one's abilities 자신의 능력을 알 수 있음 - a lot of information + experience in diverse fields 다양한 분야에서 많은 정보와 경험을 얻을 수 있음	- may lack commitment / responsibility by thinking one can always change jobs 언제든 직업을 바꿀 수 있다는 생각에 의무감 / 책임감이 부족할 수 있음 - many internship opportunities in college 대학 시절 많은 인턴십 기회가 있음

3 Physical exercise is more important for older people than for younger people. 운동은 젊은 사람들보다 나이 든 사람들에게 더 중요하다.

AGREE	DISAGREE
- body: getting older → more vulnerable to disease 몸: 나이가 들면 질병에 더욱 취약해 짐 - more prone to depression: a way to overcome 우울증 경향 ↑: 극복하기 위한 방법	- building strength for the future 미래를 위해 체력을 기름 - socialize w/others (interpersonal relationships) 다른 이들과 사귈 수 있는 기회 (대인 관계)

TOEFL®/MAP
ACTUAL TEST Writing 2

14

In North America and Eurasia, approximately 180 species of honeysuckle have been found. Honeysuckle plants are popular with gardeners due to their stunning foliage and attractive trumpet-shaped blooms. Though most of them are classified as invasive species in the United States, they provide many advantages to animals as well as plants.

Honeysuckle is valuable to wildlife. It provides homes for many kinds of birds and helps native plants as well as itself reproduce by attracting a lot of pollinators. Its sturdy branches and bark give strong support for the nests of many kinds of birds, including catbirds and wrens, and its leaves can help birds hide their nests from predators. In addition, insects such as butterflies and bumblebees help pollinate its seeds, resulting in an abundance of plants.

For many birds and other animals, honeysuckle is a great source of food all year around. Berries are always welcomed by birds, especially during harsh times when it is challenging to find anything to feed on. In summer, not only insects but also insect-eating birds visit honeysuckles for food. Dormice eat its sweet nectar-rich flowers for energy. Butterflies and bumblebees, which are two of the most common pollinators, depend heavily on honeysuckle nectar. It is especially crucial to provide butterflies such as the white admiral with nectar since its numbers are declining.

One of the most impressive features of honeysuckle is that all of its parts, including leaves, berries, seeds, and flowers, can be used as medicine. The plant is helpful for indigestion, skin problems, diabetes, and many other conditions. For example, it aids people who have a fever by lowering their temperature and by cooling their bodies by inducing perspiration.

ACTUAL TEST **14**

🎧 14-01

147

Directions You have 20 minutes to plan and write your response. Your response will be judged on the basis of the quality of your writing and on how well your response presents the points in the lecture and their relationship to the passage. Typically, an effective response will be 150-225 words.

Question Summarize the points made in the lecture, being sure to explain how they challenge specific claims made in the reading passage.

CUT PASTE UNDO REDO Hide Word Count : 0

In North America and Eurasia, approximately 180 species of honeysuckle have been found. Honeysuckle plants are popular with gardeners due to their stunning foliage and attractive trumpet-shaped blooms. Though most of them are classified as invasive species in the United States, they provide many advantages to animals as well as plants.

Honeysuckle is valuable to wildlife. It provides homes for many kinds of birds and helps native plants as well as itself reproduce by attracting a lot of pollinators. Its sturdy branches and bark give strong support for the nests of many kinds of birds, including catbirds and wrens, and its leaves can help birds hide their nests from predators. In addition, insects such as butterflies and bumblebees help pollinate its seeds, resulting in an abundance of plants.

For many birds and other animals, honeysuckle is a great source of food all year around. Berries are always welcomed by birds, especially during harsh times when it is challenging to find anything to feed on. In summer, not only insects but also insect-eating birds visit honeysuckles for food. Dormice eat its sweet nectar-rich flowers for energy. Butterflies and bumblebees, which are two of the most common pollinators, depend heavily on honeysuckle nectar. It is especially crucial to provide butterflies such as the white admiral with nectar since its numbers are declining.

One of the most impressive features of honeysuckle is that all of its parts, including leaves, berries, seeds, and flowers, can be used as medicine. The plant is helpful for indigestion, skin problems, diabetes, and many other conditions. For example, it aids people who have a fever by lowering their temperature and by cooling their bodies by inducing perspiration.

honeysuckle → provides many advantages to wildlife 인동덩굴 →야생 생물에 많은 이점을 제공함

❶ valuable to wildlife 야생 생물들에게 중요함

- provides home for birds → sturdy branches / bark: strong support for nest
  새들에게 집을 제공 → 단단한 나뭇가지 / 나무 껍질: 둥지에 튼튼한 받침

- attracts pollinators → abundance of plants 수분 매개체를 끎 → 풍부한 식물

> **Paraphrasing Example** The honeysuckle provides homes for wildlife and helps with the proliferation of vegetation.

❷ honeysuckle: great source of food 인동덩굴: 먹이 공급원

- birds: berries during harsh season / dormice: flower / butterflies + bumblebees: nectar
  새: 혹독한 계절에 베리 / 겨울잠쥐: 꽃 / 나비 + 벌: 꿀

- especially important to butterflies + bumblebees ∵ #s are ↓ 특히나 나비 + 벌에게 중요함 ∵ 숫자 ↓

> **Paraphrasing Example** The honeysuckle provides food for many birds and other animals.

❸ medicinal feature 약효가 있는 특성

- all parts (leaves, berries, seeds, and flowers) can be used as medicine
  모든 부분 (잎, 베리, 씨앗, 꽃): 약으로 사용될 수 있음

- used for ingestion, skin problems, and diabetes 소화 불량, 피부 트러블, 당뇨병에 사용됨

> **Paraphrasing Example** All parts of the honeysuckle are used for medical purposes.

WORD REMINDER

honeysuckle 인동덩굴   stunning 놀랄 만큼 아름다운   foliage 잎   bloom 개화   invasive 침입하는   reproduce 번식하다
attract 끌다   pollinator 수분 매개체   sturdy 단단한   bark 나무 껍질   catbird 고양이 새   wren 굴뚝새   predator 포식자
pollinate ~에 수분하다   abundance 풍부   harsh 혹독한   feed on ~을 먹고 살다   dormice 겨울잠쥐   white admiral 흰줄나비
indigestion 소화 불량   diabetes 당뇨병   perspiration 땀

honeysuckle: difficult to eradicate → threat to the environment
인동덩굴: 근절하기 어려움 →환경에 위협

❶ invasive species: highly adaptable to environment 침범: 환경에 굉장히 잘 적응함

- traits: rapid reproduction, spreading, growth → strangles other plants → monoculture of invasive species
  특성: 빠른 번식, 확산, 증가 → 다른 식물들을 질식시킴 → 침입종의 독점

> **Paraphrasing Example** The honeysuckle is highly invasive and possesses features that are common to invasive species.

❷ –ve consequences on birds: berries → junk food 새에게 부정적 영향: 베리 → 불량 식품

- less fat + nutrients → can slow pace of migration 적은 지방 + 영양분 → 이동 속도를 늦출 수 있음

> **Paraphrasing Example** The honeysuckle has negative effects on birds. An insufficient amount of nutrients and fat will prevent birds from maintaining a steady speed during migration.

❸ honeysuckle: medicinal → medical proof ✕ 인동덩굴: 약효가 있음 →의학적 증거 ✕

- controversial ex) honeysuckle can be applied to skin for inflammation → possible infection
  논란 염증에 대해 인동덩굴을 피부에 바를 수 있음 →감염 가능

> **Paraphrasing Example** There is little evidence that the plants have any medical uses, and more research needs to be conducted.

WORD REMINDER

hedge 울타리   eradicate 근절하다   threat 위협   typical 전형적인   trait 특성   reproduction 번식   strangle ~을 질식시키다   hinder 방해하다
maple 단풍나무   oak 참나무   hickory 히코리   dominate 점령하다   consequence 영향   migration 이동   boast 자랑하다
controversial 논란의   inflammation 염증   infection 감염   treat 치료하다

The lecturer argues that the honeysuckle poses a serious hazard to the natural environment. This directly challenges the reading passage's claim that the honeysuckle is invaluable to both wildlife and humans.

First, according to the professor, the honeysuckle is highly invasive and possesses features that are common to invasive species. She explains that it climbs and throttles other plants. She also mentions the maple tree as an example to show how the honeysuckle inhibits reproduction by blocking sunlight, creating a monoculture. This goes against the reading passage's assertion that the honeysuckle provides home for wildlife and helps with the proliferation of vegetation.

Moreover, the lecturer contends that the honeysuckle has negative effects on birds. Recent studies show that the berries from the honeysuckle lack fat and nutrients and instead act as junk food. According to the lecturer, an insufficient amount of nutrients and fat will prevent birds from maintaining a steady speed during migration. This contradicts the reading passage's assertion that the honeysuckle provides food for many birds and other animals.

Finally, the professor dismisses the medicinal effects of the honeysuckle. She elaborates by explaining that there is little evidence that the plant has any medical uses and that more research needs to be conducted. This casts doubt on the reading passage's idea that all parts of the honeysuckle are used for medical purposes.

WORD REMINDER

pose 야기하다   hazard 위험   invaluable 매우 귀중한   possess 소유하다   throttle ~을 질식시키다   inhibit 억제하다   proliferation 확산, 증식
vegetation 식물   insufficiency 부족   hamper 방해하다   dismiss 일축하다   elaborate 상세히 말하다   little 거의 없는   conduct 시행하다

Hide Word Count : 0

Directions Read the question below. You have 30 minutes to plan, write, and revise your essay. Typically, an effective response will contain a minimum of 300 words.

Question

Do you agree or disagree with the following statement?

Environmental issues can be solved or improved in the future.

Use specific reasons and examples to support your answer.

📝 NOTE-TAKING

- *matter of concern for many companies* 많은 기업들에게 관심사
  - inventions + improvements to filtering facilities 정화 시설 발명 + 개선
    - Ex corporations in the past: didn't take seriously 과거의 기업: 심각히 받아들이지 않았음
      - → now: install systems to reduce toxic waste 현재: 독성 폐기물을 감소시킬 장치를 설치
  - develop a filtering system 정화 시스템 개발

- *green movement* 환경 운동
  - more people are concerned about situation 더 많은 사람들이 상황에 대해 관심을 가짐
    - Ex recycling campaigns 분리수거
      - → food waste: ground + dried → process → fertilizer 음식물 쓰레기: 분쇄하여 건조시킴 → 과정 → 비료

INTRODUCTION

generalization: development of tech → many advantages + environmental damage
일반화: 과학 기술의 발전 → 많은 이로움 + 환경 파괴

⬇

attention → solutions + global responses
관심 → 해결책 + 국제적 대응

⬇

thesis: agree (investment, attitudes toward environmental concerns)
논제: 찬성 (투자, 환경 문제에 대한 사고방식)

- *environmental damage → faster than restoration* 환경 파괴 → 복구보다 더 빠름
  - Ex trees: cut down 나무: 벌목
    - new trees: shallow root structures 새로운 나무: 얕은 뿌리 조직
      - → susceptible to erosion → natural disasters 침식에 취약 → 자연재해

- *problems w/the attitudes that some companies + individuals have*
  일부 기업 + 개인이 가진 태도의 문제
  - profit-oriented objective → worsens the effect 이윤 지향적 목표 → 결과를 악화시킴
    - Ex corporations: concerned about making revenue 기업: 이득을 내는데 관심이 있음
      - → meet safety standards → no further improvements to filtering systems
      안전 기준 충족 → 정화 시스템 더 이상의 개선 ✗

INTRODUCTION

generalization: development of tech → many advantages + environmental damage
일반화: 과학 기술의 발전 → 많은 이로움 + 환경 파괴

⬇

attention → solutions + global responses
관심 → 해결책 + 국제적 대응

⬇

thesis: disagree (pace of destruction, attitudes toward environmental concerns)
논제: 반대 (파괴의 속도, 환경 문제에 대한 사고방식)

The development of technology has provided people with a lot of advantages; however, it has also caused a tremendous amount of environmental damage. As environmental concerns have attracted the attention of many people, there are numerous solutions and global responses that have been proposed or initiated. Though some people contend that environmental damage is irreversible, I strongly believe that nature can be restored in the future. I believe this will happen due to support from big corporations and green campaigns.

First, environmental issues have become a major matter of concern for a number of companies. To illustrate, most corporations in the past did not take seriously environmental effects such as air pollution and noxious materials. However, as the devastating consequences came to the notice of corporations, they started to install systems to reduce toxic waste and to develop filtering systems, which will eventually be able to remove all pollutants from factory emissions.

In addition, the green movement has spread worldwide. Compared to the past, today, many more people are concerned about the environmental situation, which could have a direct effect on generations to come. For instance, almost everyone in Korea participates in recycling campaigns. Hence, people have become habituated to sorting plastics, aluminum cans, and cardboard into recycling bins. Furthermore, food waste is ground and dried and then goes through a special process with chemicals to turn it into fertilizer. These examples show that our environmental circumstances will gradually get better.

It is true that an enormous amount of time and effort will be required to restore the Earth's damaged environment. On the other hand, there are many companies striving to improve their systems for filtering toxic materials. In addition, people are taking part in preservation campaigns and are trying to rehabilitate the environment for their descendants. Therefore, I firmly agree with the statement that environmental issues can be solved or improved in the future.

WORD REMINDER

tremendous 굉장한   initiate 시작하다   irreversible 되돌릴 수 없는   restore 회복시키다, 복원하다   noxious 유해한   install 설치하다
emission 방출   recycle 재활용하다   habituate 습관이 되다   sort 분류하다   bin 큰 상자   grind 갈다   fertilizer 비료   strive 노력하다
preservation 보존   descendant 자손

TIPS for SUCCESS

부정대명사 Indefinite Pronoun

부정대명사는 any, every, some 또는 no 등의 단어로 시작하는 경우가 대부분이다. 불특정 사람이나 사물을 가리키며, 일부는 단수, 일부는 복수, 또 다른 경우는 둘 다(복수 및 단수)에 쓰일 수 있다.

단수형 부정대명사	another, anybody, anyone, anything, each, either	everybody, everyone, everything, little, much, neither	nobody, no one, nothing, one, other	somebody, someone, something
복수형 부정대명사	both, several	(a) few	many	others
단/복수형 부정대명사	all, any	more, most	none	some

The development of technology has provided people with a lot of advantages; however, it has also caused a tremendous amount of environmental damage. As environmental concerns have attracted the attention of many people, there are numerous solutions and global responses that have been proposed or initiated. Though some people contend that nature can be restored in the future, I strongly argue that the environmental destruction that has already occurred is irreversible. I believe this is true because of the speed of destruction and the lack of interest in the issue.

To begin with, the environment is being damaged faster than it is being restored. For example, every year, many trees are cut down in order to meet demand for furniture, houses, and fuel. Though new trees are planted to avoid deforestation, the newly planted trees have relatively shallow root structures that are susceptible to erosion. This situation can cause numerous natural disasters, including landslides and floods.

In addition, there are still companies as well as individuals who do not take this issue seriously. To illustrate, there are many corporations that are more concerned with making money than with preserving the environment. This attitude discourages them from improving their filtering systems as long as the amount of pollutants produced during manufacturing processes does not exceed safety standards. In addition, because some people ignore environmental issues, the restoration of nature becomes even more difficult.

It is true that the green movement is slowly changing our natural surroundings. However, what is being done to decrease environmental damage is far from enough to restore nature, and the Earth is suffering from disastrous consequences. In addition, there are many companies and individuals who do not realize the severity of the harmful effects and are not taking any action, Therefore, I firmly disagree with the statement that environmental issues can be solved or improved in the future.

WORD REMINDER

fuel 연료   avoid 막다   deforestation 삼림 벌채   shallow 얕은   susceptible 취약한, ~의 영향을 받기 쉬운   erosion 침식   disaster 재앙
revenue 수익   discourage 단념시키다   exceed 초과하다   surrounding 환경   realize 깨닫다   severity 심각성

TIPS for SUCCESS

병치 Parallelism

비교급을 쓸 때는 품사를 일치시켜 주어야 한다는 점을 기억해야 한다. 세 번째 단락의 문장을 살펴보자.

To illustrate, there are many corporations that are more concerned with **making** money than with **preserving** the environment.

간혹 ~ that are more concerned with making money than to preserve the environment라고 써서 실수를 하는 경우가 있는데 동명사는 동명사, 부사는 부사, 명사는 명사 등 같은 품사를 사용해야 한다는 것을 잊지 말자.

1 Governments should pay more attention to environmental problems than to health problems.

정부는 보건 문제보다 환경 문제에 더 많은 관심을 쏟아야 한다.

AGREE	DISAGREE
- environmental damage → related to health problems 환경 파괴 → 건강 문제와 관련 있음 ex) disease from pollutants 오염 물질에서 발생하는 질병 - changes in ecosystems 생태계 변화 ex) global warming 지구 온난화	- health: directly related to humans 건강: 인간과 직접적인 연관이 있음 - many corporations already invest a lot of money in green campaigns 이미 많은 기업들이 환경 운동에 많은 돈을 투자하고 있음

2 What governments can do to improve their health systems is to clean the environment.

정부가 보건 제도를 개선하기 위해 할 수 있는 것은 환경을 깨끗이 하는 것이다.

AGREE	DISAGREE
- sanitary: crucial to preventing diseases from spread 위생: 질병이 퍼지는 것을 예방하는데 중요함 - help individuals keep clean: habituation 청결을 유지하려는 개인에게 영향을 미침: 습관화	- need more investment in medical research 의학 연구에 대한 더 많은 투자 필요 - other factors can improve health systems 보건 제도를 개선하기 위한 다른 요소들도 있음 ex) physical exercise, diet 운동, 식단

3 Environmental issues are so complex that individuals cannot do anything about them.

환경 문제는 너무 복잡해서 개인이 할 수 있는 것은 없다.

AGREE	DISAGREE
- government: sizable research + campaigns → greater effect 정부: 큰 연구 + 캠페인 → 더 큰 효과 - can take corresponding measures 상응하는 조치를 취할 수 있음	- individual's effort: builds up → national movement 개인의 노력: 축적함 → 국가적 운동 - daily routine that requires an individual's participation 개인의 참여를 요하는 일상 생활 ex) recycling and taking public transportation instead of driving a car 분리수거, 자동차 운전 대신 대중교통 이용

4 Many people are trying to preserve the environment now; nevertheless, it is impossible to improve the environment in the future. 많은 사람들은 환경을 보존하기 위해 노력한다. 그럼에도 불구하고, 미래에 환경을 개선하는 것이 불가능하다.

AGREE	DISAGREE
- too much destruction 너무 많은 파괴 ex) Japan 일본 - ongoing development + urbanization 계속되는 개발 + 도시화	- technological improvement 과학 기술의 발달 - regrowth of organisms 생물의 재성장 ex) trees 나무

ACTUAL TEST **14**

TOEFL® MAP

ACTUAL TEST Writing 2

15

Approximately fifty-five million years ago, the Eocene Epoch began. It lasted for roughly twenty-one million years. The Eocene Epoch is noted for both the rise of mammals during it and the marked increase in global temperatures, with the average temperature rising between five and seven degrees Celsius.

Some researchers attribute the global warming that occurred then to disruptions in ocean currents. According to these scientists, the currents in the ocean actually stopped flowing. Normally, one result of flowing currents is that warm water is displaced by cooler water. These currents can strongly affect the temperatures of the lands they pass near. However, when the ocean currents ceased flowing, warm water remained in place, which caused surface temperatures in numerous regions to rise.

Other experts attribute the Eocene warming to one or more major asteroid strikes on the planet. Around the time the Eocene Epoch began, an asteroid impacted North America and formed Chesapeake Bay, which is located in the eastern United States. There were some other large strikes in Siberia in Russia around that time as well. The impacts from these strikes could have caused debris and ash to go high in the atmosphere and stay there for years. As a result, a greenhouse effect would have occurred and made the Earth's temperatures rise significantly.

Finally, some believe that the release of massive amounts of methane into the atmosphere caused a global greenhouse effect. At the bottom of the oceans, there is a large amount of methane trapped in ice. Any warming of the Earth's oceans could have made the ice melt. This would have released the methane into the atmosphere. With so much methane in the air, the Earth's temperatures would have continued rising until much of it dissipated.

🎧 15-01

> **Directions** You have 20 minutes to plan and write your response. Your response will be judged on the basis of the quality of your writing and on how well your response presents the points in the lecture and their relationship to the passage. Typically, an effective response will be 150-225 words.

Question Summarize the points made in the lecture, being sure to explain how they cast doubt on specific points made in the reading passage.

CUT PASTE UNDO REDO   Hide Word Count : 0

Approximately fifty-five million years ago, the Eocene Epoch began. It lasted for roughly twenty-one million years. The Eocene Epoch is noted for both the rise of mammals during it and the marked increase in global temperatures, with the average temperature rising between five and seven degrees Celsius.

Some researchers attribute the global warming that occurred then to disruptions in ocean currents. According to these scientists, the currents in the ocean actually stopped flowing. Normally, one result of flowing currents is that warm water is displaced by cooler water. These currents can strongly affect the temperatures of the lands they pass near. However, when the ocean currents ceased flowing, warm water remained in place, which caused surface temperatures in numerous regions to rise.

Other experts attribute the Eocene warming to one or more major asteroid strikes on the planet. Around the time the Eocene Epoch began, an asteroid impacted North America and formed Chesapeake Bay, which is located in the eastern United States. There were some other large strikes in Siberia in Russia around that time as well. The impacts from these strikes could have caused debris and ash to go high in the atmosphere and stay there for years. As a result, a greenhouse effect would have occurred and made the Earth's temperatures rise significantly.

Finally, some believe that the release of massive amounts of methane into the atmosphere caused a global greenhouse effect. At the bottom of the oceans, there is a large amount of methane trapped in ice. Any warming of the Earth's oceans could have made the ice melt. This would have released the methane into the atmosphere. With so much methane in the air, the Earth's temperatures would have continued rising until much of it dissipated.

📝 NOTE-TAKING

global warming during the Eocene Epoch 시신세 동안의 지구 온난화

❶ *disruptions in ocean currents* 해류의 분열

- no flowing: warm water stays in place 흐름 ✕ : 따뜻한 물이 한 곳에 머무름

The modification of ocean currents would have trapped warm water in specific places.

❷ *asteroid strikes* 소행성 충돌

- debris + ash → atmosphere → temp. ↑ 잔해 + 재 → 대기 → 온도 ↑

After asteroid strikes, debris and ash thrown into the atmosphere resulted in rising temperatures during the period.

❸ *release of methane* 메탄의 방출

- ice melt → methane into atmosphere → temp. ↑ 녹은 얼음 → 대기로 메탄 유입 → 온도 ↑

Methane trapped under the ice was released into the atmosphere when the ice melted, causing the temperature to increase.

WORD REMINDER

approximately 대략   noted for ~으로 유명한   rise 상승   attribute ~에 돌리다   disruption 붕괴   current 흐름 displace 바꾸어 놓다
cease 중지하다   in place 제자리에   surface 표면   asteroid 소행성   impact 충돌하다   debris 잔해, 파편   significantly 상당히
release 방출하다   massive 엄청나게 큰   trap 좁은 장소에 가두다   atmosphere 대기   dissipate 흩뜨리다

---

theories on global warming during the Eocene Epoch: erroneous
시신세 동안의 지구 온난화에 관한 이론들: 잘못되었음

❶ *ocean currents: no factual basis* 해류: 사실적 근거 ✕

- computer modeling (ocean currents + influence on temp.) 컴퓨터 모델링 (해류 + 온도에 대한 영향)
- currents + waves: carry heat → but not enough transmission 해류 + 파도: 열을 운반 → 하지만 충분한 전달 ✕

Paraphrasing Example
No factual evidence can confirm any changes in ocean currents.

❷ *asteroid impact: affects temp. faster* 소행성 충돌: 온도에 더 빨리 영향을 끼침

- global warming during the Eocene: over a thousand years 시신세 동안의 온난화: 천 년에 걸쳐 일어났음
- should've returned to normal quickly 곧 원래대로 돌아왔어야 함

Paraphrasing Example
If the temperature had been affected by an asteroid impact, the alteration in temperature should have occurred faster.

❸ *methane: takes thousands of years to have any influence on temp.*
메탄: 온도에 영향을 미치기 위해서는 수천 년이 걸림

- should have been other factors to affect the temp. 온도에 영향을 미치는 다른 요소가 있었을 것임

Paraphrasing Example
If methane alone had caused the climate to change, it would have taken much longer.

WORD REMINDER

geological 지질학의   term 용어   endure 견디다   virtually 사실상   entire 전체의   basis 근거   transmit 옮기다   scale 규모   extinction 멸종
eliminate 제거하다

The lecturer argues that the theories on global warming during the Eocene Epoch are not supported with valid proof. This directly refutes the reading passage's claim that there are three possible factors which could have caused the rising temperatures during that time.

First, no factual evidence can confirm any changes in ocean currents. It has been found that the heat carried by ocean currents and waves is not transmitted strongly enough to affect the overall temperature of the Earth. This contradicts the claim from the reading passage that the modification of ocean currents would have trapped warm water in specific places.

On top of that, the lecturer contends that if the temperature had been affected by an asteroid impact, the alteration in temperature should have occurred faster, and the temperature should have returned to its previous range once the atmosphere had been purified. This rebuts the reading passage's claim that after asteroid strikes, debris and ash thrown into the atmosphere resulted in rising temperatures during the period.

Finally, the lecturer asserts that it seem impossible that methane could have affected the temperature. If methane alone had caused the climate to change, it would have taken much longer to occur. This contradicts the idea presented in the reading passage that methane trapped under the ice was released into the atmosphere, causing the temperature to increase.

WORD REMINDER

valid 타당한   proof 증거   factor 요소   confirm 확인하다   overall 총체적인   modification 변경   specific 특정한   alteration 변화
previous 이전의   purify 정화하다

Hide Word Count : 0

Directions Read the question below. You have 30 minutes to plan, write, and revise your essay. Typically, an effective response will contain a minimum of 300 words.

Question

Should children help their families with household chores, or should they study and play?

Use specific reasons and examples to support your answer.

HOUSEHOLD CHORES

- *sense of responsibility* 책임감
    - certain jobs: regular basis → helpful for the future 특정 일: 규칙성 → 미래에 도움이 됨
        Ex studies: children doing household chores → a higher chance of displaying a strong sense of
        responsibility at work 연구: 집안일을 하는 아이들 → 직장에서 강한 책임감을 가질 확률 ↑
            → accomplishment 성취감

- *harmony + unity* 화합 + 단합
    - understand difficulties of household chores 집안일의 어려움을 이해함
        Ex after doing dishes 설거지 후
            → understand mom better 엄마를 좀 더 잘 이해함

INTRODUCTION

generalization: how parents guide their children
일반화: 부모가 아이들을 어떻게 교육시키는가

⬇

influence children for the rest of their lives
아이의 전체적 삶에 대한 영향

⬇

thesis: household chores (responsibility, understanding + respect)
논제: 집안일 (책임감, 이해심 + 존중심)

STUDYING AND PLAYING

- *physical + social development* 체력 + 사회성 발달
    - children w/the same age group → build necessary skills 또래 집단 → 필요한 능력 형성
        Ex playing: running + cooperating skills → strengthen health 노는 것: 달리기 + 협력하는 능력 → 체력 강화
            → household chores → miss a chance to play + interact 집안일 → 놀기 + 교류의 기회를 놓침

- *set own studying habits* 스스로 공부하는 습관을 기름
    - each phase of life: diff. studying skills 삶의 각 단계: 다른 공부 능력
        Ex adding + subtraction: during childhood → ready for the next step in math later
        덧셈 + 뺄셈: 아동기에 학습 → 이후 다음 단계의 수학을 대비
            → household chores: can be taught at any time in life 집안일: 일생 동안 언제든지 배울 수 있음

INTRODUCTION

generalization: how parents guide their children
일반화: 부모가 아이들을 어떻게 교육시키는가

⬇

influence children for the rest of their lives
아이의 전체적 삶에 대한 영향

⬇

thesis: study + play (physical + social development, fundamental basis of studying)
논제: 공부 + 노는 것 (체력 + 사회적 발달, 공부의 기초)

How parents guide their children is crucial in child development. Parents' approaches can influence their children for the rest of their lives. Some people contend that children should concentrate on studying and playing. However, for two reasons, I strongly believe they should be assigned some household chores. Such chores both help children learn responsibility and aid them in developing a greater understanding of and more respect toward others.

Firstly, children can develop a sense of responsibility by doing household chores. Having certain jobs that must be done on a regular basis, children can be prepared for the future. For instance, many studies have proven that children who have been trained to do household chores have a greater chance of displaying a strong sense of responsibility at work when they reach adulthood. This also results in a great feeling of accomplishment for children.

Furthermore, cooperating with other members of a family can let children feel a sense of harmony and unity with their family members. By doing household chores with their family members, children will have a chance to understand the difficulties that their parents experience when doing jobs such as cleaning, gardening, and cooking. For example, when I was young, I could not see the difficulties that my mom had to go through when preparing each meal. Conversely, after doing the dishes on my own, I was able to understand, and I thanked my mom for doing that chore for the family even at times when she wanted to take a break.

It is true that studying and playing are necessary for children. However, assigning household chores does not mean that children have to spend a tremendous amount of time doing the work. Instead, having a few jobs at home will teach children responsibility and give them a sense of accomplishment. Moreover, children have a chance to realize that they are receiving help from other family members that they used to take for granted. For the above reasons, I assert that children should help their families with household chores rather than concentrate only on studying and playing.

> **WORD REMINDER**
>
> crucial 중요한   approach 접근법   rest 나머지   assign 할당하다   chore 가사   aid 돕다   respect 존중   on a regular basis 정기적으로
> prove 증명하다   display 나타내다   accomplishment 성취감   do the dishes 설거지하다   tremendous 대단한   realize 깨닫다
> take ~ for granted ~을 당연하게 받아들이다

TIPS for SUCCESS

독립형 에세이: 본론 Triple "E"s

본론은 보통 Triple "E"s (T E E E) 방식을 기억하자. 일단 중요한 아이디어가 되는 topic sentence를 쓴 후에, 보다 자세히 설명해 주는 explanation sentence가 나온다. 그리고 의견을 뒷받침해 주는 example이 나온 후 그 예를 좀 더 자세히 말해 주는 elaborating sentence가 나온다. 물론, 중간중간에 살을 붙여 주어도 좋고, 해당 단락의 내용을 다시 한 번 정리해 주는 closing sentence가 있어도 좋다. 두 번째 단락을 살펴보자.

T: Firstly, children can develop a sense of responsibility by doing household chores.

E: Having certain jobs that must be done on a regular basis, children can be prepared for the future.

E: For instance, many studies have proven that children who have been trained to do household chores have a greater chance of displaying a strong sense of responsibility at work when they reach adulthood.

E: This also results in a great feeling of accomplishment for children.

CUT   PASTE   UNDO   REDO

How parents guide their children is crucial in child development. Parents' approaches can influence their children for the rest of their lives. Some people contend that children should help with household chores. However, for two reasons, I strongly believe they should concentrate on studying and playing. Childhood is an important period in children's physical development, and the foundation for further learning is built up during this period.

Firstly, childhood is a critical time in children's physical and social development. Hence, playing and socializing with others in the same age group can help children develop necessary skills. For instance, playing often requires running and cooperating with others. It helps children strengthen their muscles and immune systems. On the other hand, if children are stuck doing household chores, they will not have a chance to learn to play and interact with others.

Furthermore, it is necessary that children set their own study habits. Each phase of life requires a different study skill, and it is important for children to spend very much time setting goals and working hard to achieve them. For example, addition and subtraction should be taught during childhood so that children are ready to take the next step in math later. While household chores can be taught at any time during people's lives, certain study skills and habits should be accomplished at specific times.

It is true that children learn responsibility and cooperation by doing household chores. However, these skills can also be taught by doing assignments and group tasks at school. Strengthening physical skills and developing social skills through play are very important in childhood. In addition, it is essential for children to establish a basis for studying for their futures. For the above reasons, I assert that children should play and study rather than help their families with household chores.

WORD REMINDER

physical 신체의   foundation 기초   critical 중대한   socialize 어울리다   strengthen 강화하다   muscle 근육   immune system 면역 체계
stick 붙이다   interact 서로 영향을 끼치다   addition 덧셈   subtraction 뺄셈   accomplish 성취하다   specific 특정한   assignment 과제
task 직무   essential 필수적인   establish 성립시키다   basis 기초

▉ TIPS for SUCCESS

독립형 에세이: 결론

결론을 어떻게 시작할지 난감할 경우, 자신이 설득하고자 하는 진술의 반대 의견에 대한 장점에 대해 짤막하게 쓴 후, 앞 두 본론의 이유들 때문에 자신은 동의 혹은 반대한다고 결론을 지을 수 있다. 일단 자신의 의견에 대한 반대 의견의 장점을 생각해 보자.

It is true that children learn responsibilities and cooperation by doing household chores.
(집안일을 하면서 책임감과 협동심을 배운다: 맞는 주장이다)

반대 의견의 장점에 대한 해결책 또는 본인이 주장했던 의견 두 개를 나열할 수 있다.

However, these skills can also be taught by pursuing assignments and group tasks at school.
(하지만, 이런 능력들은 학교에서 과제나 단체 임무를 수행하며 배울 수 있다: 역시 맞는 주장이다)

Strengthening physical skills and developing social skills through play are very important in childhood.
(체력 강화 + 사회 능력을 기르는 것은 아동기에 매우 중요하다: 설득력 있다)

In addition, it is essential for children to establish a basis for studying for their futures.
(미래를 위한 학습의 토대를 형성하는 것은 필수적이다: 더욱 확실한 설득력이 있다)

For the above reasons, I assert that children should play and study rather than help their families with household chores.
(자신의 주장을 다시 한번 언급하며 결론을 내린다)

1 Children should play sports for fun, not for competition. 아이들은 스포츠를 경쟁이 아닌 재미로 해야 한다.

AGREE	DISAGREE
- purpose: health + social skill 목적: 건강 + 어울리는 능력 - a child may become too competitive → stress + pressure 아이가 너무 경쟁적으로 될 수 있음 → 스트레스 + 압박감	- good-faith competition → improvement 선의의 경쟁 → 발전 - recognition for good results 좋은 결과에 대한 인정

2 To become a financially responsible adult, children should learn to manage their own money at an early age. 금전적으로 책임감 있는 성인이 되기 위해 아이들은 어릴 때부터 자신의 돈을 관리하는 것을 배워야 한다.

AGREE	DISAGREE
- would be able to learn consequences of excessive spending 과소비에 관한 결과에 대해 알 수 있음 - habit of saving 저축하는 습관	- rationality: not fully developed 이성: 아직 완전히 발달 ✕ - stress + frustration 스트레스 + 좌절

3 It is better for children to have jobs similar to those of their parents.
아이들은 부모님의 직업과 비슷한 직업을 갖는 것이 좋다.

AGREE	DISAGREE
- help from parents (advice) 부모님으로부터 도움을 받음 (조언) - more familiar w/the field 그 분야에 보다 더 친숙함	- freedom to choose what they want to do 하고 싶은 것을 선택하는 자유 - should consider aptitudes 적성을 고려해야 함

ACTUAL TEST **15**

165

TOEFL® MAP

ACTUAL TEST Writing 2

16

When dinosaurs ruled the Earth more than sixty-five million years ago, they had a variety of different appearances. One interesting feature about them, though, is that a great number of the fossils which have been unearthed show that many dinosaur species had a crest on their heads. Typically made of bone, some crests were small while others extended for more than a meter. The purpose of these crests has puzzled paleontologists for decades.

One group of scientists suspects that dinosaurs used their crests to smell with. By studying the fossilized remains of some dinosaurs, paleontologists have learned that dinosaurs' nasal cavities extended into their crests. Hadrosaurs are one group of dinosaurs that had elaborate crests. Lambeosaur, corythosaurus, and parasaurolophus are three species of hadrosaurs with crests. Due to their crests, many experts believe that these dinosaurs all had highly sensitive senses of smell.

During the age of dinosaurs, the average temperature on the Earth was much higher than it is in modern times. Thus some paleontologists believe that crested dinosaurs evolved so as to adapt to these hot temperatures. They speculate that their crests enabled them to regulate their body temperatures and therefore prevented them from overheating. Many dinosaurs are known to have stayed in the water to help cool themselves off. So it is possible that those dinosaurs that were not water bound—which included many that had crests—instead relied on different methods, such as crests, to keep cool.

A more recent theory is that dinosaurs used their crests to make sounds. Some claim that lambeosaurs in particular made use of their crests to communicate. Since the size and the appearance of each crest differed, so too did the sounds that individual lambeosaurs made. This would have made it possible for dinosaurs to recognize distinctive individuals.

🎧 16-01

Directions You have 20 minutes to plan and write your response. Your response will be judged on the basis of the quality of your writing and on how well your response presents the points in the lecture and their relationship to the passage. Typically, an effective response will be 150-225 words.

Question Summarize the points made in the lecture, being sure to explain how they cast doubt on specific points made in the reading passage.

CUT PASTE UNDO REDO   Hide Word Count : 0

When dinosaurs ruled the Earth more than sixty-five million years ago, they had a variety of different appearances. One interesting feature about them, though, is that a great number of the fossils which have been unearthed show that many dinosaur species had a crest on their heads. Typically made of bone, some crests were small while others extended for more than a meter. The purpose of these crests has puzzled paleontologists for decades.

One group of scientists suspects that dinosaurs used their crests to smell with. By studying the fossilized remains of some dinosaurs, paleontologists have learned that dinosaurs' nasal cavities extended into their crests. Hadrosaurs are one group of dinosaurs that had elaborate crests. Lambeosaur, corythosaurus, and parasaurolophus are three species of hadrosaurs with crests. Due to their crests, many experts believe that these dinosaurs all had highly sensitive senses of smell.

During the age of dinosaurs, the average temperature on the Earth was much higher than it is in modern times. Thus some paleontologists believe that crested dinosaurs evolved so as to adapt to these hot temperatures. They speculate that their crests enabled them to regulate their body temperatures and therefore prevented them from overheating. Many dinosaurs are known to have stayed in the water to help cool themselves off. So it is possible that those dinosaurs that were not water bound— which included many that had crests—instead relied on different methods, such as crests, to keep cool.

A more recent theory is that dinosaurs used their crests to make sounds. Some claim that lambeosaurs in particular made use of their crests to communicate. Since the size and the appearance of each crest differed, so too did the sounds that individual lambeosaurs made. This would have made it possible for dinosaurs to recognize distinctive individuals.

uses of dinosaurs' crests 공룡의 볏의 용도

❶ *to smell* 냄새를 맡기 위해서
- nasal cavities: extended to crests 비강: 볏까지 뻗쳐 있음
  Ex hadrosaurs 하드로사우르스

   It is feasible that their crests helped dinosaurs smell effectively.

❷ *to control body temperature* 체온 조절을 하기 위해서
- avrg temp.: higher than now 평균 기온: 오늘날보다 높았음
- crest: adaptation (prevent from overheating) 볏: 적응 (과열 방지)

   Many dinosaurs living away from water would probably have used their crests to regulate their body temperatures.

❸ *to communicate* 의사소통을 하기 위해서
- each crest: diff. size + shape 각각의 볏: 다른 크기와 모양
  → diff. sound 다른 소리

  Paraphrasing Example It has recently been discovered that dinosaurs used their crests as a means to communicate.

WORD REMINDER

feature 특징   unearth 발굴하다   species 종(種)   crest 볏   extended 쭉 뻗은   paleontologist 고생물학자   suspect 추측하다
remain 유골   fossilize 화석으로 되다   nasal 코의   cavity 강(腔)   elaborate 정교한   evolve 진화하다   adapt 적응하다   speculate 추측하다
regulate 조절하다   prevent 막다   overheat 과열시키다   cool off 식히다   rely on ~에 의지하다   in particular 특히   recognize 인지하다
distinctive 특유의

none of the theories is reliable 그 어떤 이론도 타당성이 없음

❶ *olfactory: related to size of brain* 후각: 뇌의 크기와 연관이 있음
- animals w/a good sense of smell: well-developed brain 훌륭한 후각을 가진 동물: 잘 발달된 뇌
- many hadrosaurs: tiny brains 많은 하드로사우르스: 작은 뇌

   The small brain cavities made it impossible for dinosaurs to have used their crests to heighten their sense of smell.

❷ *crest: too small to control body temperature* 볏: 체온을 조절하기에는 너무 작음
- some possessed bones to keep bodies cool 일부 공룡들은 몸을 시원히 유지해 주는 뼈들을 가지고 있음
- triceratops: frills → diffuse heat + remain cool 트리케라톱스: 프릴 → 열을 분산 + 시원함 유지

  Paraphrasing Example Though it has been proposed that dinosaurs utilized their crests to cool off, the sizes were not big enough for that purpose.

❸ *communication: only one species* 의사소통: 단 한 종만 했음
- only lambeosaurs could communicate 오직 람베오사우르스만이 의사소통을 할 수 있었음

   While lambeosaurs are known for communicating among themselves by using their crests, other dinosaurs with crests did not have the ability to communicate with each other.

WORD REMINDER

notice 알아채다   outlandish 기이한   spiked 머리칼이 위로 선   hairdo 머리 모양   purpose 목적   enhance 강화하다   walnut 호두
tiny 아주 작은   lack 결핍하다   postulate 가정하다   plate 등 딱지   enormous 거대한   frill 가장자리 주름, 목 털   diffuse 발산하다 remain 남다
promise 전망, 가망   definitely 확실히   jump to conclusions 속단하다

ACTUAL TEST **16**

The lecturer argues that none of the theories about the uses of a dinosaur's crest is reliable. This directly refutes the reading passage's claim that the crests must have served some purpose and that there are many theories postulating their uses.

First, dinosaurs' small brain cavities made it impossible for them to have used their crests to heighten their sense of smell. To be specific, many dinosaurs with crests possessed very small brains, which made it implausible for their crests to have served as extensions of their olfactory organs. This fact contradicts the reading passage's claim that it is feasible that their crests helped dinosaurs smell effectively.

On top of that, the speculation that their crests were used to maintain their body temperatures is also invalid. Though it has been proposed that dinosaurs utilized their crests to cool off, the crests were not big enough for that purpose. This casts doubt on the reading passage's claim that many dinosaurs living away from water probably used their crests to regulate their body temperatures.

Finally, although lambeosaurs are known for communicating among themselves by using their crests, other dinosaurs with crests did not have the ability to communicate with one another. This disproves the idea presented in the reading passage that it has recently been discovered that dinosaurs used their crests as a means to communicate.

WORD REMINDER

reliable 믿을 수 있는   possess 소유하다   extension 확장   olfactory 후각의   organ 장기   feasible 가능한   utilize 이용하다   means 수단

TIPS for SUCCESS

관계대명사의 생략

관계대명사가 주격일 경우 be동사의 생략이 가능하다. 세 번째 단락의 문장을 살펴보자.

This casts doubt on the reading passage's claim that many dinosaurs (which were) living away from water probably used their crests to regulate their body temperatures.

위의 문장에서 many dinosaurs 다음에는 which were living away from water가 맞지만 which were 가 생략되어서 living away from water만 쓰였다.

또한, 관계대명사의 목적격 역시 생략이 가능한데, 관계대명사 다음 〈주어 + 타동사〉가 나왔음에도 불구하고 뒤에 목적어가 없거나 〈주어 + 자동사 + 전치사〉 다음 목적어가 나오지 않았을 경우에는 목적격 관계대명사가 생략된 것이다. 다음의 문장을 살펴보자.

Customers should have the right to choose products (which) they are interested in.

만약 they are가 없으면 Customers should have the right to choose products, which are interested in. 즉, 물건이 흥미를 느끼게 되므로 이상한 문장이 된다. 하지만 in이라는 전치사 다음에 목적어가 없기 때문에 목적격 관계대명사가 생략되었다는 점을 알 수 있다.

Hide Word Count : 0

Directions Read the question below. You have 30 minutes to plan, write, and revise your essay. Typically, an effective response will contain a minimum of 300 words.

Question

Neighbors are people who live near others. In your opinion, what type of neighbor is the best to have?

- Someone who is quiet
- Someone who is similar to yourself
- Someone who is supportive

Use specific reasons and examples to support your answer.

📝 NOTE-TAKING

- ***good rest @ home*** 집에서는 충분한 휴식
  - necessary to provide quiet environment for each other 서로 조용한 환경 제공: 필요함
    Ex long meeting → deserves good night's sleep 긴 회의 → 숙면 필요
  - loud music / party → impossible to relax / get enough sleep → possibility of sleep disorders
    큰 음악 소리 / 파티 → 휴식 / 숙면이 불가능 → 수면 장애 가능성

- ***privacy: most important*** 사생활: 가장 중요함
  - keeping sound ↓: basic + must-do manner 소리 ↓: 기본 + 지켜야 하는 매너
    Ex condos / apts: able to hear people upstairs 콘도 / 아파트: 위층 사람들을 들을 수 있음
  - extremely stressful → dispute 굉장한 스트레스 → 갈등

INTRODUCTION

generalization: home: security, happiness, and a sense of belonging
일반화: 집: 안전, 행복, 소속감

⬇

crucial to think about factors when choosing home → neighbor
집을 고를 때 요소에 대해 생각하는 것이 중요함 → 이웃

⬇

thesis: someone quiet (resting environment + privacy)
논제: 조용한 사람 (쉬는 환경 + 사생활)

- ***easier to understand each other*** 서로 이해하기 쉬움
  - introverted neighbor + extroverted neighbor = conflict 내성적인 이웃 + 외향적인 이웃 = 갈등
    Ex extrovert: party → introvert: stressed out 외향적인 사람: 파티 → 내성적인 사람: 스트레스
    → possible dispute 분쟁의 가능성

- ***share interests*** 흥미거리 공유
  - **Ex** watching sports and making noise → tough for one who never cheers for a team
    스포츠 경기를 보며 시끄럽게 하는 것 → 스포츠 팀을 응원하지 않는 사람에게는 힘든 일
  - both like watching sports: share thoughts / watch together
    둘 다 경기 관람을 좋아하는 경우: 생각 공유 / 함께 관람
  - able to appreciate similar hobbies / exchange opinions: joy
    비슷한 취미를 즐길 수 있는 것 / 의견을 공유할 수 있는 것: 즐거움

generalization: home: security, happiness, and a sense of belonging
일반화: 집: 안전, 행복, 소속감

⬇

crucial to think about factors when choosing home ➡ neighbor
집을 고를 때 요소에 대해 생각하는 것이 중요함 → 이웃

⬇

thesis: someone similar (understanding + share interests)
논제: 비슷한 사람 (이해심 + 흥미 분야 공유)

Someone Supportive

- ● *in case of emergency* 응급 상황일 경우
  - – irrational when facing urgent situation: stay together + help 위급 상황 시 비이성적으로 변함: 같이 있어 주고 도와줌
    Ex hurt: hard for a fam member to think logically 부상: 식구는 논리적으로 생각하기 어려움
    ➡ neighbor: calm the person down + find way to help the one injured
    이웃: 식구를 진정시킴 + 부상당한 사람을 도울 방법을 찾음

- ● *+ve reinforcement: full of energy + optimism* 긍정적 강화: 넘치는 에너지 + 긍정적인 마음
  - – cheer up / make confident + content 응원 / 자신감 + 행복
    Ex compliment on trivial matters ➡ make neighbor happy 사소한 것에 대한 칭찬 → 이웃을 기쁘게 해 줌
  - – meaningful ∵ people put too much value on privacy these days
    의미 있음 ∵ 요즘 사람들은 사생활에 너무 많은 가치를 둠

generalization: home: security, happiness, and a sense of belonging
일반화: 집: 안전, 행복, 소속감

⬇

crucial to think about factors when choosing home ➡ neighbor
집을 고를 때 요소에 대해 생각하는 것이 중요함 → 이웃

⬇

thesis: someone supportive (understanding ➡ +ve reinforcement)
논제: 힘이 되어주는 사람 (이해심 + 긍정적 강화)

CUT　PASTE　UNDO　REDO

A home provides security and happiness. Thus, it is crucial to think about some important factors when choosing a place to live. Among these factors are people's neighbors. If the place where people should feel the most comfortable turns into a place where people instead get stressed out, the home will not serve its purpose anymore. Hence, I strongly believe someone who is quiet would be the best neighbor to have. The reason is that people need a restful environment and privacy.

First of all, people need to get good rest at home. It is necessary that neighbors provide a quiet environment for one another. For instance, if a person has had a long meeting at work, he deserves to sleep well at night. On the other hand, if a neighbor turns on some loud music until late or has a party, it would be hard for the person to relax and get a good night's sleep. This could even lead to sleep disorders.

On top of that, many people consider privacy the utmost important factor when selecting a place to dwell. In order to respect others' privacy, keeping noise down is basic good manners. To be specific, this happens a lot in condos and apartments, where people can hear what is going on upstairs, especially if the building is old. The noise can be extremely stressful and often causes disputes between neighbors.

Each person has different standards when deciding on a place to live. It is true that there is no such thing as a perfect neighbor. It might be good to have neighbors who can enjoy the same hobbies together; nevertheless, anyone would admit that providing a quiet environment and respecting privacy would easily outweigh the advantages of having shared interests. Therefore, in my opinion, the best type of neighbor to have is someone who is quiet.

WORD REMINDER

crucial 중요한　factor 요인　deserve (~할 만한) 가치가 있다　utmost 최고의　dwell 거주하다　dispute 갈등　outweigh 우세하다

TIPS for SUCCESS

단수형일 때와 복수형일 때 의미가 바뀌는 단어들이 있다. 아래의 단어들을 살펴보자. (A~F)

air	공기; 태도	airs	뽐내는 꼴
arm	팔	arms	무기
condition	상태	conditions	지불 조건
content	취지; (형식에 대한) 내용	contents	내용물, 목차
custom	관습	customs	세관
damage	손해, 피해	damages	배상금
earning	획득	earnings	소득
effect	효과	effects	물품, 소유물
electronic	전자의	electronics	전자 공학
facility	쉬움; 재능	facilities	시설
feature	특징; 얼굴의 어느 한 부분	features	용모

CUT PASTE UNDO REDO

A home provides security and happiness. Thus, it is crucial to think about some important factors when choosing a place to live. Among these factors are people's neighbors. If the place where people should feel the most comfortable turns into a place where people instead get stressed out, the home will not serve its purpose anymore. Hence, I strongly believe someone with similarities to myself would be the best neighbor to have. The reason is that the neighbor can be more understanding and share the same interests.

First of all, it is difficult for people who are too different to understand one another. To be specific, if one person is introverted but the person living next door is extroverted, conflict is inevitable. For instance, if the latter person loves having parties until late at night every weekend, the other one would get extremely stressed out due to the noise and the music. This will eventually lead to a dispute between the two.

On top of that, being able to appreciate similar hobbies and exchange opinions about them can make living in a certain neighborhood more enjoyable. For instance, if only one neighbor enjoys watching sports, it can be very tough for a person who never cheers for a team to understand the neighbor, who might become very noisy during a game. However, if both of them like watching sports, they can share their thoughts and even watch games together.

Each person has different standards when deciding on a place to live. It is true that there is no such thing as a perfect neighbor. It might be good to have neighbors who are quiet and do not disturb other people's privacy; nevertheless, anyone would admit that being able to understand others and sharing common interests would easily outweigh other advantages. Therefore, in my opinion, the best type of neighbor to have is someone with similarities to myself.

WORD REMINDER

introverted 내성적인　extroverted 외향적인　conflict 갈등　inevitable 불가피한　appreciate 감상하다　disturb 방해하다　admit 인정하다

TIPS for SUCCESS

단수형일 때와 복수형일 때 의미가 바뀌는 단어들이 있다. 아래의 단어들을 살펴보자. (G~P)

glass	유리	glasses	안경
good	훌륭한	goods	상품
irregularity	불규칙	irregularities	부정 행위
letter	편지; 글자	letters	증서; 문학; 학문
manner	방법	manners	풍습, 예의범절
mean	의미하다	means	수단, 방법
moral	교훈	morals	품행, 도덕
odd	이상한, 홀수의	odds	여분
pain	아픔; 고통	pains	고생, 노력
power	힘	powers	대국, 강국
premise	전제	premises	토지, 건물
provision	규정	provisions	식량

ACTUAL TEST **16**

A home provides security and happiness. Thus, it is crucial to think about some important factors when choosing a place to live. Among these factors are people's neighbors. If the place where people should feel the most comfortable turns into a place where people instead get stressed out, the home will not serve its purpose anymore. Hence, I strongly believe someone who is supportive would be the best neighbor to have. The reason is that the neighbor can be understanding and give positive reinforcement.

First, it is crucial to have a supportive neighbor, especially in case of an emergency. People tend to become irrational facing urgent situations. Thus, it is helpful to have a neighbor who can stay calm and give a hand when needed. For instance, when someone is hurt, it is often hard for a family member not to panic. A supportive neighbor can try to calm the person down and find a way to aid the injured person.

On top of that, neighbors who constantly provide positive reinforcement are always full of energy and optimism. Reinforcers can cheer up people or make them confident. For example, giving a compliment on a trivial matter like a hairstyle or clothing is more than enough to make a person content. This, in fact, is especially meaningful nowadays as people put too much value on privacy and tend to keep away from others.

Each person has different standards when deciding on a place to live. It is true that there is no such thing as a perfect neighbor. It might be good to have neighbors who respect others' privacy; nevertheless, anyone would admit that being able to understand and continually give positive reinforcement would easily outweigh being indifferent. Therefore, in my opinion, the best type of neighbor to have is someone who is supportive.

WORD REMINDER

supportive 힘이 되는   positive reinforcement 긍정적 강화   irrational 비이성적인   urgent 긴급한   panic 공포   aid 도움이 되다
optimism 낙천주의   content 만족하는   compliment 찬사   trivial 사소한   infeasible 실행 불가능한   indifferent 무관심한

TIPS for SUCCESS

단수형일 때와 복수형일 때 의미가 바뀌는 단어들이 있다. 아래의 단어들을 살펴보자. (Q~Z)

quarter	1/4; 지역	quarters	숙소
regard	관계; 존중	regards	(편지에서의) 안부 인사
sanction	허용	sanctions	(국제법 위반에 대한) 제재 규약
sale	판매	sales	매출액
saving	절약	savings	저축
spectacle	볼만한 것	spectacles	안경
statistic	통계치	statistics	통계학, 통계표
term	기간; 말	terms	조건; (친한) 사이; 말투
time	시간	times	시대; 경험
value	가치	values	가치관
work	일	works	공사; 공장
water	물	the waters	바다; 탄산수

RELATED TOPICS

1 Which of the following values do you think is the most important to teach a young child? Use specific reasons and examples to support your choice.

어린 아이를 가르칠 때 다음 중 어떤 가치가 가장 중요하다고 생각하는가? 구체적인 이유와 예를 들어 자신의 선택을 뒷받침하시오.

- Being honest   • Being helpful   • Being patient

BEING HONEST

- fundamental factor in interpersonal relationships
  대인 관계에 있어 기본적인 요소
- can be confident in self 스스로에게 떳떳할 수 있음

BEING HELPFUL

- fundamental factor in interpersonal relationships
  대인 관계에 있어 기본적인 요소
- learn to feel happiness through help
  도움을 통해 행복을 느끼는 방법을 배움

BEING PATIENT

- fundamental factor in interpersonal relationships 대인 관계에 있어 기본적인 요소
- good training to be prepared for difficult situations 어려운 상황에 대비하는 훌륭한 연습

2 You have been given a gift of money. Which of the following would you spend it on? Use specific reasons and examples to support your choice.

당신에게 선물로 현금이 주어졌다. 다음 중 어떤 곳에 사용을 하겠는가? 구체적인 이유와 예를 들어 자신의 선택을 뒷받침하시오.

- A piece of jewelry   • A pair of concert tickets   • An expensive meal

A PIECE OF JEWELRY

- investment 투자
- able to keep it for a long time 오래 간직할 수 있음

A PAIR OF CONCERT TICKETS

- emotional wealth 감정적 풍부함
- able to enjoy my favorite hobby with a friend / family
  가장 좋아하는 취미를 친구 / 식구와 즐길 수 있음

AN EXPENSIVE MEAL

- great way to celebrate the gift 선물을 기념할 수 있는 훌륭한 방법
- able to enjoy a special moment with a friend / family 특별한 순간을 친구 / 식구와 함께 할 수 있음

3 You are going to start a new business. Which of the following do you feel is the most important to becoming successful? Use specific reasons and examples to support your choice.

당신은 새로운 사업을 시작하려 한다. 성공하기 위해서는 다음 중 어떤 것이 가장 중요한가? 구체적인 이유와 예를 들어 자신의 선택을 뒷받침하시오.

- Enough capital   • Good workers   • Great products

ENOUGH CAPITAL

- if out of money → cannot continue with the business
  돈이 떨어진다면 → 사업을 계속 진행하는 것은 불가능
- need a lot of investment in the beginning
  초반에는 투자금이 많이 필요함

GOOD WORKERS

- ability and effort will produce good results
  능력과 노력이 좋은 결과를 가져옴
- cooperation and harmony → important factors at work
  협동과 조화 → 직장에서 중요한 요소

GREAT PRODUCTS

- good quality → many buyers → success 좋은 질 → 많은 구매자 → 성공
- able to draw attention from investors 투자자들로부터 많은 관심을 끌 수 있음

TOEFL® MAP

ACTUAL TEST Writing 2

17

Prior to the rise of the Roman Republic in the sixth century B.C., the Italian Peninsula was dominated by the Etruscan people. For centuries, the Etruscans' origins have been shrouded in mystery. Yet there is evidence—from both ancient and modern sources—that the Etruscans came from an area in what is the modern-day nation of Turkey.

The first evidence linking the Etruscans to ancient Turkey is found in the writings of Herodotus, the man considered "the Father of History." Herodotus lived in the fifth century B.C., and his most famous work is *The Histories*. In one section of it, he notes that the Etruscans emigrated from Lydia, which was located in western Turkey. Herodotus wrote that there was a famine in Lydia which lasted for eighteen years. Because of the famine, half of Lydia's population was sent out of the country. They sailed from the port of Smyrna and eventually landed at Umbria, a region in Italy.

Linguists have supported Herodotus's claims by noticing some similarities between ancient Etruscan and another language found in an inscription on Lemnos, a Greek island near Lydia. Etruscan has never been translated, so its origins are unknown. Perhaps the people of Lydia made the inscription on their way to Umbria. Over time, it is possible that their language evolved and changed into Etruscan.

Finally, studies on the DNA of four ancient breeds of cows in Tuscany, Italy, have revealed that they are similar to some cows from Turkey. Only the cows in Tuscany, which was the primary region in which the Etruscans lived, had any similarities to the cows in Turkey. No other cows in Italy were related at all. Thus some conclude that both the Etruscans and their cows arrived in Italy by ships they sailed from Turkey.

🎧 17-01

Directions You have 20 minutes to plan and write your response. Your response will be judged on the basis of the quality of your writing and on how well your response presents the points in the lecture and their relationship to the passage. Typically, an effective response will be 150-225 words.

Question Summarize the points made in the lecture, being sure to explain how they challenge specific claims made in the reading passage.

CUT   PASTE   UNDO   REDO   Hide Word Count : 0

Prior to the rise of the Roman Republic in the sixth century B.C., the Italian Peninsula was dominated by the Etruscan people. For centuries, the Etruscans' origins have been shrouded in mystery. Yet there is evidence—from both ancient and modern sources—that the Etruscans came from an area in what is the modern-day nation of Turkey.

The first evidence linking the Etruscans to ancient Turkey is found in the writings of Herodotus, the man considered "the Father of History." Herodotus lived in the fifth century B.C., and his most famous work is *The Histories*. In one section of it, he notes that the Etruscans emigrated from Lydia, which was located in western Turkey. Herodotus wrote that there was a famine in Lydia which lasted for eighteen years. Because of the famine, half of Lydia's population was sent out of the country. They sailed from the port of Smyrna and eventually landed at Umbria, a region in Italy.

Linguists have supported Herodotus's claims by noticing some similarities between ancient Etruscan and another language found in an inscription on Lemnos, a Greek island near Lydia. Etruscan has never been translated, so its origins are unknown. Perhaps the people of Lydia made the inscription on their way to Umbria. Over time, it is possible that their language evolved and changed into Etruscan.

Finally, studies on the DNA of four ancient breeds of cows in Tuscany, Italy, have revealed that they are similar to some cows from Turkey. Only the cows in Tuscany, which was the primary region in which the Etruscans lived, had any similarities to the cows in Turkey. No other cows in Italy were related at all. Thus some conclude that both the Etruscans and their cows arrived in Italy by ships they sailed from Turkey.

NOTE-TAKING

READING

the Etruscans are from Turkey 에투르리아인은 터키로부터 왔음

❶ *writings by Herodotus* 헤로도투스의 저서들

- *The Histories* → famine in Lydia sent half of population to Umbria
  The Histories → 리디아의 기아가 인구의 반을 움브리아로 보냈음

Famine forced the people of Lydia to migrate to Umbria.

❷ *similarities in language in an inscription* 비문의 언어의 유사점

- language by people of Lydia → evolved + changed into Etruscan
  리디아의 사람들에 의한 언어 → 진화 + 에투르리아 언어로 바뀜

The language found on the inscription proves that the language of Lydia evolved into Etruscan.

❸ *DNA similarities of cows* 소 DNA의 유사점

- cows in Tuscany + cows in Turkey 토스카나의 소 + 터키의 소

The genetic resemblance between cows in the two places suggests that the cows were brought to Tuscany by people from Turkey.

WORD REMINDER

prior to ~에 앞서 peninsula 반도 dominate 지배하다 origin 기원, 발단 shroud 숨기다 mystery 수수께끼 source 근거 link 연결하다
emigrate 이주하다 famine 기근 linguist 언어학자 inscription (책·금석에) 새겨진 글, 비문 translate 해석하다 evolve 진화하다 breed 품종
reveal 나타내다 primary 주요한

LISTENING

the origin of the Etruscans: doubtful 에투르리아인의 기원: 의문

❶ *Herodotus: historian but also fabricator* 헤로도투스: 역사가이지만 조작자이기도 함

- wrote stories about monsters 괴물에 관한 이야기들을 집필
  ∴ not always reliable 언제나 믿을만 하지는 않음

Though Herodotus remains a renowned historian, his stories are not always factual.

❷ *inscription on Lemnos: not sure of its origin* 림노스에 새겨진 글자: 기원이 불확실함

- people from Lydia left it 리디아의 사람들이 그것을 남김
- Etruscan sailors left it (engaged in maritime trade on the Mediterranean)
  에투르리아 선원들이 남긴 것 (지중해에서 무역에 종사하였음)

There are two possible origins for the language.

❸ *DNA evidence: true DNA* 증거: 사실

- cows: imported from Asia Minor by a merchant 소: 상인에 의해 소아시아로부터 수입

Despite reliable evidence of genetic similarities between the DNA of Turkish and Tuscan cows, how the cows got to Tuscany is unknown.

WORD REMINDER

front-page 제 1면 article 기사 clear up (문제, 의문 등을) 풀다 poke (구멍을) 내다 cite 언급하다 authority 권위자 definitely 확실히
invaluable 매우 귀중한 fabricator 제작자; 이야기를 지어내는 사람 supposedly 아마도 reliable 믿을 수 있는 bear 나타내다
the other way around 역으로 engage in 종사하다 import 수입하다 merchant 상인 refugee 피난자 adapt 적응하다

ACTUAL TEST **17**

The lecturer argues that he doubts a certain theory on the origin of the Etruscans. This directly contradicts the claim made in the reading that three pieces of evidence support the theory that the Etruscans originated in Turkey.

First, though Herodotus remains a renowned and very important figure in the field of history, his stories are not always factual. He even wrote about monsters as if they actually existed. This fact casts doubt on his assertion in *The Histories*, restated in the reading passage, that a famine forced the people of Lydia to migrate to Umbria.

Furthermore, the lecturer contends that there are two possible origins for the Etruscan language. One possibility is that people from Lydia left the inscription, and the other is that Etruscan sailors left it as the Etruscans were involved in trade on the Mediterranean. This rebuts the reading passage's claim that the language found in the inscription proves that the language of Lydia evolved into Etruscan.

Finally, the lecturer asserts that despite genetic similarities between the DNA of Turkish and Tuscan cows, how the cows got to Tuscany is unknown. It is highly likely that the cows were introduced to Turkey by an Etruscan merchant. This challenges the idea presented in the reading passage that the genetic resemblance suggest that the cows were brought to Tuscany by people from Turkey.

▶ WORD REMINDER

remain 남다   renowned 유명한   factual 사실에 기반을 둔   as if 마치 ~인 것처럼   restate 다시 말하다   famine 기근   migrate 이주하다
involve in ~에 관여하게 만들다   despite ~에도 불구하고   introduce 들여오다   resemblance 유사점

■ TIPS for SUCCESS

약자Abbreviation

형식을 갖춘 에세이를 쓸 때 줄임말은 가급적 삼가는 것이 좋다. '등등'의 의미를 가지고 있는 etc.(et cetera)를 쓰는 학생들이 많은데 such as나 including을 나열된 단어들 앞에 써서 일부의 예를 나타낸다는 뜻을 전달하는 것이 더 좋다. 즉, There are many similarities, **such as** DNA, origin, language, etc.는 피하는 것이 좋다. 대신 There are many similarities, **such as** DNA, origin, and language.에서 볼 수 있듯이, such as는 모든 것이 아닌 일부의 예를 나타내는 표현이므로 2~3개를 나열한 후 마지막 단어 전에 and나 or을 쓰면 된다.

   Hide Word Count : 0

Directions Read the question below. You have 30 minutes to plan, write, and revise your essay. Typically, an effective response will contain a minimum of 300 words.

Question

Do you agree or disagree with the following statement?

A person's way of dressing is a good indicator of that individual's personality.

Use specific reasons and examples to support your answer.

AGREE

- *expectations of how others interpret them* 다른 이들이 어떻게 판단하는지에 대한 기대
  - express themselves through clothing 옷을 통해 자신을 표현
    Ex neat + organized → suit 깔끔함 + 정돈됨 → 정장
    hippies: unique way of dressing → carefree + love-oriented characters
    히피: 특이한 옷차림 → 자유 + 사랑을 지향하는 성격

- *messages to express interests / especially hates* 관심사 / 특히 싫어하는 것을 표현하는 메시지
  Ex political activists: campaigning slogan on clothing 정치 운동가: 옷에 캠페인 표어
    → liberal + active personality 자유롭고 활동적인 성격
  Ex shirt w/offensive illustrations against a radical movement
    급진적인 운동에 대항하는 혐오스러운 삽화의 티셔츠
    → conservative + defending personality 보수적 + 방어적 성격

INTRODUCTION

generalization: many factors in judging a person's character
일반화: 한 사람의 성격을 판단하는 많은 요소들

⬇

manners / attitudes, appearance, speech
예의범절 / 태도, 외모, 말투

⬇

thesis: agree (awareness toward others' interpretation, messages clothing carries)
논제: 반대 (다른 이들의 판단에 대한 자각, 옷이 전달해 주는 메시지)

DISAGREE

- *trend / influence* 유행 / 영향
  - impact on a way of wearing an outfit 옷을 입는 것에 영향을 끼침
    Ex friend: wanted to wear clothing in hip-hop style 친구: 힙합 스타일의 옷을 입고 싶어했음
      → had to listen to parents → dressed in preppy style 부모님 말씀을 들었어야 했음 → 학생 스타일로 입음

- *depending on situation / rules at work* 상황 / 직장의 규칙에 달렸음
  - corporation: practicality + unity → dress codes 기업: 실용성 + 통일성 → 복장 규정
    Ex cousin w/a cheerful personality: prefers brightly colored clothing 명랑한 성격의 사촌: 밝은 색상의 옷 선호
      → company: requires suits with dark tones 회사: 어두운 계열의 정장 요구

INTRODUCTION

generalization: many factors in judging a person's character
일반화: 한 사람의 성격을 판단하는 많은 요소들

manners / attitudes, appearance, speech
예의범절 / 태도, 외모, 말투

⬇

thesis: disagree (influence from others, circumstances + jobs)
논제: 찬성 (다른 이들의 영향, 상황 + 직장)

There are many factors that influence us when judging a person's character. These factors include one's manners or attitudes, appearance, and speech. Some contend that a person's way of dressing does not reflect his or her traits. However, I strongly believe that clothing is a good indicator of one's personality because one's way of dressing shows how one expects to be seen by others. In addition, clothing can display messages that mirror one's character.

First off, wearing certain clothes comes from our expectations of how other people will see us. Hence, people try to express their nature through their outfits. For example, people who are neat and organized prefer wearing suits to wearing hip-hop pants. On the other hand, hippies in the 1960s wore clothes that were very different and showed off their personalities. Their unique way of dressing reflected their carefree and love-oriented personalities.

On top of this, some people wear clothing with messages to let people know what they like. To illustrate, people who are interested in politics may wear shirts that feature the campaign slogan of their favorite politician. In addition, other people wear clothing that identifies their favorite sports teams, musicians, and outdoor activities. For instance, my older brother often wears shirts that have pictures of the members of his favorite rock bands on them. As a result, it is possible to learn a lot about people just by looking at the clothes that they wear.

It is true that certain jobs and circumstances require people to dress in ways that could be very different from their own styles. However, those jobs and circumstances cannot completely change people's styles. In other words, they will wear whichever clothing they want to wear once they are out of their workplace or the situation for which they must follow a dress code. Because people are aware that others may assess their personalities by looking at their clothes, dressing in a particular style is a means to show one's nature. Furthermore, people wear clothing with certain messages they would like to deliver. For the above reasons, I agree with the statement that one's way of dressing is a good indicator of one's personality.

WORD REMINDER

factor 요소   judge 판단하다   attitude 태도   reflect 반영하다   indicator 척도   expect 기대하다   mirror 반영하다   nature 성질, 본성
outfit 의상 한 벌   carefree 자유로운   feature ~을 특징으로 삼다   campaign slogan 캠페인 구호   politician 정치인
identify (신원 등을) 알아보게 하다   musician 음악가, 뮤지션   outdoor activity 실외 활동   circumstance 상황   assess 평가하다
particular 특정한   deliver 전달하다

There are many factors that influence us when judging a person's character. These factors include one's manners or attitudes, appearance, and speech. Some contend that a person's way of dressing is a good indicator of his or her personality. However, I strongly believe that clothing does not really reflect a person's traits. For one thing, other influences may affect how a person dresses. In addition, certain circumstances and jobs require a different way of dressing regardless of one's individual tastes.

First off, a desire to follow trends may keep us from dressing according to our own styles. Moreover, influence from others may have a great impact on our way of wearing outfits. For instance, my friend's parents have always been very conservative in terms of clothing and required that my friend dress to their standards. Consequently, even though my friend was once fascinated by hip-hop music and wanted to dress in a style reflecting his interest, he had to listen to his parents and wear preppy-style clothes instead.

On top of that, no matter how they wish to dress, some people have to wear appropriate clothing depending on rules at work or school. Since many corporations emphasize unity as well as practicality and set corresponding dress codes, employees are responsible for wearing clothing that will satisfy the regulations. To illustrate, my cousin has a very cheerful personality and likes to wear brightly colored clothing. Nevertheless, her job as a consultant is based on rationality and trust, so the company she works for asks her to wear suits with dark tones.

It is true that numerous people judge us according to how we dress because they believe one's appearance mirrors one's character. However, influence from other individuals or from society at large plays a crucial role in choosing clothes. Furthermore, many companies and circumstances have specific dress codes that do not necessarily reflect one's own tastes. For the above reasons, I disagree with the statement that one's way of dressing is a good indicator of one's personality.

▶ **WORD REMINDER**

trait 특성 influence 영향 affect ~에 영향을 미치다 regardless of ~에 개의치 않고 taste 취향 trend 유행 impact 영향
standard 기준 fascinated 매료된 appropriate 적절한 corporation 기업 emphasize 강조하다 unity 통일성 practicality 실용성
corresponding 상응하는 regulation 규칙 cheerful 명랑한 rationality 합리성 numerous 많은 crucial 중요한 role 역할

■ **TIPS for SUCCESS**

당위성 동사 (가정법)

말하는 사람의 요구나 권고 등의 의견을 나타낼 때 쓰이며, 어떠한 일의 당위성 혹은 중요성을 나타내는 동사가 that절을 동반할 경우 쓰인다. 〈당위성 동사 + that절 + should + 동사원형〉으로 이루어져 있으며, should는 일반적으로 생략하는 경우가 많다. 두 번째 단락의 문장을 살펴보자.

For instance, my friend's parents have always **required** that my friend **dress** to their standards.

위의 문장 중 my friend's parents have require that my friend dress에서 my friend가 단수명사임에도 불구하고 dress라는 동사원형이 쓰였다. 이는 dress앞에 should가 생략되었기 때문이다. 당위성 동사에는 desire, wish(소망하다), suggest, propose, recommend, move(제안하다), advise(충고하다), order(명령하다), demand, require, request(요구하다), decide(결정하다), insist, urge(주장하다), expect(기대하다) 등이 있다.

cf. 당위성 형용사: TEST 11 참고

RELATED TOPICS

1 How people look or dress is more important for succeeding than having good ideas.

성공하기 위해서는 좋은 아이디어를 가지고 있는 것보다 외모나 옷에 신경을 쓰는 것이 더 중요하다.

AGREE	DISAGREE
- first impression: most important in some jobs 첫인상: 어떤 직업에서는 가장 중요	- competence: most important at a company 유능함: 회사에서 가장 중요함
- halo effect 후광 효과 (하나의 장점 / 단점이 다른 모든 면에도 영향을 끼치는 것)	- clothing: no accomplishment / progress 옷: 성취 / 진척 ✕

2 People nowadays spend more time on what they want to do rather than what they have to do.

오늘날 사람들은 해야 할 일 보다는 하고 싶은 일에 더 많은 시간을 보낸다.

AGREE	DISAGREE
- less stress: more important for people 스트레스 ↓: 사람들에게 더욱 중요함	- no freedom to choose a task at workplace 하고 싶은 일을 정할 수 있는 자유 ✕
- individualized: less consideration for others 개인주의화: 다른 이들에 대한 배려 ↓	- certain duties need to be done 특정 일들은 실행되어야만 함 ex) cleaning 청소

3 Great leaders try to make employees feel that they take part in making decisions.

뛰어난 리더들은 직원들이 의사 결정에 참여하고 있다는 기분을 느낄 수 있도록 노력한다.

AGREE	DISAGREE
- motivation to work harder 더욱 열심히 일하도록 동기 부여	- each employee has his own role 각각의 직원은 자신만의 역할이 있음
- teaching a sense of responsibility 책임감을 가르침	- giving less pressure in terms of responsibility 책임감에 대한 압박 ↓

4 Advice from older people is more valuable than from peers. 나이 든 사람의 충고가 친구의 충고보다 더 가치가 있다.

AGREE	DISAGREE
- many experiences 많은 경험	- more knowledgeable in particular issues 특정 이슈에 관해서는 더욱 많은 지식을 가지고 있음
- more objective + rational (peers can be too subjective) 보다 객관적이고 이성적임 (동료들은 너무 주관적일 수 있음)	- peers: more aware of personal situations many times 친구: 종종 사생활에 대해 더욱 잘 알고 있음

5 It has become less important for families to have meals together.

가족들이 함께 식사를 한다는 것은 덜 중요해지고 있다.

AGREE	DISAGREE
- too busy w/work / study 일 / 공부로 너무 바쁨	- share conversations w/each other during meals 식사를 하며 함께 대화를 나눔
- more value on other activities 다른 활동에 더 많은 가치를 둠 ex) playing tennis together 함께 테니스를 치는 것	- life: busier → the only time to gather: during meals 삶: 더욱 바빠졌음 → 모임의 유일한 시간: 식사 시간

TOEFL® MAP
ACTUAL TEST Writing **2**

18

TOEFL® MAP **ACTUAL TEST**

VOLUME

HELP

NEXT

WRITING Question 1 of 2

00:03:00 ● HIDE TIME

Bird feeders are devices that are placed outdoors. The purpose of these bird feeders is to supply food to birds. There are many types of bird feeders, such as peanut feeders for blue jays and woodpeckers, sugar water feeders for hummingbirds, and platform feeders for mourning doves. At first glance, they may look appealing since they save birds from dying of hunger. However, they cause a lot of problems that can sometimes be serious and can even act as ecological traps.

Most birds are wild animals and need to find food by themselves; however, when there are bird feeders, they may get used to the feeders and become too dependent. Feeding birds on a regular basis means the birds could lose their natural abilities to search for food themselves. This may be a major problem when the feeders are no longer available. Excessive reliance on feeders could result in birds losing some of their natural abilities, which could eventually result in their deaths.

Researchers have discovered that a wider variety of birds species are spotted in areas with bird feeders than in areas without them. This can result in negative consequences since the introduction of a new bird species to a region can harm the native insect population. The birds will consume many insects, which will not know how to defend themselves from the invasive species. The loss of balance in the insect population can affect native plants, which could eventually change the local environment. This could ultimately harm the native bird population.

Though the chances are low, birds can transmit serious diseases such as salmonella and avian diseases to humans and other animals. The diseases can spread by a person approaching a dead bird without any proper protection. They can also be transmitted by bacteria on improperly maintained or contaminated feeders. Finches, pine siskins, and sparrows are the most common birds that get various diseases.

🎧 18-01

TOEFL® MAP **ACTUAL TEST**

VOLUME

HELP

NEXT

WRITING | Question 1 of 2

00:20:00 ● HIDE TIME

Directions You have 20 minutes to plan and write your response. Your response will be judged on the basis of the quality of your writing and on how well your response presents the points in the lecture and their relationship to the passage. Typically, an effective response will be 150-225 words.

Question Summarize the points made in the lecture, being sure to explain how they challenge specific claims made in the reading passage.

CUT | PASTE | UNDO | REDO | Hide Word Count : 0

Bird feeders are devices that are placed outdoors. The purpose of these bird feeders is to supply food to birds. There are many types of bird feeders, such as peanut feeders for blue jays and woodpeckers, sugar water feeders for hummingbirds, and platform feeders for mourning doves. At first glance, they may look appealing since they save birds from dying of hunger. However, they cause a lot of problems that can sometimes be serious and can even act as ecological traps.

Most birds are wild animals and need to find food by themselves; however, when there are bird feeders, they may get used to the feeders and become too dependent. Feeding birds on a regular basis means the birds could lose their natural abilities to search for food themselves. This may be a major problem when the feeders are no longer available. Excessive reliance on feeders could result in birds losing some of their natural abilities, which could eventually result in their deaths.

Researchers have discovered that a wider variety of birds species are spotted in areas with bird feeders than in areas without them. This can result in negative consequences since the introduction of a new bird species to a region can harm the native insect population. The birds will consume many insects, which will not know how to defend themselves from the invasive species. The loss of balance in the insect population can affect native plants, which could eventually change the local environment. This could ultimately harm the native bird population.

Though the chances are low, birds can transmit serious diseases such as salmonella and avian diseases to humans and other animals. The diseases can spread by a person approaching a dead bird without any proper protection. They can also be transmitted by bacteria on improperly maintained or contaminated feeders. Finches, pine siskins, and sparrows are the most common birds that get various diseases.

📝 NOTE-TAKING

READING

bird feeders: supply food → can cause problems + ecological traps
새 모이통: 먹이를 공급 → 문제를 일으킬 수 있음 + 생태학의 덫

 birds: get used to bird feeders → dependent 새: 모이통에 익숙해짐 → 의존적

- can result in absence of natural behavior → possible death 자연적 행동의 부재 → 죽음 가능

> **Paraphrasing Example** Providing food will make birds get used to the feeder, leading to possible death due to the loss of their natural traits.

 areas with bird feeders: more diverse range of birds 새 모이통이 있는 지역: 더 많은 종류의 새들

- introduction of new species → confusion in insect population → native bird species ↓
새로운 종의 출현 → 곤충 수의 혼란 → 토종 새 ↓

> **Paraphrasing Example** It was mostly new bird species that were spotted around the area with bird feeders, resulting in dominance by invasive birds.

 transmit serious diseases 심각한 병균의 전염

- bacteria on improperly maintained or contaminated feeders 잘못된 관리 + 오염된 모이통에 있는 박테리아

> **Paraphrasing Example** Serious diseases can be transmitted by contaminated feeders.

WORD REMINDER

blue jay 큰 어치   appealing 매력적인   ecological 생태학의   trap 덫   dependent 의존적인   trait 특성, 특징   reliance 의존   range 범위   consequence 결과   introduction 소개   native 토착의   habitat 서식지   transmit 전염시키다   avian 조류의   approach 다가오다   improperly 부적절하게   contaminated 오염된   finch 메추라기   pine siskin 검은 방울새   sparrow 참새

LISTENING

BF: helpful in maintaining ecological balance + increasing biodiversity conservation 새 모이통: 생태학 균형을 유지하는 것 + 생물의 다양성 보존에 도움이 됨

 birds' role: distribute seeds, pollinate, and control pests 새의 역할: 씨앗의 분포, 식물의 수분, 해충 방제

- supply food → birds can focus on reproduction → able to maintain population
식량 제공 → 새는 번식에 집중 가능 → 새 숫자를 유지할 수 있음

> **Paraphrasing Example** With enough food, birds can focus on reproduction that will maintain their populations.

 study: bird feeders with different foods were placed: new species
연구: 다른 종류의 모이가 든 새 모이통 설치: 새로운 종

- non-feeding locations: similar number of native + non-native birds 새 모이통이 없었던 곳: 토종 새 + 외래종 새의 숫자가 비슷
→ keeping bird feeders w/normal diet → no worries about invasive species
새 모이통에 원래 먹는 모이를 넣음 → 외래종에 대한 걱정 안 해도 됨

> **Paraphrasing Example** Though there were similar numbers of non-native birds and native birds at non-feeding locations, there were many non-native birds at feeders with different sorts of food.

❸ **diseases: avoided → wash hands, never feed birds on ground, clean bird feeders every 2 weeks** 병균: 피할 수 있음 → 손 씻기, 바닥에서 먹이지 않기, 2주에 한 번씩 모이통 청소하기

- no proof that risk of transmission is higher at bird feeders than in the wild
자연에서보다 모이통에서의 전염 위험률이 높다는 증거가 없음

> **Paraphrasing Example** The possible transmission of diseases can be avoided by following the proper steps, including cleaning feeders on a regular basis and washing one's hands thoroughly after touching feeders.

WORD REMINDER

biodiversity 생물의 다양성   crucial 결정적인   distribution 분포   pollination (식물) 수분   pest control 해충 방제   reproduction 번식   sustain 지속하다   omnivorous 잡식성의   nectar 꿀, 과즙   defecate 배변하다   surface 표면   definitive 확정적인   proof 증거   transmission 전염

ACTUAL TEST **18**

191

In the lecture, the professor argues that bird feeders can create many advantages if kept properly. This goes directly against the idea presented in the reading passage that bird feeders can cause serious problems.

First, feeding birds during harsh winters is very important for maintaining ecological balance. With enough food, birds can focus on reproduction, which will maintain their populations. This refutes the reading passage's claim that providing food will make birds get used to the feeders, leading to possible death due to the loss of their natural traits.

Moreover, the lecturer talks about a study conducted in New Zealand. Bird feeders with different kinds of food were placed in gardens. Though there were similar numbers of non-native birds and native birds at non-feeding locations, there were many non-native birds at feeders with different sorts of food. This rebuts the reading passage's argument that it is mostly new bird species that are spotted in areas with bird feeders, resulting in dominance by invasive birds.

Lastly, the possible transmission of diseases can be avoided by following the proper steps. This includes cleaning feeders on a regular basis and washing hands thoroughly after touching feeders. In addition, birds should not be fed on the ground. This is opposite the idea in the reading passage that serious diseases can be transmitted by contaminated feeders.

WORD REMINDER

create 불러일으키다　properly 적절히, 제대로　conduct 실시하다　sort 종류　spot 발견하다　proper 적절한　regularly 정기적으로
thoroughly 아주, 깨끗하게

Directions Read the question below. You have 30 minutes to plan, write, and revise your essay. Typically, an effective response will contain a minimum of 300 words.

Question

Do you agree or disagree with the following statement?

Children should be rewarded for good exam results.

Use specific reasons and examples to support your answer.

📝 NOTE-TAKING

AGREE

- **recognition for accomplishments** 성취에 대한 인정
  - further motivation 그 이상의 동기 부여
    - **Ex** cousin: prize when do well on exam 사촌: 시험을 잘 볼 때마다 상을 받음
      - → prepare harder → stimuli + good results = interested in studying
      - 더 열심히 준비 → 자극 + 좋은 결과 = 공부에 대한 흥미
      - ∴ does well even w/out rewards 상 없이도 잘 하게 됨

- **prepare for the future** 미래에 대한 준비
  - ability: assessed + evaluated based on results 능력: 결과에 입각해 사정 + 평가 받음
    - **Ex** salary: outcome of tasks 급료: 일의 결과
      - → habit of assigning a value to a result → desirable way for the future
      - 결과에 가치를 부여하는 습관 → 미래에 대한 바람직한 방법

INTRODUCTION

generalization: many ways to motivate children
일반화: 아이들에게 동기 부여를 주는 여러 가지 방법

⬇

+ve reinforcement (praise, rewards) vs. –ve reinforcement (punishment)
적극적 강화 (칭찬, 상) vs. 부정적 강화 (벌)

⬇

thesis: agree (recognition, fundamental basis in capitalistic nation)
논제: 찬성 (인정, 자본주의 국가의 근본 바탕)

DISAGREE

- **reward: ultimate goal** 상: 궁극적 목표
  - studying for prize > gaining knowledge 상을 위한 공부 > 지식 습득
    - **Ex** friend: got a gift whenever he did well on an exam 친구: 시험을 잘 볼 때마다 선물을 받았음
      - → gift: prior + more meaningful 선물: 우선적 + 더욱 의미 있음

- **result > process** 결과 > 과정
  - no learning from failure 실패로부터 배우지 않음
    - **Ex** Thomas Edison 토마스 에디슨
  - if rewarded based on results, no innovative + creative experiments
    - 결과로 상을 받았다면, 혁신적 + 창의적인 실험 x

INTRODUCTION

generalization: many ways to motivate children
일반화: 아이들에게 동기 부여를 주는 여러 가지 방법

⬇

+ve reinforcement (praise, rewards) vs. –ve reinforcement (punishment)
적극적 강화 (칭찬, 상) vs. 부정적 강화 (벌)

⬇

thesis: disagree (mistaken idea about reward, different values)
논제: 반대 (상에 대한 잘못된 생각, 다른 가치)

There are many ways to motivate children to do well on exams. Some parents use positive reinforcement such as praise and rewards while others use negative reinforcement, including punishment. Though some people contend that rewards may become the ultimate goal for children, there is no doubt that positive reinforcement acts as a means to encourage children to perform better. Thus, I strongly believe children should be rewarded for good exam results because it is a good way to recognize their efforts. Moreover, rewards are a fundamental method of recognition for work in a capitalist nation.

To begin with, getting a reward is a way to get recognition for one's accomplishments. Having received acknowledgement for his achievements, a child would be further motivated to study hard. For instance, every time my cousin did well on an exam, he got a prize from my uncle. Consequently, he worked harder to prepare for the next exam. Eventually, receiving rewards and earning good exam results led him to become interested in studying, and now he does well on his tests even without any rewards.

In addition, giving a prize according to a result is a way to prepare children for the future. Because in a capitalist nation, one's overall ability is generally assessed and evaluated based on the results of a test or the quality of one's assigned work, it is important that one try hard to achieve the best possible results. To illustrate, most companies determine an employee's salary depending on the outcome of given tasks. Thus, building a habit of assigning value to the results produced is a desirable way for children to become ready for their lives in the future.

It is true that giving rewards can yield the side effect that children may put value only on the result itself. However, providing no acknowledgement could also give children hard time adjusting to a society where rewards are used as recognition. When children are rewarded with a prize, they will be motivated to do better on subsequent work. Furthermore, children will be prepared to work in a capitalist economy in the future. For the above reasons, I agree with the statement that children should be rewarded for good exam results.

WORD REMINDER

positive reinforcement 긍정적 강화   negative reinforcement 부정적 강화   ultimate 궁극의   means 방법   recognize 인정하다
fundamental 근본적인   capitalist 자본주의자   accomplishment 성취   acknowledgement 인정   assess 사정하다   evaluate 평가하다
determine 결정하다   outcome 성과   assign 정하다   yield 초래하다   subsequent 그 후의

TIPS for SUCCESS

전치사 Preposition

전치사는 시간이나 장소 등에 대한 정보를 줌으로써 보다 자세한 정보를 제공하는 목적을 가지고 있다. 전치사는 명사(구), 대명사, 동명사(구), 또는 명사절을 동반한다. 다음의 문장들을 살펴보자.

Children should be rewarded for **good results**. (명사: 아이는 훌륭한 결과에 대해 상을 받아야 한다.)

Children should be rewarded for **them**. (대명사: 아이는 그것에 대해 상을 받아야 한다.)

Children should be rewarded for **getting good results**. (동명사구: 아이는 훌륭한 결과를 얻은 것에 대해 상을 받아야 한다.)

Children should be rewarded for **how they did on their exams**. (명사절: 아이는 그가 시험에서 한 것에 대해 상을 받아야 한다.)

ACTUAL TEST **18**

There are many ways to motivate children to do well on exams. Some parents use positive reinforcement such as praise and rewards while others use negative reinforcement, including punishment. Though there is no doubt that positive reinforcement acts as a means to encourage children to perform better, I strongly believe it is wrong to reward children for good exam results because a reward may become the children's only goal. In addition, the children may come to believe that the results are more important than the process.

To begin with, children may set a reward as their ultimate goal. In other words, instead of feeling a sense of accomplishment in gaining knowledge, children might study for a reward. To illustrate, my friend's parents always gave him a gift as a reward whenever he did well on an exam. Consequently, for my friend, the desire to get a gift has become a higher priority and more meaningful than learning and obtaining new knowledge.

In addition, it is likely that children will put more value on the results of an exam rather than the process of preparing for the exam. As a result, the children may not learn from failure. Rather, it may only cause frustration and disappointment because the children are not able to get a prize. Many famous scientists, such as Thomas Edison, learned from failure. Had he gotten rewards depending on outcomes, he would not have been challenged to try such innovative and creative experiments.

It is true that rewards can be utilized as a way to stimulate children to try harder. However, as an outcome is not always correlative to endeavor, this approach may yield a situation where children are discouraged and no longer put forth much effort. For learners, gaining knowledge, not rewards, should be the most important objective. Furthermore, sometimes children should be praised for the procedures they follow in learning rather than the results themselves. For the above reasons, I disagree with the statement that children should be rewarded for good exam results.

WORD REMINDER

priority 상위   frustration 좌절   innovative 혁신적인   utilize 이용하다   stimulate 자극하다   correlative 상관적인   endeavor 노력
approach 접근법   objective 목표   praise 칭찬   procedure 절차

TIPS for SUCCESS

because는 접속사이기 때문에 반드시 주절이 필요하다.

첫 단락의 문장을 살펴보자.

I strongly believe it is wrong to reward children for good exam results **because** a reward may become the children's only goal.

물론 한글에서는 '나는 아이가 훌륭한 시험 결과에 대해 상을 받는 것이 잘못되었다고 굳게 믿는다. 왜냐하면 상은 아이에게 있어서 유일한 목표가 될 수 있기 때문이다.'라는 두 개의 독립절이 가능하지만, 영어에서 because는 종속접속사로서, 홀로 절을 만들 수 없다. 즉, I strongly believe it is wrong to reward children for good exam results. Because a reward may become the children's only goal.에서 because절은 문장이 아닌 sentence fragment가 되는 것이다.

또한, 부사절이 주절을 앞설 경우 comma를 붙이고 (Because a reward may become the children's only goal, I strongly believe it is wrong to reward children for good exam results.), 주절 뒤에 나올 경우 comma를 붙이지 않는다.

1 Parents have barely any control over their children since children are influenced by the media and other outside factors. 아이들은 미디어와 다른 외부 요소들의 영향을 받기 때문에 부모에게는 아이들에 대한 통제력이 거의 없다.

AGREE	DISAGREE
- more time exposed to media than time spent with parents 부모와 보내는 시간보다 미디어에 노출되는 시간이 더 많음 - peer pressure: often has more influence than parents' rules 또래에게서 받는 압박감: 부모의 규칙보다 종종 더 영향력이 있음	- basic rules: may be determined by parents and children 기본 규칙: 부모와 아이들에 의해 정해질 수 있음 - education from school, religion → obedience to parents 학교, 종교의 교육 → 부모에게 순종

2 One of the best ways that parents can help teenagers prepare for adult life is to encourage them to get part-time jobs. 청소년들이 성인기를 준비하도록 부모가 도울 수 있는 가장 좋은 방법은 아르바이트를 하도록 권유하는 것이다.

AGREE	DISAGREE
- responsibility + independence 책임감 + 독립심 - a value of money 돈의 가치	- studying: basic part of student life 학업: 학생의 기본 - the ultimate goal may be to earn money 궁극적인 목표가 돈을 버는 것이 될 수 있음

3 The best way for parents to make their children more responsible is to have them take care of an animal. 부모에게 있어 아이의 책임감을 향상시키기 위한 가장 좋은 방법은 아이로 하여금 동물을 돌보게 하는 것이다.

AGREE	DISAGREE

- having duties on a regular basis 정기적으로 임무를 가짐
  ex) feeding, cleaning 사육, 청소
- animal's reliance on the child → strong will to protect the animal 동물이 아이에게 의존 → 동물을 보호해야겠다는 강한 의지
	- may result in undesirable consequences 바람직스럽지 못한 결과를 초래할 수 있음
	  ex) death of an animal 동물의 죽음
	- no reaction from certain types of animals → no accomplishment → unwilling to take care of the animal 특정 동물들은 반응이 없음 → 성취감 × → 그 동물을 돌보고 싶은 마음 ×

4 Parents should keep their children from watching television in order to make them do well at schoolwork. 부모는 자식들이 공부를 잘하게 만들기 위해 텔레비전 시청을 못하게 해야 한다.

AGREE	DISAGREE

- TV: addictive TV: 중독성 있음
- may affect a child's daily routine 아이의 일상에 영향을 줄 수 있음
  ex) spend too much time on a hairdo in order to imitate an actress 영화배우를 따라 하기 위해 머리에 너무 많은 시간을 소비
	- entertainment: release stress 오락 프로그램: 스트레스를 해소시켜 줌
	- informative programs: helpful in education 정보를 제공해 주는 프로그램: 교육에 도움이 됨
	  ex) news, documentary films 뉴스, 다큐멘터리

ACTUAL TEST 18

MEMO

MEMO

MEMO

TOEFL® MAP

ACTUAL TEST

New TOEFL® Edition

Susan Kim
Michael A. Putlack

Writing **2**

Scripts and Translations

 DARAKWON

TOEFL MAP ACTUAL TEST

New TOEFL Edition

Writing 2

Scripts and Translations

Actual Test 01

TASK 1 · INTEGRATED TASK
Anthropology: The Harappan Civilization

READING   p.015

기원전 약 3,000년에서 기원전 1,500년 까지, 세계에서 가장 뛰어난 초기 문명 중 하나가 존재했다. 오늘날의 파키스탄과 인도에 있는 인더스 강 계곡에 위치했던 이 문명은 하라파 문명이라고 알려져 있다. 하라파 사회는 주로 도시에 위치했으며 도시들은 격자 모양으로 이루어져 있었다. 그곳 사람들은 시대에 앞선 발달된 농경 기술을 사용했고, 인더스 문자라고 불리는 문자를 가지고 있었으며, 광범위한 지역 무역에 종사했다. 그러나 기원전 1,500년쯤, 하라파 문명은 갑작스러운 종말을 맞이했다.

멸망에 관해 가장 널리 인정받고 있는 이론 중 하나는 하라파인들이 외부 침입자들에게 점령을 당했다는 것이다. 많은 학자들은 중앙아시아로부터 온 인도유럽 부족인 아리아인들이 하라파의 정복과 관련이 있다고 믿는다. 기원전 약 1,500년에 그 지역에서 전쟁이 일어났으며, 당시 아리아인들이 하라파 영토로 이주하기 시작했다는 일부 증거가 존재하고 있기 때문에, 이 이론은 사실일 가능성이 높다.

다른 학자들은 하라파 문명이 자연적인 이유 때문에 멸망했다고 주장한다. 그들에 따르면, 인더스 강 계곡은 기원전 약 1,500년경 극심한 기후 변화를 겪었다고 한다. 광범위한 농경 사회를 유지시킨, 한때 우거진 땅이었던 그곳은 강우량 부족으로 메마른 사막으로 변했다. 따라서, 기근이 그 지역을 강타했고 굶주림으로 죽지 않던 사람들은 생계를 유지할 수 있는 다른 지역으로 이주해 갔다.

세 번째 이론에 따르면 여러 질병이 하라파 사회에 만연하여 멸망을 초래했다고 한다. 일부 사람들은 전염성 바이러스 질병인 콜레라가 그 원인이었다고 단정한다. 콜레라는 종종 물을 통해 확산된다. 하라파인들은 동일한 수자원을 사용했기 때문에, 콜레라 전염병이 전 주민들을 재앙으로 이끌었을 수도 있다. 너무나 많은 사람들이 죽고 죽어 가면서, 하라파 문명은 역사에서 사라졌다.

LISTENING   🎧 01-01

M Professor: One of the problems with studying archaeology is that it's virtually impossible to know precisely what happened in the past. Let's take the downfall of the Harappan civilization as an example. They had a brilliant culture, right? But they just, well, seemed to disappear around 1500 B.C. There are three primary theories about their disappearance, but all have holes in them.

The first theory involves war. Some believe the Harappan Civilization was overwhelmed by invading Aryans. It's possible, sure. But this isn't just one place we're talking about. The Harappans had major cities, including Harappa and Mohenjo-Daro. There were more than 100 other towns and cities in that region and hundreds of minor settlements. Yet almost no evidence supporting the invasion theory exists. Harappan society wouldn't have easily collapsed. At least some of the settlements would have fought, but there's no archaeological proof of any battles being fought.

The climate-change theory is popular as well. But keep in mind that Egypt and Mesopotamia were two contemporary societies of the Harappans. Both experienced changing climates. Egypt became more desert-like while Mesopotamia endured a tremendous flood. Still, the Egyptians thrived while the flood actually helped Mesopotamian agriculture. So I'm positive the Harappans also would have been able to survive any changes in their climate.

Some have speculated that a cholera epidemic wiped out the Harappans. I sincerely doubt it. You see, cholera spreads through dirty water. But remember what I told you about the Harappan cities . . . ? That's right. They had a water system which guaranteed them access to clean water. Their cities even had sewer systems designed to keep waste material that carried diseases out of their drinking water. I just don't see how an epidemic caused by cholera could have caused the downfall of an entire civilization.

교수: 고고학 연구에 있어서의 문제점 중 하나는 과거에 정확히 무슨 일이 있었는지를 알아내는 것이 사실상 불가능하다는 점입니다. 하라파 문명의 멸망을 예로 들어 봅시다. 그들은 훌륭한 문화를 가지고 있었습니다, 그렇죠? 하지만 음, 기원전 약 1,500년 전쯤 사라졌다고 보여지고 있습니다. 그들의 멸망에 관해 세 개의 주된 이론들이 있지만, 모두 결점을 가지고 있습니다.

첫 번째 이론은 전쟁과 관련이 있습니다. 일부는 하라파 문명이 침략자였던 아리아인들에게 전복되었다고 믿고 있죠. 맞습니다, 가능한 일입니다. 하지만 우리가 단지 한 곳만을 이야기하고 있는 것은 아닙니다. 하라파 사람들에게는 하라파와 모헨조다로를 포함한 주요 도시들이 있었습니다. 이들 지역에는 100개 이상의 여러 마을과 도시가 있었고 수백 개의 작은 거주지들이 존재했습니다. 그러나 침략 이론을 뒷받침하는 근거는 거의 존재하지 않습니다. 하라파 사회는 쉽게 몰락하지 않았을 것입니다. 적어도 일부 거주지에서는 싸움이 있었겠지만, 전투가 일어났다는 고고학적 증거는 존재하지 않습니다.

기후 변화 이론 역시 유명합니다. 하지만 이집트와 메소포타미아가 하라파와 동시대의 사회였다는 점을 명심해 두십시오. 양쪽 모두 기후 변화를 겪었습니다. 메소포타미아는 거대한 홍수를 견디어 냈던 반면 이집트는 사막과 같은 곳이 되었습니다. 그럼에도 불구하고, 홍수는 메소포타미아의 농업에 사실상 도움이 되었고 이집트인들은 번성했습니다. 따라서 저는 하라파인들 역시 어떤 기후 변화에서도 살아날 수 있었을 것이라고 확신합니다.

몇몇 사람들은 콜레라 전염병이 하라파인들을 몰살시켰다고 추측하고 있습니다. 그것은 정말 의심스럽습니다. 자, 콜레라는 더러운 물을 통해 확산됩니다. 하지만 하라파 도시들에 관해 여러분께 말씀드렸던 것을 기억하고 계신가요? 그래요. 그들은 깨끗한 물을 이용할 수 있도록 해 주는 급수 시설을 가지고 있었습니다. 그들의 도시에는 심지어 마시는 물에 질병을 옮기는 오물이 들어가지 않도록 설계가 이루어진 하수구 시설도 있었죠. 콜레라로 인한 전염병이 어떻게 한 문명 전체의 멸망을 가져왔는지 저로서는 이해할 수가 없군요.

Sample Essay   p.018

교수는 하라파의 멸망에 관한 가설들에 근거가 없다고 주장한다. 이는 하라파 문명의 갑작스러운 멸망을 설명해 줄 수 있는 가능한 이론들이 존재한다는 지문의 주장을 직접적으로 반박한다.

첫째로, 침략에 관한 증명을 보여주는 근거는 존재하지 않는다. 하라파와 모헨조다로 등의 주요 도시에서 아리아인들이 침략했다는 증거는 발견되지 않는다. 이는 외부인들의 침략이 하라파 문명의 멸망을 초래했다는 지문의 주장에 심각한 의문을 제기한다.

뿐만 아니라, 교수는 다른 동시대의 문명들도 멸망 없이 기후 변화를 겪었다고 주장한다. 이집트는 건조했음에도 불구하고 번영했으며, 메소포타미아는 홍수에 의해 오히려 도움을 받았다. 따라서, 하라파인들 역시 극적인 기후 변화를 겪었다고 할지라도 살아남았을 것이다. 이는 인더스 강 계곡에서의 극심한 기후 변화로 하라파인들이 멸망했다는 지문의 주장과 모순된다.

마지막으로, 교수는 콜레라가 멸망의 원인이 될 수 없었다고 주장한다. 하라파인들은 깨끗한 물을 공급해 줄 수 있었던 급수 시설뿐만 아니라 하수구 시설도 가지고 있었다. 이는 수원을 공유함으로써 나타나게 된 콜레라 등의 여러 질병 때문에 하라파가 멸망하게 되었다는 지문의 의견과 반대된다.

TASK 2 · INDEPENDENT TASK
Challenge

대부분의 사람들은 고향에 남아야 할지, 아니면 고향을 떠나야 할지에 대해 결정할 시기를 겪는다. 학교, 직장, 재정 상태, 또는 단순히 다른 환경에서 살고자 하는 바람이 그러한 결정에 영향을 미치며, 그 결과는 그들이 어떻게 새로운 환경에 적응하느냐에 달려 있다. 일부 사람들은 고향에 머무를 때가 더 행복하고 성공적이라고 주장한다. 하지만, 나는 사람들로 하여금 폭넓은 견해를 기를 수 있게 해 주고 새로운 삶에 적응할 수 있는 능력을 발전시킬 수 있게 해 주기 때문에 낯선 곳에서 생활하는 것이 사람들에게 더 많은 기회를 열어 준다고 굳게 믿는다.

첫째, 사람들은 다른 곳으로 이사를 가면, 다양한 경험을 하고 다른 이들과의 폭넓은 관계를 형성할 수 있다. 이는 그들이 보다 넓은 견해를 갖는데 도움이 되며, 그들에게 보다 많은 기회를 제공해 줄 것이다. 예를 들면, 낯선 도시로 이사를 갔을 때, 나는 그곳 사람들이 다른 생활 방식뿐 아니라 내가 살던 곳의 사람들과는 차별화된 생각을 가지고 있다는 점을 깨달았다. 따라서, 나는 다양한 관점을 공유할 수 있었는데 이는 타인들과 함께하는 직장 생활에서 큰 도움이 되었다.

뿐만 아니라, 낯선 곳으로의 이동은 사람들에게 새로운 환경에 적응할 좋은 기회를 줄 수 있다. 새로운 관습을 이해하고 새로운 사람들과 교류함으로써, 특정한 종류의 상황 및 개인에 대처하는 능력을 발달시킬 수 있다. 예를 들어, 내 사촌은 내성적이었고 만나본 적이 없는 사람들과 어울리는데 어려움을 겪었다. 하지만, 일 때문에 다른 주로 이사를 가야만 했다. 새로 배운 능력 덕분에, 이제 그녀는 여러 종류의 모임에서 새로운 사람들과 만나는 것을 즐기고 있다.

자신이 자란 곳에서 머무르면 편안함과 안정감을 얻을 수 있다는 점은 사실이다. 반대로, 과다한 편안함은 의욕을 저하시킬 수 있으며 사람을 무감각하게 만들 수 있다. 다양한 경험을 갖고 폭넓은 대인 관계를 형성하는 것은 보다 넓은 견해를 갖는데 도움이 될 것이다. 게다가, 새로운 문화를 경험하는 것은 대인 관계뿐 아니라 특정한 상황에 필요한 능력을 갖출 수 있는 기회도 줄 수 있다. 이상의 이유로 인해, 나는 고향에 머무르는 사람들보다 고향을 떠나는 사람들이 더 행복하고 성공할 가능성이 높다는 진술에 강력히 찬성한다.

대부분의 사람들은 고향에 남아야 할지, 아니면 고향을 떠나야 할지에 대해 결정할 시기를 겪는다. 학교, 직장, 재정 상태, 또는 단순히 다른 환경에서 살고자 하는 바람이 그러한 결정에 영향을 미치며, 그 결과는 그들이 어떻게 새로운 환경에 적응하느냐에 달려 있다. 일부는 다른 곳으로 이사를 가는 것이 사람들이 성공하는 것에 그리고 더 행복해지는 데에 도움이 된다고 주장한다. 하지만, 정신적인 안정감을 주고 더욱 확고한 대인 관계를 형성시켜 주기 때문에 나는 고향에 머무르는 것이 더 낫다고 굳게 믿는다.

첫째, 고향에 머무는 것으로부터 오는 편안함과 안정감과는 달리, 새로운 장소로 떠나는 것은 불안을 초래하고 많은 사람을 겁나게 할 수 있다. 예를 들면, 내 친구는 다른 주에서 직장을 얻어 처음부터 모든 것을 새로 시작해야 했기 때문에 심한 스트레스를 받았다. 가게를 찾고, 이웃을 알아가며, 새로운 의사도 찾아야 했다. 결과적으로, 그녀는 성공과 행복을 위해 일에 더욱 쏟아야 하는 노력 대신 현지 상황에 적응하느라 많은 시간을 낭비했다.

뿐만 아니라, 사람들은 자신들이 자란 지역에서 다른 이들과 보다 강한 유대감을 형성할 수 있다. 새로운 사람들과 대인 관계를 맺기 위해 우정을 키우는 것보다는 이미 형성된 관계를 유지하고 넓혀 나가는 것이 훨씬 용이하다. 예를 들어, 내 사촌은 대학에서 졸업한 직후 회사에 취직을 했고 새로운 일에 적응하느라 굉장히 바빴다. 하지만, 대부분의 동료들이 같은 고향에서 살았기 때문에 그녀에게 친숙했고, 그 친숙함은 그녀가 회사에 쉽게 적응하는데 도움이 되었다.

새로운 환경에서 생활을 하는 것이 새로운 문화를 배울 기회를 제공해 준다는 것은 사실이다. 반면, 그것은 스트레스와 시간 낭비라는 느낌을 주기도 한다. 게다가, 사람들은 이미 수년간 알고 지내온 이들과 더욱 깊은 대인 관계를 형성할 수 있기 때문에 성공에 있어서 보다 많은 기회를 갖게 된다. 이상의 이유로 인해, 나는 고향에 머무르는 사람들보다 고향을 떠나는 사람들이 더 행복하고 성공할 가능성이 더 높다는 진술에 강력히 반대한다.

Actual Test 02

TASK 1 · INTEGRATED TASK
Marine Biology: A Narwhal's Tusk

일각돌고래는 자연에서 가장 독특한 생물 중 하나이다. 치아가 있는 이 고래종은 약 5미터 길이까지 자란다. 하지만 일각돌고래의 가장 신기한 특징은 머리에 돌출되어 있는 엄니이다. 일각돌고래의 엄니는 거의 3미터까지 자랄 수 있다. 수세기 동안, 사람들은 이를 신기하게 여겨왔다. 일각돌고래는 한때 높은 가치를 인정 받았으며 심지어는 본래 마력을 지니고 있다고 믿어졌다. 오늘날 과학자들은 엄니가 다양한 용도로 쓰였을 것이라는 결론을 내리고 있다.

엄니의 첫 번째 용도는 사실상 상당히 실용적인 것이다. 일각돌고래는 북극해의 추운 바다에서 서식한다. 그들이 살고 있는 바다는 종종 두꺼운 얼음 층으로 덮여 있다. 포유류인 일각돌고래는 숨을 쉬기 위해 수면 위로 올라오지 않으면 익사한다. 그래서, 물이 얼음으로 덮여 있을 때, 신선한 공기를 들이쉴 필요가 있을 때마다 얼음을 깨기 위해 엄니를 사용한다.

일반적으로, 수컷 일각돌고래는 엄니가 있는 반면, 암컷이 엄니를 가지고 있는 경우는 매우 드물다. 그러므로 많은 해양 생물학자들은 수컷 일각돌고래가 서로 싸울 때 엄니를 사용한다고 믿는다. 여러 종의 수컷들이 영토나 암컷 때문에 경쟁을 할 때 흔히 싸움을 벌인다. 수컷 일각돌고래들은 엄니를 완벽한 무기로 사용하여, 지배권을 위한 싸움에 참가할 가능성이 높다.

마지막으로, Harvard와 다른 기관의 과학자들이 일각돌고래의 엄니에 대해 한 가지 새로운 사실을 발견했다. 엄니 바깥에 수백만 개의 신경 종말이 있다는 것을 알아낸 것이다. 이는 엄니가 일종의 센서 기능을 할 수 있도록 해 준다. 일각돌고래는 수온과 수압의 변화를 감지할 수 있으며 물속에 어떠한 종류의 입자가 있는지 알아낼 수 있다. 그리고 이들은 아마 다른 기능도 가지고 있을 것이다. 상당히 예민한 감각 기관을 가짐으로써, 일각돌고래는 매우 유용한 부속 기관을 갖추고 있는 것이다.

LISTENING 🎧 02-01

W Professor: Now, here's a picture of a narwhal . . . Obviously, its most unique feature is the long tusk here . . . In many cases, the tusk is more than half as long as the whale's entire body. Obviously, it must serve some sort of purpose. But what . . . ?

Since the narwhal dwells in the Arctic Ocean, it seems logical to assume the narwhal uses its tusk to break the ice above it when it needs to, uh, to breathe. But consider this . . . Narwhal tusks, despite being up to three meters in length, only weigh around ten kilograms. They're actually quite fragile. And narwhals often swim in areas where the surface ice is extremely thick. There's absolutely no way that their tusks are strong enough to break through that kind of ice.

Narwhals are also rather peaceful animals, so it's unlikely that they use their tusks to fight one another. All right, narwhals have been seen using their tusks to fight on rare occasions, but the lack of scars and wounds in most narwhals suggests that this isn't a common practice. It's more likely that the tusks are instead used to determine social ranking in narwhal pods.

I am, however, somewhat intrigued by reports that narwhal tusks are full of nerves that let them act like sensors. This would be highly beneficial if it were true. But there are two facts that make this theory unlikely. First, very few females have tusks. If the tusks were that useful as sensors, then it's likely that female narwhals would have evolved so that all of them have tusks. In addition, on average, female narwhals live longer than males. So it doesn't seem like these so-called sensors are of much use to the males at all. They sure don't help keep them alive longer.

교수: 자, 여기 일각돌고래의 사진이 있습니다... 분명 가장 독특한 특징은 여기에 있는 기다란 엄니입니다... 많은 경우, 엄니는 고래 몸 전체 길이의 반을 넘습니다. 당연히 어떠한 용도로 쓰이겠지요. 그렇지만 그것이 무엇일까요...?

일각돌고래는 북극해에 살기 때문에 그들이 음... 숨을 쉴 필요가 있을 때, 위에 있는 얼음을 깨기 위해 엄니를 사용한다고 가정하는 것은 논리적으로 보입니다. 하지만, 이러한 점을 생각해 보세요... 길이가 3미터까지 된다는 점에도 불구하고, 일각돌고래의 엄니는 약 10킬로그램밖에 무게가 나가지 않습니다. 엄니는 사실 매우 부서지기가 쉬워요. 그리고 일각돌고래는 종종 꽤 두꺼운 얼음 표면이 있는 곳에서 수영을 합니다. 그러한 얼음을 깰 수 있을 정도로 충분히 강력한 엄니는 결코 아닌 것이죠.

일각돌고래는 또한 꽤 평화로운 동물이기 때문에, 서로 싸우려고 엄니를 사용하는 일은 거의 없습니다. 좋아요, 일각돌고래가 매우 가끔 싸우기 위해 엄니를 사용하는 것이 목격된 적은 있지만, 대부분의 일각돌고래에 흉터와 상처가 드물다는 점은 싸움이 흔한 일은 아니라는 점을 암시해 줍니다. 오히려 엄니는 일각돌고래 무리에서 사회 계급을 결정하는데 사용될 가능성이 더 높습니다.

하지만 저는 일각돌고래의 엄니에 센서와 같은 역할을 하게 하는 신경이 가득하다는 보고에 다소 호기심을 느꼈습니다. 이러한 점이 사실이라면 많은 이점이 있을 것입니다. 그러나 이 이론을 불가능한 것으로 만드는 두 가지 사실이 있습니다. 첫째, 엄니를 가지고 있는 암컷들은 거의 없습니다. 만약 엄니가 센서로서 그렇게 유용하다면, 암컷 모두가 엄니를 갖도록 진화했을 것입니다. 게다가, 평균적으로 암컷 일각돌고래는 수컷보다 오래 삽니다. 그래서 소위 센서라 불리는 것들은 수컷에게 별 소용이 없어 보입니다. 분명 수컷들을 더 오래 살도록 해 주지는 않는 것이죠.

Sample Essay p.028

교수는 일각돌고래 엄니의 용도에 관한 여러 증거들이 의심스럽다고 주장한다. 이는 일각돌고래의 특이한 엄니가 몇몇 용도로 사용되기 위해 진화해 왔다는 지문의 주장을 정면으로 반박한다.

첫째, 얼음을 깨기 위해 엄니를 사용했다는 점은 엄니가 너무 약하다는 점에서 설득력이 없다. 게다가, 일각돌고래는 종종 두꺼운 얼음층이 있는 곳에서 수영을 하는데 이는 일각돌고래가 얼음을 깨기 위해 엄니를 사용한다는 가능성을 매우 희박하게 한다. 이는 일각돌고래가 공기로 호흡을 해야 하고 얼음을 깨는데 엄니를 이용할 수 있다는 지문의 주장과 모순된다.

다음으로, 일각돌고래는 쉽게 싸우지 않는다. 일반적으로 일각돌고래에게서 흉터나 상처가 발견되지 않는다는 사실이 이러한 주장을 뒷받침한다. 이는 엄니가 다른 경쟁자들과의, 영역이나 암컷을 차지하기 위한 싸움에 사용된다는 지문의 주장을 반박한다.

마지막으로, 두 가지 증거가 엄니에 부착된 신경 말종이 센서로 사용되는 것은 아니라는 점을 보여 준다. 첫째, 암컷들이 거의 엄니를 가지고 있지 않다는 사실은 의구심을 불러 일으킨다. 게다가, 암컷이 수컷보다 오래 살고, 이는 수컷에 의한 엄니의 사용을 불확실하게 만든다. 이러한 두 가지 사실은 수백만 개의 신경 종말이 엄니를 감각 기관으로 만든다는 지문의 주장을 반박한다.

TASK 2 · INDEPENDENT TASK
Students' Roles

Sample Essay 1 | AGREE p.031

오늘날, 많은 학생들이 학교에서 공부를 하면서 아르바이트를 하고 있다. 그들은 학비를 지불하기 위해 돈이 필요할 수도 있고, 직장 경험을 얻고 싶어 할 수도 있으며, 단순히 여가에 쓸 돈을 벌기 위해 일을 하고 싶어 할 지도 모른다. 어떤 이들은 학생들이 공부에 집중해야 한다고 말하지만, 경험과 책임감 때문에, 나는 학생들이 대학을 다니며 아르바이트를 해야 한다고 굳게 믿는다.

첫째, 학생들은 다른 사람들과 함께 일을 하고 협력함으로써 미래를 준비할 수 있다. 예를 들어, 나의 삼촌은 화학을 전공했고, 연구원으로 제약 회사에서 아르바이트를 했다. 나중에, 삼촌은 연구실에 앉아서 실험하는 것보다 학교에서 배운 지식을 활용해서 제품을 홍보하는 것에 자신이 더 뛰어나다는 점을 깨달았다. 결과적으로, 삼촌은 마케팅으로 전공을 바꿨고 궁극적인 직업을 발견했다.

더욱이, 학생들은 아르바이트를 함으로써 의무감과 책임감을 배울 수 있다. 예를 들어, 친구 중 한 명이 지난 학기 동안 아르바이트를 했는데, 기숙사에서 한 시간 떨어진 회사에서 일을 했다. 하루는, 그가 중간고사 때문에 벼락치기를 해서 굉장히 피곤해했다. 하지만, 매우 지쳤음에도 불구하고 그는 한 시간 거리의 직장에 가야 했다. 그는 좀 더 절제력을 기르고 하루의 시간을 보다 효율적으로 관리해야 한다는 점을 배웠다고 말했다.

깊은 지식을 쌓는 것이 중요한 것은 사실이며, 어떤 면에서 보면, 대학은 많은 이들에게 그들의 능력을 발전시킬 수 있는 마지막 관문일지도 모른다. 반면, 경험과 책임감의 결여는 학생들이 실제 일하는 분야에 들어갔을 때 그들을 혼란스럽게 만들고, 그들이 일에 적응하는데 어려움을 겪도록 만들 것이다. 그러므로, 나는 아르바이트가 사회로 들어가는 전환점이 될 수 있을 것이라고 믿으며, 학생들이 대학에서 공부하는 동안 아르바이트를 해야 한다고 주장한다.

Sample Essay 2 | DISAGREE   p.032

오늘날, 많은 학생들이 학교에서 공부를 하면서 아르바이트를 하고 있다. 그들은 학비를 지불하기 위해 돈이 필요할 수도 있고, 직장 경험을 얻고 싶어 할 수도 있으며, 단순히 여가에 쓸 돈을 벌기 위해 일을 하고 싶어할 지도 모른다. 어떤 이들은 학생이 일자리를 얻는 것이 중요하다고 말하지만 공부는 학생 생활의 기본적인 부분이기 때문에, 나는 학생들이 공부에 집중해야 한다고 굳게 믿는다. 덧붙여, 아르바이트가 항상 학생의 전공과 연관성이 있지는 않기 때문이다.

첫째, 아르바이트는 공부 시간을 빼앗을 뿐만 아니라, 집중을 하는 것도 방해할 것이다. 예를 들어, 장학금을 받던 내 친구는 그녀의 아르바이트로 인해 예전만큼 공부에 집중할 수가 없었기 때문에 그 다음 해에 장학금을 계속 받을 수 없었다. 그녀가 아르바이트를 하는 대신 공부에 집중을 했더라면 그녀의 장래 진로와 자금의 원천 유지 모두에 있어서 더 좋았을 것이다.

더욱이, 학생들이 하는 많은 아르바이트는 그들의 전공과 관련이 없다. 예를 들면, 나의 사촌이 대학교 2학년 때 아르바이트를 했다. 그녀는 고고학을 전공했기 때문에, 그녀가 찾던 일은 자리가 매우 제한되어 있거나, 전임으로 일할 자리를 찾는 사람들에게만 제공이 되었다. 결과적으로, 그녀는 커피숍에서 일을 했고 졸업 후 미래의 직장에서 쉽게 배울 수 있는 기본적인 책임감만을 배웠다.

책임감을 쌓고 다른 사람들과 일하는 것은 미래의 진로를 준비하는데 있어 중요하다. 하지만, 위에서 언급했듯이, 학생들은 실제 직업 분야에 들어갔을 때 사회적 능력과 책임감을 기를 수 있다. 깊은 지식을 얻는 것은 대학에 다니는 근본적인 이유이다. 게다가, 많은 아르바이트는 학생들의 전공과 무관하다. 그러므로 나는 학생들이 대학을 다니는 동안 공부에 집중해야 한다고 주장한다.

Actual Test 03

TASK 1 · INTEGRATED TASK

Marketing: Choices

READING   p.035

삶의 질의 향상 덕분에 소비자는 상품과 서비스를 구매할 때 선택의 폭이 넓다. 개개인은 본인만의 스타일과 취향을 가지고 있기 때문에 기업은 상품

선택을 많이 제공함으로써 소비자들의 취향에 맞추려 노력한다. 대부분의 사람들은 그들 것이 될 수 있는 어떤 것이든 선택의 폭이 넓은 가게를 방문할 때 기쁨을 경험한다.

많은 선택권을 가진 소비자들은 그들의 개인 취향에 맞춰 쇼핑을 할 수 있다. 많은 선택들을 갖는다는 것은 개인들이 자신을 표현할 수 있는 자유를 좀 더 많이 갖고 있다는 것이다. 이는 행복함과 창의력을 낳는다. 예를 들면, 수많은 종류의 레고 블록은 아이들로 하여금 무수한 아이디어를 떠올리게 함으로서 그들의 창의력과 상상력을 개발할 수 있도록 한다.

나은 질의 상품과 서비스는 다양한 선택에서 얻는 또 하나의 혜택이다. 각각의 소비자의 취향에 맞추기 위해 기업은 질을 높이기 위해 끊임없이 연구한다. 기업들은 그들 제품의 질의 향상뿐 아니라, 좀 더 나은 가격으로 경쟁하기도 한다. 유사 제품들의 가격을 보여주는 웹사이트도 있기 때문에 소비자들은 어떤 기업들이 더 나은 옵션을 제공하는지 쉽게 비교해 볼 수 있다. 이는 소비자들이 바가지 쓰는 것을 피할 수 있게 도와준다.

폭넓은 선택을 통해 사람들은 그들이 사거나 선택하는 것에 대한 통제력을 갖고 있다고 생각하며 이는 만족감을 준다. 이것은 직장에서도 흔한 일이다. 많은 연구가 직장에서 직원들은 그들의 일에 대한 권한이 더 있을수록 더 열심히 한다는 것을 보여준다. 자율성과 결정권을 더 많을수록 더 큰 만족감이 생기고, 따라서 몸도 더 건강하게 한다.

LISTENING   🎧 03-01

W Professor: All right . . . yesterday, I went to get a pair of runners for myself. A salesperson asked if the shoes were for running, walking, training, or every occasion. The next question was if I wanted a specific brand . . . and the store had runners from at least 15 different brands. Then, I was asked about different features like . . . arch support or cushioned insoles . . . or orthotic friendly . . . or even waterproof shoes! Okay, then I had to see if my feet were narrow, medium, or wide. And of course, I ended up with all sorts of colors to choose from before I finally made my decision. Hmm . . . Is this good or bad? Are we really happy to have so many choices?

A study was done at a supermarket near Stanford's campus. Consumers who had a choice of twenty-four different jams to taste were actually less likely to purchase any jam compared to shoppers who only had a choice of six different jams. The reason is that consumers become overwhelmed by too many choices and get exhausted and stressed out. Some shoppers even put off their purchases indefinitely.

It is also interesting that people consider a greater variety of brands as being better in terms of quality. This happens because consumers think more kinds of products being available means that a brand has more expertise in that particular field . . . and this can lead consumers to be biased and to make erroneous decisions. For instance, in one survey, consumers had samples of chocolates to try. One group of chocolates had a wide variety of selections while the other had only a few. Then, people rated the ones with many choices as better tasting even though both groups of chocolates were from the same brand.

Lastly, having many choices leaves consumers with regrets and feeling dissatisfied. People tend to overthink and . . .

교수: 자... 어제, 저는 운동화 한 켤레를 사러 갔었어요. 점원이 운동화가 러닝용인지, 걷기용인지, 트레이닝용인지, 아님 일상용인지 물어봤지요. 다음 질문은 특정 브랜드를 원하는지에 관한 것이었어요... 그리고 가게는 최소 15개의 다른 브랜드의 상품들을 갖고 있었지요. 그리고 나서 저는 다른 특성에 관한 질문을 받았어요... 발바닥의 움푹한 부분을 받쳐주는 것, 충격 완화가 되는 안창, 혹은 정형 교정 친화적인지... 또는 심지어는 방수 신발인지요!... 좋아요... 그리고 나서 저는 제 발이 좁은지, 중간인지, 혹은 넓은지에 대해 생각해야 했어요. 그리고 물론 결정을 내리기 전에 수많은 색깔 중 하나를 골라야 했어요. 이게 좋은 걸까요, 나쁜 걸까요? 수많은 선택에 놓여 있는 우리는 정녕 행복한가요?

스탠포드 캠퍼스 근처에 있는 슈퍼마켓에서 연구가 진행되었습니다. 소비자들은 24개의 다른 잼을 맛보고 골라야 했는데 사실 6개의 다른 잼을 맛보고 선택해야 하는 소비자들에 비해 어떤 잼도 구입할 가능성이 낮았어요. 이는 소비자들에게 너무 많은 선택권이 있을 경우 오히려 심리적으로 압도되며 지치고 스트레스를 받기 때문이에요. 일부 소비자들은 심지어 구매를 무기한으로 미루기까지 하지요.

또 한 가지 흥미로운 점은, 사람들은 질적인 면에서 더 많은 선택권을 주는 브랜드를 더 좋다고 생각한다는 거예요. 이는 더 많은 종류의 상품을 이용할 수 있다는 건 그 브랜드가 특정한 분야에서 더 전문적이라는 뜻이라고 받아들이기 때문에 벌어져요... 그리고 이는 소비자들이 편견을 갖게 하고 잘못된 결정을 내리게 할 수도 있어요. 예를 들면, 소비자들이 초콜릿 샘플을 맛볼 수 있었어요. 한 그룹은 몇 개의 종류만 있었던 반면, 한 그룹은 다양한 종류의 초콜릿을 맛볼 수 있었어요. 그 후, 양쪽 그룹 모두 같은 브랜드의 초콜릿을 맛보았음에도 불구하고 사람들은 다양한 종류의 초콜릿을 가진 쪽이 더 맛있었다는 평을 내렸지요.

마지막으로, 많은 선택은 소비자에게 후회와 불만족의 감정을 남깁니다. 사람들은 계속 생각하지요... 그리고 구입 후에도 그들은 끊임없이 자신에게 "만약 …했더라면?"하며 질문을 던집니다. 제한적인 선택을 가진 소비자들은 그들의 결정에 대해 보통 만족하는 반면, 다양한 선택을 가진 소비자들은 종종 미련을 겪고 이는 결국 그들이 구매한 상품에 대한 실망으로 이어집니다.

Sample Essay   p.038

교수는 너무 많은 질문과 선택은 우리의 삶을 행복하지 않게 만든다고 말한다. 이는 소비자들이 많은 선택 덕분에 많은 이득을 얻는다는 지문의 내용을 직접적으로 반박한다.

첫째, 교수는 다른 그룹은 오직 6개의 다른 종류의 잼들을 선택할 수 있었던 반면 한 그룹의 소비자들은 24개의 다른 종류의 잼을 선택할 수 있었던 슈퍼마켓에서 진행되었던 한 연구에 대해 언급한다. 결과적으로, 더 많은 옵션을 가졌던 소비자들이 지쳐서 구매를 연기했다. 이는 다양한 선택은 소비자들이 개인 선호도에 따라 쇼핑을 할 수 있는 기회를 제공한다는 지문의 내용에 반대된다.

둘째, 소비자들에게 많은 선택을 주는 것은 특정 브랜드가 질이 좋다는 잘못된 생각을 갖게 할 수 있다. 한 연구에서, 소비자들은 두 그룹으로 나뉜, 같은 브랜드의 초콜릿을 맛보았다. 한 그룹은 많은 종류가 있었고 다른 그룹은 몇 가지의 종류밖에 없었다. 모든 초콜릿이 같은 브랜드 제품이라는 것을 모

른 채, 소비자들은 전자가 더 맛있다고 평가했다. 이는 고를 수 있는 더 비슷한 물건이 있을 때, 소비자들은 더 나은 가격과 질을 접하게 된다는 지문의 내용을 반박한다.

마지막으로, 소비자들은 여러 개 중 하나를 고른 후에 그 제품에 대해 실망하는 경향이 있다. 이는 사람들이 남아 있는 물건에 대한 미련에서 오는 스트레스를 겪기 때문에 발생하는데, 이는 불만족과 후회로 이어진다. 이는 통제력과 힘을 가졌다는 기분이 소비자를 만족스럽게 한다는 지문의 내용을 논박한다.

TASK 2 · INDEPENDENT TASK
Single vs. Multiple

Sample Essay 1 | AGREE   p.041

성공하기 위해 여러 다양한 능력을 키울 것인지 아니면 하나의 특정한 능력에 집중할 것인지에 대한 질문은 언제나 행해져 왔다. 각각의 방법에는 장점뿐만 아니라 단점도 있다. 어떤 사람들은 다른 능력을 개발하기보다 하나의 분야에 집중하는 것이 우선시되어야 한다고 주장한다. 하지만, 나는 다양한 분야들이 서로 밀접한 관계에 있기 때문에 오늘날 사회에서는 다양한 분야에서의 능력을 갖추는 것이 필요하다고 굳게 믿는다. 또한, 사람들은 언제든지 상황이나 자신의 적성에 따라서 전공이나 직업을 바꿀 수 있는 결정을 내릴 수 있다.

우선, 프로젝트에서 일을 실행하기에 앞서 실제 먼저 아이디어를 발표해야 하기 때문에 직장에서는 의사소통 능력 및 설득력 등의 능력이 필수적이다. 예를 들면, 폭넓은 지식을 가지고 있는 우수한 직원이라 할지라도, 만약 자신의 생각을 표현하지 못한다면 계획을 실행시키는 것은 불가능할 것이다. 따라서, 특정 능력들은 서로 밀접히 연관되어 있으며 시너지 효과를 만들어 낸다.

게다가, 많은 능력을 키우면 개인의 재능과 흥미를 발견하는데 도움이 된다. 덧붙여, 자신의 불만족이나 상황의 변화 때문에 때때로 자신의 전문 분야를 바꾸어야 할 필요도 있을 수 있다. 예로써, 내 사촌은 스쿠버다이빙 강사였는데 일을 하다가 부상을 당했다. 그는 일을 그만두었어야 했지만, 과거에 땄던 자격증 덕분에 회계 사무실에 쉽게 취직을 할 수 있었다. 그러한 능력을 키우지 않았더라면, 그는 이전 직업을 잃었다는 점과 직업적인 성공으로부터 멀어졌다는 점으로 인해 좌절하고 낙담해 했을 것이다.

하나의 능력에 집중하는 것이 한 사람이 특정 분야에서 깊이 있는 지식을 얻는데 도움이 되는 것은 사실이다. 하지만, 그러한 능력이 상황 때문에 무용하게 되거나, 그 능력을 사용하는 것에 대한 흥미를 잃는다면, 고통과 혼란을 겪을 수도 있다. 게다가, 다른 능력을 개발하는 것은 시너지 효과를 만들어 낼 수 있다. 이 두 가지 이유로, 나는 누군가 성공을 하고 싶다면, 하나의 능력에 집중하는 것보다 많은 능력을 개발하는 것이 더 낫다는 진술에 강력히 동의한다.

Sample Essay 2 | DISAGREE   p.042

성공하기 위해 여러 다양한 능력을 키울 것인지 아니면 하나의 특정한 능력에 집중할 것인지에 대한 질문은 언제나 행해져 왔다. 각각의 방법에는 장점뿐만 아니라 단점도 있다. 어떤 사람들은 다양한 분야에서의 능력을 갖추는 것이 오늘날 사회에서 필요하다고 주장한다. 하지만, 나는 특정 분야에 집중함으로써 깊이 있는 지식을 얻을 수 있기 때문에 다른 능력들을 개발하기에 앞서 하나의 분야에 초점을 맞추는 것이 우선시되어야 한다고 굳게 믿는다. 게다가, 한 가지 능력에 집중한다면 시간을 절약할 수 있을 것이다.

우선, 대부분의 일자리는 특정 능력을 가진 직원을 필요로 한다. 업무들이 회사의 여러 부서에 나누어져 있기 때문에, 직원들은 특정 분야에서의 깊이

있는 지식을 개발하는 것이 필수적이다. 예를 들면, 회사의 한 직원이 다양한 분야에서의 많은 능력은 가지고 있으나, 특정 분야에서는 다른 직원들만큼 유능하지 못할 수도 있다. 그가 다양한 능력을 소유하고 있음에도 불구하고, 기업이 필요한 직원은 특정 분야에서의 전문적인 능력을 가진 사람인 것이다.

게다가, 다른 능력을 키우는 것은 시간 낭비일 수 있다. 다양한 분야에서 폭넓은 지식을 얻는 것은 도움이 될 수 있다. 하지만, 이는 어느 정도의 시간을 빼앗게 될 것인데, 이러한 빼앗긴 시간은 특정 분야에서의 성공에 요구되는 한 가지 능력을 갖추는데 사용될 수 있을 것이다. 예로서, 많은 연구에 따르면 대학에서 다양한 학문을 공부했던 학생들은 하나의 학문에 집중했던 학생들보다 졸업 후 좋은 직업을 가질 가능성이 낮다.

다양한 능력들이 서로 밀접한 관계를 가지고 있다는 점은 사실이다. 하지만, 기업 및 기타 조직들은 특정 분야에 전문화된 다양한 구성원들이 있는 여러 부서들을 갖추고 있으며, 각 구성원들에게는 자기의 분야에 대한 깊이 있는 지식이 기대된다. 게다가, 많은 종류의 능력을 기르는 것은 시간 및 노력의 낭비가 될 수 있다. 이 두 가지 이유로서, 나는 성공을 하고 싶다면, 하나의 능력에 집중하는 것보다 많은 능력을 개발하는 것이 더 좋다는 진술에 강력히 반대한다.

Actual Test 04

TASK 1 · INTEGRATED TASK

Communications: Social Media

READING   p.045

테크놀로지의 발달 덕분에, 사람들은 그들의 일상을 세계 다른 지역에 있는 사람들과 공유할 수 있게 되었다. 소셜 미디어가 세계의 사람들과 실시간으로 의사소통이 가능하게 해 주었지만, 그것은 또한 많은 문제들을 야기해오기도 했고, 이중 일부는 심각하며 즉각적인 관심을 필요로 한다.

소셜 미디어가 건강에 어떻게 영향을 끼치는지에 대한 많은 연구가 있다. 사람들과 얼굴을 맞대고 대화를 하며 시간을 보내는 대신, 사람들은 더 고립되고 소셜 미디어에 의존하게 되었다. 한 연구에 따르면, 소셜 미디어를 하는 시간을 줄이는 것은 고독감을 감소시켰고, 사람들의 전반적인 행복감을 증가시켰다. 또한 그 연구는 사람 간의 관계가 아닌 소셜 미디어 상의 관계는 이미 우울증이나 흔히 포모증후군이라고 알려진 고립 공포감을 겪는 사람을 더 악화시킨다는 것을 발견했다.

소셜 미디어의 보급으로 창의력을 읽어버리는 위험 또한 있다. 스스로 아이디어를 떠올리기 보다는, 사람들은 단순히 소셜 미디어에 키워드를 입력하고 아이디어를 찾으며, 그들이 좋아하는 걸 고르고, 베낀다. 많은 아이디어는 토론을 위해 직접 만났을 때 나오곤 했다. 그러나, 소셜 미디어가 그걸 방해했고, 사람들이 아이디어를 떠올리기 전에 그들의 생각을 공유하는 것은 어려워졌다.

오보는 또 하나의 심각한 문제이며 쉽게 해결될 수 없다. 이는 일부 언론사나 사람들이 소셜 미디어의 본질을 악용하기 때문이다. 일단 잘못된 정보가 나가면 정정한다 하더라도 걷잡을 수 없이 확산이 지속된다. 오보의 조회수 때문에 일부러 오보를 흘리는 사람들이 있다. 이는 사건과 연관이 없음에도 불구하고 굉장히 힘든 시간과 상황을 겪어야 하는 무고한 희생자를 낼 수 있다.

W Professor: No one would deny that our lives have been changed by social media, and it is hard to live without social media. Because social media has had such an impact on people's lives, some people are against it . . . And, of course, everything has downsides . . . but the advantages definitely make us able to tolerate it.

Have you ever heard of a woman named Cunhaporanga Tatuyo? I see some hands . . . all right . . . About one-third of this class seems to know her. Ms. Tatuyo is a member of the Tatuyo people, who inhabit the banks of the Amazon River. According to the news, she's gained 6 million followers within 18 months of opening a social media account. Since the pandemic, there have been no travelers in the region . . . so in order to introduce her culture and to attract travelers, she has started uploading daily-life pictures of the indigenous people living in the Amazon jungle. And it's been a huge success . . . Many people . . . um . . . including myself . . . and probably some of you, too . . . are waiting for new pictures and videos of a fascinating culture we are not very familiar with. This is a great example of showing how social media connects people from different sides of the world.

As many of you are probably aware, social media is the most effective tool for reaching the attention of lots of people in a short period of time. Quite often, environmental issues used to be neglected and ignored either purposely or unintentionally. However, thanks to the constant acknowledgement of environmental concerns through social media platforms, more people now have an awareness of many issues and show interest in sustainability and nature conservation.

Finally, social media helps people stay in touch. As society moves at a faster and faster pace, it has become harder to meet people. In the past, people had to spend a lot of time catching up after they hadn't seen others in a long time. But now? I know what my cousin had for her birthday dinner last night thanks to all the pictures she uploaded for her family and friends to see. Even though we are in different countries, I always feel like she is close by.

교수: 누구도 우리의 삶은 소셜 미디어에 의해 변화되었다는 것을 부정하지 않을 것이며, 소셜 미디어 없이는 살기가 힘들죠. 소셜 미디어가 사람들의 삶에 엄청난 영향을 끼쳐왔기 때문에, 일부 사람들은 그것에 맞서죠. 물론 모든 것들은 단점이 있어요... 하지만 장점은 확실히 우리가 소셜 미디어를 견딜 수 있게 해주지요.

Cunhaporanga Tatuyo라는 여성에 대해 들어본 적 있나요? 손을 든 사람들이 좀 보이네요... 좋아요... 이 반의 약 1/3 정도가 그녀를 아는 것 같군요... Tatuyo는 아마존강의 강둑에 사는 타투요 부족 사람들의 일원입니다. 뉴스에 따르면, 그녀는 소셜 미디어 계정을 시작한 후 18개월만에 600만 명의 팔로워를 갖게 되었어요. 세계적 유행병 이후, 그 지역을 찾는 관광객이 없었고... 그래서, 그녀의 문화를 알리며 관광객을 유치하기 위해 아마존 정글에 사는 원주민들의 일상 사진을 업로드 하기 시작했어요. 그리고 그건 커다란 성공이었죠... 많은 사람들이... 음... 저를 포함해서요... 그리고 아마도 여러분 일부도요 (웃음)... 우리가 익숙하지 않은 매혹적인 문화에 대한 새로운 사진과 동영상을 기다리고 있지요. 이는 소셜 미디어가 세계 다른 지역의 사람들을 어떻게 연결해 주는지 보여주는 훌륭한 예에요.

여러분 중 다수가 아시겠지만, 소셜 미디어는 단시간에 많은 사람들의 관심을 받는데 가장 효율적인 도구에요. 꽤 자주, 환경 문제들은 고의든 의도치 않게든 외면당하고 무시당하곤 하죠. 하지만 소셜 미디어 플랫폼을 통한 지속적인 환경에 대한 우려 덕분에, 더 많은 사람들이 많은 사안들에 관심이 있고, 지속 가능성과 자연 보전에 대해 흥미를 보입니다.

끝으로, 소셜 미디어는 사람들이 서로 연락을 유지할 수 있게 해줘요. 사회가 빠른 속도로 움직이기 때문에 사람들을 만나는 것은 더 어려워졌어요. 과거에는, 다른 사람들을 오랫동안 만나지 못한 후에는 근황을 따라잡기 위해 많은 시간을 보내야 했어요. 그런데 지금은 어떤가요? 저는 제 사촌이 가족과 친구들이 볼 수 있도록 그녀의 사진들을 모두 업로드한 덕분에, 어젯밤 제 사촌이 생일 저녁 식사로 무엇을 먹었는지 알아요. 비록 우리는 다른 나라에 있지만, 저는 항상 그녀가 가까이에 있다고 느껴요.

Sample Essay p.048

지문은 소셜 미디어가 심각한 문제를 초래하며 적절한 조치가 취해져야 한다고 주장한다. 그러나, 교수는 소셜 미디어가 사람들에게 수많은 이점을 가져다 주었기 때문에, 몇 가지 단점은 견디는 것이 합당하다고 주장한다.

첫째, 지문은 소셜 미디어에 너무 많은 시간을 보내는 것은 건강 문제를 일으킨다고 알려져 있다고 주장한다. 하지만, 교수는 소셜 미디어는 사람들을 이어주는데 도움이 되었다고 언급하며 아마존 강둑에 사는 여성의 예를 든다. 그녀는 소셜 미디어에서 원주민들의 일상을 공유했고 그녀의 행동은 사람들의 관심을 받는데 크게 성공했다.

뿐만 아니라, 지문은 창의력을 잃고 있는 것에 대해 주목한다. 사람을 실제로 만나서 회의를 하며 토론을 하는 대신 아이디어를 찾고 복제하는 것은 혁신과 창의력의 결핍을 초래한다. 그럼에도 불구하고, 교수는 소셜 미디어가 대중의 경각심을 끌어내는 역할을 할 수 있다고 설명한다. 그녀는 또한 소셜 미디어를 통한 자연 보존에 대한 지속적인 참여는 대중의 관심을 더 모았다고 말한다.

끝으로, 지문은 오보가 힘든 시간과 상황을 겪는 무고한 희생자를 낼 수 있다고 밝힌다. 하지만, 교수는 어떻게 소셜 미디어가 사람들이 자주 볼 수 없는 다른 사람들과 손쉽게 연락하는 것을 가능케 하는지에 관한 또 다른 장점을 설명한다.

TASK 2 · INDEPENDENT TASK

The Internet

Sample Essay 1 | AGREE p.051

인터넷의 출현으로, 우리의 삶은 바뀌었고 인터넷이 없는 우리의 삶은 상상하기 힘들다. 우리는 이메일을 쓰는 것부터 독감 접종의 예약까지, 인터넷에 굉장히 의존하고 있다. 일부 사람들은 인터넷이 삶에 많은 부정적인 영향을 가져왔다고 주장하지만, 나는 현대 사회에서 인터넷의 사용은 대부분 긍정적인 영향을 미친다는 명제에 동의한다. 이유는, 편리함과 환경 문제에 대한 관심 때문이다.

첫째, 인터넷은 우리에게 그 어느 때보다 더 편리함을 가져다 주었다. 예를 들면, 과거에, 우리는 특정 분야에 대한 정보를 찾기 위해서는 도서관에 가야 했다. 하지만, 인터넷 덕분에, 우리가 해야 할 일은 키워드를 입력하고 정보를 검색하는 것뿐이다. 이는 우리의 삶을 편리하게 해주었을 뿐 아니라,

우리가 시간을 절약하도록 도와주었다. 따라서 인터넷은 우리로 하여금 제약을 받지 않고 정보 검색하는 것을 가능케 했다.

뿐만 아니라, 그러지 않았다면 등한시되었을 만한 환경과 사회 문제가 대중으로부터 더 많은 관심을 받고, 사람들이 자연의 지속 가능성과 보존에 대해 더욱 관심을 가지게 해준다. 예를 들면, 잘 알려진 기업에서 자연에 분명히 해가 되는 공장을 운영하는 것이 SNS에 알려졌을 때, 소식은 굉장히 빠른 속도로 퍼진다. 자연 환경 문제에 관한 경각심과 지속적인 인식 덕분에, 많은 그런 사건들은 사람들이 자연 보호 법 제정을 요구하는 결과를 가져왔다.

인터넷에서 퍼지는 오보에 관한 위험이 있는 것은 사실이다. 하지만, 그것은 신문, 잡지, 그리고 심지어는 일부 책에서도 언제나 있어 왔다. 인터넷은 편리함을 제공해 왔고, 사람들 사이에서 환경과 사회적 경각심을 불러일으켰다. 그러므로 나는 인터넷의 보급은 현대 사회에서 대부분 긍정적 영향을 미친다고 굳게 믿는다.

Sample Essay 2 | DISAGREE p.052

인터넷의 출현으로, 우리의 삶은 바뀌었고 인터넷이 없는 우리의 삶은 상상하기 힘들다. 우리는 이메일을 쓰는 것부터 독감 접종의 예약까지, 인터넷에 굉장히 의존하고 있다. 일부 사람들은 인터넷이 삶에 많은 긍정적인 효과를 가져왔다고 주장하지만, 나는 인터넷 사용이 현대 사회에서 대부분 긍정적인 영향을 미친다는 명제에 동의하지 않는다. 이유는, 건강 문제와 돌이킬 수 없는 결과를 초래할 수 있는 오보 때문이다.

첫째, 인터넷은 정신뿐 아니라 신체적 문제들을 자아낼 수 있다. SNS가 건강 관련 문제에 어떤 영향을 끼치는 가에 대한 많은 연구가 실행되고 있다. 다른 사람들과 대면 대화를 하며 시간을 보내는 것 대신, 우리는 더욱 고립되고 전자 통신 기계에 더 많이 의존해 왔다. SNS상의 교류는 이미 우울증과 FOMO라고도 불리는 고립공포감을 겪고 있는 사람들의 상태를 더욱 악화시킨다는 것이 드러났다. 연구에 따르면 스마트폰이나 노트북의 사용 시간을 줄이는 것은 외로움을 감소시켰고, 전체적인 행복감은 증가시켰다.

뿐만 아니라, 오보는 인터넷이 가져온 또 하나의 심각한 문제이다. 자세히 말하자면, 일부 언론 단체와 개인들은 인터넷의 본질을 악용한다. 일단 정확하지 않은 정보가 공개되면, 수정을 한다 하더라도 걷잡을 수 없이 퍼져나간다. 이는 사건과 연관이 없음에도 불구하고 극도로 힘든 시간과 상황을 겪어야 하는 무고한 희생자를 낼 수 있다.

인터넷이 우리의 삶을 편하게 만들고 우리에게 광대한 양의 정보를 제공해주는 것은 사실이다. 하지만, 사람들의 정신적 그리고 신체적 문제에 관한 한 그럴 만한 가치가 없다. 또한, 소문이나 오보는 무고한 희생자들을 비참한 시간으로부터 고통받게 만들 수 있다. 그러므로, 나는 인터넷의 보급은 우리 삶에 많은 부정적 영향을 미친다고 굳게 믿는다.

Actual Test 05

TASK 1 · INTEGRATED TASK

Anthropology: The Amazon River Basin

READING p.055

남미의 아마존 강 유역은 지구에서 가장 다양한 생명체들을 담고 있다. 아이러니하게도, 이곳은 다수의 인간들이 살기에는 이상적인 곳이 아니었다. 실제, 역사적으로, 소수의 사람들만이 아마존 전 지역을 둘러싸고 있는 혹독

한 우림 지대에서 살아남을 수 있었다.

아마존 우림 지대는 많은 동식물들을 포함하고 있지만 상당한 규모의 인간 무리들이 살아가기에는 적합하지 않다. 그러한 이유 중 하나는 열악한 토질 때문인데, 이곳의 토양은 본래 산성을 띠고 있다. 따라서, 농부들이 한 두 시즌 정도 옥수수와 콩 같은 작물들을 재배할 수는 있지만, 그 후에는, 토양의 영양 성분들이 빠져나가 어떤 것도 재배할 수 없게 된다. 보다 발전된 농법이 사용되고 있는 오늘날조차, 아마존의 많은 수의 사람들을 부양하기에 충분한 식량은 재배될 수 없다.

과거, 아마존에는 단백질의 공급원이 존재하지 않았는데, 단백질은 인간이 생존하는데 필수적인 것이다. 소와 양 같은 식용 동물들은 유럽인들이 1500년대에 이들을 가져왔던 당시의 남미에서만 찾아볼 수 있었다. 이곳에 동물들이 유입된 이후에도, 동물들의 무리가 많은 적은 없었는데, 그 이유는 열악한 토양과 정글로 뒤덮인 토지는 동물들에게 필요한 충분한 양의 먹이를 생산할 수 없었다.

한때 미 대륙에는 세 개의 거대한 문명이 존재했다. 마야, 잉카 그리고 아즈텍이 그들이다. 이들 중 아마존에서 살았던 사람들은 없었다. 게다가, 이 세 문명권의 사람들은 석조 건물들을 지었다. 석재는 궁전과 사원의 주요 건축 자재였는데, 그것들은 고대 문명 사람들이 사실상 항상 지어왔던 것들이었다. 하지만 아마존 어디에서도 건축용으로 사용될 수 있는 석재는 거의 존재하지 않는다. 마찬가지로, 어떤 궁전이나 사원도 고고학자들에 의해 발견되거나 발굴된 적이 없는데, 이는 일정 규모 이상의 인간 거주지가 그곳에 존재했을 것 같지 않게 한다.

LISTENING　　　🎧 05-01

W Professor: Nowadays, the region around the Amazon River is sparsely inhabited. But was it always like that? After all, many areas in the Americas in the past were home to large empires, like the Aztecs and Mayas. So is it possible that a sizable civilization once existed in the Amazon? I believe the answer is yes, but the evidence has been lost.

The Amazon has plenty of vegetation that could easily support large numbers of people. After all, many species of edible plants, including nuts, berries, citrus fruits, bananas, and pineapples, grow in the jungle. In addition, while most of the soil is fairly acidic, parts of the Amazon are quite fertile. You see, uh, volcanic eruptions in the past spread copious amounts of ash, which benefits the soil. Thus Amazon farmers would have been able to raise crops in many places.

And don't forget that the Amazon is home to huge numbers of animals, which could have provided protein for humans. The Amazon River is rich in fish, an excellent source of protein. And the rainforest is teeming with birds, more than 400 species of reptiles, and 500 species of mammals. I contend that a large human population could have thrived there while consuming a diverse diet.

Finally, it's easy to explain why there's no evidence of any past civilizations: The rainforest destroyed it. Yes, there's very little stone that people could have built with. Yet not all cultures built with stone. The Amazon would have supplied an abundant amount of wood that people could have constructed buildings with. However, over time, the hot, humid weather would've worn away the majority of these buildings. And the jungle would have overtaken the rest. Any buildings that have survived until today are so covered with vegetation that they'd be practically impossible to find.

교수: 현재, 아마존 강 주위에는 사람들이 거의 거주하고 있지 않습니다. 하지만, 늘 그랬을까요? 어쨌든 과거 미 대륙의 여러 지역은, 예컨대 아즈텍이나 마야와 같은 거대 제국들의 본거지였습니다. 그렇다면 한때 상당한 규모의 문명이 아마존 지역에 존재했었다는 것이 가능한 이야기일까요? 저는 가능할 수도 있다고 생각하지만, 그에 대한 증거는 아직 없습니다.

아마존에는 많은 수의 사람들이 먹고 살 수 있는 풍부한 양의 식물들이 있습니다. 어쨌든, 많은 식용 가능한 식물들, 즉 견과류, 딸기류, 감귤류, 바나나, 파인애플 등이 밀림에서 자라고 있으니까요. 또한, 대부분의 토양이 강한 산성을 띠고 있지만, 아마존의 일부 지역은 상당히 비옥합니다. 아시다시피, 어, 과거 화산 분출로 인해 많은 양의 재가 퍼지게 되었는데, 이로써 토질이 향상되었습니다. 따라서 아마존의 농부들은 많은 지역에서 농작물을 재배할 수 있었을 것입니다.

그리고 아마존이 인간에게 단백질을 공급해 줄 수 있는 엄청난 수의 동물들의 본거지라는 점을 잊지 말아 주세요. 아마존 강에는 어류가 풍부한데, 어류는 뛰어난 단백질 공급원이 됩니다. 그리고 우림 지대는 조류, 400여종의 파충류, 그리고 500여종의 포유 동물들로 가득합니다. 저는 그곳에서 많은 인구가 다양한 음식을 섭취하며 번성할 수 있었을 것이라고 생각합니다.

마지막으로, 왜 과거의 문명에 관한 증거가 없는지에 대해서는 설명하기가 쉽습니다. 우림 지대가 파괴시킨 것이었죠. 그렇습니다, 사람들이 건축에 쓸 수 있는 석재가 거의 존재하지 않습니다. 하지만 모든 문화에서 석재로 건물을 짓는 것은 아닙니다. 아마존은 사람들이 건물을 지을 수 있도록 풍부한 양의 목재를 공급해 주었을 것입니다. 하지만, 시간이 흐르면서, 덥고 습한 날씨로 인해 대다수의 건축물들이 마멸되었을 것입니다. 그리고 남아 있는 건물들은 밀림이 삼켜 버렸을 것입니다. 오늘날까지 남아있는 건물들 조차도 식물들로 덮여 있어서 사실상 찾아내기가 불가능합니다.

Sample Essay　　　p.058

교수는 아마존에 상당한 규모의 고대 문명의 존재 가능성을 주장한다. 세 가지 이유로, 그녀는 아마존 지역에서 다수의 인구가 살 수 없었을 것이라는 지문의 주장을 직접적으로 반박한다.

첫째, 풍부한 식물들은 인간의 대규모 정착을 위한 충분한 식량을 제공해 주었을 것이다. 아마존의 일부는 상당히 비옥한 편이어서 농업을 가능하도록 만들어 준다. 또한, 화산 분출로 인한 화산재는 토양에 이점을 더해 주었다. 이는 열악한 토질로 인해 식물의 성장이 어려워서 다수의 사람들에게 공급될 수 있는 충분한 양의 식량이 자라지 않았을 것이라는 지문의 주장을 반박한다.

그리고, 교수는 아마존 강은 인간이 먹을 단백질을 지원할 수 있는 많은 물고기를 가지고 있다고 말한다. 게다가, 다양한 동물들은 상당 수의 인간에게 음식 공급을 하기에 충분하다. 이런 주장은 열악한 토질과 밀림으로 뒤덮인 토지는 인간이 동물들로부터 충분한 양의 단백질을 섭취하는 것이 어렵게 했을 것이라는 지문의 주장에 의문을 제기한다.

마지막으로, 많은 목재들의 이용 가능성은 아마존에 많은 인구가 거주하는 것이 가능하도록 했다. 교수에 의하면, 건물들이 발견되지 않고 있는 이유는 덥고 습한 날씨와 밀림에 빽빽이 들어서 있는 식물들 때문이다. 이는 궁전이나 사원의 부재가 아마존에서 거대한 문명이 존재하지 않았다라는 점을 보여 준다는 지문의 생각을 반박한다.

TASK 2 · INDEPENDENT TASK

The Government's Role

Sample Essay 1 | AGREE   p.061

교육은 한 나라의 발전에 있어서 가장 중요한 요소 중 하나이다. 따라서, 정부는 어디에 그리고 어떻게 예산을 사용할 것인지에 대해 매우 신중하게 계획을 세운다. 일부 사람들은 정부가 대학생들에게 더 많은 돈을 사용해야 한다고 주장한다. 하지만, 나는 아동 교육이 어린 학생들에게 고등 교육에 대한 기반을 제공해 주기 때문에 정부가 아이들의 교육에 보다 많은 돈을 사용해야 한다고 굳게 믿는다. 게다가, 대학생들에게는 자금을 자원받을 수 있는 다른 재원들이 많이 있다.

첫째, 기본적인 수준의 학교 교육은 보다 심도있는 교육의 토대이다. 학교는 학생들이 본인의 학습 습관과 일과를 만드는 곳이기 때문에, 정부가 어린 시절에 더 초점을 맞추는 것이 중요하다. 예를 들어, 일본에서는 많은 정부 자금이 아이들의 교육쪽으로 간다. 그 돈으로, 학교들은 스마트 보드와 같은 학습 도구를 취득할 뿐만 아니라 수업의 질도 개선시키고 있다. 따라서 학생들은 훌륭한 교사의 지도 하에 다양한 교육 자료 및 학습 방법들을 접한다. 그 결과 아이들의 이해 수준은 또래의 일반 아이들보다 훨씬 높은데, 이는 미래에 깊이 있는 교육의 기회를 열어준다.

게다가, 많은 기업들이 학생들을 위해 대학에 자금을 지원한다. 기업들은 우수한 학력을 가진 사원들이 필요하기 때문에, 연구, 장학금, 학교 시설을 포함한 많은 분야에 투자를 한다. 예를 들어, 내 사촌이 다니는 대학교는 학생들이 신청할 수 있는 다양한 장학금을 제공하고 있다. 대부분의 장학금은 한국의 여러 다양한 기업들로부터 나온다. 따라서 이런 장학금 중 하나를 받은 내 사촌은 자금 걱정을 하지 않고 연구에 집중할 수가 있다. 그런 점에서 볼 때, 대학생들은 정부 외에 재원으로부터 돈을 조달할 기회가 많다.

경력에 있어서 도약대이기 때문에 대학 교육이 중요하다는 점은 사실이다. 하지만, 고등 교육에 대비하기 위해 조기에 공부 습관을 발달시키는 아이들을 준비시키는 것이 더욱 중요하다. 게다가, 대학생들은 사기업들로부터 이미 충분한 자금을 받고 있다. 이러한 이유로 나는 정부가 대학생보다는 아이들의 교육에 투자를 해야 한다는 주장에 찬성한다.

Sample Essay 2 | DISAGREE   p.062

교육은 한 나라의 발전에 있어서 가장 중요한 요소 중 하나이다. 따라서, 정부는 어디에 그리고 어떻게 예산을 사용할 것인지에 대해 매우 신중하게 계획을 세운다. 일부 사람들은 정부가 아이들의 교육에 더 많은 돈을 사용해야 한다고 주장한다. 하지만, 대학생들이 해야만 하는 심층 학습과 연구 때문에 나는 정부가 대학생들에게 보다 많은 돈을 사용해야 한다고 굳게 믿는다. 게다가, 아이들은 이미 정부의 지원금으로 기초 교육을 받고 있다.

첫째, 대학은 대부분의 학생들이 졸업 후 일을 하기 위해 준비를 하는 기관이다. 따라서, 학생들이 더 유능할수록, 그들은 결국 국가의 경제 성장을 촉진시킬 회사에 더 기여할 수 있다. 예를 들어, 한국 정부가 예산의 일부를 대학에 사용하면서부터, 교육의 질이 획기적으로 향상되었다. 이에 따라, 해당 대학의 우수한 졸업생들 중 다수는 정부에서 일을 하고 있다. 결과적으로 유능한 노동력의 양성은 국가에 이득이 된다.

또한, 정부는 지금 그들이 하는 것보다 더 많은 돈을 아이들의 교육에 투자할 필요가 없다. 아이들은 깊이 있는 지식에 대한 수용 능력이 제한되어있기 때문에, 아이들의 교육에 투자를 더 하는 것은 과다 지출이 될 수 있다. 예를 들면, 정부는 유치원과 초등학교 같은 기초 교육에 자금을 제공하고 있다. 여기에는 이미 교사 양성과 시설 개선이 포함되어 있다. 아이들은 중요한 연구나 실험을 수행할 돈이 필요없기 때문에, 여기에 더 많은 돈을 투자한다면 예산 과다의 결과만이 나타날 것이다.

아이들이 초기에 학습 습관을 기른다는 점에서 아이들의 교육이 중요하다는 것은 사실이다. 하지만, 훌륭한 학습 습관은 끊임없이 바뀌는 교육 프로그램보다는 교사의 꾸준한 자극과 동기 부여로부터 나온다. 이러한 점에서 볼 때, 정부는 아이들의 교육에 지출을 늘릴 필요가 없다. 정부는 대신, 대학들이 학생들이 직장 생활로 전환하는 것을 돕기 때문에 대학들에 돈을 더 투자해야 한다. 이러한 이유로, 나는 정부가 대학생보다 아이들에게 돈을 투자해야 한다는 주장에 반대한다.

Actual Test 06

TASK 1 · INTEGRATED TASK

Education: Distance Learning

READING   p.065

새로운 바이러스의 출현으로 원격 학습은 그 어느 때보다 대중화되고, 많은 플랫폼이 개발 및 개선되었다. 세계의 많은 학교들은 초등과 중고등 학생들을 전통적인 교실에서 온라인 수업으로 전환을 선택하고 있다. 온라인 교육이 실제로 성공적일지에 관한 많은 논란에도 불구하고, 많은 부모, 학생 그리고 교사들은 새로운 실행에 만족하는 것이 증명되고 있다.

학생들은 자신만의 속도로 공부할 수 있다. 전형적인 전통 교실 환경에서, 학생들은 자신들의 학습 능력이나 속도에 상관 없이 교사가 정해둔 교수 학습 계획안을 따라야 한다. 반면, 온라인 교육은 학생들이 자신만의 속도와 방법을 정하도록 혜택을 제공하여 조작 및 경험 학습을 가능케 한다. 실제로, 학생들은 동영상 강의를 몇 번씩 다시 보고 교사들에게 메모를 남길 수도 있는 반면, 일부 과목에서는 더 어려운 문제를 풀거나 이미 알고 있는 부분은 건너 뛸 수도 있다. 그들이 고심하는 다른 과목들에 대한 추가 자료나 보충 설명을 이용할 수 있다.

온라인 학습은 교사와 학생들 사이의 소통을 유지할 수 있도록 도와준다. 줌 같은 일부 프로그램들은 실시간 강의를 가능케 하기 때문에 교사와 학생들은 동시에 서로 연결될 수 있다. 채팅 기능 덕분에, 학생들은 마이크 기능을 켜서 발언을 할 수 있는 것은 물론이고, 질문을 하거나 피드백을 바로 받을 수 있다. 심지어는 소회의실(breakout rooms)이라는 기능이 학생들이 토론을 위한 소규모 그룹으로 만날 수 있도록 해준다.

온라인 교육에서 가장 매력적인 요소는 편리함이다. 사람이 인터넷에 접근할 수 있는 한 세계 어디에서든 공부가 가능하다. 학생들은 학습에 가장 적합한 시간과 장소를 선택할 수 있다. 실제로, 이는 학생들이 학업과 과외 활동을 좀 더 효율적으로 조정하고 관리할 수 있도록 해준다. 많은 연구가 보여주길 언제 어디서든 공부할 수 있는 점이 학생들에게 대단한 성취감을 주며 결국 더 나은 성과로 인도한다.

LISTENING   🎧 06-01

W Professor: Humans have faced numerous challenges, including wars, natural disasters, and disease. Currently, we are experiencing an unprecedented pandemic, which has lasted much longer than expected and caused a tremendous number of deaths. The advent of the disease has changed our lifestyles in many ways, one of which is the introduction of distance learning. Although it may sound appealing that virtual learning is an innovative learning method, it also poses problems . . . uh . . . I mean significant problems.

To begin with, distance learning does let students study at their own pace. And this has actually worked well for students who have always done well in the traditional classroom setting. So no matter what the given conditions are, these students end up with good grades. The problem is with those who lack motivation. The flexibility of online classes can be very challenging for some students to stay motivated when there are many other fun things to do, like watching YouTube, shopping online, making desserts . . . you name it. So this can affect students' academic performances throughout the year.

And, uh, this type of training is not helpful for the development of communication or teamwork skills either. Even though some online learning platforms feature, um, what are called breakout rooms for group talks, they are far different from interacting in person, which is particularly crucial for younger kids. Numerous studies have shown that a lack of peer interaction results in poorer academic and social skills, so overall, distance learning is not suitable for improving interpersonal relationships.

Then there are health issues related to distance learning. By commuting and walking around campus, we are exposed to sunlight, which provides vitamin D. Besides lacking vitamin D, students can suffer from obesity by staying in one place. This can, in fact, cause more serious consequences like indigestion and at worst, even diabetes! According to recent statistics, the number of kids wearing glasses has increased by 25% since virtual learning has been implemented in most states in the United States.

교수: 인류는 전쟁, 자연 재해, 질병 등의 많은 어려움에 직면해 왔습니다. 현재, 우리는 예상했던 것보다 훨씬 오랫동안 진행 중이며 수많은 죽음을 초래한 세계적 유행병으로 전례 없던 시기를 겪고 있지요. 질병의 출현은 우리 삶의 방식을 많은 형태로 바꾸었고, 그 중 하나는 온라인 교육의 도입입니다. 온라인 교육이 혁신적인 학습 방법으로 매력적으로 들리겠지만, 그것은 많은 문제들 또한 야기해요... 음... 심각한 문제들을 말이에요.

첫째, 온라인 교육이 학생들을 자기만의 속도로 공부할 수 있게 해주는 것은 사실이에요. 그리고 이는 전통적인 교실 환경에서 항상 잘해 왔던 학생들에게는 실제로 훌륭히 이행되고 있지요. 그래서 어떤 환경이 주어지든지 간에 이런 학생은 좋은 점수를 받아요. 문제는 동기 부여가 부족한 학생들인데요. 일부 학생들에게 온라인 강의의 유연성은 유튜브를 보거나 온라인 쇼핑을 하거나 디저트를 만드는 것... 등 그 밖의 다른 많은 재미있는 일이 있을 때, 동기 부여가 지속되는 것이 굉장히 힘들 수 있지요. 그래서 이는 1년 내내 학생들의 학업 성적에 영향을 끼칠 수 있답니다.

그리고 음, 이러한 종류의 교육은 의사소통이나 협동 능력을 키우는 것에도 도움이 되지 않아요. 일부 온라인 교육 플랫폼이 음, '소회의실(breakout room)'이라 불리는 그룹 대화방의 특성을 가지고 있지만, 어린이들에게는 특히 중요한 직접 교류하는 것과는 굉장히 다르죠. 많은 연구 결과에 따르면

또래와의 교류 결핍은 더 좋지 않은 성적과 사회성을 초래한다고 해요. 그래서 전반적으로, 원격 교육은 대인 관계를 개선하는데 적합하지 않습니다.

게다가 온라인 교육과 관련된 건강 문제가 있어요. 통근을 하고 캠퍼스를 걸어 다니면서, 우리는 비타민 D를 제공해 주는 햇빛에 노출됩니다. 비타민 D의 부족 외에도, 학생들은 한 곳에 머무르는 것으로 인해 비만으로 고생할 수 있어요. 이는, 사실, 소화 불량과 최악의 경우 심지어는 당뇨병 같은 더 심각한 결과를 초래할 수 있어요! 최근 통계 자료에 따르면, 미국 대부분의 주에서는 온라인 수업이 실행된 이후 아이들의 안경 착용이 25%나 증가했다고 하네요.

Sample Essay   p.068

교수는 원격 학습이 상당한 단점을 제기한다고 주장한다. 이는 원격 학습이 이상적이고 성공적인 교육 방법이라는 지문의 주장을 직접적으로 반박한다.

첫째, 온라인 교육이 학생들에게 본인만의 속도로 공부할 수 있는 기회를 제공한다는 사실에도 불구하고, 유튜브 시청 등 다른 것들로부터 쉽게 방해를 받기 때문에 학생들은 동기 부여 상태를 유지하기가 매우 힘들다. 결과적으로, 동기 부여의 결핍은 학생의 전반적인 성과에 부정적인 영향을 끼칠 수 있다. 이는 학생이 맞춤 학습 방식의 이점을 가진다는 지문의 내용을 반박한다.

뿐만 아니라, 교수는 원격 학습이 특히 어린 학생들 사이에서 사회적 능력의 발달을 방해할 수 있다고 말한다. 다른 친구들이나 교사들과의 불충분한 교류는 결국 부족한 사회성뿐 아니라 불만족스러운 학업 성과도 초래할 수 있다. 이러한 사실은 온라인 학습이 학생들이 서로 상호 작용을 할 수 있게 해 준다는 지문의 내용을 반박한다.

마지막으로, 그녀는 원격 학습이 심지어는 심각한 건강 문제를 일으킬 수 있다고 지적한다. 예를 들면, 학생들은 비타민 D의 결핍, 비만, 그리고 소화 불량으로 고생할 수 있다. 게다가, 연구 결과가 보여주길 아이의 안경 착용이 25%나 증가했다. 이는 학습 방법의 편리함이 아이들로 하여금 그들의 학업과 과외 활동 사이에서 더 나은 균형을 유지하도록 돕는다 지문의 주장을 논박한다.

TASK 2 · INDEPENDENT TASK
Alone vs. Together

Sample Essay 1 | AGREE   p.071

사람들은 자신만의 삶의 방식을 가지고 있다. 몇몇 사람들은 하루를 빨리 시작하고 끝내는 것을 선호하는 반면, 다른 이들은 늦잠을 자는 것을 선택한다. 기술의 발달로, 맞춤 방식의 근무가 근래에 가능해졌다. 다시 말해서, 직장인들이 자택 근무를 하는 모습을 보는 것은 더 이상 흔치 않은 일이 아니다. 어떤 이들은 자택 근무가 많은 단점을 가져다 준다고 주장하지만, 이 방법은 직원들에게 보다 많은 자유를 주기 때문에 나는 회사에서 다른 이들과 함께 일하는 것보다 집에서 혼자 일하는 것이 더 낫다고 굳게 믿는다. 덧붙여, 시간도 절약된다.

첫째, 집에서 일할 때 직원들은 보다 많은 자유를 가질 수 있다. 자세히 말하면, 직원들은 그들만의 규칙이나 시스템을 갖출 수 있다. 예를 들어, 자택 근무를 하는 내 친구는 낮에 항상 낮잠을 잔다. 그는 휴식을 취한 후에 원기가 회복됨을 느끼며 더 나은 결과가 나타난다고 말한다. 그에 따르면, 회사에서 일을 했을 때, 점심 식사 후에는 졸리고 무기력했다고 한다. 따라서, 자택 근무는 사람들이 자신을 위한 근무 환경을 자신에 맞게 만들 수 있도록 해 준다.

둘째, 직원들은 시간을 절약할 수 있다. 종종 직장에 가기 위해 준비를 하

고, 출퇴근하는 시간도 많이 걸린다. 예를 들어, 내 사촌은 화장을 하고 옷을 입는 등 출근 준비를 하기 위해 한 시간 이상이 걸린다고 한다. 게다가, 그녀의 집에서 직장까지는 40분이 소요된다. 따라서, 회사에 도착할 때쯤, 그녀는 이미 지쳐 있다. 그러므로, 자택 근무를 함으로써 사람들은 시간 절약뿐 아니라 에너지도 비축할 수 있다.

몇몇 사람들은 동료들과 함께 일을 하는 것이 그들이 동기 부여를 얻을 수 있는 경쟁 가능한 환경에서 일할 기회를 준다고 주장한다. 하지만, 경쟁은 종종 직원들 사이에서 압박감을 조성하여 건강을 해칠 수 있다. 융통성과 시간 절약을 이유로, 나는 회사에서 다른 이들과 함께 일하는 것보다 집에서 혼자 일하는 것이 더 바람직하다는 진술에 동의한다.

Sample Essay 2 | DISAGREE   p.072

사람들은 자신만의 삶의 방식을 가지고 있다. 몇몇 사람들은 하루를 빨리 시작하고 끝내는 것을 선호하는 반면, 다른 이들은 늦잠을 자는 것을 선택한다. 기술의 발달로, 맞춤 방식의 근무가 근래에 가능해졌다. 어떤 이들은 자택 근무가 많은 장점을 가져다 준다고 주장하지만, 나는 회사에서 다른 이들과 함께 일하는 것이 집에서 혼자 일하는 것보다 더 낫다고 굳게 믿는다. 이는 근무 환경과 협력 때문이다.

첫째, 개인은 자기 동기 부여의 역할을 할 수 있는 경쟁심을 느낄 수 있다. 예로써, 내 사촌이 일하는 회사에서 대회가 열린 적이 있었다. 모든 직원들이 주어진 임무의 결과에 대해 발표를 하며 다른 이들과 경합을 벌이게 되었다. 우승자의 작업은 회사의 차후 프로젝트로 수행되도록 되어 있었다. 내 사촌이 작업한 것이 실제 프로젝트로 선정되지는 않았지만, 그는 그 작업에 많은 노력을 기울였고 그것으로부터 배웠다고 말했다.

둘째, 모든 직원이 같은 능력을 가지고 있는 것은 아니다. 어떤 사람들은 특정 분야에서 뛰어나고 다른 사람들은 또 다른 분야에서 유능할 수 있다. 따라서, 직원들은 자신의 지식과 능력을 사용하며 배우고 서로 협력할 수 있다. 예를 들어, 내 친구는 엑셀의 사용에는 능하지만 파워포인트에서는 그만큼 훌륭하지 않다. 그 결과, 그녀는 엑셀에 어려움을 겪는 동료들을 도와준다. 대신, 파워포인트를 하는 데 어려움을 겪을 때마다 다른 이들로부터 도움을 받는다. 이는 그녀의 부서 내에 더 좋은 생산성뿐 아니라 상승적 효과도 가져다 준다.

집에서 혼자 일하는 것이 개인에게 보다 많은 자유를 가져다 준다는 것은 사실이다. 하지만, 지나친 자유는 직원들이 그들이 수행 중인 직무에 집중하는 것을 어렵게 할 수 있다. 이는 낮은 생산성을 야기할 수 있다. 다른 이들과 함께 일하는 것은, 개인에게 보다 경쟁적인 환경에서, 스스로에게 보다 더 엄격해지도록 도와줄 수 있다. 또한, 개인은 협력하며 자신의 지식과 능력을 다른 동료들과 공유할 수 있다. 그러므로, 나는 회사에서 다른 이들과 함께 일하는 것보다 집에서 혼자 일하는 것이 더 좋다는 진술에 반대한다.

Actual Test 07

TASK 1 · INTEGRATED TASK
Zoology: Animal Play Behavior

READING   p.075

수년간, 학자들은 동물의 행동을 연구해 왔다. 그들이 관찰한 한 가지 측면은 어린 동물들이 인간의 아이들처럼 노는 것 같이 보인다는 것이다. 과학

자들은 세심한 실험을 통해, 왜 어린 동물들이 놀이를 하는가에 대한 세 가지 주된 이유가 존재한다는 결론을 내렸다.

첫째로, 학자들은 남는 에너지를 소모하기 위해 동물들이 놀이를 한다고 믿는다. 동물들이 하는 놀이의 대부분은, 자신들의 형제자매 혹은 다른 동물들과 함께하는, 달리기 및 뛰기와 같은 신체적 활동과 관련이 있다. 특히 개와 고양이 등의 일부 동물들은 발로 이리저리 칠 수 있는 공과 막대기 같은 장난감들을 가지고 놀기도 한다. 다른 동물들과 함께 또는 혼자서 놀며, 어린 동물들은 비교적 안전한 방법으로 불필요한 에너지를 소모한다. 이는, 결국, 동물들이 겪게 될 여러 종류의 스트레스를 해소하는데 도움이 된다.

놀이는 또한 어린 동물들이 성인기에 대한 준비를 하도록 도와준다. 사실 야생의 모든 동물들은 포식자가 아니면 먹이감이다. 포식자인 사자들은 어릴 때 놀며 종종 다른 사자와 가짜 싸움을 벌인다. 이러한 싸움 놀이를 하는 동안, 사자들은 먹이감에 몰래 다가가 공격하는 법뿐만 아니라 다양한 싸움의 기술들도 배우게 된다. 사자들은 성인이 되어 스스로를 부양하기 위해 필요한 중요 기술들을 새끼일 때 습득한다. 반면, 사슴과 같은 먹이감 동물들은 어릴 때 빨리 달리고 높이 뛰는 법을 배우는데, 이는 자신들을 사냥하는 포식 동물들로부터 도망치는데 필요한 기술들이다.

게다가, 어린 동물들은 함께 놀며 사회적 능력을 발달시킨다. 같은 종의 다른 새끼들과 노는 강아지나 고양이 새끼들은, 서로 교류하며 놀지 않고 자란 새끼들보다 보통 더 사회적이다. 그리고, 어린 쥐에 대한 실험 연구는 어린 쥐들이 노는 동안 뇌가 특정 화학 물질을 분비한다는 점을 보여 준다. 이러한 화학 물질은 그들이 성장했을 때 다른 쥐들을 대하는데 있어서 필요한 다양한 사회적 능력의 발달에 도움이 된다.

LISTENING   🎧 07-01

W Professor: We all love watching videos of a kitten playing with a ball of yarn or puppies play-fighting with one another. They're cute, aren't they? But lots of researchers have focused their studies on why exactly animals—particularly young animals—play both alone and with one another.

Many claim that animals play because they're expending excess energy. However, studies of animals in the wild seem to, well, disprove this. For instance, baby seals have been observed playing with one another while their mothers were away hunting. The seals were hungry yet were still playing. After their mothers returned and fed them, they continued to play. It appears that some animals just have, uh, playful natures and don't necessarily do it to rid themselves of extra energy.

Observers have noticed that some young animals, particularly predators, learn hunting skills when playing together. This has been noticed in tigers, lions, dogs, and cats, among others. Yet some experiments have shown that animals aren't necessarily learning hunting skills. Let me tell you about one test . . . One group of cats was allowed to play together while another was not. When both groups' hunting skills were tested, there was no discernable difference. Those results suggest that survival skills are instinctive and not learned by playing.

Some experts believe that playing together lets animals develop some social skills they'll need later. But in some experiments, rats were raised alone until they reached adulthood and were then introduced to communities of adult rats. These rats successfully integrated with the others and had no problems socializing. Likewise, some claim that a chemical released from rats' brains when playing helps them socialize. This chemical also gets released in the brains of older rats, which suggests that it's released when needed, not just when rats are playing.

교수: 우리 모두는 새끼 고양이가 털실 뭉치를 가지고 놀거나 강아지들이 다른 강아지와 놀며 다툼을 벌이는 비디오를 보는 것을 좋아합니다. 귀엽습니다, 그렇죠? 하지만, 많은 학자들은 정확히 어떤 이유로, 특히나 어린 동물들이 혼자서 혹은 다른 동물과 노는지에 대한 연구에 초점을 맞춰 왔습니다.

많은 이들은 동물들이 과다한 에너지를 소모하기 위해 놀이를 한다고 주장합니다. 하지만, 야생에서 이루어진 동물에 관한 연구들은, 음, 이를 반증하는 것 같이 보입니다. 예를 들어, 어미가 사냥을 나간 동안 새끼 물개들이 서로 노는 모습이 목격되었습니다. 물개들은 배가 고팠지만 여전히 놀고 있었죠. 어미가 먹이를 주기 위해 돌아왔을 때에도 그들은 계속 놀았습니다. 이는 어떤 동물들은 원래 놀기를 좋아하는 본성을 가지고 있으며 남는 에너지를 없애기 위해 놀지는 않는다는 점을 보여 줍니다.

학자들은 일부 어린 동물들, 특히 포식 동물들이 함께 놀며 사냥 능력을 배운다는 것에 주목해 왔습니다. 이러한 점은 호랑이, 사자, 개, 그리고 고양이에게서 목격되었죠. 하지만 몇몇 실험에 따르면 동물들이 반드시 사냥 방법을 배우는 것은 아닙니다. 하나의 실험에 대해 이야기해 보도록 하죠... 한 무리의 고양이들은 함께 놀게 하고 다른 무리는 그렇게 하지 못하게 했습니다. 두 무리의 사냥 능력을 시험해 보았을 때, 뚜렷이 다른 점은 없었습니다. 그러한 결과는 생존 능력이 본능적인 것이며 따라서 놀며 배울 수 있는 것이 아니라는 점을 나타내 줍니다.

몇몇 전문가들은 함께 노는 것이 동물들로 하여금 나중에 필요하게 되는 사회적 능력을 발달시켜준다고 믿고 있습니다. 하지만, 몇몇 실험에서, 들쥐들은 성인기에 이를 때까지 홀로 자란 후 다 자란 쥐의 무리에 들어가게 되었습니다. 이러한 들쥐들은 다른 쥐들과 성공적으로 동화되었으며 서로 어울리는데 문제가 없었습니다. 마찬가지로, 일부 사람들은 놀이를 할 때 뇌에서 분비되는 화학 물질이 사회성을 돕는다고 주장합니다. 이 화학 물질은 나이 든 들쥐의 뇌에서도 분비가 되는데, 이러한 사실은 그 화학 물질이 단지 놀 때만 분비되는 것이 아닌, 필요할 때에 분비되는 물질이라는 점을 나타냅니다.

Sample Essay   p.078

교수는 어린 동물들의 노는 행동에 대한 본문의 이론은 잘못되었고, 이런 노는 행동에는 특정한 이유가 없다고 주장한다. 이는 어린 동물들이 왜 노는가에 대한 세 가지 특정한 이유가 존재한다는 지문의 주장을 직접적으로 반박한다.

첫째로, 노는 것과 남는 에너지를 소모하는 것 사이에는 아무런 상관관계가 없다. 예를 들면, 새끼 물개들은 배고플 때도 놀고 어미가 식량을 구해왔을 때도 놀이를 하는데, 이러한 사실은 그들이 놀기를 좋아하는 본성을 가지고 있다는 점을 보여 준다. 이는 어린 동물들이 남는 에너지를 소모하기 위해 놀이를 한다는 지문의 주장과 모순된다.

뿐만 아니라, 교수는 생존 능력이 경험을 통해 배워지는 능력이 아닌 선천적인 특성이라고 주장한다. 그녀는 같이 노는 것이 허용되었던 고양이 집단과 그렇지 않았던 고양이 집단 사이에 크게 다른 점이 없었다는 점을 보여 주는 연구 사례에 대해 이야기한다. 이는 놀이가 어린 동물들에게 여러 생존 기술 및 사냥 기술들을 가르쳐 주며 그 결과 성인기로의 준비에 도움이 된다

는 지문의 주장을 반박한다.

마지막으로, 교수는 어린 동물들에게 사회적 능력을 제공해 주는 화학 물질이 필요할 때마다 분비되는 것이라고 주장한다. 이러한 점은 홀로 자란 쥐가 성인기에 도달하면 다른 쥐들과 함께 지내는데 별 문제가 없었다는 몇몇 실험에서 명백히 드러난다. 이는 놀 때 뇌에서 분비되는 특정 화학 물질이 어린 동물들의 사회성 형성에 도움이 된다는 지문의 내용과 반대된다.

TASK 2 · INDEPENDENT TASK
Teachers' Roles I

Sample Essay 1 | AGREE   p.081

교수법의 질은 교육에 있어서 항상 논란이 되어왔다. 교사가 얼마나 잘, 열정적으로 가르치는가는 학생의 성적에 막대한 영향을 끼칠 수 있다. 일부는 학생의 성과가 교사의 보수를 결정하기 위한 적절한 척도가 될 수 없다고 주장한다. 하지만, 나는 교사들이 학생의 성과에 따라 보수를 받아야 한다고 굳게 믿는다. 이는 교사의 노력을 인정하는 방법이 된다. 게다가, 이러한 방식은 교사들로 하여금 교수법을 끊임없이 개선시키고 개발하도록 자극할 것이다.

첫째로, 자본주의 사회에서 사람들의 보수는 긍정적 강화의 역할을 할 수 있다. 성과급은 교사들이 보다 많은 열의를 가지고 수업을 하도록 동기 부여를 해 주며, 성취감을 느낄 수 있게 해 주고, 노력에 대해 인정을 받고 있다는 자부심을 안겨 준다. 예를 들면, 교사의 보수가 학생들의 시험 성적에 따라 책정된 후 학생들의 전반적인 성적이 상당히 향상되었다는 연구 결과가 있다. 이러한 상황은 교사가 학생들을 지도하는데 보다 많은 책임감과 열정을 가질 수 있도록 해 준다.

뿐만 아니라, 학생의 성적에 따라 교사의 보수가 결정될 때 교육의 질은 향상된다. 각각의 교사는 하나의 특정 과목을 전문으로 하고 있으므로, 해마다 비슷한 내용을 가르치는 것은 수업을 매너리즘에 빠뜨릴 수 있다. 반면, 결과에 따른 보수 방식은 교사들이 특정 주제라 할지라도 다양한 방법으로 접근하도록 자극한다. 예를 들어, 선생님인 나의 삼촌은 항상 새로운 교수 방법 및 수업 자료를 고안해 내서 학생들이 수업 교재를 보다 쉽게 이해하게끔 하고 있다. 따라서, 최신 교육 도구와 참고 자료들로, 학생들은 개념을 보다 효과적으로 이해할 수 있고 시험 성적도 향상시킬 수 있다.

학생들의 성적이 즉시 향상되지 않을 수 있다는 점은 사실이다. 학생의 교육은 또한 교사의 통제를 벗어난 많은 요소에 의해 영향을 받는다. 이는 나태함, 결석, 학대하는 부모, 그리고 학습 장애가 있는 학생 등을 포함한다. 그럼에도 불구하고, 결과에 따른 보수 지급 방식은 교사들에게 보다 열심히 일을 하도록 하는 자극이 되고 동기 부여가 될 것이다. 더 나아가, 교사들로 하여금 끊임없이 그들만의 교수법을 연구하고 개선시키도록 할 것이다. 위의 이유로서, 나는 교사들이 학생의 성과에 따라 보수를 받아야 한다는 진술에 강력히 찬성한다.

Sample Essay 2 | DISAGREE   p.082

교수법의 질은 교육에 있어서 항상 논란이 되어왔다. 교사가 얼마나 잘, 열정적으로 가르치는가는 학생의 성적에 막대한 영향을 끼칠 수 있다. 일부는 교사들이 학생의 성과에 따라 보수를 받아야 한다고 주장한다. 하지만 나는 수업이 지나치게 성적 지향적으로 이루어질 수 있고, 결과에 바탕을 둔 체제는 교사들 사이에서 긴장감을 일으킬 수 있기 때문에 학생의 성적은 교사의 보수를 결정하는데 있어서 적절한 측도가 될 수 없다고 굳게 믿는다.

첫째로, 오직 시험 및 과제의 결과에만 수업의 초점이 맞추어질 수 있다.

이는 학생들이 지식을 얻기보다는 시험에서 더 좋은 성적을 얻을 수 있는 전략을 배우는 것에만 집중하는 결과를 낳을 수 있다. 예를 들면, 많은 연구가 보여 주듯이 학생들의 결과에 따라 교사들이 보수를 받았을 때, 대부분의 교사들은 시험과 관련된 주제에만 집중을 했고, 이로써 학생들은 일정 주제에 관해 포괄적인 이해를 얻기보다는 요점만 배우는 식이 되어 버렸다. 게다가, 교사와 학생 모두에게 과정보다는 결과에 더 많은 가치를 두는 경향이 나타난다.

뿐만 아니라, 학생들의 성과가 그들이 얻은 지식을 항상 반영해 주지는 않는다. 일부 주제는 보다 많은 시간과 연습을 요한다. 예를 들어, 나는 영어 수업에서 많은 문법 용어와 개념에 대해 배웠다. 그것들이 무엇인지, 작문에 어떻게 응용하는지 알고 있었음에도 불구하고, 그 방법들을 실제 작문에 적용시키기까지는 많은 시간이 걸렸다. 따라서, 이러한 접근법은 교사들뿐만 아니라 학생들에게도 스트레스와 좌절감을 안겨 줄 것이며 결국 열정을 사라지게 할 것이다.

결과에 따른 보수 지급 방식이 교사들로 하여금 교수법을 향상시키도록 자극할 것이라는 점은 사실이다. 하지만 학생의 교육은 교사의 통제를 벗어난 많은 요소에 의해 영향을 받는다. 이는 나태함, 결석, 학대하는 부모, 그리고 학습 장애가 있는 학생 등을 포함한다. 또한, 교사들은 지식 자체보다는 시험 결과에 과다한 중요성을 부여할 수도 있고, 일부 과목은 성적 향상이 천천히 나타날 수 있기 때문에 교사들 사이에서 압박감과 불안감을 일으킬 수도 있다. 위의 이유로서, 나는 교사들의 학생의 성과에 따라 보수를 받아야 한다는 진술에 강력히 반대한다.

Actual Test 08

TASK 1 · INTEGRATED TASK

Astronomy: The Existence of Life on Mars

READING   p.085

우주에서 인간만이 홀로 존재하는가에 관한 수수께끼는 1984년 남극에서 발견된 1.9킬로그램의 운석으로 증명될 수 있었다. 신중한 분석 후, 나사(NASA) 과학자들은 화성에서 온 것이라고 자신들이 주장하는 그 운석에 외계에서 비롯된 생물체가 한때 포함되어 있었다고 발표했다.

운석은 1984년에 발견되었지만, 나사의 과학자들은 2009년이 되어서야 그것에 과거 수십억 년 전 화성에 생물이 존재했다는 강력한 증거가 포함되어 있다고 주장했다. 발표가 늦어지게 된 이유는 최근에야 전자 현미경이 발달되어 과학자들이 이전에는 볼 수 없었던 운석의 다양한 특징들을 살펴볼 수 있게 되었기 때문이다. 고성능의 전자 현미경으로 발견한 것은 운석 표면에 있는 극도로 작은, 박테리아와 같은 유기 물질의 화석 증거였다. 이는 화성에 적어도 미시적인 차원에서 생명체가 있었다는 점을 명백히 나타내는 지표가 되었다.

과학자들은 운석이 약 36억년에서 40년 전쯤 화성에서 형성되었다고 믿고 있다. 그 후, 화성은 오늘날 보다 훨씬 더 따뜻하고 습해졌다. 물이 암석의 갈라진 틈으로 들어갔다. 그리고 나서, 생명체가 연이어 생겼으며 그 갈라진 틈 안에 보금자리를 만들었다. 과학자들은 암석에서 발견된 탄산염 광물을 언급하며 자신들의 이론을 방어하고 있다. 그들이 추측하기에 이러한 광물들은 생명체에 의해서만 형성될 수 있는 것이다.

생명체의 존재에 대한 또 다른 증거는 운석에 자철광이 포함되어 있다는 점이다. 연구에 따르면 운석 내 자철광의 약 1/4은 작은 결정체 모양을 띠고 있다. 이런 결정체들은 화학적으로 순수하고 구조적으로 완벽하며, 유기 물질이 아닌, 생명체에 의해서만 형성될 수 있는 고유한 3차원 형태를 지니고 있다. 종합해 보면, 이들 과학자들은 자신들이 우주 어딘가에 생명체가 존재하고 있다는, 혹은 적어도 존재했다는 증거를 가지고 있다고 확신한다.

LISTENING   🎧 08-01

M Professor: I'm sure you've all seen the news that scientists have found proof that life once existed on Mars. I'm sorry, but I've read countless articles like this before. I'm simply not satisfied with what the NASA scientists have offered as proof of their discovery.

For instance, they claim to have used an electron microscope set at a high power of magnification to discover evidence of, uh, nanobacteria. Now, keep in mind that electron microscope technology isn't perfect. The microscopes are easily contaminated during the preparation process. The bacteria could have come from the microscope itself. The photographic process is imperfect, too. At resolutions that high, the images created often aren't realistic. Hmm . . . So what we're seeing may not be evidence of bacteria at all.

But let's assume there actually is some kind of fossilized bacteria in that rock. And let's also assume the rock is Martian in origin. It's still highly likely that it became contaminated with bacteria after it reached Earth, not before it got here. It's estimated that the meteorite landed on Earth 11,000 years ago. That's plenty of time for bacteria to have moved inside it. I contend that the bacteria in the meteorite are probably of terrestrial, uh, that is, Earth, origin.

Finally, an article I read cited the presence of magnetite in the rock as proof that it contained extraterrestrial organisms. Again, I need to mention electron microscopes. The magnetite found in the rock was extremely tiny. Microscopic even. The scientists said that the magnetite had perfect shapes, but they determined this by manipulating the pictures they took. The evidence is flimsy. We can't trust the images the microscope produced. Until our technology further improves, we cannot be certain whether or not the magnetite is evidence that there really once was life on Mars.

교수: 과학자들이 화성에 한때 생명체가 존재했다는 증거를 발견했다는 뉴스를 여러분들 모두가 접해본 적이 있을 것이라고 생각합니다. 미안하지만, 저는 전에도 이런 기사를 셀 수 없이 많이 읽어 보았습니다. 나사의 직원들이 발견의 증거로서 제시하고 있는 것은 불만족스러운 것이죠.

예를 들면, 그들은 나노 세균의 증거를 발견하기 위해 고성능의 확대력을 가진 전자 현미경을 사용했다고 주장합니다. 자, 전자 현미경의 기술은 완벽하지 않다는 점을 기억해 두세요. 현미경은 준비 과정에서 쉽게 오염될 수 있습니다. 박테리아는 현미경 자체에서 나왔을 수도 있는 것입니다. 사진 촬영 과정 역시 완벽하지 않습니다. 그 정도로 높은 해상도에서 생겨나는 상은 종종 현실적이지 않습니다. 흠, 따라서 우리가 보는 것이 박테리아에 대한 증거가 전혀 아닐 수도 있습니다.

하지만, 일종의 화석화된 박테리아가 그 암석에 실제로 있다고 가정해 봅시다. 그리고 그 암석이 화성에 기원을 두고 있다고 가정해 보죠. 박테리아가 지구로 오기 전이 아닌, 그 이후에 오염되었을 가능성은 여전히 높습니다. 운석은 11,000년 전에 지구에 도달했다고 추정되고 있습니다. 박테리아가 그 안에 들어가기에 충분히 긴 시간입니다. 저는 운석에 있는 박테리아가 아마도 지구에서 나온, 즉 그 근원지가 지구라고 생각합니다.

마지막으로, 제가 읽었던 기사에서는 외계 생명체를 포함하고 있었다는 증거로 암석의 자철광이 언급되고 있었습니다. 또 다시, 전자 현미경을 설명해야겠군요. 암석에서 발견된 자철광은 극도로 작았습니다. 현미경으로만 볼 수 있을 뿐이었죠. 과학자들은 자철광이 완벽한 형태를 가지고 있었다고 했지만, 이는 그들이 찍은 사진을 조작해서 결정한 것입니다. 증거가 너무 빈약합니다. 현미경이 만들어 낸 상을 믿을 수는 없습니다. 과학 기술이 더 발달할 때까지는 자철광이 화성에 한때 생명체가 실제 존재했다는 것의 증거가 될 수 있는지 혹은 그렇지 않은지에 대해 확신할 수 없습니다.

Sample Essay p.088

교수는 화성에 생명체가 존재했다는 것은 가능한 일이 아니라고 주장하며 자신의 주장에 대해 세 가지 이유를 제시한다. 이는 지구에서 발견된 운석이 화성에 한때 생명체가 존재했었다는 점을 증명해 준다는 지문의 주장과 직접적으로 반대된다.

첫째, 교수는 기술이 아직 완벽하지 않았고 오염에 취약해서 전자 현미경의 사용에 결점이 있었다고 주장한다. 게다가, 찍힌 사진은 선명하지 않아서 우리는 과학자들이 본 것이 박테리아라고 말할 수 없다. 이는 전자 현미경을 통해 운석을 살펴봄으로써 박테리아와 같은 생명체의 화석을 과학자들이 찾아냈다는 지문의 주장을 반박한다.

둘째, 교수는 박테리아가 지구로부터 비롯된 것일 가능성이 있기 때문에 박테리아가 화성에서 왔다고 믿는 것은 신뢰할 수 없다고 강조한다. 다시 말해서, 운석은 화성에서 왔지만, 박테리아가 그 안으로 들어갔을 수 있다는 것이다. 이 주장은 생명체에 의해서만 형성될 수 있는 탄산염 광물이 암석에서 발견되었다는 지문의 주장에 의문을 제기한다.

마지막으로, 암석에서 찾아낸 자철광은 받아들여지기 좋은 그것의 이미지로 보기에는 너무 작다. 게다가, 과학자들은 여전히 개발 중에 있던 현미경에 의해 찍힌 사진을 수정했고, 이는 그 이미지들을 믿을 만하지 못하게 한다. 이는 자철광 결정체에서 발견된 특성은 오직 생물이 있는 경우에만 발생할 수 있는 것이라는 지문의 주장을 반박한다.

TASK 2 · INDEPENDENT TASK
Choosing a Method

Sample Essay 1 FINDING INFORMATION ABOUT A PROBLEM BY USING THE INTERNET p.092

모든 사람은 매일 문제에 직면한다. 커피를 쏟는 등의 사소한 일부터 직장 동료와 마찰을 겪는 등의 좀 더 심각한 문제까지, 사람들의 삶에 문제가 일어나는 것은 불가피하다. 어려운 문제가 있을 때, 나는 인터넷을 사용해서 정보를 찾아 문제를 해결하는 것을 선호한다. 이 방법은 내가 시간을 절약하고 좀 더 객관적인 관점에서 문제를 볼 수 있도록 해 준다.

첫째, 인터넷에서 정보를 찾는 것은 시간과 노력을 아껴준다. 대부분의 사람들은 비슷한 문제를 겪으며, 인터넷에서 그들이 겪고 있는 문제에 대한 충고를 얻는 것은 쉽다. 예를 들어, 인터넷에서 비슷한 경우와 해결책에 관한 것을 읽거나 어떤 책을 추천 받음으로써 우리는 동료와의 마찰을 해결할 수 있다. 그러므로 문제를 해결하기 위해 시간을 낭비하며 힘들어하는 대신 인터넷에서 검색하여 문제를 푸는 것은 굉장히 효율적인 방법이다.

게다가, 사람들은 문제를 좀 더 객관적인 관점에서 바라볼 수 있다. 예를 들어, 연구 결과에 따르면 사람은 가까운 친구나 식구들에게서는 편향된 조언을 들을 가능성이 높다. 그 이유는 친구나 식구들은 단순히 밀접한 관계가 있기 때문일 수도 있고, 친구들이 그 사람의 입장에서만 이야기를 듣기 때문일 수도 있다. 하지만 인터넷에서는 다른 사람들이 다양한 의견들을 공유할 수 있으므로 해결 방안들이 좀 더 객관적이다.

사람들은 항상 문제를 다루어야 하며, 각자 그 문제를 풀어나가는 방법에 대한 자신의 의견과 그 의견에 대한 이유가 있다. 인터넷은 사람들이 시간과 노력을 아끼도록 도울 수 있다. 게다가, 인터넷에서 접하는 조언이나 지도는 편견이 없을 가능성이 조금 더 높다. 그러므로 나는 인터넷에서 정보를 찾는 것이 문제를 해결하는 가장 효율적인 방법이라고 생각한다.

Sample Essay 2 TAKING A LONG TIME TO THINK ABOUT A PROBLEM p.093

모든 사람들은 매일 문제에 직면한다. 커피를 쏟는 등의 사소한 일부터 직장 동료와 마찰을 겪는 등의 좀 더 심각한 문제까지, 사람들의 삶에 끊임없이 문제가 일어나는 것은 불가피하다. 어려운 문제가 있을 때, 나는 문제에 대해 오랫동안 생각하며 해결하는 것을 선호한다. 이 방법은 내가 문제의 본질을 볼 수 있게 해주며 예상치 못한 결과를 최소화시켜 준다.

첫째, 나 스스로 문제를 푸는 것은 언제나 가치가 있다. 단순히 인터넷에서 방법을 찾는 것은 특정 문제는 해결해 줄 수 있으나, 그것은 단지 단기간의 해결책일 것이다. 예를 들면, 내가 직장 동료, 친구, 또는 가족 등 다른 사람들과 마찰이 생길 때면, 나는 그 사람과 나 사이의 근본적인 문제를 찾는데 많은 시간을 보낸다. 그러므로 문제에 대해 생각할 시간을 갖는 것은 결국 내게 통찰력을 주고 미래에 같거나 비슷한 문제를 해결하는 능력을 길러줄 것이다.

게다가, 모든 사람은 다르다. 따라서 다른 사람들 말을 듣거나 인터넷에서 검색하는 것은 예상치 못한 결과를 초래할 수 있으며 심지어는 상황을 악화시킬 수도 있다. 예를 들어, 내가 나 자신과 직장 동료 사이에서의 마찰을 해결하려 할 때, 나는 상대방과 대화를 나눌 적절한 시간을 찾는 것에서부터 대화에 적절한 장소를 찾는 것까지, 많은 점을 고려해야 한다. 다시 말해, 내가 문제를 해결하고 싶을 경우, 충분한 시간에 거쳐 면밀히 검토하는 것이 필요하다.

일부 사람들은 문제에 대해 생각하며 많은 시간을 보내는 것은 시간 낭비이므로 효율적이지 못한 방법이라고 주장할 수도 있다. 하지만, 문제를 일으키는 진짜 원인을 알아내는 것은 사람들이 반복되는 실수를 하지 않게 할 수 있다. 또한, 이는 사람들이 예상하지 못한 상황들에 잘 대처할 수 있게 도울 수 있다. 따라서 나는 문제를 해결하기 위한 가장 좋은 방법은 그 문제에 대해 생각하는 데 오랜 시간을 들이는 것이라고 강력히 믿는다.

Sample Essay 3 ASKING SOMEONE WITH MORE EXPERIENCE FOR ADVICE ABOUT A PROBLEM p.094

모든 사람은 매일 문제에 직면한다. 커피를 쏟는 등의 사소한 일부터 직장 동료와 마찰을 겪는 등의 좀 더 심각한 문제까지, 사람들의 삶에 끊임없이 문제가 일어나는 것은 불가피하다. 삶에서 어려운 문제가 있을 때, 나는 그 문제에 대해 좀 더 경험이 있는 사람에게 조언을 구하는 것을 선호한다. 이 방법은 내가 시간과 노력을 절약할 수 있고 조금 더 객관적일 수 있도록 해 준다.

첫째, 이미 같거나 비슷한 경험이 있는 사람의 이야기를 듣는 것은 내 시간과 노력을 절약해 줄 수 있다. 다시 말해, 나는 문제를 다룰 때 실패로 이끌 수도 있는 불필요한 단계를 피할 수 있다. 예를 들어, 내가 직장에서 일하는데 문제가 생기면, 좀 더 경험이 있는 내 상사에게 물어보는 것이 낫다. 그러므로 인생에서 문제를 해결할 때, 좀 더 경험이 있는 사람들의 말을 듣는 것은 확실히 시간과 노력을 절약해줄 수 있다.

게다가, 나는 문제를 좀 더 객관적인 관점에서 바라볼 수 있다. 통계에 따르면, 사람들은 자기 자신의 관점으로 이야기를 할 가능성이 높아서 그들은 자신의 문제를 객관적으로 생각할 수 없다. 다른 관점을 지닌 타인의 조언을 들음으로써, 나는 좀 더 합리적이고 공정해질 수 있다. 그러므로 문제에 대해 더 경험이 있는 사람에게 조언을 구하는 것은 중요하다.

인터넷에서 충고를 찾는 것이 문제를 다루는 아주 좋은 방법이기는 하지만, 사람들은 직접 조언을 듣는 것이 더 중요하다. 경험이 더 있는 사람의 조언을 듣는 것은 시간과 노력을 절약해줄 뿐 아니라, 그들이 좀 더 합리적이고 현명할 수 있도록 이끌어 준다. 그러므로 나는 문제가 생길 때, 문제를 해결하는 가장 좋은 방법은 더 경험이 많은 누군가에게 그 문제에 대한 조언을 구하는 것이라고 강력히 믿는다.

Actual Test 09

TASK 1 · INTEGRATED TASK
Food Technology: Food Irradiation

READING   p.097

식품 방사선 처리는 음식 안에 있는 미생물들을 무해하게 만들고 식품의 저장 기간을 늘리기 위해 특정 종류의 음식에 적은 양의 방사선을 쪼이는 것이다. 일반적으로 방사선 처리되는 식품은 감자 등의 덩이뿌리, 망고나 파파야 같은 열대 과일, 그리고 가금류와 생선을 포함한 육류이다. 일반 대중 사이에서는 식품을 방사선 처리하는 것이 안전하지 않으며 해롭다고 인식되고 있지만, 이는 모두 잘못된 생각이다.

첫째, 식품은 적은 양의 방사선에 노출되는데, 이는 인간에게 전혀 해를 끼치지 않는다. 하지만 방사선은 식품의 표면 또는 내부에 있는 미생물의 DNA를 파괴시킬 만큼은 강하다. 이로써 미생물들은 식품이 부패하거나 먹는 사람에게 해를 입히지 못하게 된다. 게다가, 사실상 식품에 있는 100%의 박테리아가 방사선 처리 과정에서 파괴되며, 바이러스나 곰팡이 같은 다른 균들도 파괴된다.

방사선 처리의 또 다른 장점은 식품이 부패하는 과정을 지연시킨다는 점이다. 이는 열대 과일을 그것들이 재배되는 곳에서부터 세계 각지에 있는 가게까지, 엄청난 거리를 이동하게 해 준다. 그 결과, 동남아 국가들의 농부들은 신선한 농산물을 미국과 유럽의 소비자들에게 판매할 수 있다. 방사선 처리는 또한 식품이 슈퍼마켓에 도착한 후 진열대 위에 보다 오래 있을 수 있도록 해 준다. 따라서 바로 판매되지 않더라도 식품이 부패하거나 상하지 않는다.

마지막으로, 식품이 방사선에 노출되었을 때, 영양 가치의 손실은 거의 없다. 사실, 그와 같은 변화는 무시할 만하다. 그래서 미생물, 박테리아, 그리고 다른 병균들은 제거되는 반면, 식품은 동일한 양의 비타민과 무기질을 유지한다. 방사선 처리의 최종 결과는 보다 안전하고, 보다 오래 지속되며, 영양분이 풍부한 식품이다.

W Professor: For decades, companies have been irradiating various food products. They claim that doing so kills pathogens and makes food take longer to spoil. But there's widespread belief among consumers that irradiated food can be harmful. I must admit that I understand why they feel that way.

For instance, one supposed advantage of irradiating food is that it kills any pathogens in it. Well, it's actually impossible to know if they're all killed. Even if just, say, one percent of those pathogens survive, they're likely to be super resistant to irradiation, and, uh, they might reproduce more pathogens with similar resistance. You know, that's similar to how some viruses have developed strains resistant to antibodies. If some pathogens develop a resistance to radiation, we might do more harm than good by irradiating our food.

Now, um, irradiation definitely can slow down how quickly some foods spoil. But it can actually cause the ripening process to halt. Take bananas as an example. Farmers often pick green bananas and ship them to market. By the time the bananas reach the supermarket, they're yellow and ripe. But when some green bananas get irradiated, they stop ripening. Who's going to eat green bananas? They aren't ripe, don't taste good, and lack vitamins and minerals.

Oh, that's another thing I should mention. Don't believe those studies claiming that irradiated food loses none of its nutritional value. Some scientists conducting research have determined that some foods may lose nutrients during the irradiation process. Additionally, other scientists believe that storing food for longer than nature typically allows it to stay good before spoiling, uh, reduces its nutritional value. So, sure, you can drink milk that's been on the shelf for longer, but it might not be as good for you as fresh milk is.

교수: 수십 년 동안, 기업들은 여러 종류의 식품에 방사선 처리를 하고 있습니다. 그들은 그렇게 하는 것이 병균을 죽이고 식품을 오랫동안 상하지 않도록 해 준다고 주장합니다. 하지만 소비자들 사이에는 방사선 처리된 음식이 해로울 수 있다는 믿음이 널리 퍼져 있습니다. 저는 사람들이 그렇게 생각하는 이유를 이해할 수 있다고 해야 할 것 같군요.

예를 들어, 식품 방사선 처리의 이점이라고 알려져 있는 것 중 하나는 그로 인해 식품 안에 있는 병균들이 죽는다는 점입니다. 글쎄요, 병균들이 모두 죽었는지를 아는 것은 사실상 불가능합니다. 만약, 가령, 1퍼센트의 병균이라도 살아 있다면, 그것들은 방사선에 대한 강력한 내성을 가지고 있을 수 있으며, 그리고, 음, 비슷한 저항력을 가진 더 많은 병균들을 생산해 낼 수 있습니다. 음, 그것은 몇몇 바이러스들이 항체에 저항할 변종을 발달시킨 방법과 비슷합니다. 만약 일부 병균들이 방사선에 대한 내성을 기르게 된다면, 식품 방사선 처리는 득보다 실이 많은 것이 될 수 있습니다.

자, 음, 방사선 처리는 확실히 몇몇 식품들의 빠른 부패를 지연시켜 줄 수 있습니다. 그러나 이는 사실상 후숙 과정을 중단시킬 수도 있습니다. 바나나를 예로 들어 봅시다. 농부들은 종종 덜 익은 바나나를 수확해서 매장으로 운송합니다. 바나나가 슈퍼마켓에 도착할 무렵에는, 노랗게 익어 있죠. 하지만 몇몇 덜 익은 바나나들은 방사선 처리가 되어, 후숙을 멈춥니다. 누가 덜 익은 바나나를 먹을까요? 그 바나나들은 익지 않았기 때문에 맛도 없으며, 비타민과 미네랄도 결핍되어 있습니다.

아, 언급해야 할 사항이 하나 더 있군요. 방사선 처리된 식품들의 영양 가치가 전혀 손상되지 않는다고 주장하는 연구들은 믿지 마십시오. 연구를 수행한 일부 과학자들은 몇몇 식품이 방사선 처리 과정에서 영양분을 잃을 수도 있다고 결론지었습니다. 게다가, 다른 과학자들은 상하기 전 자연이 통상 허용하는 것보다 오래 식품을 저장하면, 어, 영양학적인 가치가 감소한다고 믿고 있습니다. 따라서, 물론, 더 오랫동안 보관된 우유를 마실 수는 있겠지만, 신선한 우유만큼 좋지는 않을 것입니다.

Sample Essay   p.100

교수는 식품 방사선 처리가 인체에 해로운 영향을 초래할 수 있다고 주장한다. 이는 방사선 처리가 식품을 보다 더 오랫동안 보관하는데 효과적인 방법이 된다는 지문의 주장을 직접적으로 반박한다.

첫째, 식품 방사선 처리는 박테리아 전체를 제거하지 못할 수도 있다. 살아남은 병균들은 방사선에 대한 강한 내성을 키워서, 자손들에게 비슷한 내성을 물려줄 것이다. 이는 방사선 처리가 식품 부패의 주된 원인인 박테리아를 죽이기 때문에 멸균에 효과적인 방법이 된다는 지문의 주장을 반박한다.

뿐만 아니라, 교수는 방사선 처리로 인해 식품의 후숙 과정이 방해를 받을 수 있다고 주장한다. 교수에 따르면, 바나나들의 후숙 과정이 중단되면 만족스럽지 못한 맛이 초래될 뿐만 아니라 비타민과 무기질의 결핍 현상도 초래한다. 이는 방사선이 식품의 부패 과정을 지연시켜 식품의 장거리 운송을 가능하게 해 준다는 지문의 주장을 반박한다.

마지막으로, 방사선 처리 과정 중 영양 가치가 손실될 수도 있다. 식품의 유효 기간은 늘어날 수 있겠지만, 영양소가 파괴될 가능성이 있다. 이는 박테리아가 성공적으로 제거됨에도 비타민과 미네랄은 똑같이 남아 있으므로 방사선 처리된 식품에서는 영양 손실이 거의 없게 된다는 지문의 내용과 반대된다.

TASK 2 · INDEPENDENT TASK
Future Life

Sample Essay 1 | AGREE   p.103

사람들은 빠르게 변화하는 오늘날의 사회에 적응하면서 그 어느 때보다 훨씬 더 바빠졌다. 따라서, 요리법과 식품 기술의 발달로 조리 방법 및 조리 과정이 더욱 편해지고 시간도 절약되고 있다. 일부 사람들은 인스턴트 식품이 천천히 조리된 음식에 그 자리를 내어 주고 있다고 주장하지만, 인스턴트 식품의 수요가 증가하고 식품 기술이 급속히 발전하고 있기 때문에 나는 앞으로 20년 후에는 요리 준비 시간이 단축될 것이라고 굳게 믿는다.

첫째로, 많은 가족들이 저녁 식사에 함께 모이는 것이 어렵다. 이는 각자 자신의 일로 바쁘기 때문이며, 한 명이 각기 다른 시간에 각 가족 구성원에게 음식을 준비해 주는 것을 힘들게 만든다. 따라서, 인스턴트 식품의 수요가 빠르게 증가하고 있다. 예를 들면, 나는 종종 일이 늦게 끝나서 식구들과 함께 저녁 먹는 것이 불가능하기 때문에, 어머니께서는 편리하고 조리 시간이 짧은 라면을 준비해 주신다. 보다 많은 사람들이 조리, 준비, 그리고 정리 시간을 절약해 주는 인스턴트 식품의 편리함과 신속함에 만족한다. 결과적으로, 가까운 미래에는 대부분의 사람들이 요리하는데 더 적은 시간을 사용하게 될 것이다.

게다가, 식품 기술의 끊임없는 발전은 사람들로 하여금 더 짧은 시간에 요리를 할 수 있도록 만들어 준다. 인스턴트 식품의 맛이 천천히 조리하는 음식

의 맛과 매우 비슷하기 때문에, 대다수의 사람들은 보다 더 쉬운 조리법을 선호하고 있다. 예를 들어, 내 동료는 일이 끝난 후 저녁을 먹기 위해 항상 냉동 음식을 구입하여, 집에서 이를 간단히 전자레인지에 돌린다. 이로써 조리와 정리 시간을 절약할 수 있을 뿐만 아니라, 식당에서 나오는 것과 같은 맛을 느낄 수 있다.

인스턴트 음식은 그 일부가 다른 나라에서 왔음에도 불구하고 대부분 맛이 똑같은 것은 사실이다. 하지만 사람들은 레스토랑에서 다른 맛의 음식을 즐길 수 있고, 그래서 사람들은 원한다면 그것들을 먹을 수 있다. 대부분의 사람들은 집에서 편리함 때문에 주로 인스턴트 식품을 요리하는 것에 익숙해질 것이다. 게다가, 발전하는 과학 기술로 인스턴트 식품은 소비자의 입맛에 맞게 만들어 질 것이다. 이상의 이유로, 나는 앞으로 20년 후에는 조리에 보다 더 적은 시간이 사용될 것이라는 진술에 확고히 동의한다.

Sample Essay 2 | DISAGREE   p.104

사람들은 빠르게 변화하는 오늘날의 사회에 적응하면서 이전보다 훨씬 더 바빠졌다. 따라서, 요리법과 식품 기술의 발달로 조리 방법 및 조리 과정이 더욱 편해지고 시간도 절약되고 있다. 일부 사람들은 요리 준비 시간이 20년 후에는 더욱 단축될 것이라고 주장한다. 하지만, 사람들은 건강에 더욱 관심을 갖고 있으며 천천히 조리된 음식은 사람들의 문화를 나타내 주기 때문에, 나는 준비 시간이 현재와 같거나 아니면 더욱 길어질 것이라고 굳게 믿는다.

첫째로, 영양은 현대 사회에서 가장 중요한 이슈가 되었다. 인스턴트 식품은 편리성 및 시간에 대한 요구를 충족시켜 주기 때문에 인기가 있다. 하지만, 새로운 질병과 비만 등의 문제들이 표면화되면서, 많은 사람들이 인스턴트 식품에 의해 일어날 수 있는 위험성을 깨닫게 되었다. 예를 들어, 많은 연구는 다수의 인스턴트 식품이 영양가가 떨어진다는 것을 증명해 주었다. 실제로 일부 식품에는 해로운 화학 물질까지 포함되어 있다. 반대로, 음식이 저온에서 천천히 조리될 때, 훨씬 더 맛이 부드럽고 영양가가 높아진다. 따라서, 건강에 대한 자각이 사람들로 하여금 천천히 조리된 음식을 선호하도록 만들고 있다.

게다가, 천천히 조리하는 것은 개인의 문화와 어린 시절의 추억을 보존한다. 사회가 요구하는 것이 더욱 많아지면서, 사람들은 어린 시절에 대한 향수를 느끼고 있다. 각 문화는 고유의 조리법과 스타일을 가지고 있기 때문에 음식의 준비는 맛만큼이나 중요하다. 예를 들어, 가족 모임에서 조리하는 동안 나오는 냄새가 과거를 상기시켜 주기 때문에, 많은 사람들이 아직도 천천히 익힌 갈비찜을 선호하고 있다.

인스턴트 식품이 처음 나온 후 수십 년간 큰 인기를 얻어왔다는 점은 사실이다. 하지만, 편리함 때문에 아파트를 선호했던 많은 사람들이 최근 정원이 있는 전통 가옥으로 되돌아 오고 있다. 이처럼, 천천히 조리된 음식은 장차 제자리를 다시 찾게 될 것이다. 사람들은 천천히 조리된 음식이 인스턴트 식품보다 더 좋다는 것을 알고 있다. 게다가, 이는 어릴 때의 추억을 불러 일으키며 개인의 문화를 반영해 준다. 이상의 이유로, 나는 앞으로 20년 후에는 조리에 더 적은 시간이 사용될 것이라는 진술에 동의하지 않는다.

Actual Test 10

TASK 1 · INTEGRATED TASK
Environment: Fast Fashion

READING   p.107

패스트 패션은 소비자의 수요에 맞추기 위해 아주 빠른 속도로 유명 인사의 문화나 패션쇼 무대에서의 디자인을 복제한 옷을 설명하는데 쓰이는 용어이다. 패스트 패션은 쇼핑객들이 아주 합리적인 가격에 유행하는 옷을 구입하는 것을 어느 때보다 쉽게 만들었다. 이는 비록 의류 산업에 비할 데 없는 이윤을 가져왔지만, 관심을 가져야 할 필요가 있는 많은 문제들 또한 야기시켜 왔다.

패스트 패션은 비용을 최소화하기 위해 통상 낮은 질의 원료를 사용해서, 대부분의 옷은 비생분해성 원료로 만들어진다. 예를 들면, 폴리에스터는 석유로 만들어지며, 분해하는데 200년까지 걸릴 수 있다. 게다가, 가장 흔한 직물 중 하나인 면화의 재배는 해로운 살충제의 사용은 말할 것도 없고, 엄청난 물을 필요로 한다.

열악한 기업 윤리는 많은 직원들을 위험에 놓이게 한다. 일부 기업들은 개발 도상국의 법을 이용해서, 대부분, 그들은 근로 시간에 따른 법률을 따르지 않거나 노동자들에게 어떠한 혜택도 주지 않는다. 사람들이 수많은 정신적뿐 아니라 신체적 학대를 겪음에도 불구하고, 많은 직원들, 특히나 아이들은 언제든 해고당할 수 있기 때문에 이 문제들을 신고하는 것을 꺼려한다.

의류가 질 낮은 원료로 만들어졌기 때문에, 옷이 그리 오래가지 못할 것이라는 것은 명백하고, 결국 더 많은 소비와 의류쓰레기를 만들어낸다. 소비자들은 새로운 제품들이 낮은 가격에 끊임없이 나오기 때문에 가게에 더 자주 가도록 부추겨지며, 결국 구입하게 된다. 최근 연구가 보여주기를 사람들이 지속 가능한 브랜드에서 살 의향이 있다고 말을 하지만, 그들은 거의 그렇게 하지 않는다. 많은 이들에게 유행의 정상에 머물고 싶은 욕망을 포기하기란 쉽지 않다.

LISTENING   🎧 10-01

M Professor: Many of you, I am sure, are familiar with slow food. But how many of you are familiar with the term slow fashion . . . ? Well . . . it's more popularly known as ethical fashion . . . People were tired of the fast pace of society and wanted to relax and really enjoy the taste of food . . . so the slow-food movement began. Inspired by slow food, the slow-fashion movement was born in 2007, and some of the principles include sustainable materials, fair trade, and minimizing waste. Let me explain these principles in detail.

Most people are aware that the oil industry is the largest polluter in the world . . . but not many are aware that the fashion industry is the second. In order to reduce environmental damage, companies that are part of the slow-fashion movement use biodegradable materials like . . . organic or recycled cotton, organic linen, and silk. Many companies are putting very much effort into becoming eco-friendly . . . In fact, numerous corporations now grow cotton with rainwater . . . Even though higher-quality garments are usually more expensive, they will last longer, and their production will be less harmful to the environment.

Work ethics is not considered a problem in the slow-fashion industry. Hmmm . . . Can you imagine yourself not being able even to go to the restroom for 10 hours . . . ? Or constantly getting abused or harassed by supervisors? Terrible work ethics are never seen in the slow-fashion industry, where companies hire local workers who are protected by labor laws. They provide workers with good working conditions . . . so no forced labor, no child labor, no violence, and no discrimination.

Most importantly, consumers need to have awareness of the negative environmental consequences fast fashion is causing. There are even companies nowadays that actually tell shoppers to repair garments rather than to buy new ones . . . It might sound funny . . . but I, in fact, would like to make a purchase from those particular brands if I need clothing in the future. Nevertheless, nothing will change unless everyone makes an effort and develops better habits, like buying less, buying better quality, choosing sustainable brands, and choosing clothes made in countries with stringent environmental regulations.

교수: 여러분 중 다수는, 제가 확신하는데, 슬로푸드에 대해 익숙할 거예요... 하지만 슬로우 패션이라는 용어에 익숙한 사람은 몇 명일까요...? 자... 윤리 패션이라고 더 많이 알려져 있지요.. 사람들은 급박히 돌아가는 사회에 지쳤고, 쉬며 진정으로 음식의 맛을 즐기고 싶어했어요... 그렇게 슬로푸드 운동이 시작되었죠. 그러니까, 슬로푸드에서 영감을 받아, 슬로우 패션은 2007년에 생겼고, 지속 가능한 원료, 공정 무역, 그리고 쓰레기의 최소화 등의 몇 가지 원칙을 가지고 있습니다. 이러한 원칙들에 대해 좀 더 자세히 설명해 보도록 할게요.

대부분의 사람들은 세계적으로 원유 산업이 가장 큰 오염원이라는 것을 알고 있어요... 하지만 많지 않은 사람들만이 패션 산업이 두 번째라는 것을 알고 있지요. 환경 파괴를 줄이기 위해, 기업들은 슬로우 패션 운동에 동참하고 생분해성 원료를 사용해요. 유기농 혹은 재생 면, 유기농 리넨, 그리고 실크... 같은 것들 말이에요. 많은 회사들이 친환경적이 되기 위해 아주 많은 노력을 기울입니다... 사실 다수의 기업들은 이제 빗물로 면화를 재배합니다. 보통 높은 질의 의류가 더 비싸긴 하지만, 더 오래 가고, 생산이 환경에 덜 해로울 것이에요.

기업 윤리는 슬로우 패션 산업에서는 문제될 것이 없어요. 흠... 10시간 동안 화장실도 못 가는 것이 상상이 가나요?... 혹은 관리자로부터 끊임없이 괴롭힘이나 학대를 당하는 건요? 끔찍한 기업 윤리는 노동법으로부터 보호 받는 현지 근로자를 고용하는 회사들이 있는 슬로우 패션 산업에서는 절대 볼 수 없어요. 회사는 노동자들에게 훌륭한 노동 환경을 제공합니다... 즉, 강요된 노동도, 아동 노동도, 폭력도, 차별도 없어요.

다른 무엇보다도, 소비자들이 패스트 패션이 야기하는 환경의 부정적인 결과에 대해 경각심을 가질 필요가 있습니다. 요즘엔 심지어는 소비자들에게 새로운 옷을 사지 말고 고쳐 입으라는 말을 실제로 하는 기업들도 있어요... 웃기게 들릴 수도 있어요... 하지만 사실 저도 미래에 옷이 필요하면 그런 특정 브랜드들에서 구매하고 싶어요. 어쨌거나, 모두가 노력하고 더 나은 습관을 기르지 않는 이상 아무것도 바뀌지 않을 거예요. 이를테면 더 적게 사고, 더 나은 질의 물건을 사며, 지속 가능한 브랜드의 물건을 고르고, 엄격한 환경 규제가 있는 나라에서 만든 옷을 고르는 것들이요.

교수는 슬로우 패션 운동이 어떻게 실천되는지 설명한다. 이는 패스트 패션이 환경을 위협한다는 지문의 내용에서 언급된 문제들에 대해 해결책을 제시한다.

첫째, 교수에 따르면, 지속 가능한 원료들인 유기농 면, 실크, 그리고 유기농 리넨 등이 슬로우 패션 옷에 사용되고 있다. 높은 가격에도 불구하고, 그 옷들은 쉽게 닳지 않아서, 소비자들은 옷들을 오랜 시간 동안 소유할 수 있다. 이는 패스트 패션이 환경에 해로운 비생분해성 물질을 사용한다는 지문의 내용을 설명해 준다.

다음으로, 교수는 슬로우 패션 산업의 회사들은 근무 윤리를 따른다고 주장한다. 많은 슬로우 패션 운동 기업들은 아동 노동, 차별, 그리고 폭력 금지 같은 원칙을 따른다. 이는 패스트 패션 산업 내 특정 기업들이 노동자들을 위한 정해진 명확한 규정이 없는 장소들로부터 부당한 이익을 취한다고 하는 지문에 묘사된 내용에 반한다.

마지막으로, 교수는, 소비자들이 환경에 대한 자신들의 태도를 바꾸지 않는 이상 그들이 옷을 더 적게 사고, 더 좋은 품질에 더 많이 지불하며, 더 강력한 환경 규제를 가지고 있는 곳에서 만들어진 옷감을 찾게 하는 것은 어려울 것이라고 경고한다. 이는 많은 소비자들이 유행을 따라가는 것을 포기하는 것을 여전히 꺼려한다는 지문의 내용을 정확히 설명해 준다

TASK 2 · INDEPENDENT TASK

Manufacture

세계화가 이루어짐에 따라, 국가 간의 경쟁은 불가피하며, 한 나라에서 또 다른 나라로의 제품의 수출입은 일반적인 관행이 되고 있다. 따라서, 기업들은 홍보, 판촉, 서비스를 통해 자국 소비자의 관심뿐만 아니라 해외 소비자의 관심을 끌기 위해 노력하고 있다. 일부 사람들은 소비자들이 사고 싶은 것을 선택할 수 있는 자유를 누려야 한다고 주장한다. 하지만, 나는 두 가지 이유로써, 비록 가격이 높다고 하더라도 소비자들은 자국 제품을 구매해야 한다고 굳게 믿는다. 우선, 국가 경제에 통화를 유지시킴으로써 시너지 효과가 일어날 것이다. 또한, 새로운 제품에 대한 연구 및 개발 역시 촉진될 것이다.

첫째, 자국 제품의 구매는 그 나라의 경제 성장을 촉진시켜 줄 것이다. 예를 들어, 만약 한 나라의 국민들이 그 나라에서 생산된 주요 제품의 구입을 거부하고, 대신 수입 제품의 구입을 선호한다면, 완성된 제품을 생산하는 기업들과 특정 부품이나 부속을 생산하는 하청업체들 모두 어려움을 겪게 될 것이다. 그 결과로 전체 산업이 경제적 어려움으로 인해 고통을 받게 될 가능성이 있다.

뿐만 아니라, 기업들은 자신들의 제품을 소비자가 구매해 줄 때 품질을 개선시키고 향상시킬 동기 부여를 얻게 된다. 기업들은 소비자의 기대를 만족시켜야 한다는 책임감을 갖는다. 예를 들면, 일본인들은 외국에서 생산된 다른 제품들보다 가격이 높아도 자국의 제품을 구입하는 것으로 잘 알려져 있다. 이러한 현상은 일본 기업들이 수익 증대의 일환으로 보다 좋은 제품을 생산하도록 만들었다. 이러한 관행은 보다 높은 수익을 낳고, 기업들로 하여금 제품의 품질 기준을 향상시키도록 함으로써 그 결과 시너지 효과를 가져오게 될 것이다.

사실 민주적 시장의 개념 중 하나는 소비자가 원하는 것에 돈을 지불할 수 있는 자유가 있어야 한다는 점이다. 하지만, 만약 대부분의 사람들이 더 나은 품질과 더 낮은 가격의 수입 제품을 선호한다면, 그 국가는 수입 상품에만 의존해야 하는 결과를 낳을 수도 있을 것이다. 경제 성장과 제품 개발의 이유

로, 나는 소비자가 가격이 높더라도 자국의 제품을 구입해야 한다는 의견에 동의한다.

세계화가 이루어짐에 따라, 국가 간의 경쟁은 불가피하며, 한 나라에서 또 다른 나라로의 제품의 수출입은 일반적인 관행이 되고 있다. 따라서, 기업들은 홍보, 판촉, 서비스를 통해 자국 소비자의 관심뿐만 아니라 해외 소비자의 관심을 끌기 위해 노력하고 있다. 일부 사람들은 소비자들이 가격이 높더라도 자국의 제품을 구입해야 한다고 주장한다. 하지만, 나는 두 가지 이유 때문에, 소비자들은 사고 싶은 것을 선택할 자유를 누려야 한다고 굳게 믿는다. 우선, 경쟁이 발전을 촉진시킬 것이다. 또한, 자유는 민주적 시장의 기본적인 개념이다.

첫째, 경쟁은 발전을 가져온다. 소비자들은 같은 가격이면 더 나은 품질의 제품을 선호할 가능성이 많다. 따라서, 기업들은 소비자들에게 만족을 주기 위해 많은 노력을 할 수 있다. 예를 들어, 수십 년 전, 한국 밖에 사는 사람들은 한국의 전자 제품 기업들에 대해 거의 알고 있지 못했다. 하지만 한국에 많은 전자 제품 기업들이 생기고 경쟁이 치열해지면서, 각 기업들은 우수한 연구원들을 양성하고 전략적 이득을 얻기 위해 많은 자금을 투자했다. 결과적으로, 한국의 전자 제품 산업은 세계적인 선도 산업 중의 하나로 인정을 받고 있다.

뿐만 아니라, 각 개인은 구매를 하는데 있어서 필요에 따른 서로 다른 취향과 선호를 가지고 있기 때문에 소비자들에게는 자신들의 의지에 따라 제품을 선택할 권리가 있어야 한다. 예를 들면, 나는 물건을 구입할 필요가 있을 때마다 가격을 가장 먼저 고려한다. 학생이기 때문에, 나는 더 높은 가격의 더 좋은 품질을 가진 제품 보다는 가장 낮은 가격의 제품을 선택한다. 따라서, 만약 내가 더 높은 가격의 같은 품질을 가진 제품을 사야 한다면, 불쾌감을 느끼게 될 것이다.

자국의 제품을 사는 것이 기업들로 하여금 제품의 질을 더 향상시키도록 하는 동기를 부여할 수 있다는 것은 사실이다. 하지만, 상황에 관계 없이, 소비자들이 수입 제품보다 현지에서 만들어 진 제품을 더 선호할 것이라는 확신으로 인해 일부 기업들은 품질 향상을 위한 노력을 하지 않을 수도 있다. 선의의 경쟁과 선택의 자유라는 이유로, 나는 소비자가 가격이 높더라도 자국의 제품을 사야 한다는 의견에 반대한다.

Actual Test 11

TASK 1 · INTEGRATED TASK

Anthropology: The Mayan Empire

잉카와 아즈텍과 함께 콜롬버스 이전 시대의 세 개의 가장 훌륭한 미주 제국 중 하나는 마야 제국이었다. 마야 제국은 주로 멕시코, 과테말라, 그리고 벨리즈에 걸쳐 있는 중앙아메리카 지역에 위치해 있었다. 마야는 약 300년부터 800년 사이에 가장 강력했다. 마야인들은 잘 발달된 도시를 가지고 있었고, 농업에 대해 알고 있었으며, 자신들만의 달력을 가지고 있었고, 고급 수학을 이해했으며, 고유의 문자 체계를 발전시켰다. 그 후, 약 800년부터 900년 사이, 그들은 사라져 버렸다.

마야의 멸망은 역사상 가장 어려운 수수께끼 중 하나이다. 그들의 몰락에

관한 여러 이론이 있다. 가장 유력한 것은 마야가 전쟁에서 패배했기 때문이라는 것이다. 멕시코의 톨텍 사람들은 마야인들과 동시대인이었다. 그들은 호전적인 사람들이었다. 많은 고고학자들은 톨텍의 한 차례 침략으로, 혹은 거의 한 세기 동안 계속된 연속적인 침략으로 마야가 급속히 쇠약해 져서 결국 멸망했다고 믿는다.

또 다른 유명한 이론은 마야가 자신들의 성공적인 문화 때문에 인구가 갑작스럽게 급증을 했다는 것이다. 하지만, 모두를 부양할 수 있는 충분한 작물을 재배할 수는 없었다. 마야는 종종 그들이 경작하고자 하는 지역의 산림을 개간하기 위해 화전법을 사용했다. 그러나, 이 방법은 토질에 해로웠기 때문에, 두 세 번의 작물의 생장기를 거치면 땅은 종종 쓸모 없게 되었다. 마야가 단순히 스스로를 부양할 수 없어서 광범위한 기근이 초래되었다고 하는 것은 가능한 일이다.

마야인들이 한때 살았던 대부분의 지역은 오늘날 다우림인 반면, 수세기 전에는 그렇지 않았다. 당시는 훨씬 더 건조했다. 일부 사람들은 마야가 농사를 불가능하게 만든 장기간의 가뭄을 겪었다고 추측한다. 그 지역에 대한 지질학적 연구에 따르면 이 이론에는 어느 정도의 사실성이 있다. 물이 없었기 때문에, 마야 제국이 멸망했거나 혹은 살기 위한 노력의 일환으로 이들은 다른 곳으로 옮겨 갔을 것이다.

W Professor: As you can see, the Maya had an extremely advanced culture for their time. But sometime between the years 800 and 900, they ceased to exist as a people. Sure, some of them lived on. Even today, there are a few million descendants of the Maya. Yet the empire was essentially gone by the year 900. Why is that? Nobody knows for sure. And every theory has flaws.

For instance, a common theory is that a foreign invader such as the Toltec conquered the Maya. There are two problems with that belief. The first is that the only archaeological evidence for warfare in Mayan lands dates back to the years between 500 and 600. That's about two centuries prior to the Mayan collapse. The second is that the Toltec didn't engage in military adventurism until after 900. So it couldn't have been the Toltec that caused the Maya to fall.

Some people claim that the Mayan population increased so much that the empire's farmers couldn't grow enough food to feed everyone. I doubt that. First, the Maya were incredibly knowledgeable when it came to farming. They would have overcome any difficulties by planting new crops or devising new methods. Plus, even if they did have problems feeding everyone, the entire population wouldn't have died. The Maya collapsing due to agricultural problems is simply inconceivable.

Finally, there is some geological and tree ring evidence which supports the theory that there was an extended drought in Mayan lands. Yet, um, this drought occurred in the northern part of Mayan territory. But the archaeological evidence shows that it was the southern part of Mayan territory that was the first to fall. I believe that proves a drought didn't cause an end to the Maya Empire either.

교수: 아시다시피, 마야인들은 시대에 비해 상당히 발전된 문화를 가지고 있었습니다. 하지만, 약 800년에서 900년 사이, 그들은 하나의 민족으로서 존재하지는 않게 되었죠. 물론, 일부는 살아 남았습니다. 심지어 오늘날에도 수백만의 마야 후손들이 있으니까요. 그렇지만 마야 제국은 약 900년경 완전히 사라졌습니다. 왜일까요? 아무도 정확히는 모릅니다. 게다가 모든 이론들에는 결점이 있습니다.

예를 들어, 일반적인 하나의 이론에 따르면 톨텍 같은 외부 침입자들이 마야를 정복했다고 합니다. 그에 대해서는 두 가지 문제점이 있습니다. 첫째는 마야 지역에서의 전쟁에 대한 유일한 고고학적 증거는 그 연대가 500년에서 600년 사이로 거슬러 올라갑니다. 이는 마야의 붕괴 시점보다 약 두 세기 앞선 것입니다. 두 번째는 톨텍인들이 900년 이후에야 군사적 모험주의에 참여했다는 점입니다. 따라서 마야의 멸망을 초래한 존재가 톨텍인들이 될 수는 없는 것입니다.

일부 사람들은 마야 인구가 너무 급증해서 마야 제국의 농부들이 모두를 부양하기에 충분한 식량을 재배할 수가 없었다고 주장합니다. 저는 그렇지 않다고 생각합니다. 첫째, 마야인들은 농업에 있어서 놀랄 정도로 박식했습니다. 새로운 농작물을 재배하거나 새로운 농법을 고안해 냄으로써 어떠한 어려움도 극복했을 것입니다. 게다가, 모두를 부양하는 데는 문제가 있었다 할지라도, 전체 인구가 사망하지는 않았을 것입니다. 농업 문제 때문의 마야가 멸망했다고 하는 것은 터무니없는 말입니다.

마지막으로, 마야 지역에서 장기간에 걸친 가뭄이 일어났다는 이론을 지지하는 지질학적인, 나이테 증거가 있습니다. 그런데, 음, 이 가뭄은 마야 영토의 북부에서 일어났습니다. 하지만 고고학적 증거에 의하면 먼저 붕괴되기 시작한 곳은 마야 영토의 남쪽이었습니다. 이는 제가 생각하기에 가뭄 역시 마야 제국의 멸망을 가져온 것이 아니라는 점을 입증해 줍니다.

교수는 마야 문명의 멸망의 원에 관해 누구도 확신하고 있지 못하다고 주장한다. 이는 마야 제국이 갑자기 붕괴했는지에 대한 세 가지 이유가 존재한다는 지문의 주장을 직접적으로 반박한다.

첫 번째로, 침략을 주장하는 이론은 두 가지 이유로 가능성이 없다. 첫째, 마야인들이 전쟁에 참여했던 시기가 멸망하기 두 세기 전이었기 때문이다. 둘째, 또 다른 문제는 톨텍인들이 900년 전에는 전쟁에 참여하지 않았다는 점에 있다. 이는 톨텍과의 전쟁에 패배하여 마야가 멸망하게 되었다는 주장을 반박한다.

다음으로, 교수는 마야인들은 농사에 대해 박식했기 때문에 적절한 해결책을 생각해 냈을 것이라고 주장한다. 교수는 이러한 점은 농작물의 부족으로 전체 인구가 사라지게 되었을 것이라는 가능성을 희박하게 만든다고 말한다. 이는 갑작스런 인구 증가로 식량이 부족해져 그 결과 극심한 기근이 일어났다는 지문의 주장을 반박한다.

마지막으로, 가뭄 이론에 따르면, 두 지역은 서로 일치하지 않는다. 치명적인 가뭄은 마야 제국의 북쪽에서 일어났던 반면, 문명의 붕괴는 남쪽 지역에서 시작되었다. 이는 지속적인 건기로 농사가 불가능하게 되어 기근이 일어나게 되었다는 지문의 주장과 상충된다.

TASK 2 • INDEPENDENT TASK
Problem Solving

현대 사회에서는 많은 사람들이 교류를 하기 때문에, 사람들 사이에서 문제가 일어나는 것은 불가피하다. 불쾌한 기분을 표현하는 방법에는 여러 가지가 있다. 사람들은 편지를 쓰거나, 직접 상대방에게 말을 하거나, 또는 전화로 통화를 함으로써 자신의 감정을 나타낼 수 있다. 나는 이메일이나 문자 메시지를 전송하는 것이 사람들의 생각을 더 조직화하고 공손함을 유지하는 가장 효과적인 방법이라고 굳게 믿는다.

첫째, 이메일이나 문자를 보내면, 사람들은 보다 논리적인 방법으로 자신의 생각을 정리할 수 있다. 많은 경우에 있어서, 사람들은 언짢을 때 두서없이 말하는 경향이 있다. 예를 들어, 나는 브라질로 여행을 갔었는데 열성이 없는 여행 가이드의 태도에 매우 실망을 했다. 그래서, 여행사의 책임자에게 일어났던 순서대로 있었던 일을 설명하는 이메일을 보냈고 사과와 보상을 받아낼 수 있었다.

게다가, 사람의 분노에 관한 직접적인 구두 표현은 다른 사람의 기분에 상처를 주거나 더 큰 오해를 불러 일으킬 수 있기 때문에 이메일이나 문자 메시지를 작성하면 사람들은 보다 효과적으로 자신의 화를 통제할 수 있다. 예를 들면, 내 친구는 급우에게 화가 나서, 문자를 보내기로 결심한 적이 있었다. 메시지를 작성하는 순간에는 그의 화가 문장에 직접적으로 표출되어 있었다. 하지만, 문자를 보내기 전, 내 친구는 자기 급우의 감정에 상처를 줄 수 있는 단어들을 수정했다.

전화 통화와 음성 메시지가 사람들의 감정을 전달하는데 보다 더 효과적이라는 점은 사실이다. 반면, 직접적인 언어 표현은 상황을 악화시킬 수 있다. 이메일이나 문자 메시지를 작성함으로써, 사람들은 자신의 언짢은 기분을 표현하는데 보다 더 논리적이 될 수가 있다. 더 나아가, 메시지를 작성하면 사람들은 자신의 감정을 다스릴 수 있고 그것을 전송하기 전에 내용을 수정하는 시간을 가질 수 있다. 그러므로 나는 이메일이나 문자로 문제를 해결하는 것이 문제를 해결하는 가장 좋은 방법이라고 생각한다.

Sample Essay 2 | PHONE CALLS / VOICE MAILS   p.124

현대 사회에서는 많은 사람들이 교류를 하기 때문에, 사람들 사이에서 문제가 일어나는 것은 불가피하다. 불쾌한 기분을 표현하는 방법에는 여러 가지가 있다. 사람들은 편지를 쓰거나, 직접 상대방에게 말을 하거나, 또는 전화로 통화를 함으로써 자신의 감정을 나타낼 수 있다. 나는 전화를 하거나 음성 메시지를 남기는 것이 감정을 직접적으로 표현하고 오해를 방지할 가장 효과적인 방법이라고 굳게 믿는다.

첫째, 전화로 통화를 하거나 음성 메시지를 남기는 것은 보다 더 직접적인 방식으로 화를 표출할 수 있는 효과적인 방법이 된다. 예를 들면, 매장 점원에게 화가 났을 때, 나는 강조하고 싶은 중요한 모든 단어에 강세를 두어 말했다. 결과적으로, 내가 표현하고자 했던 취지와 감정이 충분히 전달되었던다.

게다가, 목소리의 억양이나 음조가 없는 경우 사람들 간에 더 큰 오해를 불러 일으키거나 특정 상황을 악화시킬 수 있다. 예를 들면, 내 친구의 실험 동료가 회의에 나타나지 않았다. 대신, 그녀는 만나기로 한 지 한 시간 이상이 지나서야 회의에 올 수 없다는 메시지를 보냈다. 내 친구는 비꼬는 메시지를 다시 보냈다. 그는 그녀를 기다리는 동안 재미있었다고 말했다. 그는 비꼬는 방식으로 썼지만, 실험 동료는 이를 문자 그대로 받아들여 죄책감을 느끼지 않았다.

이메일이나 문자 메시지가 사람들의 생각을 보다 더 체계적으로 정리하도록 만들어 준다는 점은 사실이다. 하지만, 자신의 감정을 숨기고 지나치게 예의를 차리는 것보다는 본인의 감정을 솔직히 표현하는 것이 더 중요하다. 전화 통화나 음성 메시지는 사람들이 더 직접적으로 자신의 생각을 표현할 수 있도록 해 준다. 더 나아가, 더 큰 오해를 야기시키는 것도 막아 준다. 그러므로 나는 전화 통화나 음성 메시지로 문제를 해결하는 것이 그 문제를 다루는 가장 좋은 방법이라고 생각한다.

Actual Test 12

TASK 1 · INTEGRATED TASK
Zoology: Bonobos

READING   p.127

보노보는 아프리카 콩고 강의 남쪽에 서식하는 멸종 위기에 처한 영장류이다. 많은 영장류 동물학자들이 보노보에 대해 알게 된 것은 보노보들이 꽤 온순한 성격을 가지고 있다는 점이다. 침팬지처럼 본성이 공격적이고 난폭한 다른 영장류들과는 뚜렷이 다르다.

보노보가 온화한 성격을 가지고 있다는 점에 대한 많은 근거들이 존재한다. 전문가들은 포획된 상태의 여러 보노보들을 연구했는데 보노보들이 난폭한 성향을 가지고 있다는 증거는 거의 목격하지 못했다. 포획된 보노보들은 보통 착하고 온순하고 예민했으며, 사육사들은 보노보를 다루는 동안 별다른 문제를 겪지 않았다고 전했다. 이 점에 있어서, 보노보들은 사육사들을 공격하거나 혹은 기타 문제들을 일으키는 다른 영장류들과는 다르다.

또한 보노보들에게는 난폭한 행동을 하려는 새끼들을 제지하려는 경향이 있다. 예를 들어, 많은 동물 종의 새끼들은 종종 서로 싸우거나 격렬한 다툼을 벌인다. 이는 새끼들에게 사냥하는 법뿐만 아니라 기타 생존 기술들도 가르쳐 준다. 하지만, 나이 든 보노보들은 어린 보노보들 사이의 싸움에 개입함으로써 이러한 행동을 적극적으로 제지한다. 따라서, 새끼 보노보들은 그들의 성장 기간 동안 어떻게 싸우는지, 혹은 어떻게 공격적인 성향을 기르는지에 대해 배우지 않는다.

보노보들은 보다 난폭한 그들의 사촌 뻘인 침팬지들과 종종 대조가 된다. 침팬지들은 작은 동물들을 사냥하고, 다른 영장류 무리들을 공격하기 위해 돌이나 나뭇가지를 무기로 삼는다고 알려져 왔다. 보노보들 사이에서는 이러한 행동이 목격된 바 없다. 일부 연구원들은 보노보가 초식 동물이라는 사실 때문에 그들이 지니고 있을지도 모르는 난폭한 충동이 억제되고 있다고 믿는다. 보노보들은 초식 동물이기 때문에, 자기방어 목적 이외에는 어떠한 것도 사냥하거나 죽일 필요가 없다. 따라서, 이들은, 특히 침팬지와 비교해 볼 때, 보다 더 평화로운 동물로 진화해 왔다.

LISTENING   🎧 12-01

W Professor: You might have read about how bonobos are considered a nonaggressive species. Well, there's some truth to that, but let me point out a few problems with this widely accepted theory.

First, few long-term studies of bonobos in the wild have been conducted. After all, the first studies began in the 1970s. And there are only a few thousand wild bonobos. Instead, most research has been done on captive bonobos. There are, uh, just about 100 in captivity. That's not too many. Now, these studies on captive bonobos rave about their gentleness. However, keep in mind that many animals behave differently in captivity. A meek animal may become vicious while an aggressive animal may become calm. So although captive bonobos are gentle, we can't be sure if that's their real nature until we conduct more research on them in their natural habitats.

Additionally, bonobos aren't always as peaceful as they appear. They often engage in acts of group aggression. Here's what happens . . . Many times, young bonobos form small groups. Then, they stalk and subsequently attack an older bonobo that's by itself and which has let its guard down. That hardly sounds like peaceful behavior to me.

Finally, numerous comparisons have been made between the, uh, peaceful bonobos and violent chimpanzees. However, I feel that chimps are a product of their environment. You see, chimps' natural habitats were invaded by humans long ago. Much of the vegetation they once ate was destroyed by human settlements. As a result, chimps became omnivores. They learned to hunt, which increased their violent tendencies. Bonobos, on the other hand, live south of the Congo River in land that few humans have encroached upon. Thus bonobos' more peaceful, herbivorous lifestyles haven't been interrupted. Perhaps in the future, should their lands be invaded, they too will adapt and become more violent.

교수: 여러분은 보노보들이 어떻게 비공격적인 종으로 여겨지는지에 관해 책에서 읽은 적이 있을 것입니다. 음, 그건 사실이기도 하지만, 이처럼 널리 받아들여지는 이론에는 몇 가지 문제점들도 있다는 점을 지적해 보도록 하겠습니다.

첫째로, 야생에서의 보노보에 관한 장기간의 연구는 거의 진행된 적이 없었습니다. 아무튼, 초기 연구는 1970년대에 이루어졌죠. 덧붙이면 야생 보노보는 몇 천 마리에 불과합니다. 대신 대부분의 연구는 포획된 보노보를 대상으로 행해졌습니다. 음, 포획된 보노보는 약 100마리 정도죠. 많은 것이 아닙니다. 자, 포획된 보노보에 대한 이러한 연구들은 보노보의 온순함에 대해 이야기를 해줍니다. 하지만, 포획된 상태에서는 많은 동물들이 다르게 행동한다는 것을 기억하세요. 온순한 동물이 포악하게 변할 수도 있고, 공격적인 동물은 온순해 질 수도 있습니다. 그러니까, 포획된 보노보들이 온순하다고 할지라도, 우리는 자연 서식지에 있는 보노보들을 더 연구할 때까지는 온순함이 그들의 진정한 본성인지 알 수가 없습니다.

뿐만 아니라, 보노보들은 보이는 것과 달리 항상 평화롭지만은 않습니다. 종종 집단적인 공격을 벌이기도 하죠. 자, 이렇게요... 주로, 어린 보노보들이 작은 무리를 형성합니다. 그리고 나서, 혼자 있는 무방비 상태의 나이 든 보노보에게 몰래 접근한 후 공격합니다. 저에게는 이것이 평화적인 행동으로 보이지는 않는군요.

마지막으로, 음... 온순한 보노보들과 난폭한 침팬지들 사이에 많은 비교가 이루어졌습니다. 하지만, 저는 침팬지들이 환경의 영향을 받았을 뿐이라고 생각합니다. 저기... 침팬지의 자연 서식지는 오래 전에 인간들에 의해 침범을 당했습니다. 그들이 한때 섭취했던 대부분의 식물들은 인간의 정착에 의해 파괴되었습니다. 결과적으로, 침팬지들은 잡식성이 되었습니다. 그들은 난폭한 성향을 증가시키는 사냥 방법을 배우게 되었습니다. 보노보들은, 반면, 인간들이 거의 침범하지 않았던 콩고 강의 남쪽 땅에서 살았습니다. 그래서 보노보들의 평화롭고 초식 중심의 생활 방식은 방해를 받지 않았던 것입니다. 아마도 장래에 자신들의 땅이 침범을 당한다면, 그들 또한 그에 적응하게 되어 보다 더 난폭하게 변할 것입니다.

교수는 보노보의 온순한 성격에 관한 이론에 몇 가지 문제가 있다고 주장한다. 이러한 주장은 보노보의 온화한 행동이 세 가지 증거로서 입증될 수 있다는 지문의 주장과 반대된다.

첫째, 교수는 야생 상태에 있는 보노보에 관해 장기적으로 연구가 실행된 적이 거의 없었고 대부분의 연구가 포획된 보노보에 집중되어 있다고 말한다. 포획된 동물들은 다르게 반응하기 때문에, 보노보가 자연 서식지에서 어떻게 반응할지는 확실하지 않다. 이는 포획된 보노보가 온순한 성격을 설명해 줄 수 있다는 지문의 주장을 반박한다.

게다가, 교수는 보노보가 보이는 것처럼 호의적이지 않다고 말한다. 실제로, 새끼 보노보들은 가끔 무리를 형성하여 혼자 있는 나이 든 보노보를 공격한다. 이러한 주장은 보노보들이 새끼들에게 난폭한 행동을 금지시킴으로써 평화를 유지한다는 지문의 주장에 의문을 제기한다.

마지막으로, 보노보와 종종 비교되는 침팬지의 성격은 환경에 영향을 받았을 가능성이 높다. 따라서, 이론적으로는 보노보의 서식지가 인간에 의해 파괴된다면, 보노보들도 침팬지들처럼 난폭한 행동을 하게 될 것이다. 이러한 점은 침팬지가 동물들을 사냥하고 다른 영장류를 공격하는 반면 보노보의 초식성은 이들의 난폭한 성향을 감소시킨다는 지문의 주장을 반박한다.

TASK 2 · INDEPENDENT TASK
Teachers' Roles II

교육 기관은 학생들이 필요로 하는 것에 맞추고 가장 바람직한 교육 환경을 제공하기 위해 최선을 다한다. 따라서, 이런 목적을 달성하기 위해 교육 단체가 실행하는 많은 방법과 제도가 있다. 다른 과목을 다른 교사가 담당하는 것도 몇 가지 이점이 있지만, 나는 초등학교는 한 학급에 단 한 명의 교사만 있어야 한다고 굳게 믿는다. 이는 학생들의 좀 더 많은 관심 받기 그리고 효율적인 교실 관리와 관계가 있다.

아이들은 특히 어렸을 때, 한 명의 교사로부터 더 많은 관심이 필요하고 교사 및 학우들과 강한 유대 관계를 형성할 필요가 있다. 이는 교사와의 탄탄한 관계가 학생의 동기 부여 수준을 강화시킬 수 있기 때문이다. 예를 들면, 한 연구는 한 학급에서 한 명의 교사의 지도하에 있는 학생들은 하루에 서너 명의 다른 교사들을 만나는 학생들에 비해 더욱 행복하고 안전한 기분을 느낀다는 것을 보여준다. 이는 학생들이 한 선생님에 의해 가르침을 받을 때 효과적이라는 것을 보여준다.

게다가, 모든 과목은 서로 연관되어 있기 때문에, 교사는 한 과목에서 가르친 지식을 다른 과목에 적용시킬 수 있다. 이는 또한 학기말에 성공적인 학업 성취로 이끈다. 예를 들어, 교사는 국어 수업에서 가르친 독해 기술을 사회 시간에 학생들에게 역사적 인물을 가르칠 때 적용시킬 수도 있다. 따라서, 한 교사가 학급 전체를 관리하면, 교사는 학생들의 요구와 능력을 더 쉽게 파악할 수 있고 다른 과목을 가르칠 때 그런 것들을 고려할 수 있다.

다른 교사로부터 각각의 과목을 배우는 것은 각각의 과목을 다른 선생님에게 배우는 것이 학생들을 다른 교수 유형에 노출시킬 것임은 사실이다. 하지만, 아이들이 다른 방식과 관점을 구분하기에는 너무 어리다. 학생들은 한 선생님에게 배울 때 더 안전하고 편안하게 느껴 더 나은 학업 성취를 이끈다. 나아가, 한 교사가 학생들을 지도하는 것은 교사로 하여금 통합된 교과 과정을 통해 더 나은 교육 목표에 도달할 수 있도록 해준다. 그러므로 나는 초등학교에서는 한 명의 교사가 모든 과목을 가르쳐야 한다고 굳게 믿는다.

교육 기관은 학생들이 필요로 하는 것에 맞추고 가장 바람직한 교육 환경을 제공하기 위해 최선을 다한다. 따라서, 교육 단체가 실행하는 많은 방법과 제도가 있다. 모든 과목을 한 명의 교사가 관리하는 것에 대한 이점이 몇 가지 있지만, 나는 초등학교는 각 과목에 다른 교사들을 배정해야 한다고 굳게 믿는다. 이는 각 교사의 전문화와 학생들이 한 교사에게 너무 많이 의존할지 모른다는 사실 때문이다.

학생들은 전문적인 기술을 가진 다른 교사들로부터 다양한 교육 방법을 통해 배울 수 있다. 다시 말해서, 특정한 교수법에 적응하기 보다 학생들은 배움의 다양한 방법에 노출되는 기회가 생긴다. 예를 들면, 다른 교사들은 전통적인 교수법을 유지하는데 출중한 반면 일부 교사들은 기술을 활용하는데 전문가일 수 있다. 각각 다른 방법은 학생들로 하여금 많은 방법을 경험하고 다양한 관점을 개발하도록 도와주어 교육의 향상된 질로 이끌어 준다.

더 나아가, 과목별로 다른 교사들이 있는 것은 학생들이 좀 더 훈련될 수 있도록 도와준다. 단일 교사의 인도 하에, 학생은 그 교사를 지나치게 편하게 느낄 수 있다. 예를 들면, 학생은 교사가 이해해 줄 것이니 과제를 조금 늦게 제출해도 괜찮다고 생각할 수 있다. 이는 책임감 부재를 초래하며 학생이 교사에게 더욱 의존하도록 만든다. 게다가, 아이들은 미래에 결국 다른 교사들에게서 배울 것이다. 그러니, 특히 학업 부담이 요구 되지 않는 어린 나이에는 그러한 환경에 적응하는 것이 낫다.

하나의 교사만 있는 것은 학생들과 교사들 사이에 더 친밀한 관계를 가질 가능성을 줄일 수 있다. 하지만, 학생들은 다른 교육 방법에 노출되는 것이 더욱 좋다. 덧붙여, 학생들이 한 명의 교사에게 적응이 된다면, 그들은 교사와 너무 편해질 수 있으며 너무 의존적으로 될 수 있다. 따라서, 나는 어린 학생들은 각 과목을 다른 교사들에게서 배워야 한다고 강력히 주장한다.

Actual Test 13

TASK 1 · INTEGRATED TASK

Oceanography: Coral Degradation

산호초는 바닷속 조직으로 부식과 태풍으로부터 해안을 보호하는 수중구조물이다. 산호초는 전체 물고기와 다른 해양 생물의 약 25%의 서식지이고, 그들은 해양 생태계에 굉장히 중요한 역할을 한다. 하지만, 여러 요인으로 인해, 산호초는 멸종 위기에 놓여졌다. 산호초의 파괴는 산호 붕괴라고 불리며 즉각 해결되어야 할 필요가 있다.

산호가 맞닥뜨리는 가장 큰 문제는 산호 표백이고, 산호 표백의 주된 원인은 기후 변화이다. 바다 온도의 상승은 산호들이 산호 안에서 살며 색깔, 식량, 그리고 영양소를 공급하는 조류들을 밀어내게 된다. 조류가 없이는, 산호들은 흐려지고 마치 표백이 된 것처럼 하얗게 보인다. 결국 이는 온도 하강으로 조류들이 다시 산호로 돌아오지 않는 이상 그들을 죽게 만들 것이다.

많은 원인들 중 하나는 비료, 석유, 그리고 인간과 동물의 분뇨를 포함한 공해이다. 플라스틱 쓰레기는 산호 조직에도 물리적인 손상을 일으켜 산호를 파괴시킨다. 둥둥 떠다니는 쓰레기는 또한 산호초가 살아 있게 하는 햇빛을 산호초가 받지 못하게 한다. 채광, 도로 건설, 그리고 농업을 포함한 지상 활동 역시 산호들을 위험에 빠뜨리게 한다. 농업에 사용되는 비료 안의 과도한

영양분은 산호초에 특히나 위험하다.

남획, 스쿠버 다이빙, 그리고 산호 수확 같은 인간의 행위 역시 산호초의 손상에 기여한다. 남획은 세계 산호초의 55% 이상을 위협하고, 동남아의 산호는 특히 이런 행위에 취약하다. 게다가, 많은 산호들은 여행객을 유치하기 위해 잡혀서 수족관에 전시될 뿐 아니라, 꺾어서 보석이나 기념품으로 팔려지기도 한다. 환경적 문제는 많은 여행객들이 산호에게 치명적인 옥시벤존이라 불리는 화학 물질이 들어간 자외선 차단제를 바르기 때문에 더욱 악화되고 있다.

M Professor: Have you ever had a chance to go scuba diving? Once you enter the underwater world, you will be welcomed by wonderful corals of different colors and shapes. However, these astonishing corals are in great danger due to human activities. This problem should be taken quite seriously since it can affect the entire ecosystem. Let's look more closely at the consequences we are about to face in the near future.

Lots of you probably think the beautiful colors corals possess merely serve an aesthetic purpose . . . and I wish I could say you're right. But, unfortunately, coral bleaching can pose a catastrophic problem to the entire reef ecosystem. Countless underwater animals, including fish, turtles, and sea birds, depend on coral reefs for food, protection, and shelter. We need to take this very seriously because once they die, it is almost impossible to get the reefs back.

Coral degradation due to human activities can also bring about disasters. Coral reefs act as underwater seawalls and protect shorelines from storms, floods, and waves . . . This is very important because without them, the results could be devastating . . . uh . . . as there would be a loss of life, erosion, and property damage. Coastal communities will always be exposed to the danger of natural disasters. Many of you might wonder how an overabundance of nutrients can destroy the reefs . . . well . . . Too much is never good . . . so . . . excess nutrients can increase the amount of algae and end up smothering corals . . . hmm . . . eventually causing death.

The loss of coral reefs can result in significant impacts on some countries' economies. Think about communities which depend on the ocean for fishing, tourism, and food supplies . . . If those sources disappear one day, it is inevitable that the whole community will suffer from an economic crisis. Let me give you an example of the fishing industry. It is not just corals that will die . . . but other marine animals that feed on corals will also die . . . and that can affect the entire ecosystem. Fishermen will be deprived of their main source of income and will have to do something else for a living.

교수: 스쿠버 다이빙을 해볼 기회가 있었던 사람 있나요? 바닷속을 들어가면, 다른 색깔과 무늬의 아름다운 산호에게서 환영을 받을 거예요. 하지만, 이러한 놀랄만한 산호들은 인간의 행위로 인해 굉장한 위험에 처해 있습니다. 이 문제는 생태계 전체에 영향을 끼칠 수 있기 때문에 꽤 진지하게 받아들여져야 합니다. 조만간 우리가 직면하기 직전인 결과에 대해 좀 더 자세히

보도록 하지요.

여러분 중 다수는 아마도 산호의 아름다운 색깔에 단지 아름다움의 목적만 있다고 생각하실 겁니다... 그리고 저도 여러분이 맞다고 말하고 싶어요. 하지만 불행히도 산호 표백은 산호 생태 전체에 비극적인 문제를 가져올 수 있어요. 물고기, 거북이, 그리고 바다 새 등의 셀 수 없는 바다 동물들은 식량, 보호, 그리고 거처의 이유로 산호에 의존해요. 일단 산호가 죽으면, 산호초를 되찾는 것이 거의 불가능하기 때문에 우리는 이것을 굉장히 사려 깊게 받아들여야 합니다.

인간 행위 때문에 산호 붕괴는 재난도 야기시킬 수 있어요. 산호초는 바닷속의 제방 역할을 하고 태풍, 홍수, 그리고 파도로부터 해안가를 보호하지요... 이는 산호초들 없이는 그 결과가 충격적일 수 있기 때문에 매우 중요합니다... 음... 생명의 손실, 침식, 그리고 아마도 토지의 파손이 있을 것이니까요. 해안 마을은 자연재해에 항상 노출되어 있을 것입니다. 여러분 중 많은 분들은 어떻게 과잉 영양분이 산호초를 파괴할 수 있는지 궁금하실지도 몰라요... 음... 과다한 건 언제나 좋지 않지요... 그러니까... 과잉 영양분은 조류의 양을 증가시켜서 산호를 질식시킬 수 있어요... 음... 결국 죽음을 초래하지요.

산호초 손실은 일부 국가의 경제에 굉장한 영향을 미칠 수 있습니다. 어업, 관광업, 식량 공급 등으로 바다에 의존하는 사회에 대해 생각해 보세요... 만약 그런 원천이 하루 아침 사라진다면, 사회 전체가 경제난을 겪을 거라는 것은 불가피합니다. 어업에 대한 예를 드리죠. 산호 뿐 아니라 산호를 먹는 다른 해양 식물들도 죽을 거예요... 그리고 그것은 생태계 전체에 영향을 끼치겠지요. 어부들은 수입의 주된 원천을 박탈당하고 생계 수단으로 다른 것을 찾아야 할 것입니다.

Sample Essay   p.140

교수는 적절한 조치가 취해지지 않는 한 가까운 미래에 산호 붕괴가 파괴적인 결과를 가져다 줄 것이라고 경고하고 설명한다. 이는 산호초가 멸종 위기에 있다는 지문에서 설명된 의견을 지지한다.

첫째, 산호 표백은 산호 생태계 전체를 위험에 빠뜨릴 수 있다. 만약 산호가 색깔을 잃어버리고 죽는다면, 다른 해양 동물들 역시 위험에 빠질 것이다. 이는 기후 변화로 인한 바다 온도의 상승이 산호들이 조류를 내쫓게 하고, 산호 표백과 산호이 죽음을 초래한다는 지문의 내용을 옹호한다.

뿐만 아니라, 교수는 해안 지역이 그 어떠한 자연 장벽이 없이 자연 재해를 직면할 것이라고 주의를 준다. 산호초 없이는, 해안가는 태풍, 홍수, 그리고 파도에 취약할 것이다. 덧붙여, 과잉 영양분은 조류 급증을 일으킬 것이고, 산호를 질식시켜 죽일 것이다. 이는 공해와 지상 활동들이 산호초에게 해를 가할 수 있다는 지문의 입장을 설명한다.

끝으로, 해양 활동에 크게 의존하는 일부 국가들은 경제난을 겪을 것이다. 만약 산호가 죽으면, 산호를 잡아먹는 다른 동물들이 먹이 원천의 결핍으로 고통 받거나 죽을 것이다. 이는 해양 여행, 남획, 그리고 산호 수집 등의 인간 활동이 산호초의 파괴에 기여한다는 지문의 내용을 설명해 준다.

TASK 2 · INDEPENDENT TASK

Influence

Sample Essay 1 | AGREE   p.143

젊은 사람들은 미래의 사회를 이끌어 갈 사람들이다. 따라서, 사회적 쟁점에 대한 그들의 참여는 미래에 커다란 영향을 미칠 수 있다. 어떤 사람들은 오늘날 젊은 사람들이 중요한 결정을 내리는데 상당한 역할을 해왔다고 주장한다. 하지만, 나는 젊은 사람들이 미래의 사회에 영향을 끼칠 수 있는 주

요 결정에 거의 영향을 미치지 못했다고 굳게 믿는다. 일단, 많은 젊은 사람들은 사회적 쟁점에 대한 관심을 잃었다. 게다가, 관료제가 종종 젊은 사람들이 자신들의 생각을 표현하는 것을 막고 있다.

첫째, 사회가 더욱 더 요구가 많고 경쟁적으로 변해 가면서, 젊은 사람들은 보다 더 개인주의적으로 변하고, 자신에게 직접적인 영향을 미치지 않는 사회적 쟁점들에 대해서는 관심을 잃게 되었다. 예를 들어, 미래의 환경 파괴의 결과에 대해 생각하는 젊은 사람들은 많지 않다. 따라서, 다수의 젊은 사람들은 환경을 보호하는 운동에 자신들의 시간을 사용하여 그에 동참하는 것을 꺼리고 있다.

뿐만 아니라, 사회적 이슈들을 인식하고 자신들의 의견을 개진하는 젊은 사람들이 여전히 존재하고 있음에도 불구하고, 권력을 유지하고 관행을 따르려는 목적으로 관료제가 빈번하게 개입한다. 예를 들면, 많은 젊은 사람들이 새롭고 혁신적인 사회 구조들을 실험하고자 한다. 종종, 그들은 변화를 외친다. 그럼에도 불구하고, 이들의 생각은 사회적 권력과 오랜 관습을 유지하고 싶어하는 기성 집단에 의해 무시되고 있다.

일부 젊은 사람들이 사회의 중요한 문제들을 인식하고 미래의 결정에 영향을 끼칠 수 있는 일에 참여하려고 노력하는 것은 사실이다. 하지만, 젊은 사람들의 삶의 대부분이 자기중심적이고, 그들은 자신의 일을 관리하느라 바쁘다. 게다가, 바람직하지 않은 관료제는 젊은 사람들로 하여금 사회에 자신들의 생각을 표현하는 것을 막는다. 이상의 이유로, 나는 오늘날 젊은 사람들이 사회의 미래를 결정하는 중요한 결정에 영향을 미치지 않는다는 진술에 동의한다.

Sample Essay 2 | DISAGREE   p.144

젊은 사람들은 미래의 사회를 이끌어 갈 사람들이다. 따라서, 사회적 쟁점에 대한 그들의 참여는 미래에 커다란 영향을 미칠 수 있다. 어떤 사람들은 오늘날 젊은 사람들이 중요한 결정에 영향을 거의 끼치지 못한다고 주장한다. 하지만, 나는 그들이 미래의 사회에 영향을 끼칠 수 있는 결정을 내리는데 보다 많은 역할을 하고 있다고 굳게 믿는다. 일단, 젊은 사람들은 서로를 연결해 주는 인터넷의 힘을 이용한다. 게다가, 시위를 할 자유가 그들의 생각을 표현할 수 있도록 해 준다.

첫째, 인터넷의 부급으로 사회의 중요 이슈들에 대한 개인들의 영향력이 증대되고 있다. 대부분 젊은 사람들은 소셜 네트워크 서비스에 가입되어 있기 때문에, 특정 관심사에 대한 생각은 매우 빠르게 확산된다. 예를 들어, 환경 문제는 젊은 사람들 사이에서 심각한 주제가 되었다. 따라서, 그들은 온라인상으로 서로 토론하고, 세계 각지의 소식을 포함한 많은 정보를 접하고 있다. 젊은 사람들은 미래를 위해 자연을 보존하자는 전 세계적인 운동을 활성화시키고 있다.

뿐만 아니라, 젊은이들은 자신들의 생각을 표현할 수 있는 많은 방법들이 있다. 서명 운동이나 시위 등의 방법은 때때로 법을 개정시키는 결과를 낳는다. 예를 들면, 많은 젊은 사람들은 정규직 자리를 찾는데 어려움을 겪는다. 오히려, 그들의 계약은 일 년 단위로 갱신된다. 이러한 상황은 그들로 하여금 종종 회사의 단점과 불공정을 묵인하도록 만든다. 오늘날에는, 많은 젊은 사람들이 항의나 시위를 통해 부당함에 맞서는 행동을 보이고 있다. 그 결과, 정부는 그러한 상황을 인식하고 부당한 대우로부터 노동자들을 보호할 수 있는 법안을 통과시키는 중이다.

편리함을 목적으로 기존 관행을 유지시키려는 압력 때문에 때때로 젊은 사람들이 자신들의 생각을 나타내지 못하고 있다는 점은 사실이다. 반면, 인터넷을 통해 젊은 사람들의 생각이 급속히 확대되면서 그러한 단점은 극복되어 왔다. 게다가, 젊은 사람들은 중요한 결정에 영향을 끼칠 수 있는 많은 행사에 적극적으로 참여하고 있다. 이상의 이유로, 나는 오늘날 젊은 사람

들이 사회의 미래를 결정하는 중요한 결정에 영향을 미치지 않는다는 진술에 반대한다.

Actual Test 14

TASK 1 · INTEGRATED TASK

Botany: Honeysuckle

READING   p.147

북미와 유라시아에서는, 약 180종의 인동덩굴이 발견되었다. 인동덩굴은 그들의 아름다운 잎과 트럼펫 모양의 매력적인 꽃 덕분에 많은 정원사들 사이에서 인기가 많다. 대부분의 인동덩굴은 미국에서 침입종이라고 분류되지만, 그들은 야생 식물뿐 아니라 야생 동물에게도 많은 이점을 제공한다.

인동덩굴은 야생 생물에게 귀중하다. 그것은 많은 새들에게 집을 제공하며, 많은 수분 매개체들을 끌어서 자신 뿐 아니라 다른 토종 식물들 역시 번식하도록 돕는다. 인동덩굴의 단단한 나뭇가지 혹은 나무 껍질은 고양이 새와 굴뚝새를 포함한 많은 종류의 새들의 둥지에 튼튼한 버팀이 되고, 나뭇잎은 포식자들로부터 둥지를 숨기려는 새들을 도울 수 있다. 또한, 나비나 벌 등의 곤충들은 그것의 씨앗이 수분하는 것을 돕고 식물을 풍부하게 한다.

많은 새들과 다른 동물들에게 있어 인동덩굴은 일년 내내 훌륭한 음식 공급원이다. 베리류는 특히, 어떤 먹을 것도 찾기 힘든 시기 동안 새들에게 언제나 환영을 받는다. 여름에는, 곤충들뿐 아니라 곤충을 먹는 새들도 먹이 때문에 인동덩굴을 찾는다. 겨울잠쥐는 에너지를 위해 그것은 달콤하고 꿀이 풍부한 꽃을 먹는다. 가장 흔한 수분 매개체 중 둘인 나비와 벌은 인동덩굴의 꿀에 굉장히 의존한다. 그 수가 감소하고 있기 때문에, 흰줄나비들에게 꿀을 제공하는 것은 특히나 중요하다.

인동덩굴의 가장 인상적인 특성 중 하나는 잎, 베리, 씨앗, 꽃을 포함한 모든 부분이 약으로 쓰일 수 있다는 것이다. 그 식물은 소화불량, 피부 트러블, 당뇨, 그리고 많은 다른 질환에 도움을 준다. 예를 들면, 인동덩굴은 땀을 빼서 몸을 식힘으로써 열이 있는 사람이 체온을 낮출 수 있게 돕는다.

LISTENING   🎧 14-01

W Professor: Thanks to their beautiful flowers and wonderful scents as well as usefulness as hedges, many people consider planting honeysuckles in their backyard. Honeysuckles are known to be easy to grow and are low growing. However, people should be very careful of these plants since they are extremely difficult to eradicate. These drought-tolerant plants can survive without water for a long time. Let me explain how these plants can be a threat to the natural environment.

Honeysuckles are very invasive . . . They really kill all the native plants around them . . . They are highly adaptable to the environment and have typical traits of invasive species, such as rapid reproduction, spreading, and growth. Just like other invasive plants, honeysuckles can easily climb other plants and affect their health by strangling them. Honeysuckles also hinder reproduction of such valuable

trees as maple, oak, and hickory, whose leaves create lots of shade on the forest floor. This creates a monoculture of invasive species where one species dominates the ground and eliminates other species . . . Pretty scary, huh?

And yes . . . honeysuckles are a great food source for birds . . . but a number of studies have recently found that these plants have negative consequences for birds. The berries from honeysuckles are like . . . bird junk food or fast food . . . So yes . . . they are probably tasty, and birds love them . . . but they have less fat and nutrients compared to native berries. This poses a problem particularly for migrating birds because the lack of nutrients and fat can slow their pace of migration.

All right . . . Many people believe that honeysuckle can benefit people's bodies in many ways. Well . . . I read an article that it can even be used to treat cancer. But when you read to the end of these articles, you can find that most of them point out that there is little medical proof in these studies or that further research needs to be conducted. It is very controversial . . . Some say honeysuckle can be applied to the skin for inflammation . . . but, in fact, it can actually cause serious infections if not treated properly. Though they may be effective for certain diseases, it is certain that more studies should be done.

교수: 울타리로서의 유용성뿐 아니라 아름다운 꽃과 훌륭한 향기 덕분에, 많은 사람들은 그들의 뒷마당에 인동덩굴을 심을 생각을 하지요. 인동덩굴은 기르기 쉽고 낮게 자란다고 알려져 있어요. 하지만, 인동덩굴은 근절하기 굉장히 어렵기 때문에 사람들은 이 식물을 정말 조심해야 합니다. 가뭄도 견뎌내는 이 식물들은 물 없이 꽤 오래 살 수 있어요. 이러한 식물들이 어떻게 자연 환경에 위협이 될 수 있는지 설명할게요.

인동덩굴은 상당히 침입적이에요... 그들은 그들 주위에 있는 토종 식물들을 정말 죽이지요... 그들은 환경에 굉장히 잘 적응하고, 빠른 번식, 확산, 성장 등의 전형적인 침입종들의 특성을 가지고 있어요. 다른 침입 식물처럼, 인동덩굴은 다른 식물들을 타고 올라가 질식시킴으로써 그들의 건강을 영향을 끼쳐요. 인동덩굴들은 또한 숲 바닥에 수 많은 그림자를 생기게 해서 단풍나무, 참나무, 히코리 같은 중요한 나무들의 번식을 막기도 한답니다. 이는 하나의 종이 숲의 지면을 점령하며 다른 종들을 없애버려서 침입종의 독점을 초래해요... 꽤 무섭죠?

그리고 맞아요... 인동덩굴들은 새들에게 좋은 먹이 공급원이에요... 하지만 최근 많은 연구들이 찾아내기를, 이러한 식물들은 새들에게 악영향을 끼친다는 거에요. 인동덩굴의 베리들은 음... 이를테면 조류 불량 식품이나 패스트푸드 정도 되겠네요... 그러니까 맞아요... 그것들은 아마도 맛있고 새들이 좋아할 거에요... 하지만 그 베리들은 지방과 영양분이 다른 토종 베리들에 비해 낮게 있어요. 이는 특히나 철새들에게는 문제를 일으켜요. 왜냐하면 영양분과 지방의 결핍은 이동의 속도를 늦출 수 있기 때문이죠.

좋아요... 많은 사람들이 인동덩굴이 사람의 신체에 여러 방식으로 유용하다고 믿습니다... 음... 저는 인동덩굴이 심지어 암은 치료하는 데에도 사용된다는 기사를 읽은 적도 있어요. 하지만 그러한 기사들을 읽을 때, 대부분 이러한 연구에는 의학적 증거가 거의 없다거나 더 많은 정보가 연구될 필요가 있다고 지적하는 것을 찾을 수 있어요. 굉장히 논쟁의 여지가 있구요... 일부는 인동덩굴이 염증 (치료)를 위해 피부에 발려도 괜찮다고 말하죠... 하지만 사실, 그것은 올바르게 다뤄지지 않는다면, 심각한 감염을 초래할 수 있어요.

특정 질병에는 효과적일 수도 있겠지만, 더 많은 연구가 있어야 된다는 것은 확실합니다.

Sample Essay   p.150

교수는 인동덩굴이 자연환경에 심각한 위험을 야기한다고 주장한다. 이는 인동덩굴이 야생 생물과 인간 세계 모두에게 매우 귀중하다는 지문의 주장에 이의를 제기한다.

첫째, 교수에 따르면, 인동덩굴은 굉장히 침범적이고, 침입종들이 흔히 가지고 있는 빠른 번식 등의 특성을 소유하고 있다. 그녀는 인동덩굴들은 다른 식물들을 타고 올라가 질식시킨다고 설명한다. 그녀는 또한 단풍나무를 예로 들며, 인동덩굴이 어떻게 햇빛을 막아 번식을 막고 독점을 꾀하는지 설명한다. 이는 인동덩굴이 야생 생물들에게 집을 제공하고 식물의 증식에 도움을 준다는 지문의 주장에 반대된다.

게다가 교수는 인동덩굴이 새들에 악영향을 미친다고 주장한다. 최근 연구에 따르면 인동덩굴에서 나는 베리류는 지방과 영양소가 부족하고 오히려 정크 푸드같은 역할을 한다고 한다. 교수에 따르면 불충분한 양의 영양과 지방은 새들이 이동 시 일정한 속도를 유지하는 것을 방해할 것이다. 이는 인동덩굴이 많은 새들과 다른 동물들에게 먹이를 제공한다는 지문의 내용을 반박한다.

끝으로, 교수는 인동덩굴의 의학적 효과를 일축한다. 그녀는 그 식물의 사용에 대한 의학적 증거가 거의 없으며 더 많은 연구가 실행되어야 한다고 설명하며 그녀의 주장을 상술한다. 이는 인동덩굴의 모든 부분이 의학의 목적으로 사용된다는 지문의 생각에 의문을 던진다.

TASK 2 · INDEPENDENT TASK

Environmental Problems

Sample Essay 1 | AGREE   p.153

과학 기술의 발전은 사람들에게 많은 이로움을 제공해 왔다. 하지만, 이는 막대한 양의 환경 파괴를 야기하기도 했다. 환경에 대한 우려가 많은 사람들로부터의 관심을 불러 모음에 따라, 제안되거나 행해진 수많은 해결책과 국제적 대응이 있다. 일부 사람들은 환경 파괴가 돌이킬 수 없는 것이라고 주장하지만, 나는 미래에 자연이 다시 복구될 수 있을 것이라고 굳게 믿는다. 나는 이것이 대기업의 지원과 친환경 운동 때문에 벌어질 것이라고 믿는다.

우선, 환경 문제는 여러 기업들에게 중요한 관심사가 되었다. 예를 들면, 과거 한국에서 대부분의 기업들은 제조하는 동안 발생하는 대기 오염이나 유해 물질과 같은 환경적 영향을 심각하게 받아들이지 않았다. 그러나, 기업들이 그러한 엄청나게 파괴적인 결과를 인식하면서, 그들은 독성 폐기물들을 감소시킬 수 있는 장치들을 설치하고, 결국에는 공장에서 방출되는 모든 오염 물질을 제거할 수 있는 정화 시스템을 개발하기 시작했다.

게다가, 환경 보호 운동이 전세계적으로 확산되고 있다. 과거에 비해 오늘날 많은 사람들이 다음 세대에게 직접적인 영향을 끼칠 수 있는 환경적 상황을 우려하고 있다. 예를 들어, 한국에 있는 거의 모든 사람들은 재활용 운동에 동참하고 있다. 따라서, 사람들은 플라스틱, 알루미늄 깡통, 그리고 판지 등을 분리 수거하는 일에 익숙해지게 되었다. 더 나아가, 음식물 쓰레기는 분쇄되고 건조되어 화학품과 함께 특수 과정을 거쳐 비료로 바뀌고 있다. 이러한 예는 우리의 환경이 점차 좋아질 것이라는 것을 입증해 준다.

지구의 파괴된 환경을 회복시키는 데는 엄청난 양의 노력과 시간이 필요하다는 점은 사실이다. 반면, 독성 물질의 정화 시스템을 개선시키기 위해 노력하는 많은 기업들이 있다. 게다가, 사람들은 환경 보호 운동에 참여하며 후

손들을 위해 자연을 회복시키기 위한 노력을 계속하고 있다. 그러므로, 나는 미래에 환경 문제가 해결되거나 개선될 수 있다는 주장에 강력히 동의한다.

Sample Essay 2 | DISAGREE   p.154

과학 기술의 발전은 사람들에게 많은 이로움을 제공해 왔다. 하지만, 이는 막대한 양의 환경 파괴를 초래하기도 했다. 환경에 대한 우려가 많은 사람들로부터의 관심을 불러 모음에 따라, 제안되거나 행해진 수많은 해결책과 국제적 대응이 있다. 일부 사람들은 자연이 미래에 회복될 수 있다고 주장하지만, 나는 이미 파괴된 환경은 되돌릴 수 없다고 강력히 주장한다. 나는 이것이 파괴의 속도와 그 문제에 대한 인식의 부족 때문에 사실이라고 믿는다.

우선, 환경은 회복되는 것보다 더 빠른 속도로 파괴되고 있다. 예를 들어, 매년 가구, 집, 그리고 연료에 대한 수요를 충족시키기 위해 많은 나무들이 벌목되고 있다. 산림 벌채를 막기 위해 새로운 나무들이 심어지고 있지만, 새로 심어진 나무들은 비교적 얕은 뿌리 조직을 가지고 있기 때문에 침식에 취약하다. 이러한 상황은 산사태나 홍수를 포함한 많은 자연 재해들을 일으킬 수 있다.

게다가, 여전히 이러한 문제를 심각하게 받아들이지 않는 개인 및 기업들이 있다. 예를 들면, 환경을 보존하는 것보다 수익 창출에 더 많은 관심을 보이는 기업들이 많다. 이러한 태도는 기업들로 하여금 제조 과정 동안 배출되는 오염 물질의 양이 안전 기준을 초과하지 않는 한, 정화 시스템을 개선하는 것을 막는다. 또한, 몇몇 사람들은 환경 문제들을 무시하기 때문에, 자연 회복은 더욱 어려워지고 있다.

환경 보호 운동이 자연 환경을 조금씩 변화시키고 있는 것은 사실이다. 하지만, 환경 파괴를 감소시키기 위해 실시되고 있는 일은 자연을 복구하기에 결코 충분치 않으며, 지구는 처참한 결과들로 인해 고통받고 있다. 게다가, 많은 기업들과 개인들은 악영향의 심각성을 깨닫지 못하고 아무런 조치도 취하지 않고 있다. 그러므로, 나는 환경 문제가 미래에 해결되거나 개선될 것이라는 주장에 강력히 반대한다.

Actual Test 15

TASK 1 · INTEGRATED TASK

Meteorology: The Eocene Warming

READING   p.157

약 5천 5백만 년 전, 시신세(始新世)가 시작되었다. 시신세는 2천 1백만 년 정도 지속되었다. 시신세는 포유류가 유래된 시기라는 점과 지구 온도의 급격한 상승으로 평균 기온이 섭씨 5도에서 7도 사이가 된 시기로 유명하다.

몇몇 연구원들은 당시 일어났던 지구 온난화가 해류의 분열 때문이라고 생각한다. 이들 과학자들에 따르면, 해류의 흐름이 실제 멈추었다고 한다. 보통, 흐르는 해류의 한 가지 결과는 따뜻한 물이 차가운 물에 의해 교체된다는 점이다. 이러한 해류는 지나치는 근처의 육지의 온도에 상당한 영향을 끼친다. 그러나, 해류의 흐름이 멈추면, 따뜻한 물은 그 자리에 남아 있게 되며, 그로 인해 많은 지역의 표면 온도가 상승하게 된다.

다른 전문가들은 시신세의 온난화가 하나 혹은 그 이상의 주요 소행성들이 지구에 충돌한 결과라고 생각한다. 시신세가 시작될 때쯤, 한 소행성이 북미 지역에 충돌해서 미 동부에 위치한 체사피크 만을 형성했다. 러시아의 시베리아에도 그 당시 몇 번의 커다란 충돌이 있었다. 이러한 충돌의 영향으로

그 잔해와 재가 위로 올라가 수년간 대기에 머물렀을 것이다. 그 결과, 온실 효과가 나타났을 것이고, 지구의 온도는 급상승하게 되었을 것이다.

마지막으로, 일부 사람들은 어마어마한 양의 메탄이 대기로 방출되어 전 세계에 온실 효과를 일으켰다고 믿는다. 해저에는 엄청난 양의 메탄이 얼음 속에 갇혀 있다. 지구의 해양이 따뜻해져서 이 얼음들이 녹았을 것이다. 이로써 메탄이 대기로 방출되었을 것이다. 대기에 있는 많은 양의 메탄은 대부분 흩어져 없어질 때까지 지구의 온도 상승을 지속시켰을 것이다.

LISTENING 🎧 15-01

W Professor: Fifty-five million years ago, the Earth's atmosphere became much warmer over a period of around one thousand years. That's rather quick in geological terms. This started the Eocene Epoch, which endured high global temperatures for virtually its entire twenty-one million years.

Okay, so, uh, some scientists have claimed that ocean currents slowed down . . . or possibly even stopped flowing . . . and that caused temperatures to rise. It's an interesting theory, but it doesn't really have any factual basis. You see, um, scientists have done a lot of computer modeling on ocean currents and how they affect temperatures. And we've learned that while currents and waves do carry heat, they don't transmit enough of it to have an effect on a global scale. So it wasn't ocean currents that caused the rise in temperatures.

Some have attributed the rising temperatures to an asteroid impact. It's true that asteroid impacts can have global effects. An asteroid likely killed the dinosaurs sixty-five million years ago, and asteroid strikes have resulted in mass extinctions at other times in the Earth's past. But . . . remember that the Eocene warming occurred over a period of about a thousand years. An asteroid impact would have affected global temperatures much faster. And temperatures would have likely returned to normal fairly soon after the atmosphere cleared up. So it wasn't an asteroid either.

The thousand-year rise of the planet's temperature also eliminates from contention the theory that the release of methane from the oceans caused global warming to occur. Again, yes, some amount of methane was released. But any warming that occurred due to the release of methane would have taken thousands of years to happen. No, something else caused this sudden—er, geologically speaking—rise in the Earth's temperature. It just wasn't methane that did it.

교수: 5천 5백만 년 전, 지구의 대기는 약 천 년의 기간에 걸쳐 보다 더 따뜻해졌습니다. 지질학에 있어서는 다소 짧은 기간이죠. 이는 사실상 2천 1백만 년 동안 지구의 온도가 높게 유지되었던 시신세 때 시작되었습니다.

좋아요, 자, 일부 과학자들은 해류가 느려졌다고 주장하고 있습니다... 또는 심지어 흐름이 멈추었을지도 모른다고 합니다... 그리고 그로 인해 온도가 상승되었을 것이라고 합니다. 흥미로운 이론이지만, 아무런 사실적 근거가 없습니다. 저기, 음, 과학자들은 해류와 해류가 어떻게 온도에 영향을 미치는지에 관해 컴퓨터 모델링을 많이 했습니다. 그리고 해류와 파도가 열을 운반하기는 하지만, 전 세계적인 규모로 영향을 미칠 정도로 열을 옮기지는 않는다는 점을 알아냈죠. 따라서, 온도의 상승을 일으킨 것은 해류가 아니었던 것입니다.

일부는 온도의 상승을 소행성 충돌 탓으로 돌리고 있습니다. 소행성 충돌이 지구 전체에 영향을 끼칠 수 있다는 점은 사실입니다. 6천 5백만 년 전 소행성이 공룡을 멸종시켰을 수 있고, 과거 다른 시기에도 소행성 충돌로 집단 멸종이 일어난 경우도 있습니다. 하지만... 시신세 온난화는 약 천 년의 시기에 걸쳐 일어났다는 점을 기억해 두십시오. 소행성 충돌은 지구의 온도에 훨씬 더 빠르게 영향을 미쳤을 것입니다. 그리고, 온도는 대기가 정화된 후 곧 정상으로 되돌아왔을 가능성이 큽니다. 그러니까 소행성 역시 아니라는 것이죠.

또한 천 년 간의 지구 온도 상승은, 해양에서 나온 메탄의 방출로 지구 온난화가 발생했다는 이론을 논쟁에서 제외시켜 줍니다. 다시 말하면, 그래요, 어느 정도의 메탄은 방출되었습니다. 하지만 메탄의 방출 때문에 온난화가 일어나려면 수천 년이 걸릴 것입니다. 아니, 무엇인가 다른 것이 이렇게 갑작스럽게, 음... 지질학적으로 말해서, 지구의 온도를 상승시킨 것이죠. 단지 메탄만은 아니었던 것입니다.

Sample Essay p.160

교수는 시신세 동안의 지구 온난화에 관한 이론이 타당한 증거로 뒷받침되지 않는다고 주장한다. 이는 그 시기에 기온 상승을 초래할 수 있었던 세 가지 가능한 요인들이 있다는 지문의 주장을 직접적으로 반박한다.

첫째, 해류의 그 어떤 변화를 확인할 수 있는 사실적 증거가 존재하지 않는다. 해류와 파도에 의해 운반된 열은 지구의 전반적인 온도에 영향을 끼칠 정도로 충분히 이동되지 않는다는 것이 밝혀졌다. 이는 해류의 변화가 특정 지역들에 따뜻한 물을 가두어 놓았을 것이라는 지문의 의견과 모순된다.

게다가, 교수는 만일 소행성 충돌에 의해 기온이 영향을 받았다면 온도 변화는 더 빨리 이루어졌을 것이며, 일단 대기가 정화되면 온도는 기존의 수준을 회복했을 것이라고 주장한다. 이는 소행성 충돌 후, 그 잔해와 재가 대기로 올라가서 당시의 온도 상승을 일으켰다는 지문의 주장을 반박한다.

마지막으로, 교수는 메탄이 기온에 영향을 주는 것은 불가능해 보인다고 주장한다. 만약 요인이 메탄 하나였다면, 시간이 훨씬 더 오래 걸렸어야 한다. 이는 얼음 밑에 매장되어 있던 메탄이 대기로 방출되어 온도 상승을 이끌어 냈다는 지문의 주장과 반대된다.

TASK 2 · INDEPENDENT TASK

Children's Roles

Sample Essay 1 | HOUSEHOLD CHORES p.163

부모가 어떻게 아이들을 지도하는가는 아동 발달에 있어서 매우 중요하다. 부모의 접근 방식은 아이들의 남은 삶에 영향을 끼칠 수 있다. 일부 사람들은 아이들이 공부하고 놀아야 한다고 주장한다. 하지만, 나는 두 가지 이유로, 아이들이 집안일의 일부를 담당해야 한다고 굳게 믿는다. 집안일들은 아이들에게 책임감을 배우도록 해 주고 다른 이들에 대한 더 많은 이해심 및 배려심을 기르도록 도와준다.

첫째, 아이들은 집안일을 함으로써 책임감을 기를 수 있다. 규칙적으로 이루어져야 하는 특정한 일들을 맡음으로써, 아이들은 미래를 준비할 수 있다. 예를 들어, 많은 연구들은 집안일을 하도록 교육받은 아이들이 성인이 되어 직장에서 강한 책임감을 나타낼 가능성이 더욱 높다는 점을 입증해 주었다. 이는 또한 아이들이 높은 성취감을 느낄 수 있도록 해 준다.

더 나아가, 집안의 다른 구성원과 협력하는 것은 아이들이 가족 구성원들과의 화합과 단합의 감정을 느낄 수 있게 한다. 가족 구성원들과 함께 집안일을 함으로써, 아이들은 자신의 부모가 청소, 정원일, 그리고 요리와 같은 일을 할 때 겪는 어려움들을 이해할 수 있는 기회를 가질 것이다. 예를 들면, 나는 어렸을 때 매끼 식사 준비를 하실 때, 어머니께서 겪으신 어려움을 알지 못했다. 하지만, 내가 스스로 설거지를 하게 된 후, 쉬고 싶었던 시간에도 가족을 위해 그런 집안일을 했던 어머니에 대해 이해하고 감사할 수 있었다.

아이들에게 공부와 놀이가 필요하다는 것은 사실이다. 하지만, 집안일을 할당해 주는 것이 아이들이 그 일을 하는데 막대한 양의 시간을 쏟아야 한다는 것은 아니다. 오히려, 몇 가지 해야 할 집안일이 있다는 것은 아이들에게 책임감과 성취감을 가르쳐 줄 것이다. 게다가, 아이들은 당연하게 여겼던, 다른 가족 구성원들의 도움을 자신들이 받고 있다는 점을 깨닫게 될 것이다. 이상의 이유로, 나는 아이들이 공부와 노는 것에만 집중하는 것보다 집안일을 하며 가족에게 도움을 주어야 한다고 주장한다.

Sample Essay 2 | STUDYING AND PLAYING   p.164

부모가 어떻게 아이들을 지도하는가는 아동 발달에 있어서 매우 중요하다. 부모의 접근 방식은 아이들의 남은 삶에 영향을 끼칠 수 있다. 일부 사람들은 아이들이 집안일을 도와야 한다고 주장한다. 하지만, 나는 두 가지 이유로, 아이들이 공부하고 노는 것에 집중해야 한다고 굳게 믿는다. 아동기는 아이들의 체력 발달에 중요한 시기이고, 더 깊은 배움에 대한 기초가 그 시기에 형성되기 때문이다.

첫째, 아동기는 아이들의 체력과 사회적 발달에 있어서 중요한 시기이다. 따라서, 또래의 다른 아이들과 놀며 사회 활동을 하는 것은 아이들이 필요한 능력을 기르는데 도움을 줄 것이다. 예를 들어, 노는 것은 종종 다른 이들과 함께 뛰거나 협동하는 것을 요구한다. 이는 아이들의 근육이나 면역 체계를 강화시키는데 도움이 된다. 반면, 아이가 집안일을 떠맡고 있다면, 다른 아이들과 함께 놀며 교류하는 것을 배울 기회가 없을 것이다.

더 나아가, 아이들이 스스로의 공부 습관을 기르는 것이 필요하다. 삶의 각각의 단계는 서로 다른 학습 능력을 요구하고 아이들이 목표를 설정하는데 아주 많은 시간을 보내고 그것들을 성취하기 위해 열심히 일하는 것은 중요하다. 예를 들면, 아이들이 수학의 다음 단계로 갈 준비를 하기 위해 덧셈과 뺄셈은 아동기에 배워야 한다. 집안일은 사람들의 삶 동안 어느 시기에든 배울 수 있는 반면, 일부 학습 능력과 습관은 특정한 시기에만 형성될 수 있다.

아이들이 집안일을 함으로써 책임감과 협동심을 배운다는 것은 사실이다. 하지만, 이러한 능력들은 학교에서 과제나 단체 임무를 하며 배울 수도 있다. 아동기에는 노는 것을 통해 체력을 기르고 사회적 능력을 발달시키는 것이 중요하다. 게다가, 아이들이 자신의 미래를 위해 공부의 기초를 닦아 두는 것은 필수이다. 이상의 이유로, 나는 아이들이 집안일을 하며 가족을 돕는 것보다 놀며 공부를 해야 한다고 주장한다.

Actual Test 16

TASK 1 · INTEGRATED TASK

Paleontology: The Functions of a Dinosaur's Crest

READING   p.167

6천 5백만 년 이전 공룡들이 지구를 지배했을 때, 그들은 다양한 외형을 가지고 있었다. 그렇지만, 그 중 한 가지 흥미로운 특징은 발굴된 화석에서 많은 공룡 종들의 머리에 볏이 있었다는 점이다. 통상 뼈로 이루어진 볏은, 1 미터가 넘게 뻗어있는 것들도 있었던 반면, 일부는 그 크기가 작았다. 이 볏의 용도가 무엇인지는 수십 년간 고생물학자들을 당황하게 만들었다.

한 과학자 단체는 공룡들이 냄새를 맡기 위해 볏을 사용했다고 추정한다. 일부 공룡의 화석 유골을 연구함으로써 고생물학자들은 공룡의 비강이 볏까지 뻗어있다는 것을 알아냈다. 하드로사우르스는 정교한 볏을 가진 공룡들이다. 람베오사우르스, 코리토사우르스, 그리고 파라사우롤로푸스가 볏을 가진 하드로사우르스의 세 종이다. 볏으로 인해, 많은 전문가들은 이러한 공룡들이 상당히 민감한 후각을 가지고 있었다고 믿는다.

공룡 시대에는, 지구의 평균 기온이 현재의 기온보다 훨씬 높았다. 따라서 일부 고생물학자들은 볏이 있는 공룡들이 이러한 더운 기후에 적응하기 위하여 진화했다고 믿고 있다. 그들은 볏이 공룡들로 하여금 체온을 조절할 수 있도록 해 주었으며, 따라서 신체가 과열되지 않도록 했다고 추측한다. 많은 공룡들이 몸을 식히기 위해 물속에 머물렀던 것으로 알려져 있다. 따라서, 볏이 있는 많은 종들을 포함하여, 물속에 살지 않는 공룡들은 그 대신 몸을 차갑게 유지하기 위해 볏과 같은 다른 방편들에 의존했을 것이다.

보다 최근의 이론은 공룡이 소리를 내기 위해 볏을 사용했다고 한다. 몇몇 학자들은 특히 람베오사우르스가 의사소통을 하기 위해 볏을 사용했다고 주장한다. 각 볏의 크기나 모양이 달랐기 때문에, 각각의 람베오사우르스가 내는 소리 또한 달랐다. 이로써 공룡들은 다른 개체를 인식하는 것이 가능했을 것이다.

LISTENING   🎧 16-01

M Professor: Look at these pictures of dinosaurs here . . . here . . . and here . . . Notice their heads. In particular, take a look at the tops. Do you see those crests? Some are rather, uh, outlandish in how they're shaped, right? Check out this one . . . It looks like some kind of spiked hairdo, doesn't it?

Anyway, what's puzzling about these crests is how the dinosaurs used them. They must have had some purpose since animals typically don't develop unneeded body parts. One theory is that dinosaurs used them to enhance their sense of smell. That's unlikely, however, because animals with good senses of smell often have well-developed brains. Dinosaurs had incredibly small brain cavities. Stegosaurus, for instance, had a brain the size of a walnut. Many hadrosaurs, which were crested dinosaurs, had tiny brains, too. It's highly unlikely, therefore, that dinosaurs used their crests to smell. They simply lacked the brainpower to process the smells.

The idea that dinosaurs used their crests to cool themselves off has been postulated by some. Hmm . . . Well, it's true that some dinosaurs had bones that helped them keep cool. For instance, some had bony plates all over their bodies. Triceratops had an enormous frill around its head that helped it diffuse heat and remain cool. But dinosaurs' crests were too small to cool off these enormous animals. The crests just weren't big enough.

Now, one theory does have some promise. It states that dinosaurs used their crests to communicate with one another. There's some pretty strong evidence that lambeosaurs could do that. But . . . please note that this is just a single species. Numerous others dinosaurs had crests, you know. Just because lambeosaurs could likely use their crests to communicate doesn't mean every other crested dinosaur could do the same. You definitely shouldn't jump to any conclusions. Okay?

교수: 여기 이 공룡들 사진을 보십시오... 여기... 그리고 여기도... 그들의 머리에 주목해 주세요. 특히, 맨 위를 보세요. 볏이 보이나요? 일부는 음, 모양이 이상하죠, 그렇죠? 이것도 보세요... 위로 뻗어 있는 머리털 같군요, 그렇지 않나요?

어쨌든, 이 볏들에 관해 난해한 점은 공룡들이 어떻게 그것을 사용했는지에 대한 것입니다. 동물들은 일반적으로 불필요한 신체 부위를 발달시키지 않기 때문에, 볏에는 어떠한 용도가 있었음에 틀림없습니다. 한 가지 이론은 후각을 강화시키기 위해 공룡이 볏을 사용했다는 것입니다. 하지만 후각이 뛰어난 동물들은 종종 발달된 두뇌를 가지고 있기 때문에 그 이론은 가능성이 없습니다. 공룡들은 놀랄 만큼 작은 뇌강을 가지고 있었습니다. 예를 들면, 스테고사우르스는 호두 만한 크기의 뇌를 가지고 있었죠. 볏을 가지고 있었던 여러 하드로사우르스 역시 매우 작은 뇌를 가지고 있었습니다. 그러므로, 공룡들이 냄새를 맡기 위해 볏을 사용했다는 것은 가능성이 거의 없어 보입니다. 후각을 처리할 지능도 부족했던 것이죠.

공룡들이 열을 식히기 위해 볏을 사용했다는 의견이 몇몇 사람들에 의해 제기되고 있습니다. 흠... 글쎄요, 일부 공룡들이 몸을 식히기 위해 도움이 되는 뼈들을 가지고 있었던 것은 사실입니다. 예를 들어, 몇몇은 온 몸에 뼈판을 가지고 있었습니다. 트리케라톱스는 머리 주위에 거대한 프릴을 가지고 있어서 열을 분산시키고 몸을 식힐 수 있었죠. 하지만, 공룡의 볏은 이 거대한 동물들을 식혀주기에는 너무나 작았습니다. 충분히 크지 않았던 것이죠.

자, 어느 정도의 가능성이 있는 하나의 이론이 있습니다. 공룡들이 서로 의사소통을 하기 위해 볏을 사용했다는 것입니다. 람베오사우르스가 의사소통을 할 수 있었다는 꽤 유력한 증거들이 있기는 합니다. 하지만... 이는 단 한 종이라는 것을 염두에 두세요. 여러분도 알고 있듯이, 많은 다른 종들도 볏을 가지고 있었습니다. 람베오사우르스가 의사소통을 하기 위해 볏을 사용했을 것이라고 해서 볏을 가진 다른 모든 공룡들이 같은 것을 할 수 있었다는 것은 아닙니다. 결코 성급한 결론을 내려서는 안 되는 것이죠. 그렇죠?

Sample Essay　　　　　　　p.170

교수는 공룡의 볏의 사용에 관한 이론 중 그 어느 것도 신뢰할 만한 것은 없다고 주장한다. 이는 볏에 어떠한 목적이 있었으며, 그것의 용도에 관해 가정하고 있는 이론이 많다는 지문의 주장을 직접적으로 반박한다.

첫째, 공룡들의 작은 뇌강은 그들이 자신의 볏을 후각을 강화시키기 위해 사용하는 것을 불가능하게 만들었다. 구체적으로는, 볏을 가진 많은 공룡들이 다소 작은 뇌를 가지고 있었기 때문에, 볏이 후각을 담당하는 하나의 기관이었다는 점은 받아들이기가 힘들다. 이는 공룡들이 냄새를 잘 맡을 수 있도록 볏이 도움을 주었을 것이라는 지문의 주장과 모순된다.

게다가, 그들의 볏이 자기 체온을 유지하는데 사용되었다는 추측 역시 근거가 없다. 공룡들이 열을 식히기 위해 볏을 활용했다는 주장이 있지만, 그 용도로 사용하기에 볏은 충분히 크지 않았다. 이는 물가에서 멀리 사는 많은 공룡들이 자신의 체온을 조절하기 위해 그들의 볏을 사용했을 것이라는 지문의 주장에 의문을 제기한다.

마지막으로, 람베오사우르스 간에 의사소통이 이루어졌던 것으로 알려져 있지만, 볏을 가진 다른 공룡들에게도 서로 의사소통을 할 수 있는 능력이 없었다. 이는 공룡들이 의사소통의 수단으로 볏을 사용했다는 점이 새롭게 밝혀졌다는 지문의 주장에 반증을 제시한다.

TASK 2 · INDEPENDENT TASK
Neighbors

Sample Essay 1 ┃ SOMEONE QUIET　　　　　　p.174

집은 안전, 행복, 그리고 소속감을 제공한다. 따라서 거주할 곳을 고를 때 몇몇 중요한 요소들을 생각하는 것은 중요하다. 이런 특성들 중에 사람들의 이웃이 있다. 만약, 가장 편해야 하는 장소가 사람들이 오히려 스트레스를 받는 장소가 된다면, 집은 더 이상 목적에 부합하지 않는다. 그러므로 나는 조용한 사람이 이웃으로 최고라고 굳게 믿는다. 그 이유는 사람들은 쉴 수 있는 환경과 사생활이 필요하기 때문이다.

첫째, 사람들은 집에서 잘 쉴 필요가 있다. 이웃들은 서로에게 조용한 환경을 제공하는 것이 필요하다. 예를 들면, 만약 누군가가 회사에서 긴 회의 시간을 가졌다면, 그는 밤에 잘 잘 권리가 있다. 하지만, 만약 이웃이 늦게까지 음악을 크게 켜거나 파티를 한다면, 휴식이나 숙면을 취하는 것이 불가능하고, 이는 심지어 수면 장애까지 이끌 가능성이 있다.

뿐만 아니라, 많은 이들은 거주지를 선택할 때 사생활을 가장 중요한 요소로 생각한다. 다른 이들의 사생활을 존중하기 위하여, 소리의 볼륨을 낮추는 것은 기본적인 좋은 예절이다. 자세히 말하자면, 이런 일은 특히 건물이 오래 되었다면, 위층에서 무슨 일이 일어나는지 사람들이 들을 수 있는 콘도와 아파트에서 많이 일어난다. 소음은 극심한 스트레스를 받게 하며 종종 이웃 간의 갈등을 유발한다.

개개인은 거주할 곳을 결정할 때, 각각 다른 기준을 가진다. 완벽한 이웃 같은 것이 없다는 것은 사실이다. 같은 취미를 함께 즐길 수 있는 이웃이 있는 것은 좋을 수 있다. 하지만, 조용한 환경을 제공하고 사생활을 존중하는 것은 흥미를 공유한다는 이점을 쉽게 능가한다는 것은 누구나 인정할 것이다. 그러므로 내 생각으로는, 이웃으로서 최고의 유형은 조용한 사람이다.

Sample Essay 2 ┃ SOMEONE SIMILAR　　　　　p.175

집은 안전, 행복, 그리고 소속감을 제공한다. 따라서 거주할 곳을 고를 때 몇몇 중요한 요소들을 생각하는 것은 중요하다. 이런 특성들 중에 사람들의 이웃이 있다. 만약, 가장 편해야 하는 장소가 사람들이 오히려 스트레스를 받는 장소가 된다면, 집은 더 이상 목적에 부합하지 않는다. 그러므로 나는 자신과 비슷한 사람이 최고의 이웃이라고 굳게 믿는다. 그 이유는 더 이해하며 같은 흥미를 공유할 수 있기 때문이다.

첫째, 서로 너무 다를 때 사람들은 이해하기 힘들어 한다. 좀 더 자세히 말하자면, 한 명이 내성적이고 옆집에 사는 사람은 외향적이면, 갈등은 피할 수 없다. 예를 들면, 후자인 사람이 주말마다 밤늦게까지 파티를 한다면, 나머지 사람은 소음과 음악 때문에 굉장한 스트레스를 받을 것이다. 이는 두 사람 사이를 결국 분쟁으로 이끌 것이다.

뿐만 아니라, 비슷한 취미를 영위할 수 있고 그것들에 대한 의견을 교환하는 것은 특정 동네에 사는 것을 더 즐겁게 만들어 줄 수 있다. 예를 들면, 만약 한 이웃이 스포츠를 보는 것을 좋아하면, 운동 팀을 응원하고 환호하는 것을 전혀 하지 않는 사람은 경기를 보는 동안 매우 시끄러운 그 이웃을 이해하는 것이 굉장히 힘들 수 있다. 하지만, 만약 두 명 모두 스포츠를 좋아한다면, 그들은 생각을 공유하거나 심지어는 게임을 같이 볼 수도 있다.

누구나 거주할 곳을 결정할 때, 각각 다른 기준을 가진다. 완벽한 이웃 같은 것이 없다는 것은 사실이다. 조용하고 다른 이들의 사생활을 방해하지 않는 이웃이 있는 것은 좋을 수 있다. 하지만, 다른 이들을 이해하고 공통된 흥미를 공유할 수 있다는 것이 다른 이점들을 쉽게 능가한다는 것은 누구나 인정할 것이다. 그러므로 내 의견으로는 이웃으로 최고의 유형은 비슷한 점이 있는 사람이다.

집은 안전, 행복, 그리고 소속감을 제공한다. 따라서 거주할 곳을 고를 때 몇몇 중요한 요소들을 생각하는 것은 중요하다. 이런 특성들 중에 사람들의 이웃이 있다. 만약, 가장 편해야 하는 장소가 사람들이 오히려 스트레스를 받는 장소가 된다면, 집은 더 이상 목적에 부합하지 않는다. 그러므로 나는 도움을 주는 사람이 이웃으로 가장 좋다고 믿는다. 그 이유는 더 너그럽고 긍정적 강화를 주기 때문이다.

첫째, 특히 응급 상황의 경우에는 힘이 되어 주는 이웃을 갖는 것이 중요하다. 사람들은 긴급한 상황을 직면하면 비이성적으로 되는 경향이 있다. 따라서 침착하고 도움이 필요할 때 도움을 주는 이웃을 갖는 것은 정말 도움이 된다. 예를 들면, 누군가 다쳤을 때, 가족은 종종 공포에 빠지지 않게 되기가 어렵다. 도움을 주는 이웃은 사람을 진정시키며 다친 사람을 도울 방법을 찾을 것이다.

게다가, 끊임없이 긍정적 강화를 주는 이웃은 언제나 에너지와 낙관적 생각으로 가득 차 있다. 강화시키는 사람은 사람들을 북돋아 주고 자신감을 가지게 만든다. 예를 들면, 이웃을 만날 때 머리 스타일이나 옷 같은 사소한 것에도 칭찬을 하는 것은 그 사람을 행복하게 만들기에 충분하고도 남는다. 이것은, 사실, 사생활에 너무 많은 가치를 두고 서로에게서 멀어지는 경향이 있는 현대 사회에서 특히나 의미가 깊다.

누구나 거주할 곳을 결정할 때, 각각 다른 기준을 가진다. 완벽한 이웃 같은 것이 없다는 것은 사실이다. 다른 이들의 사생활을 존중하는 이웃이 있는 것은 좋을 수 있다. 하지만, 다른 이들을 이해하고 끊임없이 긍정적 강화를 주는 것이 오히려 무관심을 쉽게 능가할 것이라는 것은 누구나 인정할 것이다. 그러므로 내 의견으로는 지내기 가장 좋은 이웃의 유형은 힘이 되는 사람이다.

Actual Test 17

TASK 1 · INTEGRATED TASK

History: The Origin of the Etruscans

기원전 6세기 로마 공화국이 발생하기 이전, 이탈리아 반도는 에투루리아 사람들의 지배를 받았다. 수세기 동안, 에투르리아인의 기원은 비밀에 싸여져 있었다. 하지만, 고대 및 현대로부터 나온 증거에 의하면 에투르리아인은 오늘날의 터키로부터 왔다.

에투르리아인과 고대 터키를 연결해 주는 첫 번째 증거는 '역사의 아버지'라 불리는 헤로도투스의 집필이다. 헤로도투스는 기원전 5세기에 살았으며 그의 가장 유명한 작품은 The Histories이다. 그는 이 책의 한 부분에서 에투르리아인이 터키의 서쪽에 위치해 있던 리디아로부터 이주해 왔다고 기록하고 있다. 헤로도투스는 리디아에서 18년간 기근이 지속되었다고 기록했다. 기근 때문에, 리디아 인구의 반이 국가를 떠났다. 이들은 서머나 항에서 항해를 시작하여 마침내 이탈리아의 한 지역인 움브리아에 상륙했다.

언어학자들은 고대 에투르리아인의 언어와 리디아 인근 그리스의 섬이었던 림노스에 새겨진 다른 언어 사이의 유사성에 주목하여 헤로도투스의 주장을 지지해 왔다. 에투르리아어는 해석된 적이 없기 때문에, 그 기원은 알려져 있지 않다. 아마도 리디아 사람들이 움브리아로 가는 도중에 비문을 남겨놓았을 것이다. 시간이 지나면서 이들의 언어가 진화하여 에투르리아어가 되었을 가능성이 있다.

마지막으로, 이탈리아 토스카나의 네 종의 고대 소 품종의 DNA 연구는 이들이 터키의 일부 소들과 유사하다는 점을 보여 주었다. 에투르리아인들이 살았던 주요 지역이 토스카나에 있는 소마이 터키의 소들과 유사성을 가지고 있었다. 이탈리아의 다른 소들은 전혀 관련이 없었다. 따라서, 일부 사람들은 에투르리아인과 그들의 소가 터키로부터 항해한 배를 타고 왔다는 결론을 내리고 있다.

M Professor: There was a front-page article in the paper on Saturday about the Etruscans, whom we just studied, having possibly originated in Turkey. Well, it sounds nice to have cleared up that historical mystery, but, uh, but let me poke some holes in the story.

First, the article cited Herodotus as an authority. We read some Herodotus. Remember? He was definitely an invaluable historian. I mean, uh, he pretty much started the field of history. But he was also something of a, well, a fabricator. He often wrote stories about monsters that supposedly existed, including, uh, one story about giant insects big enough to eat humans. I hope I never meet them. My point is that, well, Herodotus wasn't always reliable. We can't trust everything he wrote.

The article, if I remember correctly, pointed out that there's an inscription found on Lemnos which bears some similarities to ancient Etruscan. I suppose it's possible that people from Lydia on their way to Italy left it. But, you know, it could have been the other way around, too. It could have been Etruscan sailors who left the inscription on Lemnos. The Etruscans did, after all, engage in maritime trade on the Mediterranean.

Finally, the article focused on the genetic similarities between ancient cows in Tuscany and Asia Minor, as Turkey was once called. The DNA evidence doesn't lie. But, again, we can't prove that these cows were brought to Italy by refugees from Lydia. Remember that there was a great amount of trade in the Mediterranean Sea, even during ancient times. So, yes, those cows were probably imported from Asia Minor . . . but by a merchant, not by refugees. Then, the cows were bred, and, most likely, they adapted to the land, so their numbers increased. That's all there is to it.

교수: 토요일 신문의 일면에 우리가 얼마 전 공부했던, 에투르리아인이 터키로부터 온 것일 수도 있다는 기사가 실렸습니다. 자, 역사적 수수께끼를 풀어낸 것은 멋져 보이지만, 음, 그에 관한 몇 가지 빈틈을 지적해 보도록 하겠습니다.

첫째로, 신문 기사는 헤로도투스를 권위자로 언급합니다. 우리도 헤로도투스 작품을 몇몇 읽었습니다, 기억나요? 확실히 그는 매우 귀중한 역사가입니다. 제 말은, 음, 그가 역사학을 창시한 것이었죠. 하지만, 그는 음, 일종의 조작가이기도 했습니다. 종종 사람을 잡아먹을 만큼 컸던 거대한 곤충 이야기를 비롯하여 존재했을 법한 괴물들에 관한 이야기를 썼습니다. 저는 그 괴물들을 만나지 않았으면 좋겠네요. 요점은, 헤로도투스를 항상 신뢰할 수만은 없다는 점입니다. 그가 저술했던 모든 것을 신뢰할 수는 없습니다.

만약 제가 제대로 기억하는 것이라면, 그 기사는 고대 에투르리아어와 몇몇 유사점을 가진 림노스의 비문에 관해 지적하고 있었습니다. 리디아 사람들이 이탈리아로 가면서 그 글을 남겼을 것이라는 점은 가능한 이야기라고 생각합니다. 하지만, 그 반대일 수도 있죠. 에투르리안 선원들이 림노스에 글자를 남겼을 수도 있다는 것입니다. 에투르리아인들은 지중해와의 해상 무역에 종사하고 있었습니다.

마지막으로, 그 신문 기사는 토스카나의 소와 한때 소아시아라고 불렸던 터키의 소 사이에 유전적 유사점이 있다는 점에 초점을 맞추었습니다. DNA 증거는 거짓말을 하지 않죠. 하지만, 마찬가지로, 우리는 이 소들이 리디아에서 온 피난민들에 의해 이탈리아로 들어온 것인지 증명할 수가 없습니다. 심지어 고대에도 지중해에서는 상당히 많은 무역이 이루어졌다는 점을 기억해 보세요. 그래서, 그래요, 그 소들은 아마도 소아시아로부터 들어왔을 것입니다... 하지만 피난민이 아닌 상인에 의해서인 것이죠. 그리고 나서, 소들이 사육되면서, 아마도 그 지역에 적응하여 숫자가 늘어났을 것입니다. 그것이 전부이죠.

Sample Essay   p.182

교수는 에투르리아인의 기원에 관한 한 특정 이론에 의문점이 있다고 주장한다. 이는 에투르리안인이 터키로부터 왔다는 이론에 세 가지의 증거가 존재한다는 지문의 주장을 직접적으로 반박한다.

첫째로, 비록 헤로도투스는 유명한 역사학자로 남아 있지만, 그의 이야기들이 항상 사실에 기반을 둔 것은 아니다. 그는 심지어 괴물들이 실제 존재했던 것처럼 글을 썼다. 이러한 사실은 지문에서 재차 언급된 *The Histories*에서 기근으로 인해 리디아의 사람들이 움브리아로 가게 되었다는 주장에 의문을 제기한다.

더 나아가, 교수는 에투르리아어의 기원에 관해서도 두 가지 가능성이 있다고 주장한다. 그 중 하나는 리디아 사람들이 비문을 남겼다는 것이고, 또 다른 하나는 에투르리아인들이 지중해에서 무역에 종사했기 때문에 에투르리아 선원들이 비문을 남겼다는 것이다. 이는 비문에서 발견된 언어가 리디아어가 에투르리아어로 진화했다는 점을 입증해 준다는 지문의 내용을 반박한다.

마지막으로, 교수는 터키의 소와 토스카나 소의 DNA간의 유전적인 유사점들에도 불구하고 소들이 어떻게 토스카나까지 갔는지는 알려져 있지 않다고 말한다. 소들이 에투르리아 상인에 의해서 터키로 유입되었을 가능성이 매우 높다. 이는 유전적 유사성이 사람들에 의해 이 소들이 터키에서 토스카나로 이동되었다는 점을 시사한다는 지문의 주장을 반박한다.

TASK 2 · INDEPENDENT TASK
Attire

Sample Essay 1 | AGREE   p.185

사람들의 성격을 판단할 때, 영향을 미치는 많은 요인들이 있다. 이러한 요인에는 예의 범절이나 태도, 외모, 그리고 말투가 포함된다. 일부는 옷을 입는 방법이 사람들의 특성을 거의 반영해 주지 못한다고 주장한다. 하지만, 옷차림은 타인에 의해 자신이 어떻게 보여지기를 바라고 있는지 나타내 주기 때문에 나는 옷차림이 사람의 성격에 대한 훌륭한 척도가 된다고 생각한다. 게다가, 옷은 한 사람의 성격을 반영해 주는 메시지를 나타낼 수도 있다.

첫째, 특정 옷을 입는 것은 다른 이들이 우리를 어떻게 볼 것인지에 관한 기대로부터 나온다. 따라서, 사람들은 자신들의 성격을 옷을 통해서 표현하려고 노력한다. 예를 들면, 깔끔하고 단정한 사람들은 힙합 바지보다 정장을 입는 것을 선호한다. 반대로, 60년대의 히피족들은 매우 색다르고 자신들의 성격을 잘 나타내 주었던 옷을 착용했다. 즉 그들의 독특한 옷 입는 법은 자

유로우며 사랑을 지향했던 자신들의 성격을 반영해 주었다.

뿐만 아니라, 몇몇 사람들을 사람들이 그들이 좋아하는 것을 알 수 있도록 메시지가 있는 옷을 입는다. 예를 들어, 정치에 관심이 있는 사람들은 그들이 좋아하는 정치인의 캠페인 구호가 포함된 셔츠를 입을 수도 있다. 게다가, 다른 사람들은 자신이 좋아하는 스포츠 팀, 음악가, 야외 활동을 나타내주는 옷을 입는다. 예를 들어, 우리 형은 종종 그가 좋아하는 록 밴드 멤버의 사진이 있는 셔츠를 입는다. 결과적으로, 단지 그들이 입는 옷을 봄으로써, 사람들에 대해 많이 알게 되는 것이 가능하다.

특정 직업이나 상황으로 인해 자신의 스타일과는 매우 다른 방법으로 옷을 입어야 한다는 점은 사실이다. 하지만, 그러한 직업과 상황이 사람들의 스타일을 완전히 바꾸어 놓을 수는 없다. 다시 말해서, 복장 규정을 따라야 하는 직장이나 상황에서 일단 벗어나면, 사람들은 원하는 대로 옷을 입는다. 다른 이들이 자신의 옷을 봄으로써 자신의 성격을 판단할지도 모른다는 것을 알고 있기 때문에, 특정 스타일의 옷을 입는 것은 자신의 성격을 보여 주는 하나의 방법이 된다. 게다가, 사람들은 그들이 전하고자 하는 특정 메시지가 있는 옷을 입는다. 위의 이유로, 나는 옷차림이 한 사람의 성격을 나타내 주는 훌륭한 척도라는 진술에 찬성한다.

Sample Essay 2 | DISAGREE   p.186

사람들의 성격을 판단할 때, 영향을 미치는 많은 요인들이 있다. 이러한 요인에는 예의 범절이나 태도, 외모, 그리고 말투가 포함된다. 일부는 옷차림이 사람들의 성격을 나타내 주는 훌륭한 척도라고 주장한다. 하지만, 나는 옷차림이 실제 사람들의 특성을 반영해 주지는 않는다고 굳게 믿는다. 우선, 다른 요인들이 사람이 어떻게 입는지에 영향을 미칠 수 있다. 게다가, 본인의 취향과 상관없이 특정 상황과 직업이 다른 형태의 옷차림을 요구한다.

첫째, 유행을 따라가고 싶은 욕구로 인하여 자신의 스타일에 따른 옷차림을 입지 않을 수도 있다. 게다가, 다른 사람들의 영향으로 인해 개인의 옷 입는 방법이 막대한 영향을 받을 수도 있다. 예를 들면, 내 친구의 부모님은 옷차림에 관해 매우 보수적이며, 내 친구가 당신들의 기준에 맞는 옷을 입도록 요구하신다. 그 결과, 그 친구가 한때 힙합 음악에 매료되어 자신의 관심사를 반영하는 스타일의 옷을 입고 싶어했지만, 그는 대신 부모님의 말씀에 따라 모범생 스타일의 옷을 입어야만 했다.

뿐만 아니라, 어떻게 옷을 입고 싶은지에 상관없이, 일부 사람들은 직장이나 학교의 규칙에 맞춰 적절한 옷을 입어야 한다. 많은 기업들이 실용성뿐만 아니라 통일성을 강조하여 복장 규정을 마련해 놓고 있기 때문에, 직원들은 그러한 규정을 만족시키는 옷을 입어야 한다. 예를 들어, 내 사촌은 매우 명랑한 성격을 가지고 있고 밝은 색상의 옷을 입는 것을 좋아한다. 그럼에도 불구하고, 컨설턴트인 그녀의 일은 합리성과 신뢰성이 바탕이 되므로 회사는 그녀가 어두운 계열의 정장을 입기를 요구하고 있다.

외모가 한 사람의 성격을 반영해 주기 때문에 많은 사람들이 옷을 입는 방법에 따라 사람을 판단하는 것은 사실이다. 하지만, 다른 사람들이나 크게는 사회로부터의 영향이 옷을 선택하는데 있어서 중요한 역할을 한다. 게다가 여러 기업이나 특정 상황에서는, 개인의 취향을 반드시 반영하지는 않는, 복장 규정이 존재하기도 한다. 위의 이유로, 나는 옷차림이 한 사람의 성격을 나타내 주는 훌륭한 척도라는 진술에 반대한다.

Actual Test 18

TASK 1 · INTEGRATED TASK

Ornithology: Bird Feeders

READING

p.189

새 모이통은 야외에 설치하는 장치이다. 이러한 새 모이통들의 용도는 새들에게 먹이를 제공하기 위함이다. 큰 어치와 딱따구리를 위한 땅콩 모이통, 벌새를 위한 설탕물 모이통, 그리고 애도의 비둘기를 위한 대(臺) 모이통을 비롯한 많은 종류의 새 모이통이 있다. 언뜻 보기에는 새 모이통이 굶주려 죽는 새들을 구할 수 있다는 점에서 꽤 매력적으로 보일 수 있다. 하지만 가끔은 심각해 보이는 것을 포함해 많은 문제를 일으킬 수 있으며 심지어는 생태학적 덫으로 작용할 수도 있다.

대부분의 새들은 야생 동물이며 스스로 먹이를 찾아야 한다. 하지만, 새 모이통이 있으면 새들은 모이통에 적응이 되어 의존하게 될 수도 있다. 주기적으로 새들에게 모이를 먹이는 것은 그들이 스스로 먹이를 찾아내는 선천적 특성을 잃어버릴 수 있다는 뜻이다. 이는 모이통이 더 이상 이용 가능하지 않을 때 큰 문제가 될 수 있다. 모이통에 대한 지나친 의존은 새들이 그들의 타고난 능력 중 일부를 잃게 할 수도 있는데 이는 결과적으로 그들의 죽음을 야기할 수 있다.

연구원들은 더 다양한 종류의 새들이 그것이 없는 장소보다 새 모이통이 있는 장소에서 발견되는 것을 알아냈다. 이는 새로운 조류 종의 지역으로의 도입이 토종 곤충개체군에 해를 끼치는 부정적인 결과가 될 수 있다. 새들은 많은 곤충들을 섭취할 것이고 그 곤충들은 침입종들로부터 자신을 지키는 법을 모를 것이다. 곤충개체군의 균형 상실은 토종 식물들에게 영향을 미칠 수 있으며, 결국 지역 환경을 변화시킬 수 있다. 이는 궁극적으로 토종 새 개체군에 해를 끼칠 수 있다.

가능성은 낮지만, 새는 살모넬라 균과 조류 병균 같은 심각한 병균을 사람과 다른 동물들에게 옮길 수 있다. 병균은 사람이 올바른 방호를 하지 않은 상태에서 죽은 새들에게 다가감으로써 퍼질 수 있다. 그것은 또한 올바르지 못하게 관리가 되거나 오염된 모이통에 있는 박테리아에 의해 옮겨질 수도 있다. 메추라기, 검은 방울새, 그리고 참새가 질병을 갖는 가장 흔한 새들이다.

LISTENING

🎧 18-01

M Professor: Today, it is easy to spot bird feeders when you walk around a neighborhood. They offer a fun and educational way, especially for kids, to see birds up close and to connect with nature. It really is important to keep the bird population stable even during the harsh winter . . . um . . . especially now that some parts of the world are going through such dramatic changes in climate . . . so that we can maintain ecological balance in local ecosystems and increase biodiversity conservation.

It is important to maintain bird populations because birds play a crucial role in the distribution of seeds, pollination, and pest control, which are necessary for maintaining ecological balance. Thus, feeding birds during times . . . um . . . I'd say before and after winter . . . when food is scarce, birds are dependent on feeders for their survival . . . In fact,

bird populations in certain areas depend on winter feeding. So bird feeders allow birds to focus on reproduction, making it possible for them to sustain their populations.

A study was done in New Zealand. Bird feeders with different kinds of food . . . such as slices of bread and seeds . . . were placed in gardens. Then, the researchers found that the number of native and non-native birds were similar at non-feeding locations whereas the number of new species increased a lot at the food stations. This tells us that non-native birds are highly likely omnivorous in contrast to native birds, which eat nectar, insects, and fruit. So as long as people keep bird feeders with a normal feeding diet, they will not have to worry about invasive bird species becoming dominant.

Yes, it is possible that humans can get diseases or germs from bird feeders . . . but this can be avoided by practicing a few methods. One of them is for people to wash their hands thoroughly after handling feeders. And one should never feed birds on the ground or have a platform where birds can defecate on the surfaces of the feeders. Most importantly, feeders need to be cleaned at least every two weeks and kept dry. And . . . there is no definitive proof that the risk for disease transmission is higher at bird feeders than it is in the wild.

교수: 오늘날, 동네를 걸어 다니며 새 모이통을 보는 일은 쉬워요. 새 모이통은 특히나 아이들에게 새를 가까이 보며 자연과 연결시켜주는 즐거우면서도 교육적인 방법이지요. 혹독한 겨울 동안에도 새의 숫자를 안정적으로 유지하는 것은 정말 중요해요... 음... 특히나 지구의 일부 지역은 굉장한 기후 변화를 겪으니까요... 그래서 우리가 생태계의 균형을 유지하고, 생물의 다양성 보존을 높일 수 있도록요.

새들은 생태계 균형을 유지하기 위한 씨앗의 분포, 식물의 수분, 그리고 해충 방제에 있어 결정적인 역할을 하기 때문에 새들의 수를 지키는 것은 중요합니다. 그래서 새에게 모이를 먹이는 것은 음... 겨울 전후로 말이지요... 식량이 귀할 때요, 새들은 생존을 위해 모이통에 의존합니다... 사실, 일부 지역에서는 새의 수가 겨울 먹이에 달려 있어요. 그래서, 이러한 새 모이통들은 새들로 하여금 번식에 집중하게 하며 그들의 숫자를 유지할 수 있도록 해 줍니다.

뉴질랜드에서 연구를 진행했어요. 각각 다른 음식... 그러니까 빵 조각이나 씨앗 같은 걸 넣은... 새 모이통이 정원에 놓여졌지요. 그 후 연구원들이 알아낸 바로는 음식이 담긴 새 모이통에는 외래종의 숫자가 늘었던 반면 새 모이통이 없었던 곳에는 토종과 외래종의 숫자가 비슷하다는 거에요. 이는 꿀, 곤충, 그리고 과일을 먹는 토종 새들에 반해 외래종들은 잡식성일 가능성이 높다는 점을 알려줍니다. 그러니까, 사람들이 평소대로 먹이를 넣어주는 이상 외래종이 많아질 거라는 걱정은 안 해도 되겠지요.

맞아요, 새 모이통에서 인간이 병을 얻을 가능성은 있어요... 하지만 이건 몇 가지 조치를 행해서 피할 수 있어요. 그 중 하나는 사람들이 모이통을 만진 후 손을 깨끗이 씻는 거에요. 그리고 그 누구도 바닥에서 새에게 모이를 주거나, 새가 대변을 볼 수 있는 모이통 표면에 플랫폼을 설치하면 안돼요. 가장 중요한 점은 모이통을 적어도 2주에 한번은 청소해야 하고 건조시켜야 합니다. 그리고... 야생에서보다 새 모이통에서 병균 전염의 위험이 더 높다는 확정적인 증거가 없어요.

강의에서 교수는 새 모이통이 제대로 유지된다면 많은 이점을 만들어 낼 것이라고 주장한다. 이는 새 모이통이 심각한 문제를 일으킬 수 있다는 지문의 내용을 직접적으로 반박한다.

혹독한 겨울 동안 새에게 먹이를 주는 것은 생태학 균형을 유지하는데 굉장히 중요하다. 충분한 먹이로 새들은 자신들의 개체수를 유지시킬 번식에 집중할 수 있다. 이는 먹이를 제공하는 것은 새들이 모이통에 의존하게 하며 그들의 자연 습성의 부재로 인한 죽음으로도 이끌 가능성이 있다는 지문의 내용을 반박한다.

게다가, 교수는 뉴질랜드에서 실행된 연구에 대해 이야기한다. 다른 종류의 먹이가 들어있는 새 모이통이 정원에 배치되었다. 모이통을 놓지 않은 곳의 토종 새와 외래종 새의 숫자가 비슷했던 반면, 다른 종류의 음식이 들어있었던 모이통에는 외래종들이 많았다. 이는 대부분의 새로운 종류의 새들은 모이통이 있는 지역에서 발견되었으며 결과적으로 외래종의 지배를 초래한다는 지문의 내용을 반박한다.

마지막으로 가능한 질병들의 전염은 올바른 단계를 따름으로서 예방할 수 있다. 이는 정기적으로 모이통을 청소하는 것과 모이통을 만진 후 손을 깨끗이 씻는 것을 포함한다. 또한, 새들이 땅에서 먹이를 먹게 해서는 안된다. 이는 오염된 모이통으로 인해 심각한 병균이 전염될 수 있다는 지문의 내용을 반대한다.

TASK 2 · INDEPENDENT TASK

Parents' Roles

아이들이 시험을 잘 보도록 동기 부여를 해줄 수 있는 많은 방법들이 있다. 어떤 부모들은 처벌 등의 부정적 강화를 사용하는 반면, 다른 부모들은 칭찬과 보상 등의 긍정적 강화를 사용하기도 한다. 일부 사람들은 아이들에게 보상이 궁극적인 목표가 되어 버릴 수도 있다고 주장하지만, 긍정적 강화가 아이들이 더 잘 할 수 있게 격려하는 수단으로 작용한다는 점에는 의심의 여지가 없다. 그러므로 아이들의 노력을 인정해 주는 훌륭한 방법이 되기 때문에, 나는 좋은 시험 결과에 대해 아이가 보상을 받아야 한다고 굳게 믿는다. 게다가 보상은 자본주의 국가에서 노력을 인정해 주는 기본적인 방법이기도 하다.

우선, 보상을 받는 것은 개인의 성과를 인정받는 하나의 방법이 된다. 성과에 대한 인정을 받음으로써, 아이는 열심히 공부하도록 더 큰 자극을 받는다. 예를 들면, 내 사촌은 시험을 잘 볼 때 마다 삼촌으로부터 상을 받았다. 결과적으로, 사촌은 더욱 열심히 공부하며 다음 시험을 준비했다. 결과적으로, 보상을 받고 훌륭한 시험 결과를 이루어 냄으로써, 내 사촌은 공부에 흥미를 갖게 되었고, 이제는 보상이 없어도 시험을 잘 보고 있다.

덧붙여, 결과에 따라 보상을 주는 것은 아이들이 미래를 준비할 수 있도록 해 주는 방법이 된다. 자본주의 국가에서는, 개인의 종합적인 능력이 주로 시험이나 주어진 일의 결과에 기반하여 사정되고 평가되기 때문에, 할 수 있는 한 최고의 결과를 얻기 위해 열심히 노력하는 것이 중요하다. 예를 들면, 대부분의 회사는 주어진 업무의 결과에 따라 직원의 급여를 책정한다. 따라서, 결과에 가치를 두는 습관을 기르게 하는 것은 아이들이 미리 인생을 대비하도록 하는데 바람직한 방법이 된다.

보상을 주는 것이 아이들로 하여금 결과 자체에만 가치를 두게 하는 부작용을 일으킬 수도 있다는 점은 사실이다. 하지만, 전혀 인정을 해 주지 않으면, 보상이 인정의 방편으로 사용되고 있는 사회에 아이들이 적응하느라 힘든 시기를 겪을 수도 있다. 보상을 받을 때, 아이들은 다음 번 일을 더 잘해야

겠다는 자극을 받게 될 것이다. 게다가, 차후 자본주의 경제 사회에서 일을 할 준비가 되어 있을 것이다. 이상의 이유로, 나는 아이들이 좋은 시험 결과에 대해 보상을 받아야 한다는 주장에 찬성한다.

아이들이 시험을 잘 보도록 동기 부여를 해줄 수 있는 많은 방법들이 있다. 어떤 부모들은 처벌 등의 부정적 강화를 사용하는 반면, 다른 부모들은 칭찬과 보상 등의 긍정적 강화를 사용하기도 한다. 긍정적 강화가 아이들이 더 잘 할 수 있게 격려하는 하나의 수단으로 기능한다는 점에는 의심의 여지가 없지만, 보상이 아이들에게 유일한 목표가 되어 버릴 수가 있기 때문에 나는 훌륭한 시험 결과에 대해 보상을 해 주는 것은 잘못되었다고 확신한다. 게다가, 아이들은 결과가 과정보다 더 중요하다고 생각할 수도 있을 것이다.

우선, 아이들은 상을 궁극적인 목표로 삼을 수 있다. 다시 말해서, 지식을 습득함으로써 성취감을 느끼는 대신, 아이들은 보상을 받기 위해 공부를 할지도 모른다. 예를 들면, 내 친구의 부모님은 친구가 시험을 잘 볼 때마다 항상 선물을 주셨다. 결과적으로, 내 친구에게 있어서 새로운 지식을 배우고 얻는 것보다는 선물을 받는 것이 더 우선시되고 더 의미 있는 것이 되었다.

덧붙여, 아이들은 시험을 준비하는데 그 과정보다 시험의 결과에 더 많은 가치를 부여하게 될 가능성이 높다. 이로써 아이들은 실패로부터 배우지 못하게 될 수도 있다. 오히려, 보상을 받을 수 없기 때문에 좌절과 실망만을 얻게 될 수도 있다. 토마스 에디슨은 같은 수많은 유명한 과학자들은 실패로부터 배움을 얻었다. 만약 그가 결과에 따라 보상을 받았더라면, 그렇게 혁신적이고 창의적인 실험을 시도하려고 하지는 않았을 것이다.

보상이 아이들로 하여금 더 열심히 노력하도록 고무시키는 하나의 방법으로 사용될 수 있다는 점은 사실이다. 하지만, 결과가 항상 노력과 상관관계를 이루고 있지는 않기 때문에, 이러한 방법은 아이들이 용기를 잃고 더 이상의 노력을 하지 않는 결과를 낳을 수도 있다. 학습자에게는, 보상이 아닌, 지식을 얻는 것이 가장 중요한 목표가 되어야 한다. 게다가, 때때로 아이들은 결과 자체 보다는 배우면서 겪은 과정에 대해 칭찬을 받아야 한다. 이상의 이유들로, 나는 아이들이 좋은 시험 결과에 대해 보상을 받아야 한다는 주장에 반대한다.

MEMO

MEMO

MEMO

MEMO

MEMO

MEMO

MEMO

TOEFL MAP

ACTUAL TEST
New TOEFL Edition

Writing **2**